Power At Work

Work in Global and Historical Perspective

Edited by
Andreas Eckert, Sidney Chalhoub, Mahua Sarkar,
Dmitri van den Bersselaar, Christian G. De Vito

Work in Global and Historical Perspective is an interdisciplinary series that welcomes scholarship on work/labor that engages a historical perspective in and from any part of the world. The series advocates a definition of work/labor that is broad, and specially encourages contributions that explore interconnections across political and geographic frontiers, time frames, disciplinary boundaries, as well as conceptual divisions among various forms of commodified work, and between work and 'non-work.'

Volume 16

Power At Work

A Global Perspective on Control and Resistance

Edited by
Marcel van der Linden and Nicole Mayer-Ahuja

DE GRUYTER
OLDENBOURG

ISBN 978-3-11-108235-6
e-ISBN (PDF) 978-3-11-108655-2
e-ISBN (EPUB) 978-3-11-108692-7
ISSN 2509-8861

Library of Congress Control Number: 2023932371

Bibliographic information published by the Deutsche Nationalbibliothek
The Deutsche Nationalbibliothek lists this publication in the Deutsche Nationalbibliografie;
detailed bibliographic data are available on the internet at http://dnb.dnb.de.

© 2023 Walter de Gruyter GmbH, Berlin/Boston
Cover image: Randy Faris/The Image Bank/Getty Images
Printing and binding: CPI books GmbH, Leck

www.degruyter.com

Table of Contents

Acknowledgments

This volume has a long history. The seeds were planted in the international research centre Work and Human Lifecycle in Global History at Humboldt-Universität zu Berlin. Over the course of 12 years, until July 2021, 149 fellows have joined re: work, as this institution is commonly known, to carry out their research. Just across the street from Berlin Friedrichstrasse station, it is located at the heart of Germany's old and new capital. Many re:work fellows have been senior and internationally renowned specialists on issues of work and lifecycle, whereas others were in the initial stages of their academic careers (for an overview see: https://re-work.hu-berlin.de). The founders, Jürgen Kocka and Andreas Eckert, come from the field of global history, but they have invited colleagues from anthropology, from the social sciences and other academic disciplines, and sometimes even journalists or artists, to join the centre. Over the years, re:work has developed into a highly attractive meeting point for scholars from the Global North as well as from the Global South, who have enjoyed the rare privilege of being granted, above all, time. Time to reflect on their own findings – but also time to discuss them with colleagues focusing on a wide range of historical periods and world regions, with different perspectives on, but a common interest in, work, labour, and employment, and to develop new ideas on the basis of this exchange.

The spirit of re:work is hard to describe. It is having dragged yourself to a lecture that you would never even have considered attending were it not for the disciplining effects of peer pressure – and to find yourself partaking in an inspiring discussion that changes your take on your own research. It is being caught up in a lively debate over pots and saucepans in the centre's kitchen, where the heat of the argument combines with the heat of the Indian spices being roasted in preparation for the weekly fellows' lunch to set off the building's fire alarm, forcing all residents to assemble outside (often in the middle of Berlin's freezing winter) until the fire brigade allows you to return to the office – and of course to the kitchen, since fellows compete to produce the best and most adventurous menu. It is the joy of being crammed into re:work's narrow hallways after a day of inspiring discussions at the annual conference where fellows present their work, continuing academic as well as political debates, listening to good music, and going dancing with scholars whose books you read and admired as a student. It is the intellectual challenge of establishing global perspectives on changes in the world of work, informed by highly specialised research on a very specific historical period and region. It is the enormous benefit you receive from being part of a constantly growing academic network that stretches across the globe, providing access to colleagues, discussions, conferences, and publications that would have remained out

https://doi.org/10.1515/9783111086552-001

of reach without re:work. It is, finally, being part of a truly global scholarly exchange that supports the emergence of new perspectives on work and the human lifecycle, and the experimental exploration of unexpected connections and interrelations between phenomena and dynamics that are usually not found in academic discussions.

How can this kind of spirit be captured, at least in its strictly academic respects, now that re:work's time is up? When Mamadou Diawara, Frederick Cooper, Hilda Sabato, and the editors, as members of the centre's advisory board, discussed this question with Jürgen Kocka, Andreas Eckert, and Felicitas Hentschke, the organisational heart and soul of re:work, we quickly agreed that we should produce three volumes to document at least some of the most important lines of discussion that had shaped the intellectual life at the centre. One of these volumes (edited by Andreas Eckert and Jürgen Kocka) focuses on conceptual questions of global labour history. Another volume (edited by Josef Ehmer and Carola Lentz) is dedicated to analysing historical, sociological, and anthropological perspectives on the human life course, work, and labour. In this volume, the power relations between capital and labour take centre stage, resulting as they are from the materiality of production, the specific ways in which the labour process is organised, coordinated, and controlled, and from the interrelations between these politics in production on the shopfloor, on the one hand, and (state) politics of production beyond the company premises and workers' struggles, on the other.

As editors, we have tried to assemble an intellectually stimulating collection of contributions that seek to do at least some justice to the wide range of topics and approaches covered by re:work, although a lot of fascinating work by other fellows has, by necessity, been omitted. First of all, we would like to thank the authors for being part of this endeavour, which has proved considerably more time consuming and nerve-rattling than originally envisaged. The Covid-19 pandemic meant that some authors had to look after their children when schools and kindergartens were closed, while others had to postpone interviews or could not access the relevant archives. Even under these complicated conditions, during the lonely months of pandemic lockdowns, and while the centre had to cut back on its operations, in the last stage of funding, re:work provided a safe and reliable haven for the work on this volume. Just like during the last 12 years, we once again greatly profited from the support and advice provided by the competent and surprisingly cheerful staff, and especially Felicitas Hentschke, Farah Barakat, and Sebastian Marggraff. The editors were invited to spend time at re:work whenever required for the production process of this volume, and Nicole Mayer-Ahuja was even granted a re:visiting grant during the winter term 2020/2021. While this may not have prevented the repeated shattering of deadlines, it did enable us to bring this challenging publication project to a good and (hopefully) readable end. Helen Veitch persuaded authors as well as editors to improve their thinking and writing tremendously through her thorough and helpful copy-editing. And of course there are so many others who contributed to the discussions documented in this volume, as fellows and guests of re:work, as colleagues and friends who were part of the global village that evolved in Berlin, Georgenstrasse 23, without whom this volume would not have been possible. We hope that we will keep in touch, even when re:work is history, since there is still plenty to do for scholars who wish to analyse the world of work, and also to change it. As Andreas Eckert used to say: Once a fellow – always a fellow.

Berlin, January 2023

Marcel van der Linden   Nicole Mayer-Ahuja

Tables and Figures

Tables

Figures

Marcel van der Linden

1 Introduction

Every enterprise of any size has a hierarchy – a complex system with a "boss," comprising a number of subordinate subsystems, which also have "bosses" who are the immediate subordinates of the general "boss" of the system.[1] Such a hierarchy is inevitable if larger groups of people want to coordinate their activities:

> in all labour where many individuals cooperate, the interconnection and unity of the process is necessarily represented in a governing will, and in functions that concern not the detailed work but rather the workplace and its activity as a whole, as with the conductor of an orchestra. This is productive labour that has to be performed in any combined mode of production.[2]

There are two possibilities. Either the workers appoint the "bosses" themselves through mutual consultation and have the right to recall them if they do not live up to their expectations (autonomy or self-management), or the activities of the workers are coordinated by external agents whom they do not control (heteronomy). From a quantitative point of view, autonomous cooperation carries much less weight than heteronomy. Currently, there are about ten million autonomously cooperating workers across the world,[3] while the total number of heteronomous workers (predominantly wage-earners) is approaching three billion.

In this volume, we discuss heteronomous power in employment relations. Much has already been written about this, but most of the literature has significant weaknesses: it tends to neglect the historical dimension and, insofar as it is interested in the past, it is almost completely Eurocentric. Fundamental works, such as Sidney Pollard's *The Genesis of Modern Management*, and everything of importance that followed on from this seminal tome, discuss the development of management as a purely European ("industrial") innovation; they ignore contemporary or earlier trends in colonial countries, or what is now referred to as the Global South. The rise of modern labour-management techniques is, therefore, usually explained in terms of the technological changes brought about by the Industrial Revolution as an isolated event. The colonies, unfree labour, and the Global South are blind spots; they are almost never part of the story. This is not to deny that very

---

1 Formally speaking, this description only covers a subset of all possible hierarchies. See: Herbert A. Simon, "The Architecture of Complexity," *Proceedings of the American Philosophical Society* 106, 6 (December 1962): 467–482.
2 Karl Marx, *Capital*, Vol. III. Trans. David Fernbach (Harmondsworth: Penguin, 1981), 507.
3 According to the International Co-operative Alliance.

https://doi.org/10.1515/9783111086552-002

important work has been done during the last few decades in the field of management history and that we now understand many aspects of the way in which employers have dealt with their employees much better than we used to.

Throughout the 12 years of its existence, the Berlin-based research centre "re: work" has attempted to open up this historical *problématique*. How does the coordination of work processes take place? How do supervisors and managers try to control the workforce? And what kind of means do workers use to maintain or increase their influence on labour relations? A number of research fellows have explored various aspects of the issues at hand. This collection presents a selection of their findings.

Power and Counterpower

Heteronomous labour-coordination is always based on specific power relations, on the strategies put in place by those in charge to regulate the behaviour of those who work for them, and on the attitudes of the latter who then either accept that kind of regulation or adjust it (at least partly) to their own needs.[4] Behaviour that is considered to be improper is punished and proper behaviour is rewarded. These punishments and rewards can be discretionary (i.e., at the convenience of superiors), or they could be bound by formal or informal rules. The more unfree workers are, the stronger employers' or management's discretionary power. Supervisors on slave plantations, for example, could often punish workers at will. But even their power was not always absolute. Already in 1685, the French *Code Noir* provided a legal framework for slavery. Among other things it stipulated that slaves should not work on Sundays or holidays, that they should have a day per week to work for their own ends, that their masters should not torture, mutilate, or kill them, and that slaves who were not fed, clothed, and supported by their

---

4 We distinguish three dimensions of power: (i) decision-making power, that is, power in the Weberian sense, as "every chance (no matter whereon this chance is based) to carry through the own will, *even* against resistance." See: Max Weber, *Wirtschaft und Gesellschaft*, in *Grundriss der Sozialökonomik.* Abteilung III (Tübingen: J. C. Mohr [Paul Siebeck], 1925), 28. Here we follow the careful translation given in Isidor Wallimann et al., "Misreading Weber: The Concept of 'Macht,'" *Sociology* 14, 2 (1980): 264). (ii) non-decision-making power, that is the possibility to set the agenda in debates and to make certain issues unacceptable for discussion in public forums. This dimension was presented in Peter Bachrach and Morton S. Baratz, "Two Faces of Power," *American Political Science Review* 56, 4 (1962): 947–952. And (iii) ideological power, that is the possibility to influence people's wishes and thoughts, even making them want things that go against their own self-interest (such as causing women to support a patriarchal society). This dimension is elaborated in Steven Lukes, *Power: A Radical View* (London: Macmillan, 1974).

masters according to the law had the right to notify an attorney of this and give him their statements.[5] These were, of course, "official" statements, and it is doubtful whether any masters actually obeyed the law, or if slaves – if they were even aware of the Code – would dare to launch formal proceedings if their master breached the law. Much later, during the last decades before the Civil War of 1860 to 1865, the courts in the South of the United States also began to limit the rights of slave owners, preventing them from brutalising slaves and requiring them to provide adequate clothing.

Historically, workers have generally been in favour of restricting employers' discretionary power as much as possible, and of expanding the domain of rules and meta-rules (rules about the making of rules).[6] In the case of "free" wage labour, the sociologist Philip Selznick has spoken about the transition from a "'prerogative' contract – according to which the sale of labour power carries with it few, if any, proscriptions or prescriptions on its consumption by management – to the 'constitutive contract' and to 'creative arbitration,' which does establish procedures and regulations for the utilization of labour."[7] Michael Burawoy adds to this: "Restrictions on managerial discretion and arbitrary rule, on the one hand, and enhanced protection for workers, on the other, reflect not only the ascendency of unions and internal government, but also indirect regulation by agencies of external government."[8] In the case of a highly developed "constitutive contract," the rules system "ensures the reproduction of relations in production by protecting management from itself, from its tendency toward arbitrary interventions that would undermine the consent produced at the point of production."[9]

Between working men and women (which may include "free" wage earners, chattel slaves, indentured labourers, sharecroppers, domestic servants, and many others) and those employing them, there has always been a constant – mostly silent but sometimes overt – struggle concerning employers' discretionary power and over the interpretation of formal and informal rules. There is a constantly shifting "frontier of control," that is, an ongoing struggle for control in the workplace, with managers and supervisors time and again using direct and in-

---

5 https://fr.wikisource.org/wiki/Code_noir/1685, accessed 10 February 2023.
6 This could result in unintended consequences. Sanford M. Jacoby, *Employing Bureaucracy: Managers, Unions, and the Transformation of Work in American Industry, 1900–1945* (New York: Columbia University Press, 1985), has, for example, argued that trade-union opposition against managerial discretionary power has furthered the bureaucratization of American industrial firms.
7 Philip Selznick, *Law, Society and Industrial Justice* (New York: Russell Sage Foundation, 1969), 154.
8 Michael Burawoy, *Manufacturing Consent. Changes in the Labor Process under Monopoly Capitalism* (Chicago and London: Chicago University Press, 1979), 116.
9 Burawoy, *Manufacturing Consent*, 117.

direct means to try to increase their power over their subordinates, and their subordinates, in reaction, trying to maintain and increase their relative autonomy.[10] This concept assumes, therefore, that there is a never-ending conflict between the high and low levels of all hierarchical work organisations. This incongruity is an immediate result of the fact that every labour process represents the transformation of the workers' labour capacity (labour power) into actual labour. This transformation is then never fully circumscribed until the labour process starts.

The balance of power articulated by the frontier of control could vary widely. Sometimes management mainly used its decision-making power, and sometimes it applied non-decision-making and ideological power. At some worksites, workers had a relatively large amount of manoeuvring space. For example, for the nineteenth-century anthracite miners in the United States, the rule applied that the foreman was not allowed to interfere with the work: "Always sit down when the boss is around" – that is, never work in the presence of a supervisor or manager.[11] At other sites, rules would prescribe – down to the minute – when workers had to start their activities, how many times a day they could go to the toilet, how long their breaks were, and so on, with violations often severely punished.

Even under conditions of developed capitalism and formally "free" labour, the frontiers of control remain contested. During the decades after World War Two, the establishment of "standard employment relationships" resulted in a reduction of employers' discretionary power, both on the shop floor and beyond. Since wage labour was increasingly bound to systems of social security provision, labour law was extended and "social property" expanded (Robert Castel). Karl Marx referred to this as the "silent coercion of economic circumstances," which reduced workers' capacity to confront management, lost at least some of its power. This was especially true for the so-called welfare states of the Global North. Under conditions of rapid economic growth, a massive boom in industrial mass production, the ideological competition between East and West during the Cold War, and growing trade union organisation, the position of working men and women vis-à-vis employers was generally strengthened, even beyond the centres of capitalist production. After the end of the postwar boom, employers' discretionary power tended to in-

---

10 The pioneering work on this is: Carter L. Goodrich, *The Frontier of Control. A Study in British Workshop Politics*. Foreword R. H. Tawney (New York: Harcourt, Brace, and Howe, 1920).

11 Harold W. Aurand, "The Anthracite Miner: An Occupational Analysis," *The Pennsylvania Magazine of History and* Biography 104, 4 (1980): 466. Further reflections on this in David Montgomery, *Workers' Control in America: Studies in the History of Work, Technology, and Labor Struggles* (New York: Cambridge University Press, 1979).

crease once again, as unemployment figures rose, precarious jobs spread, and unions lost members and power in many parts of the world.[12]

Such changes in what Burawoy calls the "politics of production" (comprising, for instance, the political regulation of labour) are closely intertwined with politics *in* production,[13] the concrete relations between capital and labour on the shop floor within the organisational boundaries of an enterprise. An enterprise can be considered a special type of rules system, with its own "grammar" to answer a whole series of questions: who is in – a member of the organisation or a specific part of it – and who is out; which activities, resources, purposes, and outcomes are proper and legitimate; when and where should specific activities take place?[14] The rules in any organisation are only formal in part, that is, laid down in by-laws and regulations. Informal rules always play an important role. These rules often reflect the formal rules, but not necessarily. Formal rules are sometimes difficult to implement fully as they do not cover all practises in the labour process and they are often contested. The formal structure of an organisation is always to some extent, to use the expression coined by John Meyer and Brian Rowan, a "ceremonial façade." It is a "façade" because the formal structure does not fully determine organisational practise. The façade restricts the room for organisational manoeuvre, but the formal and the practical levels nevertheless remain more or less loosely coupled. The attribute "ceremonial" points to a second loose coupling: the formal structure needs to be somewhat congruent with the organisation's economic environment and its institutional environment (as constituted, for instance, by the relations of production) if the organisation wants to acquire the legitimacy that is required for its survival.[15] Changes in the "external government of labour" (whether exerted by the state, by associations of workers and employers, or by third parties such as NGOs) tend to have an impact on the relations between capital and labour at the workplace. At the same time, shifts in these workplace relations can have an effect on standards of labour regulation beyond the limits of the organisation, since they have an impact on factors such as the strength of trade unions and the influence of labour on political regulation. Changes in coordination

---

12 Nicole Mayer-Ahuja, "Die Globalität unsicherer Arbeit als konzeptionelle Provokation: Zum Zusammenhang zwischen Informalität im Globalen Süden und Prekarität im Globalen Norden," *Geschichte und Gesellschaft. Zeitschrift für Historische Sozialwissenschaft* 43, 2 (2017): 264–296.
13 Michael Burawoy, *The Politics of Production. Factory Regimes under Capitalism and Socialism* (London and New York: Verso, 1985).
14 Tom R. Burns and Helena Flam, *The Shaping of Social Organization. Social Rule System Theory with Applications* (London: Sage, 1987), 107.
15 In as much as the institutional environment itself comprises different societal sectors with separate logics and meaningful orientations, ambivalencies and contradictions may result.

and control, and thus the limits of discretionary power, must be analysed with regard to this complex field of force.

But all forms of power are also accompanied by forms of counterpower, since, as Michel Foucault aptly noted, "where there is power, there is resistance."[16] Counterpower always challenges one or more aspects of power. It opposes certain decisions, addresses "unquestionable" grievances, and/or creates the possibility of other perceptions, cognitions, and preferences. In labour relations, the permanent confrontation between power and counterpower creates the frontier of control.

Power and Counterpower at Work: Some General Considerations

Much has been written about the balance of power in the workplace. But the literature predominantly treats the two sides in the confrontation as isolated, that is, without studying how changes in a top-down strategy lead to changes in the strategy from below and vice versa. In short, shifts in the frontier of control are often – but certainly not always – omitted from consideration. Nevertheless, the available literature does help us to identify our questions about the frontier of control.

Here, it is important to understand that power struggles are not always confrontational. Following Antonio Gramsci, we can distinguish between two different social conditions. In a non-hegemonic system, social relationships are primarily reproduced through coercion, threats, and force. In a hegemonic system, on the other hand, subordinate workers consent to their exploitation. Coercion still exists, but only as a last resort.[17] In hegemonic systems, the powerful will try to convince the subordinate that it is in their best interests to cooperate in their exploitation. For example, the feudal lord who has his serfs perform *corvée* and justifies this with the protection he can provide against external aggression. All forms of exploitation can be hegemonic or non-hegemonic, but some forms of exploitation tend more towards one pole and some more towards another. Chattel slavery, for example, is frequently based on pure coercion, while wage labour is more likely to lend itself to hegemony.

---

16 Foucault, *La volonté de savoir* (Paris: Gallimard, 1976), 125–126.
17 Antonio Gramsci, *Selections from the Prison Notebooks*. Edited and translated by Quintin Hoare and Geoffrey Nowell Smith (London: New Left Books, 1971).

Recruitment

Let's take a closer look at some aspects of heteronomous labour relations.[18] First in the sequence is the recruitment of potential workers (the people who embody labour capacity or labour power) by a future employer. Broadly speaking, employers can acquire employees through physical coercion or by hiring them. Physical coercion occurs when people are put to work under duress. This would include slaves, convict labourers in the prison-industrial complex, or the villagers in Africa and elsewhere who were forced by colonial rulers to build roads or harvest cotton. In a hiring arrangement, workers present themselves to potential employers without visible coercion. They are "free" to sell their labour power, as Marx has noted, even though they are structurally forced to do so since they are "free" of other forms of property. This is, of course, the usual form of recruitment in the advanced capitalist countries.

Even during the recruitment phase, there is great potential for tension and resistance, especially in cases of physical coercion. Prospective workers sometimes resist their recruitment violently, as in the case of uprisings or suicides on slave ships. It is estimated that

> roughly 15 percent to 20 percent of the ships which left Africa never made it to the "new world." Thousands of vessels were overtaken by the enslaved Africans on board. During some of these takeovers, these Africans, who were sometimes warriors, rose up and killed every white man on these ships. Some of these ships were sailed back to Africa by the once captured men, thousands of the ships disappeared at sea, and many never made it far from the African shores before being overrun.[19]

The threat of uprisings caused the slave traders to limit the freedom of movement of their "merchandise" as much as possible, but this never fully succeeded.

Hiring employees was often made more difficult because many potential employees were reluctant to enter into a heteronomous employment relationship, especially if it meant being separate from home and hearth and having to work in an ominous building such as a factory. Handloom weavers in Lancashire, in the first half of the nineteenth century, were said to have a "general repugnance to mill life"

---

18 In what follows, I will borrow some examples from my book *Workers of the World. Essays toward a Global Labor History* (Leiden and Boston: Brill, 2008).

19 *Atlantic Black Star* (7 February 2014). On suicides by newly enslaved people, see: William D. Piersen, "White Cannibals, Black Martyrs: Fear, Depression, and Religious Faith of Suicide Among New Slaves," *Journal of Negro History* 62, 2 (1977): 147–159.

and be "willing to starve rather than submit to factory discipline."[20] This resistance has occurred repeatedly. In the first decades of the twentieth century, Sudan Government Railways "had great difficulty attracting local Sudanese to wage employment. Typically, rural people were not willing to abandon their farming and pastoral activities for low-paying and arduous railway work."[21] Employers were then forced to entice or mislead employees, which could later lead to protests once the new recruits discovered the real nature of their employment relationship.

Adaptation

After the recruitment phase, the conversion of labour capacity into labour – the labour process proper – can begin. The balance of power between employer and employee can differ considerably between the first and the second phases. One south Russian example illustrates this. The following concerns the hiring market for seasonal agricultural labourers near Taganrog in the Don Oblast in the early 1860s, and depicts negotiations between a group of workers (a so-called *artel*) and a future employer:

> Usually negotiations are conducted with the uncle (*s diad'koi* [the artel head]; the others all lay on the ground in very free and easy poses, and only rarely, in chorus, interfere in the conversation, [which is] of extreme interest to them. Their half crude and even insolent treatment of the employer during negotiations represents a strange and funny contrast with their deferential and even servile behavior with regard to that same employer, if, by mutual consent, they become his *batraki*. The rude treatment before hire is, as if, a farewell to freedom, which they sell for four whole months to their employer. The tone of the employer likewise changes somewhat, but in inverse ratio: before hire, he is mainly exhorting (*uveshchatelen*), fawning and to the highest degree kind (*dobr'*), especially when he contends to the workers, that it is [more] advantageous for them to hire cheaply to him than to another more expensively. After hire he adopts a tone imperious and strict and no longer talks with them amicably, but limits himself to orders.[22]

---

20 Arthur Redford, *Labour Migration in England 1800–1850,* 2nd edition, edited and revised by W.H. Chaloner (Manchester: Manchester University Press, 1964 [First edition 1926]), 40.

21 Ahmad Alawad Sikainga, *"City of Steel and Fire": A Social History of Atbara, Sudan's Railway Town, 1906–1984* (Portsmouth, NH: Heinemann, 2002), 28–29.

22 Dmitri Alferaki, "Zametki o vol'nonaemnykh rabochikh v Novorossiiskom krae, a imenno vozle Taganroga," *Trudy Imperatorskago Vol'nago Ekonomicheskago Obshchestva* 2, 2 (1863): 105; cited here as translated in Timothy Mixter, "The Hiring Market as Workers' Turf: Migrant Agricultural Workers and the Mobilization of Collective Action in the Steppe Grainbelt of European Russia, 1853–1913," in *Peasant Economy, Culture, and Politics of European Russia, 1800–1921,* edited by Esther Kingston-Mann and Timothy Mixter (Princeton: Princeton University Press, 1991), 301.

Managerial control – "the ability of capitalists and/or managers to obtain desired work behaviour from workers" – in its tightest form comprises three elements: (i) direction, or a mechanism or method by which the employer directs work tasks, specifying what needs to be done, in what order, with what degree of precision or accuracy, and in what period of time; (ii) evaluation, or a procedure whereby the employer supervises and evaluates to correct mistakes or other failures in production, to assess each worker's performance, and to identify individual workers or groups of workers who are not performing work tasks adequately; (iii) discipline, or an apparatus that the employer uses to discipline and reward workers, in order to elicit cooperation and compliance with the capitalist's direction of the labour process.[23] These elements are not of equal importance in all work processes. Some activities, for example, do not lend themselves to supervision because the workplace is difficult for the employer to access.

Where direction, evaluation, and discipline play a greater role, employees usually find it more difficult to adjust when they enter the worksite for the first time. Generally, adaptation is more difficult for employees who have not been subjected to heteronomous discipline before, as shown by a large number of anthropological and historical studies:

> Centuries are required before the "free" worker, owing to the greater development of the capitalist mode of production, makes a voluntary agreement, i.e. is compelled by social conditions to sell the whole of his active life, his very capacity for labour, in return for the price of his customary means of subsistence, to sell his birthright for a mess of pottage.[24]

Many cultures do not recognise the concept of "work" as a separate human activity distinguished from other activities such as eating and sleeping. A Native American chief of the Tlingit (British Columbia, Canada) said, for example, to an official:

> I don't know how to work at anything. My father, my grandfather, and uncle just taught me how to live, and I have always done what they told me – we learned this from our fathers and grandfathers and our uncles how to do the things among ourselves and we teach our children in the same way.[25]

Moreover, heteronomous labour implies unequal power relations at work. Frequently, "newcomers" would less easily accept the authority of supervisors, espe-

---

23 R.C. Edwards, *Contested Terrain. The Transformation of the Workplace in the Twentieth Century* (Basic Books: New York, 1979): 17–18.
24 Karl Marx, *Capital*, I, 382.
25 Cited in Cole Harris, "How Did Colonialism Dispossess? Comments from an Edge of Empire," *Annals of the Association of American Geographers* 94, 1 (2004): 172.

cially if they had a different cultural or ethnic background. A case study on the Porgeran people in Papua New Guinea reveals that keeping

> Porgeran workers under non-Porgeran workers' control became a nightmare as they deserted their crew and joined a leader they knew to be of Porgeran origin. [...] They often accorded kinship terms to the crew leaders, despite having no direct relationship or even if they were from another part of the Enga province. They would say, "we are working with our father/ brother or brother-in-law," rather than "under" their leadership that often implied. Or as they saw it, the leader was part of the group rather than its head, and his status was accepted but not his power to direct others.[26]

Adaptation was often a laborious process that led to resistance. Even employees who had already been used to hierarchical labour relations had, for example, to learn the multifaceted peculiarities of the factory game:

> It meant that workers interrupted daily routines not just by turning out but also by covertly and individually stopping machines (to give themselves temporary respites) or by stealing material (to award themselves informal wage supplements). It meant that inasmuch as labourers grew increasingly enmeshed in factory work (so an employment record of brief stints might actually involve years of moving among factory berths), there emerged cohorts of operatives who took advantage of tight labour markets by using the possibility of switching jobs as a softly voiced yet crucial bargaining chip with their employers. It meant that workers, displaying remarkable energy and ingenuity, confronted the novelty of factory conditions – the inescapable divisions of industrial labour, the discipline and supervision, and sometimes the "perpetual" machines – by unilaterally constructing standards of "acceptable" factory work.[27]

Confronted with factories, workers sometimes developed "rejectionist orientations: orientations that had given heavy play to simply quitting factory toil and also, now and again, to efforts (or rumors of efforts) aimed at outright destruction of concentrated industrial facilities."[28]

---

26 Benedict Y. Imbun, "Mining Workers or 'Opportunist' Tribesmen? A Tribal Workforce in a Papua New Guinea Mine," *Oceania* 71, 2 (2000): 142–143.

27 Jonathan Prude, "Capitalism, Industrialization, and the Factory in Post-Revolutionary America," *Journal of the Early Republic* 16, 2 (1996): 254.

28 Arson was often applied. See, for example: Gary Kulik, "Pawtucket Village and the Strike of 1824: The Origin of Class Conflict in Rhode Island," *Radical History Review* 17 (1978): 5–37.

Discipline, Creativity, and the "Zone of Acceptance"

In any heteronomous work process, employers expect employees to perform the work adequately. In addition to certain employee characteristics (e. g., physical strength, intelligence, skills), work performance mainly depends on two elements: discipline and creativity. Discipline, says Max Weber, "is the probability that by virtue of habituation a command will receive prompt and automatic obedience in stere[o]typed forms, on the part of a given group of persons."[29] Discipline includes a wide variety of behaviours, such as "punctually arriving at work; conscientiously performing one's job; respecting machinery, materials, and products; obeying the instructions of foremen, and other responsible personnel; and minimising absence from work."[30] Creativity is necessary for every labour process as it is impossible for all elements of performance in a labour contract to be spelled out. Harvey Leibenstein was justified in noting that a good deal is always left to "custom, authority, and whatever motivational techniques are available to management as well to individual discretion and judgement."[31] Both factors are essential for the functioning of any enterprise, although their relative importance can differ from worksite to worksite. Supervision, incentives, and penalties allow managers to regulate a significant part of employee behaviour, but employees always retain some leeway.[32] The boundaries within which employees can be expected to obey orders are, following Herbert Simon, known as "zones of acceptance":

> The zone of acceptance is also sometimes called a "zone of indifference", for the choice among alternative behaviors, while of major importance to the employer, may be of little or no concern to the employee. A secretary, for example, usually has little or no preference for typing a letter to one of the company's customers rather than another, and little interest in the content of the letter. Even a factory manager will accept, within wide limits, whatever mix of products the factory is ordered to produce in a given month.[33]

Managers always need some degree of voluntary cooperative effort from their workers. The fact that "working to rule" can be an effective form of employee ac-

---

29 Max Weber, *The Theory of Social and Economic Organization* [*Wirtschaft und Gesellschaft*, Part I]. Trans. A.R. Henderson and Talcott Parsons (London [etc.]: William Hodge & Co., 1947), 139.
30 William Chase, *Workers, Society and the Soviet State: Labor and Life in Moscow, 1918–1929* (Urbana and Chicago: University of Illinois Press, 1987), 35.
31 Harvey Leibenstein, "Allocation Efficiency and 'X-Efficiency,'" *American Economic Review* 56 (1966): 407.
32 Reinhard Bendix, *Work and Authority in Industry*, 2nd ed. (Berkeley: University of California Press, 1974), 251.
33 Herbert A. Simon, "Organizations and Markets," *Journal of Economic Perspectives* 5, 2 (1991): 31.

tion proves this point: if workers carry out instructions to the letter, then it becomes transparent that these instructions are always incomplete and partly inconsistent; the labour process breaks down.[34] Absolute control is impossible, even under extreme circumstances.[35] The zone of acceptance means that employees can try to explore and, if possible, push the boundaries of their room for manoeuvre. This is how shirking can arise:

> When I worked at a *chaeböl* in the late 1980s, I was struck by how many people went around saying "I am busy" in lieu of ordinary greetings. Although they were busily pacing to and fro or conspicuously shuffling papers at their desk, I noticed over time that their punctuality and overt expressions of diligence masked a variety of efforts to avoid work. Managerial gaze targeted discernible features, such as tardiness, early departure, or relaxed demeanor. The constant refrain "I am busy" not only reminded superiors and colleagues about their busy-ness (and therefore their excellence) but also warded off additional business that would otherwise be foisted upon them.[36]

Shirking and other such behaviour can be rational from a strictly economic point of view. Just as it can also be rational for the employer not to keep to an agreement:

> Indeed, it always pays for a party not to perform its part of an agreement if that non-performance does not decrease the probability that the other parties will fulfill their obligations and if it suffers no loss (penalties, foregone future earnings or loss of 'goodwill') as a consequence of non-performance.[37]

---

34 Pierre Chaulieu [Cornelius Castoriadis], "Sur le contenu du socialisme," *Socialisme ou Barbarie* 17 (1955): 1–25; 22 (July-September 1957): 1–74; and 23 (1958): 81–125; Yvon Bourdet, "Les contradictions de l'hétérogestion," *Autogestion* 8 (June 1969): 135–170; Ulrich Beck and Michael Brater, "Grenzen abstrakter Arbeit," *Leviathan* 4, 2 (1976): 178–215.

35 On the Nazi concentration camps, Barrington Moore, Jr. observes: "[T]he officials could not control, through fear or other sanctions, absolutely every detail of the prisoner's life. Some areas of autonomy, or at least pseudo-autonomy, have to be left to prisoners in order to get them to do such simple things as march to their eating and sleeping quarters at the appropriate moment." In Barrington Moore, *Injustice: The Social Bases of Obedience and Revolt* (Armonk, NJ: M.E. Sharpe, 1978), 70.

36 John Lie, "What Makes Us Great. *Chaeböl* Development, Labor Practices, and Managerial Ideology," in *Transformations in Twentieth-Century Korea*, edited by Chang Yun-Shik and Steven Hugh Lee (London and New York: Routledge, 2006), 143.

37 Victor P. Goldberg, "Bridges over Contested Terrain. Exploring the Radical Account of the Employment Relationship," *Journal of Economic Behavior and Organization* 1, 3 (1980): 253.

Work Incentives

In heteronomous industrial relations, the two components of work motivation (discipline and creativity) result from a combination of three factors: compensation, coercion, and commitment, which together explain why workers are more or less motivated to do their jobs according to the employer's standards: compensation, or the offer of contingent rewards like wages and other benefits; coercion, or the threat to inflict harm; and commitment, or the invocation of loyalty.[38] In this view, the relative weight of these three motives, which varies over time and from job to job, defines the various work-incentive systems.

Compensation can be divided into three categories: (i) direct wages, i.e., money wages. These can be further subdivided in (a) compensation for the time people work (time rates); (b) compensation for the results of people's work (piece rates: payment for each item produced; commission (for salespeople): workers receive a fraction of the value of the items they sell; gainsharing: group-incentives that partially tie gains in group productivity, reductions in cost, increases in product quality, or other measures of group success; profit-sharing and bonus plans (which relate wages to the enterprise's profits); (c) a hybrid of time and result-based wages. (ii) Indirect wages, such as insurance arrangements, pay for holidays and vacations, services, and perquisites. "Inasmuch as these are generally made uniformly available to all employees at a given job level, regardless of performance, they are really not motivating rewards. However, where indirect compensation is controllable by management and is used to reward performance, then it clearly needs to be considered as a motivating reward."[39] (iii) Invisible wages, i.e. the non-contractual appropriation by employees of enterprise goods and services. This category covers a range of wage-forms, including open and legal perks, semi-legal pilfering, and outright theft.[40]

The above-mentioned existence of zones of acceptance and always-incomplete control systems implies that employers face

> a trade-off between spending more money on improving the effectiveness of monitoring or paying higher employment rents. Such efficiency wages are a form of negative class compro-

38 Chris Tilly and Charles Tilly, *Work Under Capitalism* (Boulder, CO, and Oxford: Westview Press, 1998).
39 Stephen P. Robbins, *Organizational Behavior: Concepts, Controversies, Applications* (7th Edn, Englewood Cliffs, NJ: Prentice Hall, 1996), 660.
40 Jason Ditton, "Perks, Pilferage, and the Fiddle: The Historical Structure of Invisible Wages," *Theory and Society* 4, 1 (1977): 39–71.

mise insofar as the higher wages are an alternative to more purely coercive strategies by employers in the face of strategies of resistance (shirking) by individual workers.[41]

Coercion comprises disciplinary rules and their sanctioning. It can be applied to enforce discipline, but hardly as a punishment for a lack of creativity. Coercion operates in three areas:[42] (i) disciplinary liability, i.e. the breaking of work rules, punishment for which can include castigation, demotion (transfer to other lower-paid work for a certain period), and dismissal; (ii) criminal liability, i.e. the breaking of criminal law, with corresponding punishments; (iii) material liability, where punishment includes restitution in cash or kind to the enterprise for damage to its property resulting from an infringement of labour discipline.

Commitment comprises incentives based on four main motives: "(i) pride in craftsmanship, in record achievements or the company one is working for; (ii) local loyalties; (iii) desire for public recognition and approbation; (iv) a generalized desire to serve the community."[43] These motives are very much linked to the cultural context. Illustrative is what the English observer G.R. Barker wrote in the 1950s:

> The stimuli most widely used in the USSR, for example, would generally prove useless or worse in our conditions. The honours awarded to categories of people regarded as socially valuable in the way of uniforms, medals, decorations and badges would provoke not competition for them, as visible tokens of high status, but embarrassment and possibly even contempt.[44]

Examples of commitment-incentives include: the enterprise "Book of Honour," publicity for model-workers, honorific titles ('Hero of Labour'), selection as "employee of the month," medals, and badges.

Hidden Forms of Resistance

Subaltern workers may resort to a wide range of strategies. Just exactly what forms of protest are used depends on many factors, but in all cases the strength of the workers' bargaining position is important. Even the weakest segments of the working class can resort to methods such as pretending to misunderstand assignments,

---

41 Erik Olin Wright, "Working-Class Power, Capitalist-Class Interests, and Class Compromise," *American Journal of Sociology* 105, 4 (2000): 966.
42 G.R. Barker, *Some Problems of Incentives*, 98–99.
43 G.R. Barker, *Some Problems of Incentives*, 113.
44 G.R. Barker, *Some Problems of* Incentives, 113–114.

delivering substandard work, shirking, or collective theft.[45] Violent methods have often been a means to exert pressure. Arson occurred on many plantations in the "New World," but also in Europe. In East Anglia (in England) such incidents increased dramatically after 1830, during the agrarian protest movement of "Captain Swing" and following the invention of the "strike-anywhere match."[46] Edward Thompson made the following observation:

> It is exactly in a rural society, where any open, identified resistance to the ruling power may result in instant retaliation – loss of home, employment, tenancy, if not victimization at law – that one tends to find the acts of darkness: the anonymous letter, arson of the stack or outhouse, houghing of cattle, the shot or brick through the window, the gate off its hinges, the orchard felled, the fishpond sluices opened at night. The same man who touches his forelock to the squire by day – and who may go down to history as an example of deference – may kill his sheep, snare his pheasants or poison his dogs at night.[47]

Covert measures may also include secretly ridiculing those in power, sending anonymous letters, and breaking windows.[48]

Overt forms of resistance

Resistance becomes more visible when workers coordinate reductions in output to provide a larger number of workers with employment, to improve piecework rates, or to pressure the employer or management in some other way. This method is also known as "go-slow," "ca'canny," or "gold-bricking" and has been applied by "free" and "unfree" workers alike. During a three-day protest campaign in 1904, the indentured Chinese hammer-men on the North Randfontein gold-mine in Transvaal drilled no more than "thirteen inches of rock or drilled less than twelve inches."[49] In Chicago in 1900,

> the lathers limited their day's work to twenty-five bundles and were paid three dollars, whilst formerly they handled thirty-five bundles a day for one dollar and seventy-five cents. The gas

---

45 See, for example: Robin Cohen, "Resistance and Hidden Forms of Consciousness Amongst African Workers," *Review of African Political Economy* 19 (1980): 8–22.

46 John E. Archer, *"By a Flash and a Scare": Arson, Animal Maiming, and Poaching in East Anglia, 1815–1870* (Oxford: Clarendon Press, 1990), 251–254.

47 Thompson, *Customs In Common* (New York: The New Press, 1991), 66.

48 See, for example: James C. Scott, *Domination and the Arts of Resistance. Hidden Transcripts* (New Haven, CT: Yale University Press, 1990).

49 Peter Richardson, "Coolies and Randlords: the North Randfontein Chinese Miners' 'Strike' of 1905," *Journal of Southern African Studies* 2, 2 (1976): 166–167.

fitters, steam fitters, plasterers and plumbers in the same city had reduced their exertion in a similar way. The plumbers had a specially low standard of exertion, their day's work being only sufficient to keep a man busy for half or two-thirds of a day.[50]

In 1946, miners in Enugu (Nigeria) launched a "ca'canny"; their leader Isaiah Okwudili Ojiyi "indigenized the term by calling it '*welu nwayo*' in Igbo and spent days in the mines teaching the men."[51]

What dockworkers in New Zealand in the twentieth century called "spelling" relates to go-slow methods. Historian Anna Green observed the following:

> The precise definition of spelling varied a little. The manager of the Waterfront Control Commission described it as the 'taking of rest periods', a definition with which the watersiders would have agreed. Spelling involved the absence from the job of one or more men, the gang taking it in turns to have a spell or rest period. The precise number spelling on any given occasion fluctuated according to the cargo being worked, but up to half of the gang might be spelling at any one time. Although this was usually on an hour about basis, it appears to have stretched on occasion, by the late 1940s, to a week about.[52]

Protest tactics could be more violent as well. Machine breaking (Luddism) was a well-known practise in early nineteenth-century Europe, and later occurred in the Ottoman Empire, Brazil, and China.[53] Such protests could also come from transport workers:

> In September 1924, the 8,000 rickshaws coolies in Hangkou went on strike until car traffic was stopped again. Modern means of transport, in particular, aroused hatred. Already during the Boxer Rebellion, the canal boatmen and porters, who felt threatened with unemployment by the Peking-Tientsin Railway, were in the foremost ranks of the xenophobes. In Swatou in 1927,

---

50 John Martin, "Do Trade Unions Limit Output?," *Political Science Quarterly* 17, 3 (1902): 371.
51 Carolyn A. Brown, *"We Were All Slaves": African Miners, Culture, and Resistance at the Enugu Government Colliery* (Portsmouth: Heinemann, Oxford: James Currey, and Cape Town: David Philip, 2003), 295.
52 Anna Green, "Spelling, Go-Slows, Gliding Away and Theft: Informal Control over Work on the New Zealand Waterfront, 1915–1951," *Labour History* 63 (1992): 107.
53 See, for example: Frank E. Manuel, "The Luddite Movement in France," *Journal of Modern History* 10 (1938): 180–211; Eric J. Hobsbawm, "The Machine Breakers" (1952), in *Labouring Men. Studies in the History of Labour* (London: Weidenfeld and Nicolson, 1964), 5–22; Malcolm I. Thomis, *The Luddites: Machine Breaking in Regency England* (Newton Abbot: David & Charles, 1970); Donald Quataert, "Machine Breaking and the Changing Carpet Industry of Western Anatolia, 1860–1908," *Journal of Social History* 19, 13 (1986): 473–489; Teresa Meade, "'Living Worse and Costing More': Resistance and Riot in Rio de Janeiro, 1890–1917," *Journal of Latin American Studies* 21 (1989): 241–266; Robert Y. Eng, "Luddism and Labor Protest Among Silk Artisans and Workers in Jiangnan and Guangdong, 1860–1930," *Late Imperial China* 11, 2 (December 1990): 63–101.

coolies smashed the buses, in Beijing thousands of them lay down on the rails of the tram to prevent them from opening.[54]

Sometimes dynamite was used, if available. In 1890, gold miners at the Anglo-Tharis mine (South Africa) responded to a cut in pay by blowing up the manager's house.[55] Physical and sexual violence was also used against hated employers, their family members, or their representatives among all groups of subaltern workers. "Nearly every year, in virtually every state in the South [of the United States], slaves were indicted for killing their owners."[56] In South Africa in around 1900, a Zulu-dominated secret society existed, the Izigebengu, whose adherents would rape white mistresses to punish them for abusing black "houseboys."[57] Even today, workers resort to violent means if institutional means of conflict resolution are non-existent or blocked (for instance, if cases are filed but not dealt with by the courts, or if existing laws are not implemented).[58]

A protest can also be largely symbolic. In contemporary Southeast Asia, factory women regularly express their discontent by crying, screaming, or having "epileptic" fits en masse.[59] Mock trials were also very popular in the past, such as the "court hearing" described by Robert Darnton, where eighteenth-century Parisian journeymen punished several cats to censure their master and his wife for conduct that they considered unjustified.[60] Such symbolic protests were a frequent alternative to "economic" action. Prior to 1917, Petrograd metal workers had very few formal means for staging protests. They therefore took to humiliating their despised

---

54 Otto Mänchen-Helfen, "Der Weg des chinesischen Proletariats," *Die Gesellschaft* II (1931): 262 [my own translation].

55 Peter Richardson and Jean Jacques van Helten, "Labour in the South African Gold Mining Industry, 1886–1914," in *Industrialization and Social Change in South Africa*, edited by Shula Marks and Richard Rathbone (London: Longman, 1983), 92; Robin Cohen, *The New Helots. Migrants in the International Division of Labour* (Aldershot: Gower, 1987), 204.

56 John Hope Franklin and Loren Schweninger, *Runaway Slaves. Rebels on the Plantation* (New York: Oxford University Press, 1999), 78.

57 Charles van Onselen, *Studies in the Social and Economic History of the Witwatersrand, 1886–1914*, Vol. 2: New Nineveh (Harlow: Longman, 1982), 54–55.

58 One example may suffice: in July 2012, workers' violence in the Maruti Suzuki car manufacturing plant in Manesar (India) left a senior HR executive dead and nearly 100 other officials injured, which led to the conviction of 31 workers. See *Hindustan Times* (14 January 2022).

59 See, for example: Aihwa Ong, *Spirits of Resistance and Capitalist Discipline. Factory Women in Malaysia* (Albany, NY: SUNY Press, 1987); Ines Smyth and Mies Grijns, "*Unjuk Rasa* or Conscious Protest? Resistance Strategies of Indonesian Women Workers," *Bulletin of Concerned Asian Scholars* 29, 4 (1997): 20.

60 Robert Darnton, *The Great Cat Massacre and Other Episodes in French Cultural History* (Harmondsworth: Penguin, 1984), 79–104.

superiors by wheeling them out of the factory in a wheelbarrow.[61] Some workers presented petitions, to which they sometimes added bribes "to sweeten the petition-receiver's temperament."[62]

An important form of struggle used by all categories of workers is the refusal to work. The most familiar form is of course the strike, where a group of workers collectively stops working to enforce economic, social, and/or political demands that matter to those directly concerned and/or others.[63] Because the aim of a strike is to inflict economic damage on the employer, strikers may take additional measures. They might block the use of means of labour, either by cutting off the supply of raw materials, semi-manufactures, and the like, or by tampering with equipment; they might block the sale of labour products by preventing their transport, through a consumer boycott, or by rendering goods or services useless; they may take court action; they might try to influence the credit line available to the firm; or they might commit personal acts of violence against the employer, the shareholders, or their representatives. These methods can obviously not be applied in all cases. The options depend on the broader political and legal context. If used, these methods could coincide with a strike, although they may also precede or follow one.

It is important to note that employees do not always leave the worksite during a strike. There are several kinds of strikes where they stay put. One variant is the 'sit-down' or 'stay-in,' where workers occupy the workplace without working. This strategy was first applied in the nineteenth century and became a veritable international trend during the 1930s. Another form is the 'work-in.' Here, production continues during the occupation of the firm. In Italy this practise is known as a "reverse strike" (*sciopero a rovescio*). In addition to occupying the premises, workers take control of the production process – there is a fluid transition to a production cooperative. Such forms of action implicitly or explicitly call into question the

---

61 Steve Smith, *Red Petrograd* (Cambridge: Cambridge University Press, 1983), 56–7.

62 This happened during the rickshaw pullers' strike in Changsha, Hunan Province, China, in 1918. See Angus W. McDonald Jr., *The Urban Origins of Rural Revolution. Elites and the Masses in Hunan Province, China, 1911–1927* (Berkeley: University of California Press, 1978), 148. David McCreery reports that on coffee plantations in Guatemala around 1900, petitions were "by far the most common mode of resistance." See David McCreery, "Hegemony and Repression in Rural Guatemala, 1871–1940," in *Plantation Workers: Resistance and Accommodation*, edited by Brij V. Lal, Doug Munro, and Edward D. Beechert (Honolulu: University of Hawaii Press, 1993), 217–239. See also Lex Heerma van Voss, ed., *Petitions in Social History.* Supplement 9 of the *International Review of Social History* (Cambridge: Cambridge University Press, 2001).

63 Strikes are often organised by trade unions. But even major strikes can take place without unions. See, for example, Jörg Nowak, *Mass Strikes and Social Movements in Brazil and India: Popular Mobilisation in the Long Depression* (Cham: Palgrave Macmillan, 2019).

frontier of control in and of itself. The next step is the 'collective exit,' a spectacular form of protest where a group of workers leave the workplace with the intention never to return. Such exits seem to have occurred especially among workers who were unable to assert their interests in the workplace collectively, or could do so only at great personal risk. The most important examples are found among slaves, indentured labourers, journeymen, and wage earners working in 'total institutions,' such as sailors. Due to the definitive character of such an exit, the frontier of control loses its meaning, with employees refusing to accept the employer's power any longer.[64]

Divide and Rule

Obviously, entrepreneurs tend to try to counteract employees' attempts to shift the frontier of control in their own favour as much as possible. As mentioned above, managers can always rely on various work incentives to motivate employees. But if these incentives prove insufficient, employers have many other methods to achieve their goal. Key here are attempts to undermine employee unity by emphasising ethnic, racial, and gender divisions. This applies in particular to "free" wage earners who, after all, "are in constant competition among themselves."[65] Such attempts are more visible in split labour markets, where employees are divided into higher and lower segments along lines of gender and race. John Stuart Mill already observed the following in 1848:

> So complete, indeed has hitherto been the separation, so strongly marked the line of demarcation, between the different grades of labourers, as to be almost equivalent to a hereditary distinction of caste; each employment being chiefly recruited from the children of those already employed in it, or in employments of the same rank with it in social estimation, or from the children of persons who, if originally of a lower rank, have succeeded in raising themselves by their exertions.[66]

If such methods do not achieve sufficient effect and employees nevertheless unite in unions or similar organisations, then employers have numerous other anti-la-

---

64 A more extensive comparative analysis of work refusals can be found in Marcel van der Linden, *Workers of the World. Essays toward a Global Labor History* (Leiden and Boston: Brill, 2008), 175–207.
65 Friedrich Engels, "The Condition of the Working-Class in England", *Marx-Engels Collected Works*, Vol. 4 (London: Lawrence & Wishart, 2010), 375.
66 John Stuart Mill, *Principles of Political Economy with Some of Their Applications to Social Philosophy*, Vol. 1 of 2 (London: Parker, 1848), 462.

bour (union busting) strategies at their disposal. Perhaps it makes sense to distinguish four methods: (i) Fear Stuff, (ii) Sweet Stuff, (iii) Evil Stuff, and (iv) Subversive Stuff. Fear Stuff refers to the intimidation of workers by threatening to cut their wages, to dismiss or imprison them, or to physically to assault them. Sweet Stuff refers to attempts to lure workers away from the labour movement by offering paternalistic or nationalistic 'alternatives,' such as corporate housing or yellow unions. Evil Stuff is about attempts to show, through propaganda and 'revelations,' that the labour movement has concluded a pact with the devil and intends to betray the fatherland, the white race, or something similar. Subversive Stuff seeks to undermine workers' organisations by means of espionage, provocation, and so on.[67]

The Need for an Encompassing Approach

The foregoing makes it clear that the battle at the frontier of control has an extraordinary number of variants and manifestations. Moreover, this battle is not always a zero-sum game, where one side loses what the other side wins. In a classic study of a group of 14 operators at Western Electric in the years 1927 to 1932, sociologist George Homans found that the men

> had a clear idea of a proper day's work: about two completed equipments, or 6,600 connections, for a man working on connectors, 6,000 for a man working on selectors. The wiremen in the room felt, as they had felt in the department, that no more work than this should be turned out, and this much was well within the capacity of most of them. They tended to work hard in the morning, until the completion of a day's work was in sight, and then to take it easy in the afternoon as quitting time approached. As the pressure lessened, conversation, games, and the preparation of tools and equipment for the next day's work took more and more time. It appears impossible to determine how the figure of two equipments per day was reached. Perhaps a good round number was wanted, with no connections left over. Moreover, the figure was not objectively low. *The output of the department was considered wholly satisfactory by the company.* [...] Yet output was clearly not as great as it would have been if it had been limited only by fatigue. [...] Many workingmen would have called it 'doing a fair day's work for a fair day's wage.'[68]

---

67 The first three terms are taken from Donald F. Roy, "Fear Stuff, Sweet Stuff and Evil Stuff: Management's Defences Against Unionization in the South," in *Capital and Labour. Studies in the Capitalist Labour Process*, edited by Theo Nichols(London: The Athlone Press, 1980), 395–415, although my interpretation of them is slightly different from his.
68 George C. Homans, *The Human Group* (London: Routledge & Kegan Paul, 1951), 60 [italics my own]. The operators strictly monitored the agreed amount of output: "If a man did turn out more than was thought proper, or if he worked too fast, he was exposed to merciless ridicule.

Half a century later, Michael Burawoy, on the basis of participant observation at Allied Corporation, also came to the conclusion that "foremen actively assisted operators in making out":

> When operators handed in more than the acceptable limit (140 percent), not only fellow workers but shop management might protest. Thus, the superintendent frequently returned time cards to operators when they showed more than 140 percent, requesting them to reduce the number of pieces and bank the remainder.

This behaviour was completely rational since an increased output per operator could lead to a rise of the piece rates.

> Assigning a new rate to a job could mean turnover of personnel, since workers tend to transfer to jobs where the rates are easier to make. As a result, there would be training costs, lower levels of output, more scrap, and so forth. Alternatively, operators would engage in 'goldbricking' because the new rate was "impossible", and this too implied lowered levels of output.[69]

This shows that at least lower level management may cooperate in the game of making out, while upper management usually strongly opposes this game.[70] The location of the frontier of control is itself controversial.

A second misconception is that the means of struggle for employees and employers always differ fundamentally. For example, it is not correct that only employees reduce output. Thorsten Veblen already pointed out that the "captains of industry" themselves also restrict output when this promotes their company's profitability. He spoke of a "conscientious withdrawal of efficiency," which he referred

---

He was called a 'rate-buster' or a 'speed king,' but at the same time a man who turned out too little was a 'chiseler.' He was cutting down the earnings of the group. [...] A game called 'binging' was played in the Observation Room [...]. If, according to the rules of this game, a man walked up to another man and hit him as hard as he could on the upper arm – 'binged' him, the other then had the right to retaliate with another such blow, the object being to see who could hit the harder. But binging was also used as a penalty. A man who was thought to be working either too fast or too slow might be binged." (60–61)

69 Michael Burawoy, *Manufacturing Consent. Changes in the Labor Process under Monopoly Capitalism* (Chicago: Chicago University Press, 1979), 80.

70 "Why is there a struggle within management? Because upper management is very conscious of the fact that profits would be maximized if output restriction could be ended, but they do not understand – nor would they have to directly deal with – what would happen on the shop floor were a serious attempt made to end output restriction." See Dan Clawson and Richard Fantasia, "Beyond Burawoy: The Dialectics of Conflict and Consent on the Shop Floor," *Theory and Society* 12, 5 (1983): 677.

to as sabotage.[71] The economist Harvey Leibenstein noted the following in a famous article:

> The simple fact is that neither individuals nor firms work as hard [...] as they could. [...] There are four reasons why given inputs cannot be transformed into predetermined outputs: (a) contracts for labor are incomplete, (b) not all factors of production are marketed, (c) the production function is not completely specified or known, and (d) interdependence and uncertainty lead competing firms to cooperate tacitly with each other in some respects, and imitate each other with respect to techniques, to some degree.[72]

In combination, both insights reveal that neoclassical and Marxist models of factories and other companies that like oiled machines cannot achieve maximum production because of the opposition from the personnel have little to do with reality. In the real world, employees and employers occupy symmetrical positions: "Each is seeking, by its own lights and given its opportunity set, its advantage. To this end, individual businesses (and therefore business as a whole) restrict output in pursuit of profit, and workers restrict output in pursuit of higher wages."[73]

In addition, employee resistance and subordination are not mutually exclusive and do not exist completely in isolation. This, then, has two implications:

> [T]o understand and analyse resistance (or, for that matter, subordination) we cannot adopt absolutist categories which imply a settled, determined and foreclosed character; and secondly, we cannot assume that these traditions of resistance are at most marginal and at best 'economist' aspects of labour's history.[74]

Frontiers of control are constantly evolving. There are always broader social factors that influence their ever-changing course. They also do not develop linearly in one direction but are more likely to exhibit a certain cyclical behaviour since the frontier shifts according to the broader political, economic, and ideological balance of forces.[75] Most likely, broader social relationships play an essential role in

---

71 Thorstein Veblen, *The Engineers and the Price System* (New York: B.W. Huebsch, 1921), 38.
72 Leibenstein, "Allocative Efficiency vs. 'X-Efficiency'": 407.
73 Warren J. Samuels, "On 'Shirking' and 'Business Sabotage': A Note," *Journal of Economic Issues* 28, 4 (1994): 1250.
74 Richard Price, "Rethinking Labour History", in *Social Conflict and the Political Order in Modern Britain*, edited by James E. Cronin and Jonathan Schneer(London and Canberra: Croom Helm, 1982), 198–199.
75 See, for example, the pioneering analysis in: Harvie Ramsay, "Cycles of Control: Worker Participation in Sociological and Historical Perspective," *Sociology* 11, 3 (1977): 481–506.

this. Alexis de Tocqueville suggested that in feudal societies the relationship between "master" and "servant" takes on kinship-like traits:

> So among aristocratic peoples, the master comes to envisage his servants like an inferior and secondary part of himself, and he often interests himself in their fate, by a final effort of egoism. On their side, the servants are not far from considering themselves from the same point of view, and they sometimes identify with the person of the master, so that they finally become an accessory, in their own eyes, as in his.[76]

Of course, there is also a frontier of control in such a feudal relationship, but we can surmise that it takes shape differently than in a bureaucratic enterprise. Under feudal relations, for example, "working to rule" is unlikely, while under "impersonal systematization" that is an obvious form of resistance.[77]

This Volume's Contributions

A great deal is thus known about managerial power and employees' counterpower. But much is also still unclear. How do power mechanisms work in practise? What kind of broader social factors influence their development? Which micro-influences play a role? The essays in this collection aim to shed some light on this. Applying a sectorial logic, we open this collection with two studies on agriculture, then move on to industrial labour, and end with transportation and logistics.

The first essay is about Assam's tea plantations – India's biggest employer of labour. Rana Pratap Behal describes how, from the 1860s onwards, for over a century, the labour force was recruited from Bihar, Bengal, Orissa, and Uttar Pradesh through the notorious "coolie trade." He reconstructs the changing production relations on the plantations during this period. Under colonial rule, those in power dominated by deploying coercion and extra-legal authority, aided and abetted by the colonial state. Early in the post-colonial era, in 1951, the Indian Parliament passed the Plantation Labour Act, which sought to provide for the welfare of labour and to regulate the conditions of workers in plantations. Trade unions were formed and recognised. Behal explores the economic, social, and cultural implications of these shifts for the "coolies" and their families.

---

76 Alexis de Tocqueville, *Democracy in America*. Historical-critical edition of *De la démocratie en Amérique*. Ed. Eduardo Nolla. Trans. James T. Schleifer. Vol. I (Indianapolis: Liberty Fund, 2010), 1011–1012.
77 Reinhard Bendix, *Force, Fate, and Freedom. On Historical Sociology* (Berkeley: University of California Press, 1984), 84–85.

Focusing on collective farm work in China (especially in Xingping County, Shaanxi) from the 1950s to the 1980s, Jacob Eyfert asks how the state was able to achieve control over labour processes, despite the fact that agricultural work is difficult to standardise and that the state had little disciplinary power over its "employees" – who were not on the state's payroll and could not be laid off or demoted. He demonstrates that the central government enforced very labour intensive methods of cultivation, in the face of resistance from rural people. Almost the entire able-bodied population was drawn into productive work and the length of the average workday was greatly increased, to an extent that the routine reproduction of life in the household became a problem. The state's actions used administrative fiat, physical coercion, ideological mobilisation, and material incentives, but the causal configuration as a whole has not yet been fully mapped.

From a different perspective, Ju Li traces in her case study of the "Nanfang" steel company in the mountainous area of Sichuan, the changing mode and efficiency of labour resistance movements as adopted by two generations of state-owned-enterprise workers from the 1960s to the present. Using both archival and oral sources, she reveals a remarkable contrast between the older and the younger generation of wage earners. Despite the absence of effective trade unions, the retired workers, who still harboured vivid memories of the more militant working-class traditions that had emerged during the Cultural Revolution, launched a number of successful contentious collective actions during the 1980s, while the contemporary workers, who were more directly influenced by carrot and stick policies, were largely compliant and even cooperative – thus resigning themselves to the new capitalist labour relations.

Building on a wide variety of sources, Görkem Akgöz analyses how in 1930s republican Turkey a new ideology of women's work began to be articulated, which would shape state, employer, and trade union policies in subsequent decades. Appealing to a narrative of women's citizenship rights and duties related to work, the state attempted to increase female industrial labour participation. This attempt as such did not have much effect, but nevertheless many women were recruited, driven by poverty. Focusing on the textile and tobacco industries, Akgöz describes how they were integrated into the gendered shop floor hierarchy. It wasn't until the 1950s that female workers started to question such gender divisions, resulting, in the 1960s and 1970s, in industrial disputes.

Christian Strümpell reports on his long-term ethnographic research into the Rourkela Steel Plant (Odisha), one of India's biggest steel plants. He shows how from the 1950s to the 1980s, ethnic and caste identifications played a major role in labour recruitment and the structuring of labour processes. The workers, in attempts at collective action, sometimes succeeded in crossing these dividing lines, but often failed. Since the 1990s, in the wake of India's transition to economic liberalisation, employment status replaced ethnicity and caste as the major fault line between workers at the plant. This new differentiation was not only economic, but increasingly also social and political. Power relations at work can therefore not be studied in isolation but should always be seen as being co-shaped by wider society.

Toby Boraman's contribution, however, cautions against an overemphasis on the role of employers, markets, and the state. There is a danger of marginalising worker and labour-union agency and neglecting labour processes, especially everyday social relations, experiences, and struggles on the shop floor. Focusing on the meat processing industry in Aotearoa New Zealand in the 1970s and 1980s, he shows how informal resistance and overt strikes were much inspired by indigenous Maori meatworkers, who made up almost half of the workforce and played an important role in grassroots workplace organisation. These bonds allowed workers and unions to often disregard the formal dispute resolution mechanisms, and to take direct action for better wages and conditions.

Sabine Rutar's essay discusses developments in the northeastern Adriatic port city of Rijeka (Croatia) during the postwar period until the 1970s. She focuses both on managers' ideas and practises towards controlling the shop floor and workers' resistance. She looks, in particular, at the shipyard 3. Maj, Yugoslavia's largest shipbuilding enterprise. Her analysis of labour relations and shop floor practices at the time of partial democratisation between 1966 and 1971 shows that the economic reforms initiated in the mid-1960s produced new freedoms but also new discontent. Two large, and in part aggressive, strikes in June 1969 and June 1971 revealed that the authoritarian embedding of the system of "workers' self-management" led to "ever more extensive regulation, and, ultimately, a veritable fragmentation of relations on the shop floor." In the mid-1970s, the possibilities for democratization had thus been exhausted.

The last three studies cover maritime labour. Ravi Ahuja studies the British shipping industry from the 1880s to the late 1920s. At the time, the steamships combined cutting-edge technology in the engine-room with labour intensive, low-technology work processes in the stokehold. Especially in the so-called liner business, the inflexible schedules demanded a high degree of punctuality. One of the ways in which labour management could provide this was through the recruitment of cheap "lascars" from the colonies. "Racial management" made it possible to form internal labour reserves that minimised the risk of delays and service interruptions – while keeping the wage bill down.

The next chapter also looks at the crews of steamships in the southern African region, from the 1870s to the formalisation and extension of apartheid in 1948. Focusing on ports on the southern African littoral (South West Africa, Natal, the Cape, and Portuguese-ruled Mozambique and Angola), Jonathan Hyslop argues that the political struggles and military power of the British state were crucial in giving particular forms to the lifeworld of maritime labour. In a similar vein to Ahuja, he points to the importance of "racial management," but also emphasises not only that the legal rights of colonised workers were weak, but that the white sailors were not fully "free" either. Despite repeated repression, groups of maritime workers continued to organise strikes and unions. If that proved impossible, they would resort to informal resistance, especially desertion.

Daniel Tödt's study draws attention to an often-neglected aspect of maritime labour: his study of the Congolese seafarers working on Belgian steamships from the 1920s to the 1950s reveals how crews were also monitored as much as possible ashore. To prevent sailors from being indoctrinated with anti-colonial and communist ideas, their leisure activities were monitored by means of Catholic seafarers' homes in Antwerp and Matadi. Despite the surveillance, the sailors managed to use their stay on shore to smuggle goods. The shifting discretionary power of employers and other external agents is especially evident in the conflicts over such "invisible wages."

In her concluding chapter, Nicole Mayer-Ahuja seeks to approach a global perspective on power at work by summarising and rearranging the lines of argument that are central to several of the case studies in this volume. She identifies management strategies that shift the frontiers of control towards capital in different spatio-temporal constellations. These include technological and organisational rationalisation and the relocation of production and workers, as well as companies attempting to divide and rule the workforce by changing its composition along the lines of gender, ethnicity, and employment status. Since management strategies cannot be easily equated with actual changes in the distribution of power on the shopfloor, however, the most important mitigating influences will be discussed, ranging from the materiality of production to workers' counterpower and (changing) state policies of labour regulation. Presenting highly specialised research with reference to unfamiliar contexts, periods, and regions can provoke new and unexpected questions; it can shed light upon unlikely interrelations, and seemingly self-explanatory phenomena may demand explanation when viewed from an alienating perspective. It was this kind of experimental approach that characterised re: work.

Rana Partap Behal

2 Burra Sahibs versus Coolies: Discipline and Resistance. Labour in the Assam Valley Tea Plantations

Tea plantations (or gardens/estates, in planters' parlance) in the Assam Valley were the earliest capitalist ventures set up by private British capital in colonial India during the 1840s. The opening up of these plantations is a part of the global history of modern times.[1] The colonial state facilitated the opening up of tea plantations by offering vast tracts of land at throwaway prices and mobilising large numbers of migrants to produce tea for the global market. It built infrastructure that was financed from public revenues and at no cost to the planters. The mobilisation of labour was a critical problem as the local agrarian communities did not find plantation employment attractive. Planters resorted to recruiting and transporting labour from other parts of British India. Nearly three million migrants (two million for the Assam Valley alone) were mobilised from among agrarian communities in Bihar, Bengal, Orissa, and the United Provinces between 1873 and 1947.[2] The recruitment process continued for a couple of decades even after Independence.

These plantations expanded spectacularly during the late nineteenth century, followed by steady growth in the twentieth century. The acreage under tea cultivation in the Assam Valley increased from just over 33 thousand to over 300,000 in 1947, the labour population increased from over 7,000 in 1877 to over 83 thousand in 1947, and production increased from 7 million pounds in 1872 to over 299 million pounds in 1947. The British tea companies controlled over a million acres of land in

---

1 This chapter is based on the paper: "From Indentured 'Coolie' to *Adivasi:* Labour in the Assam Valley Tea Plantations", presented at the Authors' Workshop at the International Research Centre, Work and Human Lifecycle in Global History, Humboldt University, Berlin, 27 to 31 May 2020. Modern industrial capitalism and the colonisation of Asia, Africa, the Caribbean, and other parts of the world by the British triggered a massive mobilisation of marginalised agrarian communities from the Indian subcontinent to work as a labour force in the plantations, both within British India and to the overseas colonies. Adam McKeown, "Global Migration 1846–1940," *Journal of World History* 15, 2 (2004): 155–189; Prabhu P. Mohapatra, "Coolies and Colliers. Study of the Agrarian Context of Labour Migration from Chotanagpur 1880–1920," *Studies in History* 1, 2 (1985): 247–303; Sunil S. Amrith, *Migration and Diaspora in Modern Asia* (Cambridge: Cambridge University Press, 2011).
2 Rana Partap Behal, *One Hundred Years of Servitude: Political Economy of Tea Plantations in Colonial Assam* (New Delhi: Tulika Books, 2014).

https://doi.org/10.1515/9783111086552-003

the Assam Valley by the end of colonial rule.[3] An interesting feature of these plantation enterprises was the monopolistic domination by British capital that produced as well as marketed tea on the global market. At the end of the nineteenth century, the seven top British firms controlled nearly 61 percent of all tea gardens.[4] Overall, British capital controlled 92 percent of the tea plantations in Assam in 1942. The average size of a tea estate was around 1,000 acres. Today, the labour communities associated with tea plantations constitute nearly 20 percent of the population of Assam. Assam tea plantations are the largest producers of tea and one of the biggest employers of labour in India.

The absence of a labour market in the tea areas was frequently cited as the reason for the long-distance recruiting. Suitable catchment areas for mobilisation of labour for the northeast tea plantations were found among the tribal and aboriginal communities of Bihar, Orissa, and Bengal. Large-scale assisted recruitment and transportation of these migrants, dubbed the "coolie trade" both by contemporary officials and non-officials, became an annual feature in the 1860s and remained in vogue till the 1960s. It also became a highly lucrative business activity of the British agency houses. The intervention of the colonial state in the recruitment and transportation of migrant labour to the Assam plantations was crucial. Massive mortality during the transit and on arrival in the plantations in the early 1860s warranted state intervention in the form of labour legislation in 1863 and 1865, which was further modified in 1881 and 1901. This legislation introduced the indenture system into the Assam tea plantations. Its special feature was the penal contract, which made non-compliance a criminal offense. The contract stipulated minimum monthly wages (five rupees for men, four rupees for women, and three rupees for children), a three-year term (extended to five years in 1881), a nine-hour working day, and the appointment of a labour inspector with the power to cancel the labour contract if there were any complaints of ill treatment. This gender-based wage differential was arbitrary and discriminatory as it extracted the same amount of labour from men and women alike.

The main provision of the contract act lay in the power bestowed upon the planters to arrest labourers for breach of contract and desertion without a warrant within the limits of the district. Contractual non-compliance by labourers, in-

---

3 Behal, *One Hundred Years of Servitude*, see chapter 5.
4 Amiya Kumar Bagchi, *Private Investment in India* (Cambridge: Cambridge University Press, 1972), 161–162; Rana Partap Behal and Prabhu P. [P.] Mohapatra, "'Tea and Money versus Human Life': The Rise and Fall of the Indentured System in the Assam Tea Plantations 1840–1908," in *Plantations, Peasants and Proletarians in Colonial Asia*, edited by E. Valentine Daniel, Henry Bernstein and Tom Brass (London: Frank Cass, 1992), 145.

cluding desertion, was punishable with imprisonment.[5] If convicted under this provision, the period of imprisonment would be added to the term of the contract.[6]
The planters also frequently relied on the Workman's Breach of Contract Act
XIII of 1859 that remained in force until the mid-1920s. Thus, despite formalising
the minimum wage and labour contract, the law turned unfreedom into an integral part of the indenture system. The issue of free and unfree labour has been
debated among labour historians.[7] The working and living conditions in the
Assam tea plantations may have been akin to those of the slaves in the antebellum
era plantations of the Southern United States but the dependency relationship in
the Assam plantations was an integral part of modern capitalist relations. While
containing elements of a contractual relationship, superficially resembling capitalist relations in form, in substance it was coercive exploitation for capitalist ends
with the support of the colonial state.[8]

The majority of the labour force in the Assam Valley tea plantations was recruited from Chota Nagpur, Santhal Parganas, Bihar, Bengal, Orissa, the Central
Provinces, and the Madras Presidency. A large section was drawn from among
the social communities – categorised by census officials as aboriginal, semi-abo-
riginal, and tribal – of Mundas, Oraons, Kharias, Kols or Hos, Bhumij and Santhals,
Kurmis and Murasis. The second most important group of migrants was from semi-
aboriginal castes such as the Ghasis and Goraits, Bauris and Turi. Finally, a smaller
number were drawn from low caste Hindus such as the Bhogtas, Rautias, Chamars,
and Dasadhs. The aboriginals and tribals, often referred to by the planters and the
colonial officials as "junglies," represented the most economically and socially marginalised strata of society in the recruiting regions.[9] The indentured regime was
transforming these migrant agrarian communities into labouring "coolies."

---

5 For more details, see Behal and Mohapatra, "Tea and Money": 145–150.
6 Rajani Kanta Das, *Plantation Labour in India* (Calcutta: R. Chatterji, 1931), 31–32; *Report of Assam Labour Enquiry Committee, 1906.*
7 Tom Brass and Henry Bernstein, "Proletarianization and Deproletarianization on the Colonial Plantations," in *Peasants, Proletarians, and Peasants in Colonial Asia*, edited by E. Valentine Daniel, Henry Bernstein and Tom Brass (London: Frank Cass, 1992), 1–40; Marcel van der Linden, *Workers of the Word: Essays Towards a Global Labour History* (Leiden and Boston: Brill, 2008); Marcel van der Linden and Prabhu P. [P.] Mohapatra, "Introduction", in *Labour Matters: Towards Global Labour Histories: Studies in Honour of Sabyasachi Bhattacharya*, edited by Marcel van der Linden and Prabhu P. Mohapatra (New Delhi: Tulika Books, 2009).
8 Walter Rodney put it succinctly when he argued that "capitalism in its colonial variant operated with certain peculiarities. The plantation was par excellence a colonial form. It was perhaps the most effective of the colonial forms of exploitation that had been established." Walter Rodney, "Plantation Society in Guyana", *Review (Fernand Braudel Center)*, 4, 4 (1981): 662.
9 Behal, *One Hundred Years*, chapter 6.

Rationale for Residential Compulsion: The Labour Process for Tea Production

Residential compulsion within the plantation complex for workers, office clerks, and the supervisory managerial staff was an important feature of the indenture regime. It was determined by the nature of the labour process in the cultivation and manufacturing of tea. Having failed to coerce the local communities to produce tea commercially for them by traditional methods, early British pioneer planters adopted labour-intensive methods instead of deploying the Chinese tradition of peasant-based production. The work process required the presence of labour in all seasons – hence the residential compulsion inside the plantations. The frenetic pace of expansion of the tea plantations between the 1860s and 1900, starting with the "tea mania" years (1860s), generated a huge demand for labour.[10] This led to the mobilisation of a migrant labour force from other parts of India. The mobilised labour force was immobilised on arrival within the plantation complex to be available for long hours of work from sunrise until sunset. They were to live and work under a power hierarchy dominated and headed by the omnipresent *Burra Sahibs* – the British managers – and *Chhota Sahibs* – the assistant managers – who often resorted to extra-legal authority and physical coercion in order to control, tame, and discipline labour. They were assisted by *Sirdars* and *Muhrirs* at the lower rungs of this hierarchy as well as the Indian office staff. Flogging of recalcitrant labour symbolised this extra-legal authority.

An understanding of the nature of the labour process adopted by the planters for the cultivation and manufacturing of tea will explain the rationale behind this residential compulsion. The process of tea cultivation and manufacture evolved during the early two decades of its inception through experimentation with the Chinese and indigenous methods of using manual labour. Charles Alexander Bruce, the superintendent of the government tea experimental station in Upper Assam, learnt and adopted tea cultivation and manufacturing methods from the native Singphos, in the Muttuck country in Upper Assam, with the help of Chinese tea makers brought in from China.[11] Singphos produced tea for self-consumption at their own leisure and convenience, based on a particular manual process. Unable to persuade the Singphos to produce tea for the market, Bruce brought seeds and plants from these areas, planted them in the government experimental station, fol-

---

10 Behal, *One Hundred Years*, chapter 1.

11 C.A. Bruce to Captain F. Jenkins, 1 October 1836, Parliamentary Papers, 1939: 84–5; C.A. Bruce, *An Account of the Manufacture of the Black Tea as Now Practiced in Suddeya in Upper Assam* (Calcutta: G.H Huttmann, Calcutta Military Orphan Press, 1838).

lowed their methods, and developed a new work process for the production of tea with the help of hired Chinese tea makers and local labour.[12] But unlike the Chinese tea production process, which was predominantly based on the use of peasant household labour, Bruce began producing tea with the help of hired labour.[13] The production of tea involved two processes: agricultural cultivation and manufacturing. The cultivation and manufacturing methods were further refined and modified by later planters to improve production and productivity. The cultivation process, almost entirely based on manual labour, went through different stages and seasons: site selection and clearance; production and sowing of seed; the establishment of nurseries; transplanting; digging, weeding, and hoeing; pruning; and finally plucking.[14]

Nurseries and Transplanting

The geographic locations where tea plantations were opened in the Assam Valley were heavily forested. After the selection and clearing of forest sites, the production process began at the nursery beds, where the tea seeds were carefully sown, reared, and prepared for this purpose. When the plants had grown in the nurseries for several months, they were transplanted. The transplanting was generally done during the rainy weather so that the plants would have the best opportunity of taking root in their new environment. The hot and humid climate of Assam was conducive for the growth of the tea plant and within three to six years it became fully productive. Tea bushes remain productive for over 50 years.

---

12 Parliamentary Papers, 1839: 109–114.

13 Robert Gardella, *Harvesting Mountains: Fujian and the China Tea Trade, 1757–1937* (Berkeley: University of California Press, 1994), 45.

14 I am personally indebted to the late Krishna Kamal Bhuyian, senior manager of the Adhabari Tea Estate in the Tezpur district, who explained the intricacies of tea production during my field trips in the 1970s and 1980s. For detailed descriptions of the processes of tea cultivation and manufacture, see Edward Money, *Cultivation;* David Crole, *Tea: A Text Book of Tea Planting and Manufacture,* (London: Crossby Lockwood and Son, 1897); J. C. Kydd, *The Tea Industry,* (London: Humphrey Milford, Oxford University Press, 1921); C. R. Harler, *The Culture and Marketing of Tea* (London: Oxford University Press, 1933); Nitin Varma, *Coolies of Capitalism: Assam Tea and Making of Coolie Labour* (Berlin: De Gruyter Oldenbourg, 2016).

Plucking

The plucking of leaves constituted the most significant task in the production process and was performed mostly during the summer months between April and September. The work of plucking began when new shoots had developed five leaves and a bud in addition to a small leaf at the foot of the shoot known as the sheath leaf or *jhannum*. Plucking was considered a skilled task and mostly performed by women and young girls. "Single *banji*" (barren leaves) were picked through "fine plucking." They carried a basket on their backs, supported by a strap around the forehead, into which leaves were thrown while plucking with both hands from the bushes. The plucking season was a very busy time in the plantations, and all available hands had to be put to work. Plucking involved a very strong element of continuity in the production process. A week or two after the first flush had been plucked, the second flush appeared as shoots growing from the axils or nodes, as they were called, between the leaves left on the first shoot and the stem of the shoot. Ordinarily this second flush was harvested as soon as it was possible to let two leaves remain on the new shoot. After the bud and the two leaves of the second flush had been plucked, the third flush would soon follow, and so on. Thus, plucking had to go on almost continuously from the time of the first flush in April or early May into August or September. During this period the factory, too, was kept busy manufacturing the leaf that was brought in. In the aftermath of the plucking season began the cold weather season, involving treating the tea bushes and soil for the next season's crop. The cold weather season lasted from November to March.

Pruning

The first task after the bushes ceased to flush was pruning. Regular pruning prevented the tea plant from becoming a full-grown tree and kept it as a low leafy bush. The bush was to be maintained at a height of two to two-and-a-half feet, within plucking reach of the women labourers. Although pruning stunted the growth of the plant, it did not make it less healthy or productive. The purpose of pruning was to encourage flushing for as large a bearing as possible, which could be attained by removing all dead or injured wood. A tea bush could not be left without pruning indefinitely, for with each season the unpruned leaves would become smaller and more difficult to gather, and flowers would be produced at the expense of leaves. Pruning had to be conducted between December and January every year. If not, the crop for the coming summer would be lost.

Hoeing

Hoeing was crucial for cleaning the soil. The soil around the bushes – because of the rain, scorching heat, and it having been trodden down by the pluckers' feet – would undergo caking and become overgrown with weeds. To maintain a healthy bush, the clearing of weed and grass was crucial. Consequently, it required single hoeing at least once a month, and often more especially between May and September. Double hoeing of the soil had to be done immediately after the pruning was completed. Child labour was used for cleaning the stems of the bushes and adjacent grounds using bamboo stakes (*koorpies*).

Digging and Cutting Nullahs (Drains)

The digging and cutting of drains was yet another important task and also the heaviest work in the gardens. The subject of drainage received the most careful consideration, as stagnant water was considered fatal for the proper growth of a tea bush, and therefore tea land had to be protected from inundation. Drains had to be well maintained and kept clear of obstructions for draining water and preventing inundation.[15] Other deep digging work was carried out around the plants once a year after the end of the rainy season. The digging was done using a straight garden fork with a short handle. In addition to the annual digging, occasional light forking was required to clear the weeds, which could grow during the spring and early summer rains. Apart from the work directly related to the tea plant, the labourers were also tasked with building and repairing roads, bridges, wells, and coolie huts within the gardens on a regular basis. These were important tasks in the tea plantations, where housing and other infrastructure were in constant need of repair and maintenance due to the harsh tropical weather conditions.

Manufacturing

The manufacturing process began after the plucking of the green leaf had been completed. During the early decades, the manufacturing tasks were also performed manually. After plucking, the green leaf went through several processes

---

15 David Crole, *Tea: A Text Book of Tea planting and Manufacture* (London: Crosby Lockwood and Son, 1897), 62.

on its way to becoming the final product. These involved withering, rolling, fermenting, drying and firing, sorting, and the final heating before packing. Most of these tasks were performed in the factory. From the 1870s onward, the use of machinery and technology was introduced, which was crucial for raising the productivity of tea manufacturing to larger scales in order to meet growing export demand. Though manual labour continued to be used in the factories, the mechanisation of the manufacturing process reduced its numbers.

Withering

Withering was carried out after the green leaf was brought from the field. The withering process was most important as it involved removing a great part of the water from the leaf. The leaf was exposed to the air for a considerable period, which resulted in physical and chemical changes. The green leaf was hoisted into lofts built for this purpose, where it was thinly spread out on trays. A gang of children under close supervision was often employed for this work because of their tender handling. The length of the withering process varied depending on the temperature and state of the leaf.

Rolling

After the withering, came the process of rolling. The rolling operation broke up the cells of the leaf and set free the juice or sap which was inside. Rolling had to be done in such a way as to bruise and distort the cells in order to liberate the juices and thereby facilitate the next process, fermenting.

Fermenting and Drying

Fermentation is a natural process to bring about certain chemical changes in the leaf under conditions that were put in place in the fermenting room. The room was generally separate from the factory, for it was considered important to keep the temperature low. Fermentation changed the colour of leaf from green to yellowish copper. From the fermenting room, the tea was taken back to the factory for it to dry out. This prevented further fermentation and the drawing out of all the moisture from the leaf, to enable it to retain the juices or the essential oils and other properties that gave it its chief value. Once fully dried, the tea was sorted, sifted, and packed as the final product for marketing.

Working in the factory did not mean higher wages or better status for either men or women. Nor is there evidence of any new hierarchy based upon specialised skills that would have emerged from factory employment, in contrast to field work. The plucking of leaves was the only work that was assigned, more or less exclusively, to women. A coolie remained a coolie in the eyes of the *Sahib*, whether employed on the field or in the factory. There is no mention of higher wages or better working conditions for factory employment in the annual labour or production reports. During the peak season, the factory operated twenty-four hours a day, demanding longer working hours. It is more likely that factory employment shrank to some extent with the mechanisation of the manufacturing process. Factories employed about 10 percent of the total labour force on the tea plantations.

The Indenture Regime

Tea production developed features of organised capitalist production, as plantations employed wage labour on a large scale. The indenture labour regime in the Assam tea plantations was formally based on the modern industrial notion of wage labour. The labour relations under the indenture regime in the Assam tea plantations, however, as reflected in the actions and attitudes of the planters, displayed features akin to Atlantic and Caribbean slave plantations. But unlike the American South and the Caribbean with their older plantations, Assam did not have a history of slave-based production. Unlike Caribbean planters, who transitioned from managing slavery to indenture-based plantations, the British tea planters in Assam had no prior experience of managing slave-based production. They nevertheless became "coolie-drivers" and turned the power structure of the plantation into an authoritarian regime.[16] This was recognised by both their contemporary supporters and critics. "Coolie lines" (labour residential clusters) and work places were under strict surveillance to prevent desertion and resistance.

The colonial state was fully aware and supportive of both features of this indenture regime. While it claimed to protect the interests of labour, in reality it legitimised the exercise of extra-legal authority by the planters. This balancing act was performed through various legislative interventions. The overall perception and official justification for labour legislation and the penal contract was put forward by a senior official of the Assam government in paternalist tones: labour legislation in the case of emigrants going to the Assam tea gardens was important for

---

16 Rana Partap Behal, "Coolie Drivers or Benevolent Paternalists? British Tea Planters in Assam and Indenture Labour System," *Modern Asian Studies* 44, 1 (2010): 29–51.

the "protection" of emigrant labourers who were "extremely ignorant," and government intervention was required so that they would not be "imposed upon." Since these emigrants were to travel a long distance, government supervision was necessary to prevent "overcrowding, disease, and consequent mortality." Because of the climate and unfamiliar food in the new country, the emigrants were liable to serious sickness, with often fatal results. Therefore, it was necessary to provide the "requisite comforts, medical attendance, and other appliances for his well-being," which would be enforced by law.[17] At the same time, however, it was argued, that some regulations were required to effectively enforce the contractual provisions between labour and capital as "demanded by justice." After all, the employers had spent a lot of money on importing the labourers and providing them with the "comfort" that was required by the law:

> The employer is compelled by law to guarantee the coolie a minimum wage; and it is only equitable that the law should provide him with the means of obtaining the due fulfilment of the contract by the coolie, whose only capital is his labour, and who ought not to be allowed capriciously to withdraw himself from the service of the employer [....] A penal labour law and government protection to the labour are thus correlative terms.[18]

Thus, this legislation was couched, at one level, in the language of paternalist concerns for the colonial state for the "helpless" and "ignorant" migrant coolies and, at the same time, criminalised labour relations by introducing penal provisions.

This power hierarchy based on coercion and extra-legal authority, aided and abetted by the colonial state, evolved with the introduction of the indenture system at the height of the speculative boom of the 1860s tea mania years. Over the next couple of decades, this power structure evolved to operate at two levels. At the top level, the tea companies, with their headquarters in the United Kingdom and their managing agents in Calcutta, instituted a centralised authority in the form of an apex body, the Indian Tea Association (ITA), in 1881. This apex body, manned by senior tea company executives and retired Indian civil servants, functioned as a lobby group for the industry in the corridors of power, while the planter implemented its strategies of production organisation and labour policies in the plantations. The ITA's influence was bolstered by the industry's social and political connections with the colonial authority to influence policies on matters of labour, particularly for preventing legal impediments against the use of extra-legal and coercive forms of labour control in the plantations. The ITA used its organisational connections and political clout to influence the colonial state and its policies on

---

17 Edward Albert Gait, *Assam Immigration Manual*, Calcutta (1893): 2.
18 Gait, *Assam Immigration* Manual: 2.

matters concerning recruitment, transportation, and legislation. Most remarkably, it also displayed a cunningness to adapt to the exigencies of changing legislative and political situations in the region and manipulated them to the industry's advantage. With the formation of an elected legislative assembly in 1937 in Assam the labour issue came up for debates in the public domain. Indian Tea Association, as powerful lobby in the province, was in a position to influence Government policy on labour when trade unions emerged.[19]

However, the nature of the power structure within the plantation complex, based on specific relations of production, played a crucial role in ensuring and sustaining the planters' domination and control over labour for more than a century after its inception. From the beginning, given the nature of its production process and the use of labour-intensive methods, the tea industry's major preoccupation was labour. On the ground, these strategies and policies were enforced through a hierarchical power structure centred on the omnipresent managerial authority of the British planters, the *Burra* and *Chhota Sahibs*, and their native assistants. The *Burra and Chhota Sahibs* used *Sirdars*, *Muherirs*, and office staff to control labour on the field and in coolie lines. Labour remained under constant surveillance, both in the workplace and "at home." The key emphasis throughout was on controlling labour mobility, preventing desertion, and curbing workers' contact with the world outside the plantations. Both strategies aimed at preventing the formation of labour organisations. At both levels, the authorities operated in tandem and implemented strategies and policies prepared by the apex body with a remarkable degree of success. The dramatic expansion of plantations and their sustenance demanded stability and a regular supply of labour in large numbers. The destabilisation caused by increasing desertions by migrant labour threatened to impede the growth of the new plantation enterprises and risked a loss of the capital invested in recruiting and transporting the labour. The rationale of labour stability was also linked to the nature of the labour process for the production of tea in the Assam plantations. As pointed out above, tens of thousands of workers were mobilised in the recruitment process, only to be immobilised within the spatial confines of the plantation enclaves since there was no local labour market. The frenetic increase in acreage and the expansion of production in the face of declining tea prices could be sustained only through stable and cheap labour. The logic of all this demanded a docile, disciplined, and tamed labour force, which had to be kept under control and

---

19 Rana Partap Behal, "Power Structure, Discipline and Labour in Assam Tea Plantations under Colonial Rule," in *India's Labouring Poor: Historical Studies c. 1600–2000*, edited by Rana Partap Behal and Marcel van der Linden (Delhi: Foundation Books, 2007), 145–155.

prevented from desertion by any means, including violence and intimidation, of which flogging was a regular feature.

These strategies were tied in with another significant feature of the tea plantations: the need to keep wages very low over a long period of time. An abundant and cheap supply of labour was the mainstay of the plantation system. To sustain the profitability of the industry, it was imperative to keep labour costs as low as possible. This was achieved through a very complex system of wages in cash and kind, dependence on land grants, and the system of advances that evolved in tea plantations during the late nineteenth and twentieth centuries. This was carried out under the statutory minimum wage provisions of the contract act (in reality, the maximum wage paid), since the major function of penal sanctions was to suppress wages by preventing the operation of a labour market. The wage bill was further depressed by the practise of gender differential payments, as mentioned above. No explanation was ever presented for this variation even though women performed most types of work done by men, such as hoeing and pruning. In fact, women performed work that was described as highly specialised, such as plucking, and they made up a very significant share of the labour force. In the peak season, it was estimated that nearly 60 percent of the labourers were women engaged in plucking. Since the techniques and modes of production in the tea plantations did not undergo any radical change, and there was hardly any differentiation of skills to explain the variation between male and female labour, they all performed similar tasks and for the same number of hours. The productivity of male and female labourer also did not differ significantly either.[20]

The lower wages for women and children based on such discrimination certainly had considerable financial advantages for planters, considering that their combined employment was equal to or higher than that of men. Women and children constituted more than 50 percent of the total labour force employed in tea plantations. Moreover, they were often not paid even the statutory minimum wage. This raises the questions as to how labour survived with stagnant and low wages and high mortality rates over a long period? Most of the labour force, given their low level of earnings, lived on highly inadequate low-calorie diets – for decades, rice constituted the major item of food consumption in labour households. This explains the high incidence of undernourishment among the workers. In order to keep labouring bodies in working condition, this low wage

20 Rana Partap Behal, "Wage Structure and Labour: Assam Valley Tea Plantations, 1900–1947," NLI Research Studies Series, No. 043/2003, V.V. Giri National Labour Institute, Noida (2003).

was supplemented by wages in kind, for example rice supplied at subsidised rates, a practice still in vogue.[21]

An obvious result of low wages was a very low standard of living for the labour force. During the early decades of the opening up of tea plantations and until the end of the nineteenth century, the mortality rates among labourers were appallingly high in Assam. Lamentation and expressions of serious concern by district officials failed to change the situation. The last three decades of the nineteenth century witnessed an intensification of the labour process in order to maintain the frenetic expansion of acreage under tea production, based on clearing vast areas of forest, and increasing the mechanisation of manufacturing work. This intensification increased productivity, but in combination with a labour force subjected to an extremely precarious existence, low earnings, and consequently poor nourishment, this took a heavy toll in terms of human lives. Hard labour, imbalanced diets, and unsanitary and poor living conditions left labourers increasingly vulnerable to diseases. The phenomenal growth of the tea industry from the 1870s onward was marked by very high rates of mortality among its labour force. A scholarly demographic study of official mortality data (annual labour reports) among migrant labour on the Assam tea plantations gave primacy to the epidemiological factors for high mortality. The official data showed a declining trend in mortality rates by the late nineteenth and early twentieth centuries. This decline has been attributed to a "seasoning" process in building immunity and resistance to disease, improvement in transport facilities, and administrative and health reforms in the plantations by the colonial state and the employers.[22] That, however, disregards malnutrition, inadequate diet, and harsh working and living conditions as factors for high mortality. It also completely ignores other official information, including medical reports based on sanitary and field surveys that presented a different picture not compatible with this data.[23] Women labourers, in particular, were subjected to great hardship. Apart from the drudgery of a whole day's work they also had to bear the burden of household chores and reproduction. Subjected to physical and sexual coercion, low wages, and appalling working and living conditions, they resisted the burden of reproduction. During the last two decades of the nineteenth century, the death rate was higher than the birth rate on the plantations, which was partly due to self-induced abortions. High mortality, malnutrition, and the poverty of the labour force remained a serious issue in

---

21 Behal, *One Hundred Years*, chapter 5.
22 Ralph Shlomowitz and Lance Brennan, "Mortality and migrant labour in Assam 1865–1921", *Indian Economic and Social History Review* 27, 1 (1990): 85–110.
23 Behal, *One Hundred Years*, chapter 5.

the Assam tea plantations throughout the colonial period.[24] D.V. Rege's observations, as late as 1946, revealed a stark picture of their lives:

> The standard of living of tea garden labourers in Assam is appallingly low. They merely exist. They have hardly any belongings except a few clothes (mostly tattered) and a few pots (mostly earthen). Their womenfolk have no jewelry except German silver bangles in a few cases. Their houses presented a picture of stark poverty.[25]

Education

Another very significant characteristic of life in the Assam tea plantations was almost universal illiteracy despite the fact that employers had the statutory obligation to provide schooling to the children of their labourers. Not only were they forced to live in isolation from the world outside the plantations, but even elementary education was denied to their children. Eighty years after its inception and nearly 55 years after the introduction of labour laws,[26] the census of Assam in 1921 reported a rate of literacy of only 0.25, 0.39, and 0.36 percent among plantation labourers in the districts of Lakhimpur, Sibsagar, and Darrang respectively.[27] Across the province as a whole, only 0.64 percent of the entire tea plantation labour force was reported to be literate.[28] As late as 1948, another report stated that most plantations in Assam had no facilities for the education of children above the age of twelve.[29] Recent research has shown that the educational situation among tea labour communities in Assam is still rather dismal.

Resistance

How did the labouring communities respond to this transformation process the plantation employment hoisted upon them? Equally significant is the question of their character as human beings about which images were projected through the employers' lenses. Were they truly an ignorant, unintelligent body of men

---

24 Behal, *One Hundred Years*, chapter 5.
25 D.V. Rege, "Report on Enquiry into conditions of Labour in Plantations in India" (1946): 55.
26 Under the provision of labour laws in force, the employers were responsible for the education of the children of tea garden labourers.
27 *Census of India*, 1921, Vol. Ill, Assam, part II: 344.
28 *Census of India*, 1921, Vol. Ill, Assam, part II: 344.
29 S.R. Deshpande, "Report on an Enquiry into the Cost and Standard of Living of Plantation Workers in Assam and Bengal" (1948).

and women who resisted change, and were they prone to violence and immune to economic incentives, as argued by the planters and the colonial bureaucracy? Did they allow themselves to be tamed, disciplined, and controlled by their employers without resistance and become docile, passive, and mute sufferers in the face of physical and sexual coercion and economic exploitation?

Within the boundaries erected over isolated vast spaces by the plantation regime in order to tame and discipline labour, the workers expressed their protests in different forms over time. From the very beginning of tea plantation operations during the 1840s, there is evidence of the earliest resistance by labour in the form of absconding or desertion and even strikes in the Assam Company's tea estates. These forms of resistance persisted over time in the plantations. It is interesting to note that during the period prior to the indentured legislative enactments, the Assam Company's official correspondence did not hesitate to describe the collective action of labour as a "strike." The term "strike" disappeared from the colonial records after the indenture legislation came into operation, only to resurface in the early 1920s with increasing collective labour resistance.

The terms "desertion" or "absconding" (the latter much preferred by the planters) as an act of labour resistance acquired a different connotation and meaning during the period of tea mania and indenture from the 1860s onward. Desertion was made a criminal offence under the indenture labour law and the planters were empowered with the private right to arrest deserters. Despite the surveillance and threat of severe punishment on being captured, newly arriving migrant labourers found desertion to be the only means of escaping the harshness of their journey, as well as the disease, high mortality, and brutalities of daily life on the plantations.[30] Desertion symbolised the rejection of the relationship of servitude the migrants had been coerced into under the indentured regime in the Assam Valley tea plantations. It was sometimes an individual and sometimes a collective act of resistance, comparable to what Peter Wood described as slaves "stealing themselves" in the eighteenth-century South Carolina colony in America.[31]

---

30 Deshpande, "Report on an Enquiry.".

31 Peter H. Wood, *Black Majority: Negroes in Colonial South Carolina from 1670 through the Stono Rebellion* (New York: W.W. Norton & Company, 1974), 239. While the number and the percentage of blacks in the colony were growing, individual slaves were finding it increasingly difficult to exercise even the rudimentary aspects of independence and autonomy that had been possible during earlier decades. Personal and social initiatives among slaves were gradually being checked by the evolving economic patterns and legal codes imposed by the European settlers. Changing circumstances prompted an increasing number of runaways. In a society where slaves were defined as property and where blacks were becoming artful in appropriating things they were denied, these were the people who, in a real sense, elected to "steal themselves."

Those who could not steal themselves away did adopt strategies to put up resistance against the day-to-day chores of plantation work under coercion which included shirking and sabotaging the work process and schedule. They found ways of subverting the work process or of getting their earnings with "short" work, which in turn saw them branded as shirkers, lazy, and cheaters by their employers.

Other acts of resistance included what the officials termed cases of riot, assault, intimidation, and unlawful assembly. There were strikes, but they were not recognised as such in official reporting. Instead, under indenture law both individual and collective resistance were branded as criminal acts. There were constant reports of violence by workers in retaliation against extreme forms of physical and economic coercion, indignities, and sexual harassment of their women folk by planters. Planters resorting to violence in order to seek compliance and to suppress dissent and defiance was a constant feature of labour relations in the Assam tea plantations.[32] The punishment for such acts of resistance was extremely severe, ranging from long years of imprisonment to the death penalty. While the labourers were rewarded with rigorous and long-term imprisonment even for very mild offences, the punishments awarded to the managers were scandalously mild, even on charges of extreme violence. There were cases in which managers were let off with a small fine for beating a labourer to death.[33]

While economic grievances were important factors provoking workers' actions, there were other equally significant issues such as demands for social and cultural rights. The reports of growing acts of retaliation in the plantations put pressure on the colonial state to delete the penal provisions from the indenture law in 1908, thus creating a space for more organised and collective labour resistance.[34] During the years 1920 to 1922, resistance expanded in scale and scope with greater emphasis on economic issues, and the numbers of those involved in struggles surpassed all previous figures.[35] Between September 1920 and January 1922, manifold cases of strikes, disturbances, and riots were reported on several tea districts in Assam.[36] The colonial state helped to suppress this widespread resistance.[37] However, as a result of the revolt of 1920 to 1922, indenture law was for-

---

32 Elizabeth Kolsky, *Colonial Justice in British India* (Cambridge: Cambridge University Press, 2010).

33 Kolsky, *Colonial Justice*; Behal, *One Hundred Years*, chapter 6.

34 "Report of the Assam Labour Enquiry Committee" (Calcutta 1906).

35 The economic issue becoming a dominant factor during the events of 1920 to 1922 was a reflection of the sharp decline in the real wages causing tremendous hardship to the labourers. *Report of the Assam Labour Enquiry Committee, 1921–22;* Behal, *One hundred Years,* chapter 5.

36 Behal, *One hundred Years,* chapter 5.

37 Government of Assam, Financial Department, Immigration Branch B. Nos. 20–112, (1922): 105–107.

mally abolished in 1926. Moreover, through the preservation and practise of their cultural and social traditions, the labour communities kept the memories of their experiences alive, which helped them to cope with the everyday life of grief and wretchedness. Through a celebration of their culture and social forms they resisted being reduced to tamed and disciplined coolies.[38]

The post-indenture period in the Assam Valley also witnessed a new form of labour resistance, which was described in official reports as an "exodus," a term which acquired special currency during the Chargola Exodus (1921).[39] An exodus represented a collective expression of the labourers' rejection of the rhythm of life under the plantation regime. While an exodus fell short of becoming an organised movement in the Assam Valley, it was an advance over desertion and was distinctly political in nature. Moreover, labour responded with a series of strikes following the wage cuts during the Great Depression of 1930. These strikes, across the Assam Valley tea gardens, saw larger participation and longer duration.[40] Increased state repression did not deter them. Growing discontent led to more strikes and more exodus during the years between 1931 and 1939. That last year witnessed a fierce outburst of labour struggles throughout the province of Assam. In one important respect the events of 1939 represented a significant step in the history of tea garden labour struggles. For the first time, the emergence of labour unions in an embryonic form was reported in the Assam tea plantations. The activities of these organisations were severely restricted under the draconian Defence of India rules imposed by the colonial government at the outbreak of World War Two in 1939. But labour struggles could not be eliminated, as indicated by the continuous momentum of strikes in several plantation districts throughout the war years. It was sustained because the labour struggle outside the plantations was maturing, paving the way for the formation of a provincial labour organisation that also raised issues concerning tea plantation labour.[41]

---

38 Behal, *One Hundred Years*, Chapter 6.
39 The term "exodus" was famously linked with labour resistance in tea plantations in Surma Valley in 1921. For a detailed discussion, see Nitin Varma, "Chargola Exodus and Collective Action in Colonial Tea Plantations of Assam," *SEPHIS* e-magazine, 3 (2 January 2007). For the Assam Valley the use of the term exodus appeared later in the official reportage.
40 Government of Assam, General and Judicial Department, Immigration Branch, B, Nos. 1–15 (1931); 41–50 (1931); 108–124 (June) and 71–164 (September 1931); 16–26 (December 1931); *Assam Labour Report* (1931).
41 Behal, One *Hundred Years*, chapter 6.

Living and Working in the Assam Tea Plantations after Independence

Did the dawn of Independence in 1947 herald a new era for the labouring communities of Assam's tea plantations? What did the end of colonial rule mean for them? Did they feel emancipated and freed from the oppression of an authoritarian indenture regime? Did it mean improved economic and social conditions, more dignity and better opportunities for them and their families? Did it enable them to bargain for better wages and working and living conditions in the plantations?

Tea plantations in contemporary India employ more than a million permanent workers, and perhaps more than twice as many seasonal labourers. This makes the industry the largest private sector employer in the country. But workers depend upon the plantations for more than just employment: millions of workers and their families live on the plantations, and rely on them for basic services, including food supplies, health care, and education. These services were provided for under the Plantation Labour Act (PLA), the most significant labour legislation passed immediately after Independence by the Indian parliament in 1951. This integrated issues of welfare into the framework of labour law, including education and medical facilities, canteens, crèches for children of working mothers, fixation of hours of work and wages, leave rules, prohibition of child labour, and sickness and maternity benefits. The state governments were empowered to take feasible steps to improve the lot of the plantation workers. They were to appoint inspectors to ensure the implementation of the obligatory labour welfare provisions. This also helped in creating conditions for the emergence of worker organisations. For the first time, their right to organise in labour unions was recognised.

However, experiences under colonial labour laws were to repeat themselves, with the potential benefits promised under the PLA rarely reaching the labour force. Even a brief glance across a wide range of current literature on Assam tea labour – media coverage, reports by national and international NGOs or human rights organisations, and academic findings – reveals that it is difficult to be optimistic about the status and wellbeing of plantation workers even today. Recent research reveals that in striking contrast to PLA provisions, standardised wages and working hours have not been introduced, and management more often than not fails to provide facilities such as safe drinking water, housing, education, childcare, health care, crèches, accident cover, and protective equipment. Even where they are provided, they tend to be of very poor quality. The study concludes that the tea labourers of Assam have remained the most marginalised community of India.[42] One obvious implication of poverty is that the families living in the plantations cannot support themselves on the wages they earn. For this reason, children (and particularly girls) become vulnerable to trafficking. Scores of young women and children have been trafficked out of the state with the promise of work and education. Many end up in prostitution.[43] It is ironic that men and women, after being transported for over a century to work in the Assam tea plantations, are now increasingly pushed to travel to Indian metropolises to seek work and earn their livelihoods.

Ignorance due to illiteracy, the poor socioeconomic and political conditions, and the harsh and unhealthy living environment in former coolie lines (now termed "labour lines") expose labourers to various infectious diseases and malnutrition. A detailed study on the health of tea labourers conducted by the Assam Regional Medical Research Centre revealed malnourishment (almost 60 percent) among children and micronutrient deficiencies like anaemia (72 percent).[44] Many suffer from undernutrition and infectious diseases; nutritional problems like underweight children, thinness among adults, while micronutrient deficiency disorders such as anaemia are widespread. Common infectious diseases are worm infestation, respiratory problems, diarrhoea, skin infections, filariasis, and pulmonary tuberculosis.[45]

The health condition of women labourers, who still constitute nearly 50 percent of the labour force in the tea plantations, has remained the most vulnerable. A recent report is reminiscent of the horror stories of the plight of tea plantation labouring communities in Assam during colonial times. The most common disease among women labourers is anaemia, and in areas where overall malnutrition is at its peak, it is often fatal. The mother of a new-born does not receive maternity leave, but is expected to return to work at the earliest opportunity. Many times, women bring their children to work; few tea plantations provide a crèche. Mothers suffering from anaemia cannot produce sufficient breastmilk for their babies and resort to feeding them powdered milk. Due to unhygienic conditions and malnourishment, diseases like tuberculosis appear during infancy. Cases of tuberculosis are common among children, and the rate of infant mortality is alarmingly high.[46]

---

42 Nikunja Sonar Bhuyan, "Tea Garden Labours of Assam: A Community in Distress," *International Journal of Advance Study and Research Work* 1, 1 (April 2018): 39.

43 "Assam tea plantations become hunting ground for child trafficker," *Hindustan Times* (3 September 2015.

44 Bhuyan, "Tea Garden Labourers": 40.

45 Bhuyan, "Tea Garden Labourers": 40..

46 "The Gory Reality Of Adivasi Women Working On Assam's Tea Estates," *Youth Ki Awaz* (29 August 2017).

There are no NGOs or watchdog agencies on the premises of tea plantations to monitor the rights and interests of women. A tea plantation in Assam is still isolated and difficult to access for the traditional media. The last time a BBC journalist and his crew entered a tea estate in Assam to show the reality on the ground, they were warned by the management to stop filming as they claimed that the tea estates were private property and that filming or documenting amounted to trespassing.[47]

A report of the Human Rights Institute of Columbia Law School that focused on labour conditions in tea plantations owned by the Tata group in Assam confirmed the persistence of abusive practises, and the failure to comply with the basic requirements of the PLA 60 years after its introduction. The report is critical of the International Finance Corporation for its failure to scrutinise Tata's compliance with Indian laws that were meant to promote decent labour standards.[48] The PLA was never properly enforced. Labour lines are still characterised by dilapidated and overcrowded houses, poorly stocked medical facilities, and abandoned crèches. The survey reveals that tea plantation workers are an impoverished community living on the margins. Malnutrition is widespread, along with illiteracy. Tea plantation workers succumb to diseases of poverty such as tuberculosis and typhoid at much higher rates than the rural poor in the surrounding villages.[49] It is pointed out that even the government's own statistics indicate that inspections are infrequent and fines are non-existent. As for labour unions, the plantation managers have maintained a monopoly over the Assam Chah Sangha (ACMS), a largely discredited union known for hobnobbing with the management and compromising the interests of workers.[50]

Genevieve LeBaron, in her recent study on labour practises in the global supply chains of companies producing tea in India and cocoa in Ghana, documented the presence of forced labour, human trafficking, and other illegal labour practises. She argues that

> [o]ur research uncovers that employers systematically under-pay wages and under-provide legally-mandated essential services for workers. Employers are legally required to provide basic services for tea workers on permanent contracts and their families. However, our study found that forty-seven percent of tea workers do not have access to potable water and twenty-six percent do not have access to a toilet. In both industries, these widespread

---

47 Ankita Bhardwaj, "Prospects and Challenges of Migration on Tea Garden Labourers: An Analysis in Assam," Department of Political Science, Sikkim University, India, ND.

48 "The More Things Change..." : The World Bank, Tata and Enduring Abuses on India's Tea Plantations, Human Rights Institute, Columbia Law School, January 2014: 7–8.

49 "The More Things Change...": 7–8.

50 "The More Things Change...": 7–8.

forms of exploitation are also sometimes accompanied by physical violence, threats, verbal abuse, and/or sexual violence.[51]

Although chocolate and tea companies are highly profitable, the tea and cocoa workers at the base of their supply chains are living far below the poverty line and are routinely subjected to abuse.[52] The boundaries between forced labour and highly exploitative free labour are often blurred in the industries under review.[53]

Social Exclusion, Isolation, and Assertion of Identity

One of the major consequences of the fact that plantation workers have been forced into an immobilised residential existence for a very long time is their isolation from wider Assamese society outside the plantations. Despite the settlement of a very large number of time-expired labour on land in the vicinity of plantations this isolation is not overcome. While the forced enclave existence left the tea plantation labouring communities socially and politically isolated, this was further exacerbated by the general attitude of indifference on the part of the Assamese intelligentsia and political leadership, both during and after colonial rule. Despite having lived and worked in the Assam tea plantations for several generations, these communities continue to be treated as outsiders in the Assamese public narrative. The so-called assimilation debate remains inconclusive in the heated ethnocentric political atmosphere of northeast India.

There is, however, one important change the workers themselves brought about: they asserted an adjustment in the nomenclature of their identity. Since the use of the derogatory term "coolie" is no longer acceptable, they have fought to be called *Adivasi*. This, of course, does not alter the nature of labour relations in tea plantations. After more than one and a half centuries of toiling to produce tea in the Assam plantations, there are still reports of serious violations of work-

---

51 Genevieve LeBaron, *The Global Business of Forced Labour: Report of Finding* (Sheffield Political Economy Research Council [SPERI] & University of Sheffield, 2018), 2.
52 LeBaron, *The Global Business of Forced Labour*, 3.
53 LeBaron, *The Global Business of Forced Labour*, 14.

ers' rights, and in particular their right to unionise and push their grievances is often denied.[54]

While they still fight for their social and political rights as workers inside the plantations, outside they are denied the right to affirm their status as a Scheduled Tribe, which is linked to certain provisions. Their complaint is that tea plantation communities in Assam, as *Adivasis*, are yet to be accorded Scheduled Tribe status, which would ensure a reservation in jobs, for instance, and is granted to similar communities in the states of Jharkhand and Madhya Pradesh. As long as the labour communities of the Assam plantations are not included among the Scheduled Tribes of Assam, their exclusion from the affirmative reservation provisions will persist. This is one of the root causes of the growing restlessness among these communities.[55] When the tea industry in India went through a crisis in the 1990s, due to a fall in tea auction prices and a decline in exports, and resorted to the non-payment and curtailment of wages, workers responded with violent protests and confrontations. It was not only the sectoral crisis of Assam tea production, but also apprehension regarding future prospects, which fuelled labour unrest.[56]

Labour began to fight in a more organised manner for better wages and working conditions. According to a report in the *Business Standard*, dated 27 December 2017, the wages of 1.11 million tea garden labourers in Assam and West Bengal were still overdue for revision. Azam Monam, the chairman of the Indian Tea Association, said that 138 rupees was the daily wage of a labourer, which also includes facilities like housing, subsidised rations, water and electricity connections, and education for their children. However, the reality was very different. In 2014, even the Assam chief minister, Tarun Gogoi, asked the labour and employment department to strictly enforce the various provisions of the PLA. It was also made mandatory for a tea plantation to be equipped with all the facilities set out under the act. A judicial commission was constituted by the state government to study the working conditions in the state's tea plantations and to suggest suitable measures for an improvement in housing, health, education, and other facilities. On 16 February 2015, hundreds of plantation labourers took to the streets, protesting and seeking a revision of daily wages. Under the banner "Tea Workers Wage Revision Demand Forum," they submitted a memorandum addressing the chief minister of Assam, Sarbananda Sonowal, demanding a hike of daily wages from 137 to 350 ru-

---

54 "World Bank Finds Evidence Of Labour Abuse On The Assam Tea Plantations It Owns With The Tatas," *HuffPost* (11 July 2016).

55 Deepak K. Mishra, Atul Sarma, and Vandana Upadhyay, "Invisible chains? Crisis in the tea industry and the 'unfreedom' of labour in Assam's tea plantations," *Contemporary South Asia* 19, 1 (March 2011): 75

56 Mishra, Sarma, and Upadhyay, "Invisible chains?": 75.

pees. The forum's secretary, Ghanshyam Munda, also demanded assurances that daily and fair wages and the provisions of the Plantation Act of 1951 and Minimum Wages Act of 1948 would be implemented. Moreover, he stated, the cost of housing, medical expenses, electricity, drinking water, pension, provident fund, gratuities, and bonuses should no longer be part of the daily wages, as is the norm.[57] The struggle to attain these goals continues.

Conclusion

Opening up the tea plantations in Assam in 1840 was part of British private capital's efforts to boost the production of sugar, coffee, tea, and rubber in several parts of the British Empire. Most of these tropical commodities were produced for a growing global market in the West, and most of the plantations were labour-intensive capitalist enterprises. Large numbers of labourers from marginalised agrarian communities in different parts of British India were mobilised to work in these plantations. By the 1870s, the Assam tea plantations came under the monopolistic control of British companies based in Calcutta and the United Kingdom. The British managing agencies organised the day-to-day operation of production processes through the employment of British planters as managers and assistant managers.

A special plantocracy was established under the obnoxious indenture regime since the planters wielded extra-legal authority over their labour force. After being mobilised in the recruitment process, the labour force was strictly immobilised within the plantation complex in Assam. The long-term sustenance and profitability of the tea plantations was incumbent upon a plentiful supply of cheap, docile labour. These were capitalist plantations, operating with contract-based wage labour. However, the nature of the extra-legal authority wielded by the *Burra* and *Chhota Sahibs* over the labour force was comparable to that of the white masters over their black slaves in the antebellum era in the American South. Within this structure, the workers were subjected to physical and sexual coercion and social control, which severely restricted their mobility within and outside the plantations and isolated them from the outside world.

Within the boundaries of the indenture regime, which utilised the isolated vast spaces of the tea plantations in order to tame and discipline labour, the workers expressed their protests in different forms over time. These acts of resistance were both individual and collective. While economic grievances were important

---

57 Rajiv Dutta, "Tea plantation workers stage rally protesting low daily wage," *The Times of India* (16 February 2018).

factors provoking workers' actions, there were other equally significant issues such as demands for social and cultural rights, and dignity. It has been argued that the authoritarian nature of the indenture regime, as well as the cultural and social diversity of the migrant labour communities, has impeded collective and organised labour resistance and the formation of labour organisations. On the contrary, however, there is evidence that they transcended ethnic differences and stood in solidarity with their fellow labourers, thus retaliating against physical and sexual abuse by the planters. In solidarity they faced the grave consequences of unfair convictions and long prison terms by the colonial judiciary. Through the preservation of their cultural and social traditions, the labour communities kept the memories of their experiences alive, which helped them to cope with an every-day life of grief and wretchedness. Through celebrations of their culture and social forms, they resisted becoming tamed and disciplined "coolies." They displayed characteristic features of proletarians putting up a collective resistance against capital. After all, the dependency relationship in the Assam plantations was an integral part of modern capitalist relations in the colonial context, and neither semi-feudal nor pre-capitalist in nature.

Independence in 1947 ushered in hopes of a better future for the labouring communities of the Assam tea plantations. Indeed, the post-Independence Indian state introduced the Plantation Labour Act in 1951, including several welfare provisions and the right to form labour organisations. These hopes, however, proved illusionary. The new provisions were not implemented, as least not fully, and the status of plantation labourers remained stagnant without a great deal of improvement in their earnings, education, political empowerment, or working and living conditions, even after seven decades of Independence. They have remained impoverished, undernourished, and politically insignificant despite the formation of trade unions. Their relationship of dependency with their employers, imposed under colonial rule, has been perpetuated to the present day. Many of them have settled on small pieces of land in the vicinity of the large plantations and still have to supplement their livelihood with seasonal employment. Freedom from poverty and exploitation remains a chimera for them. Without exaggeration, their plight is not much different from the one revealed during the indenture era by Dawrkanath Ganguli and Rev. Charles Dowding during the 1880s and 1890s. No wonder the *Adivasi* of the Assam tea plantations can ruefully lament: freedom and independence for whom?

Jacob Eyferth

3 Remote Control: Field Management Regimes and the Agricultural Labour Process on Chinese Collective Farms, 1956 to 1980

Most discussions of labour and the labour process focus on the industrial workplace. Agricultural work is typically assumed to be self-directed, governed by the experiential knowledge of independent cultivators who respond flexibly to variations in the soil and climate. However, agricultural work is often heteronomous, with slaves, serfs, farm hands, and migrant harvest workers working the land while being subject to top-down discipline and coordination. One of the largest such workforces was the Chinese peasantry under socialism: for a quarter of a century, some 180 million (in 1956) to 320 million (in 1983) people worked in collective agriculture, growing crops and raising animals under the supervision of collective leaders to specifications handed down by the State Planning Committee and the Ministry of Agriculture.

The Chinese agricultural workforce was in important ways the creation of the socialist state, which not only oversaw its expansion but also changed its composition by recruiting large numbers of rural women into what had traditionally been a mostly male domain.[1] The state introduced new cultivation regimes and labour processes, trained almost every rural person in new techniques, and fundamentally altered labour relations by replacing work in return for a share of the harvest with work for a wage – albeit one that was mostly paid in grain and other agricultural products. The state also massively increased the number of workdays performed by the average rural person as well as the intensity of rural work. Labour intensification relied partly on coercion and partly on intense ideological work. To a very large extent, however, it came about through the introduction of fixed scripts that prescribed the timing and frequency of operations, with the aim of wringing more labour out of the workforce and more grain, cotton, oilseeds, fodder crops, and other products out of the land. Operational sequences were increasingly standardised, and planners resorted to almost-Taylorist prescriptions on how workers should position their bodies, bend their backs, move their hands, and coordinate hands and eyes while at work. The feminisation of agricul-

---

1 For a similar argument about the Chinese industrial workforce, see Andrew Walder, "The Remaking of the Chinese Working Class, 1949–1981," *Modern China* 10, 1 (1984): 3–48.

https://doi.org/10.1515/9783111086552-004

ture, together with the influx of young workers from the post-1949 birth cohorts, created a young and on average inexperienced workforce that was both needful of and receptive to training.

This essay presents three arguments. First, agricultural work under the collectives came to resemble industrial work – not in terms of prestige and remuneration, which remained low, but in the fact that most such work was performed by teams of people working in close coordination and under the supervision of collective leaders, that work rhythms were regulated by the clock, and that remuneration was closely tied to the intensity of labour effort. Here, as in other cases of hierarchically controlled work, it makes sense to ask the central question emphasised by labour process theorists: how is labour power, i.e. the abstract capacity to labour, converted into actual productive work?[2] Questions of skill and deskilling, of the lengthening and intensification of the labour day, of labour resistance and labour's conditional consent to its own exploitation are as relevant in agricultural as in industrial work.[3] Second, and more specific to China and other socialist countries, I argue that new labour processes were the main vehicle through which rural populations came to understand socialist modernity. Chinese socialism was nothing if not didactic: it took its message into villages, urban neighbourhoods, and even households, where party activists routinely organised "family meetings" to ensure that not only household heads but also family dependents understood and supported a given policy. Nonetheless, the formal politics of the Chinese Communist Party (CCP) left many people disenchanted or confused. It was at the level of material life, of work patterns and consumption habits, that socialism affected people's lives and shaped their understanding. In particular, it was the experience of working under supervision, following impersonal routines, and earning a fixed wage per task or per labour day that introduced rural people to the state's productivist aims and to a specifically socialist notion of modernity.[4] Thirdly, the process of habituation to supervision, routine, and quantification piggy-backed on purportedly neutral technologies that were global and often colonial in origin.

---

2 Michael Burawoy, *Manufacturing Consent: Changes in the Labor Process under Monopoly Capitalism* (Chicago: University of Chicago Press, 1979); Harry Braverman, *Labor and Monopoly Capital: The Degradation of Work in the Twentieth Century* (New York: Monthly Review Press, 1988); David Knights and Hugh Willmott, *Labour Process Theory* (London: Macmillan, 1990).
3 Glenn Davis Stone, "Agricultural Deskilling and the Spread of Genetically Modified Cotton in Warangal," *Current Anthropology* 48, 1 (2007): 67–103; Deborah Fitzgerald, *Every Farm a Factory: The Industrial Ideal in American Agriculture* (Newhaven: Yale University Press, 2003).
4 This is equally true under capitalism. The philosopher Elizabeth Anderson has argued that people in the Western world routinely accept levels of despotism at work that they would not tolerate from a government: Elizabeth Anderson, *Private Government: How Employers Rule Our Lives – and Why We Don't Talk About It* (Princeton: Princeton University Press, 2017).

Throughout the twentieth century, Chinese rural reformers imported seeds, tools, agronomic knowledge, and organisational formats from abroad – not only from the United States, where hundreds of young Chinese studied agricultural science, but also from the British and French colonial empires and the Soviet Union. These reformers may have seen themselves as technicians rather than ideologues, but consciously or not, they sought to transform and standardise the rural workforce just as they transformed and standardised the genetic makeup of their crops and the features of the landscape.

Most of the empirical evidence presented here comes from the area known as Guanzhong (the "land within the passes"), the fertile Wei River Valley extending to the east and west of the old imperial capital of Xi'an. Guanzhong forms part of Shaanxi province and is geographically and culturally distinct from the mountains of southern Shaanxi and the north Shaanxi loess plateau. In terms of per capita income, it falls in between the developed coastal provinces and the impoverished hinterlands of western China. I spent a total of 16 weeks in three different villages in the counties of Zhouzhi and Xingping, living with rural families and conducting ethnographic interviews with elderly farmers. In addition, I spent four weeks in villages in Sichuan and Jiangsu provinces, and collected archival materials from three provincial and five county-level archives.

My focus here is on cotton cultivation in northern China. Thanks to the work of Sven Beckert, Giorgio Riello, Walter Johnson, and others, cotton is recognised as an agent of social transformation on a global scale.[5] Cotton is an old crop, first cultivated 5,000 years ago and widely grown by peasant farmers in Africa, America, and Asia. Global cotton, in contrast, is of recent origin. Global cotton is *gossypium hirsutum* (American upland cotton), which accounts for about 90 percent of all cotton grown today. It is genetically standardised and is itself an agent of standardisation because it must be sown, grown, picked, and packed in specific ways in order to meet the requirements of mechanised processing. As the new global cotton literature shows, cotton cultivation for industrial processing requires massive social interventions, which have included, at different times and places, the expropriation of land, the formation of joint-stock land companies, the sedentarisation of nomads, the creation of a bonded and indebted rural workforce, the breakdown

---

5 Andrew Zimmerman, *Alabama in Africa: Booker T. Washington, the German Empire, and the Globalization of the New South* (Princeton: Princeton University Press, 2010); Sven Beckert, *The Empire of Cotton: A Global History* (New York: Alfred A. Knopf, 2014); William Moseley and Lesley Gray, *Hanging by a Thread: Cotton, Globalization, and Poverty in Africa* (Athens: Ohio University Press, 2008); Walter Johnson, *River of Dark Dreams: Slavery and Empire in the Cotton Kingdom* (Cambridge, MA: Belknap, 213); Giorgio Riello and Prasannan Parthasarathi, *The Spinning World: A Global History of Cotton Textiles, 1200–1850* (Oxford: Oxford University Press, 2009).

of traditional gender divisions of labour, the promulgation of harsh colonial labour laws, and the application of social-scientific knowledge to the reproduction of the workforce.[6] Global cotton is both reliant on and generative of state power: reliant because the massive infrastructure required for cotton-based industrialisation – including the experimental farms, extension stations, irrigation works, railways, storage facilities, market and credit networks – exceeds the resources of private investors; generative because the need to keep supplies flowing justifies state intervention at all levels of society, down to the very grassroots.

Labour Mobilisation in Socialist China

China's socialist development was an accelerated version of the Soviet model. China on the eve of its first Five-Year Plan (in 1953) was a poorer, less industrialised country than the Soviet Union at a comparable stage in its development (in 1928): per capita production of grain, coal, and cotton cloth was less than one-half of the Soviet Union; steel output was less than one-tenth.[7] Like the Soviet Union, the People's Republic prioritised heavy and defence industrialisation over light industry and agriculture. The money needed to fund rapid industrialisation could not come from industry itself, which in the early People's Republic accounted for less than 20 percent of GDP, but had to be extracted from agriculture. By 1954, all major agricultural goods, such as grain, cotton, oilseeds, sugar cane, tea, meat, and hides, and their processed products – for example, flour, cotton yarn and cloth, and edible oils – were subject to unified purchase and marketing. This meant that they could be bought and sold only by state firms, at prices that were administratively set rather than determined by the market. Under this system, farmers and agricultural collectives (collectivisation was completed in 1957) were regularly assessed for production capacity and assigned sales quotas for the surplus portion of their harvest, leaving them only with what they needed for subsistence. Prices for agricultural products were graded according to quality and adjusted every few years. Agricultural products were then processed in state-

---

6 Timothy Mitchell, *Rule of Experts: Egypt, Techno-Politics, Modernity* (Berkeley: University of California Press, 2002): 59–62, 72–4, 94–10; Andrew Zimmerman, *Alabama in Africa:* 13, 130–53; Allen Isaacman, *Cotton is the Mother of Poverty: Peasants, Work, and Rural Struggle in Colonial Mozambique* (Portsmouth: Heinemann, 1996), 44–68, 70–104, 129–44.

7 Nai-ruenn Chen and Walter Galenson, *The Chinese Economy under Communism* (Chicago: Aldine Publishing Company, 1969), 35.

owned factories and sold to domestic consumers under a rationing system or channelled to the export market.[8]

Rural-urban exchange was understood as a commodity relation: the socialist
state bought agricultural products from private or collective farms, and sold machinery, fertilizer, pesticides, and consumer goods back to them. This was different in
principle from relationships in the state-owned industrial sector, where the state
did not buy and sell but appropriated products from one unit and allocated
them to other units at cost price, that is, without extracting a profit. The distinction
between commodity exchange in agriculture and planned allocation in industry
may appear semantic: in practise, rural collectives operated under plan and
were assigned output quotas, just like state-owned factories. But it is more than
semantic because seeing rural-urban exchange as a form of trade legitimised
the taking of profit. The mechanism for this, developed in debates between Soviet
economists in the 1920s, is known as price scissors. In industrialising economies,
the cost price of industrial goods falls faster than that of agricultural products:
as industry matures, it becomes more efficient and prices come down. Under scissors pricing, these cost savings are not passed on to consumers: the price of industrial goods is kept high while that of agricultural goods is kept low, allowing the
state to extract surplus from the rural-agrarian sector and transfer it to the
urban-industrial core. In China as in the Soviet Union, price scissors served as
the main motor of accumulation. In China, cotton mills led the way: the state set
the price of raw cotton so low, and the price of finished textiles so high, that
state mills earned their investment back in the first year of operation and
would continue to generate healthy profits throughout the collective years.[9]

In addition to funding the country's industrialisation, agriculture also had to
support a population that doubled between the 1949 revolution and the end of
the Mao years. It had to do so with limited land resources: arable land per capita
halved from an already minuscule 0.18 hectares to 0.09 hectares.[10] Increased yields
had to be wrested from the soil with a minimum of modern inputs, with only a
small fraction of national investment allocated to the rural sector. As late as
1970, 20 years after the land reform, only 18 percent of farmland was tractor

---

8 Carl Riskin, *China's Political Economy: The Quest for Development since 1949* (Oxford: Oxford University Press, 1987); Dwight Perkins, *Market Control and Planning in Communist China* (Cambridge,
MA: Harvard University Press, 1966).
9 Chao, Kang: *The Development of Cotton Textile Production in China* (Cambridge, MA: Harvard
East Asian Monographs, 1977), 250.
10 Planning Office of the Ministry of Agriculture, Animal Husbandry, and Fishing: *Materials on the
Agrarian Economy, 1948–1983* (Beijing, 1983) (农牧渔业部计划司，农业经济资料*1949–1983*), 34–5,
46–7, 120.

farmed and 15 percent was pump-irrigated. Chemical fertilizer use remained low, not passing the two-hundred-kilogram-per-hectare mark until 1977.[11] As late as 1980, Chinese agriculture was primarily organic and reliant on phytomass derived from solar energy. More work was performed by human and animal muscles than by machinery; more nutrients derived from farm manure and other organic matter than from chemical fertilizer; more rural homes heated with crop residues than with coal.[12]

Output growth in agriculture came mostly from two sources: from scientific experiments on model farms and the application of the resulting knowledge to the fields; and from the application of ever more labour to the land. The two processes were in fact inseparable: the new high-yielding crops bred in the Mao years were selected for their responsiveness to labour input and were introduced together with field management regimes that required frequent weeding, hoeing, watering, and fertilisation. The main routes to labour intensification were irrigation and multiple cropping. Since there was not a lot of scope for increasing China's acreage, planners focused on more intensive cropping: regions that produced a single harvest in the past were told to aim for two yearly harvests; areas that double cropped were made to produce a third annual harvest.[13]

Intensive cropping required irrigation, which meant that canals had to be dug, reservoirs built, hillsides terraced, wells drilled, and alkaline soils flushed of their salt content – all by hand, with shovels, pickaxes, wheelbarrows, and bamboo baskets as the only tools. Labour demand for these tasks was intense: in my fieldwork site of Shaanxi, in the county of Xingping, tens of thousands of farmers were mobilised every year to transform a hilly and uneven terrain into a flat geometrical landscape, divided by canals and roads into fields of equal size and shape. Directives called for an extra yearly labour input, in addition to the normal farming workload, of 40 to 100 days per adult worker. Local people remembered that the time spent in flattening the land would often exceed that of routine farming.[14] Nationwide, 100 to 150 million people were mobilised each year for public works, with an average annual labour input of 30 days. Every year, rural *corvée* labour moved

---

11 *Materials on the Agrarian Economy*, 290, 291, 292.

12 Vaclav Smil, *The Bad Earth: Environmental Degradation in China* (Armonk, NY: M.E. Sharpe, 1984), 140.

13 Nicholas Lardy, *Agriculture in China's Modern Development* (Cambridge: Cambridge University Press, 1983), 82–6.

14 Xingping County Archives, 51-2-541 (1975-07-08); 51-1-598 (1977-09-10).

between five and 25 million cubic meters of earth, the equivalent of 20 to 100 Panama Canals.[15]

Despite a well-deserved reputation for industriousness, most Chinese farmers in the early twentieth century were unemployed for part of the year. According to John Lossing Buck's survey, 58 percent of rural men in the 1930s were partly idle and seven percent were idle most of the year, with an average unemployment rate of 1.7 months per able-bodied man.[16] Socialist China thus started with a surplus of underutilised labour, with the high birth rates of the early postwar years adding millions of new workers every year. However, labour demand in agriculture and construction grew faster than supply, thanks largely to massive infrastructure projects. The four years preceding collectivisation – 1952 to 1956 – saw the number of workdays performed by rural people increase by 40 percent; by 1959, at the height of the Great Leap Forward, it had risen 115 percent above 1952 levels.[17] This increase was due as much to the addition of new workers, with women mobilised to labour in the fields, as to the increase in the number of labour days performed per individual worker, as slack seasons were filled with infrastructure work.

Before collectivisation, women's participation in agriculture was mostly seasonal, although women in poor families might work outdoors all year round. Marina Thorborg's reconstruction of female labour participation shows that before collectivisation, 30 to 50 percent of able-bodied rural women worked part-time or full-time in the fields. Participation rates rose to between 60 and 75 percent during collectivisation, dropped to between 50 and 65 percent once the collectives were established, and rose to an unsustainable 80 or 90 percent during the Great Leap Forward. They stabilised at around 70 percent in the late 1960s.[18] Participation rates are an imperfect indicator since, initially, most women worked only part-time. In 1957, two-thirds of women worked fewer than 100 days in agriculture, while two-thirds of men worked more than 150 days.[19] However, women's workdays rose quickly during collectivisation: one Hebei county reported a sevenfold

---

15 James E. Nickum, "Labour Accumulation in Rural China and its Role since the Cultural Revolution," *Cambridge Journal of Economics* 2, 3 (1978): 280, 282 (1970s data)

16 John Lossing Buck, *Land Utilization in China: A Study of 16,786 Farms in 168 Localities, And 38,256 Farm Families in Twenty-Two Provinces in China, 1929–1933* (New York: Paragon Book Reprint, 1964), 294.

17 Peter Schran: *The Development of Chinese Agriculture, 1950–1959* (Urbana: University of Illinois Press, 1969), 50–55, 75.

18 Marina Thorborg, "Chinese Employment Policy in 1949–78 with Special Emphasis on Women in Rural Production," *Chinese Economy Post-Mao* (Joint Economy Committee, Congress of the United States, US Government Printing Office, 1978), 582, 584.

19 Thorborg, "Chinese Employment Policy": 590.

increase in three years, from 30 days in 1954 to 230 days in 1956.[20] Another way to gauge changes in women's labour participation is to look at official regulations. In one case documented by Thorborg, women without significant childcare or household duties were required to work 24 days a month; young mothers who could entrust their children to other family members worked 20 to 24 days a month; mothers without such help, 15 days a month. Women who were the main childcare providers and also suffered from ill health were nonetheless expected to work 12 days a month.[21]

Five features stand out in the People's Republic's attempts to mobilise the rural population and render it more disciplined and productive:

1. Eliminating empty time: The lengthening of the workday that is central to Marx's analysis of industrial capitalism reaches its limits in agriculture, where work rhythms are determined by daylight and weather. State planners sought to fill gaps in the working year, rather than the working day, by mobilising people for infrastructure work in the winter months and during midsummer, when crops ripened in the fields. Winter and midsummer were traditionally periods of rest and regeneration, when men repaired their tools and women did textile work, and times of ritual activity and intense socialising. In central Shaanxi, *mangqian* (the time before the wheat harvest) and the New Year festival were the seasons when women visited their natal families, newborn children were introduced to relatives, weddings were planned, and family ties formed or reaffirmed. The state saw little value in holidays that were associated with lavish spending and folk superstition, and targeted slack periods for labour mobilisation. Documents from the 1970s describe with enthusiasm how thousands of men and women were mobilised to dredge the Wei River during the New Year festival, China's most important holiday, and call for a "high tide of capital construction" during the winter months, when sub-zero temperatures must have made earthwork difficult.[22]

2. Progressive labour substitution: Labour mobilisation aimed not just at making more people work for longer hours but also at sorting labour by skill and strength, directing high-value labour to high-priority tasks. A 1960 document stipulated that men should not be assigned work that can be done by women; able-bodied workers should not be assigned work that can be done by half-time workers; half-time workers should not be assigned work that can be done by supplementary

---

20 Thorborg, "Chinese Employment Policy": 592.
21 Thorborg, "Chinese Employment Policy": 95.
22 Xianyang Municipal Archives, 51-2-541.

workers.[23] The cost of labour substitution fell disproportionally on those at the bottom of the structure: not the young men who moved into industry or construction, nor the young women who replaced them in the fields; but the middle-aged and elderly women who had to shoulder the tasks abandoned by the young, without seeing any diminution in their own tasks.

3. Measurement and quantification: Traditionally, small farmers relied on rules of thumb in determining inputs or forecasting harvests and had little need for precise quantification. Collective farming, by contrast, took place in the context of a planned economy, and planners needed to know in advance how much grain would be available to feed the urban population or how much cotton to supply the textile mills. Ministries in Beijing set production targets, which were then disseminated from the central government to the provinces, and from there to prefectures, counties, people's communes, and production brigades, down to the level of the agricultural production team. The downward dissemination of targets was matched by an upward flow of crop reports. Cotton-growing counties, for example, were required to report seven times a year, starting six months before planting with a statement of readiness and concluding in November with a year-end summary.[24] The aim – never fully achieved – was total visibility: ideally, ministries in Beijing would know with a few days' delay how much land had been ploughed, how much labour mobilised, and how much grain, cotton, or oilseeds planted, irrigated, and harvested.

4. Ratcheting up: The 1956 Plan for the Development of National Agriculture called for a doubling of area yields of all major crops in ten years.[25] This was to be achieved by production contests and emulation of the "advanced experience" of high-output areas. High-yield areas were to teach their advanced practises to their less productive neighbours; low-yield areas were told to work harder until they reached their neighbours' levels. By the time a low-performing team reached the level of its neighbours, these had already moved on; the process never stopped. Teams that persistently failed to level up could expect disciplinary action against

---

23 Xingping County Archives, 4–1–80 (1960–11–16): 45. Half-time workers (*banlao*) typically refers to women aged 45 to 55 and men aged 51 to 59; supplementary workers (*fuzhu lao*) refers to retired workers.

24 Sichuan Archives, *Jianchuan* 009–320: 22.

25 Grain yields in the Northeast and Northwest were to increase from 75 kilograms per *mu* to 200 kilograms; in the North China Plain from 100 kilograms to 250 kilograms; in the double-cropping South from 200 kilograms to 400 kilograms. Cotton yields were to increase from a national average of 17.5 kilograms to 50 kilograms. See *1956–1957 Outline for the Development of Chinese Agriculture, Revised Draft* (Beijing: Renmin Ribao Chubanshe, 1957) (*1956 年到1967 年全国农业发展刚要 ,修正草案, 人民日报出版社*), 6–7.

their leaders.[26] Mass mobilisation in emulation campaigns intersected with the top-down dissemination of technical information in China's powerful agricultural research and extension system. State experimental farms were constantly developing new strands of crops and testing how they responded to irrigation, fertilizers, and pesticides. The findings were passed down to the Agricultural Production Teams (the lowest level of the three-tiered collective structure, 25 households on average) through extension officers and technicians stationed at the People's Communes (the highest level, around 2,000 households). Most communes and brigades ran experimental fields, where they tested how different strains of crops responded to the local soil and climate.[27]

5. *Ideological mobilisation:* Archival documents from the Mao years show a pervasive emphasis on ideological mobilisation. All policies – whether it was the introduction of a new wheat strain or a change in the way cotton was picked – were to be accompanied by education and propaganda, and often "thought work" appears to be the only arrow in the government's quiver. Productive work itself was meant to be transformative, as it taught rural people the values of foresight, diligence, and self-reliance. Training took different forms: as we will see, the state pursued an almost-Taylorist standardisation of the labour process, but the ideal rural labourer, from the state's perspective, was not a mindless automaton but rather a proactive, self-improving agent, willing to learn from others and on the constant lookout for new challenges.

Coercion, Emulation, and Material Incentives

How did the Chinese state convince rural people to work so much harder than they had done before? Coercion alone cannot be the answer, given the fact that there were no police to speak of in the countryside and that village militias represented a cross-section of rural society and could not be relied on to enforce the will of any single leader. Leaders were elected by team members, had no expectation of a career beyond the village, and usually returned to the rank and file after a few years of service. They used coercive power in often brutal and vindictive ways when dealing with former landlords and class enemies, but they had little leverage over members of good standing, who could not be dismissed from the team and could be neither promoted nor demoted. Incentive schemes (discussed below)

---

26 Xianyang Municipal Archives, 001–03-C-0258 (1963–12–24): 34.
27 Sigrid Schmalzer, *Red Revolution, Green Revolution: Scientific Farming in Socialist China* (Chicago: University of Chicago Press, 2016).

linked income to individual effort, but overall cash and grain incomes were capped and did not grow over time. While labour input rose, cash wages and grain supplies remained frozen throughout the collective years.

Labour intensification relied on a triad of administrative fiat, ideological mobilisation, and material incentives. Administrative fiat ensured that workers turned out in sufficient numbers: every collective member – in fact, every able-bodied citizen of the People's Republic – had a legal obligation to participate in productive work.[28] Central and provincial governments rarely set labour mobilisation targets, but they set output quotas; collective units then allocated labour with an eye to meeting these quotas. In central Shaanxi, labour mobilisation took the form of biannual campaigns: a spring campaign that began with the wheat harvest and the planting of maize and cotton in May/June and continued until autumn, and an autumn campaign that started with the cotton harvest and the planting of wheat in October/November and extended into April/May. Mobilisation began months before the start of planting, with meetings at the county level; smaller meetings were then held at the commune and brigade levels. If necessary, follow-up meetings would be called to deal with events such as unexpected droughts or insect infestations.[29]

At the level of the team, turnout was mostly ensured by social pressure. Team members were summoned to work in the morning, when leaders went through the villages beating gongs, and typically worked three shifts: from sunrise to mid-morning breakfast, from breakfast to noon, and from 2pm to 6pm; during the busy seasons, a fourth shift was added. People could beg off from work from time to time but were required to make up for the time they missed. Economic pressures rather than coercion ensured that people went to work: most interviewees agreed that if they did not work, they got no work points, and without work points, they would have nothing to eat. Coercion became necessary, however, when lucrative side-lines lured people away from the collective fields. Women in cotton-growing districts often neglected agricultural work to weave cloth for the black market, earning far more than they would have done in the collective fields. Collectives responded by confiscating homespun cloth and ordering women back to the fields. Coercion was also common during the Great Leap Forward, when most men had been sent away to smelt steel or build reservoirs, and labour shortages forced teams to mobilise all women for farm work. In Guanzhong, starving

---

28 *Model Regulations for an Agricultural Producers' Co-Operative* (Beijing: Foreign Languages Press, 1956), 8, 12, 33; Constitution of the People's Republic of China (1954), Article 16: "Work is a matter of honour for every citizen of the People's Republic of China who is capable of working." Article 91: "Citizens of the People's Republic of China have the right to work."

29 Xianyang City Archives, 123–1–1836 #5 (1955–6–6): 34–36.

women declared that they would steal from the fields unless the state raised their rations. Local governments called on the teams to identify the women who were still capable of outdoor work, and use investigation, pressure, and replacement to move as many women as possible from the "rear guard" sectors of childcare and domestic work to the "frontlines" of production.[30] Some teams fined workers who did not "exert" themselves, but it seems fines were reserved for former landlords and rich peasants and rarely used with team members of a "good" class background.[31] These measures were later criticised as excessive; in general, it was scarcity, not coercion, that ensured that people turned out for work.

Following the example of the Soviet Union, the People's Republic designated model workers, publicised their stories, and encouraged others to emulate their achievements. One of the most successful rural emulation campaigns was the Silver Flower Contest, named after five women farmers from Shaanxi famed for their record cotton yields.[32] At its peak, the contest involved 120,000 activists on more than 4,000 model fields, the vast majority of them women. Silver Flower activists were nothing if not enthusiastic: one team declared that "our heads may roll, our blood may flow if we don't meet the target of 1,000 *jin* of cotton per *mu.*" The members of another team promised not to marry "until our sputniks fill the sky" (until they established new production records).[33] Yet it was precisely this heroic determination that made the movement unattractive to other rural people. Most activists were young women without domestic obligations, who could spend entire days in the fields – unlike married women, who had to shuttle between the field and home. From the perspective of older women, activists were either imposters, whose record-breaking feats were due to hidden government support, or scabs, whose blind enthusiasm pushed up output norms. Many women I interviewed had fond memories of work in the collective fields, which they experienced as joyful and egalitarian. Others, however, told mocking stories about farming experiments gone wrong (in one case, women activists so overfertilised a field that the plants collapsed under their own weight), and described activists as lickspittles and careerists.[34]

Work performed for the collective was measured in work points. Ten points represented a standard workday, namely the work that could be done by an

---

30 Xingping County Archives, 4–1–80 (1960–11–11): 30; 4–1–81 (1960–09–30): 29–30.

31 Xianyang City Archives, 001–06-D-0154 (1965–03–30): 65.

32 Gao Xiaoxian, "The Silver Flower Contest: Rural Women in 1950s China and the Gendered Division of Labour", *Gender and History* 18, 3 (2006): 594–612; Gail Hershatter, *The Gender of Memory: Rural Women and China's Collective Past* (Berkeley: University of California Press, 2011).

33 Xingping County Archives, 4–1–73 (1960–04–05): 102–103, 106. Translation is my own.

34 Zhouzhi interviews (2008–09–10).

able-bodied man working three full shifts in the fields. Most men earned ten points per day, even if their tasks were not demanding; women typically earned six to eight points per day. In theory, men and women received equal pay for equal work, but since they worked separately and performed different tasks, it was easy for collective leaders to label women's work as lighter and less skilled. In Guanzhong, men monopolised grain cultivation, while women worked in the cotton fields. Cotton cultivation is backbreaking, but it was considered light and paid less than men's work in the grain fields.[35] Tasks that needed to be done quickly (such as harvesting and planting) or were particularly onerous (such as carrying manure) were paid per task rather than per day. In theory, task rates were set in such a way that a person working at a normal speed earned the equivalent of a full workday.[36] However, young men and women working for piece rates could sometimes earn the equivalent of two or three days' work in a single day.

Work points did not have a fixed monetary value but represented shares in collective income. It was only at year's end, when teams calculated their income and expenses, that the value of the work points became known. They varied substantially between teams, depending less on natural endowments than on sales quotas and administrative quotas. A team that was permitted to grow garlic, chiles, or other lucrative cash crops, or to run a brick kiln as a collective side-line, might pay its members five or six times more per workday than a team that was assigned heavy grain production quotas and had no side-lines.[37] While collective members would not learn how much they had earned until the end of the year, they would receive advances in the form of grain, cooking oil, fuel, and other such goods throughout the year. If the value of work points earned exceeded the price of goods consumed, they would receive a cash payout from the collective coffers; if earnings fell short of consumption, the debt would be carried over to the next year.[38]

For people living close to the subsistence minimum, grain income was more important than cash – not least because grain could be exchanged for cash, but cash could not legally buy grain beyond one's ration quota. State grain procure-

---

35 Li Huaiyin quotes a man saying that "in the moment of smoking a cigarette, what a man does equals what a woman does for half a day." Li Huaiyin, *Village China under Socialism and Reform* (Stanford: Stanford University Press, 2019), 200–202.

36 Xingping County Archives, 4–1–80 (1960–09–27): 16–23.

37 Zhouzhi interviews (2010–08–08). I am indebted to Meng Fanhang for sharing his fieldnotes with me.

38 Jean Oi, *State and Peasant in Contemporary China: The Political Economy of Village Government* (Berkeley: University of California Press, 1989), 33–37; William Parish and Martin King Whyte, *Village and Family in Contemporary China* (Chicago: University of Chicago Press), 62–71.

ment policies allowed collectives to distribute about 15 kilograms of grain per person and per month, far below what international organisations consider a subsistence ration; any surplus above that level had to be sold to the state.[39] Collectives typically divided their consumption grain into two portions: a basic ration distributed per capita to provide a subsistence floor to all members; and "work point grain" used to reward labour contributions. The proportion varied over time and between teams; the most common distribution keys were "three-seven" and "four-six," that is, 30 to 40 percent paid out as work point grain, and 60 or 70 percent paid as basic ration.[40] Neither basic rations nor work point grain were wages in the proper sense: households had to pay for their grain, no matter how it was distributed. What people got by earning work points was the right to buy much-needed grain in addition to their basic rations.

This complex system functioned in some ways like a wage, in others like income sharing in a cooperative or large household. Work point incomes fluctuated in unpredictable ways and depended more on the overall economic health of the collective than individual members' efforts. Since the pool from which incomes were drawn was fixed, one member's gain was all other members' loss, a setup that generated jealousy and suspicion. Opaque and confusing in many ways, the work point system was transparent in one respect: it linked grain supplies to labour in the fields and thus compelled people to work for their survival. Basic grain rations covered about one-half to two-thirds of calorific needs, depending on the overall level of supply and on the ratio between basic and work point rations. People supplemented their insufficient rations with grain grown in garden-size private plots, and those with cash incomes sometimes bought grain on the black market. But by and large, it was the work point grain that made the difference between satiety and hunger.

The Labour Process in the Fields

Even before collectivisation, Chinese yields for most crops were high by international standards. When the CCP called for a doubling of yields in ten years, this was known to be an ambitious target. As mentioned above, output growth was to be achieved with minimal capital investment, that is, without extensive mechanisation and with little use of pesticides or synthetic fertilizers. It was to rely, first,

---

39 International aid organizations define surplus as 25 kilograms and more. See Oi, *State and Peasant in Contemporary China*, 48.
40 Oi, *State and Peasant in Contemporary China*, 38–40.

on the application of modern science, and second, on a massive increase of labour input. The CCP inherited a powerful agricultural research and extension apparatus from its Nationalist predecessors and moved quickly to implement existing plans that had been shelved during the war.[41] I focus here on changes in cotton cultivation, but similar transformations took place in other crops. Changes in cotton cultivation affected millions of rural people: around 40 percent of the rural population – 200 to 280 million people – were classified as cotton farmers, which meant that they belonged to production teams that were subject to cotton procurement quotas.[42]

Starting in the 1920s, Chinese entrepreneurs and governments sought to replace native Chinese cotton (*gossypium arboreum*) with long-staple varieties from the United States (*g. hirsutum*), but their efforts were frustrated by the tendency of such cotton to deteriorate outside its home environment. By the 1930s, research institutions in China – often staffed by United States-trained agronomists and funded by United States institutions – established programs to breed strains that were genetically stable and suited to Chinese conditions. The key here was the introduction of pure-seed districts, namely large areas in which only one type of cotton was grown. In 1950, the Ministry of Agriculture established pure-seed districts that stretched across several provinces: northwest China was to grow Stoneville No. 4, originally from Missouri; northern China grew 517 (a Chinese strain bred from Stoneville); Zhejiang and Jiangsu grew Deltapine 15, and so on.[43] Seed standardisation opened the path to the standardisation of cultivation regimes: whereas in the past, cultivation methods differed depending on the soil and climate, now it became possible to prescribe best practises for areas comprising millions of hectares and tens of thousands of production teams.

By 1955, the Chinese state controlled both ends of the cultivation process: almost all cotton was grown from improved seeds, and almost the entire harvest was procured by the state's Cotton Company, which tested it for fibre length, colour, and tensile strength and fed this information back to the planners. Improved cultivation methods were disseminated through the agricultural extension system, which reached down from central research universities to experimental stations at the level of the people's communes. Newspaper articles and handbooks written in

---

41 Schmalzer, *Red Revolution, Green Revolution.*
42 People's Republic of China, Cotton and Hemp Office of the Ministry of Trade, *Statistical Materials on Cotton* (Beijing, 1989) (中华人民共和国商业部棉麻管理局, 棉花统计资料), 321.
43 Ministry of Agriculture: "Comprehensive Report on the National Meeting on Cotton Work," in *1949–1952 Selected Archival Materials on the Economy of the People's Republic of China: Agriculture* (Beijing: Zhongguo Shehui Kexueyuan, 1991) (农业部: "全国棉产工作会议总结报告", *1949–1952* 中华人民共和国经济档案资料选编:农业卷), 296–306.

accessible language gave advice on farming techniques, and clapper songs – short sketches written to musical accompaniment – taught farmers how to battle the bollworm, the whitefly, and the cotton borer.

Published guidelines prescribe in exhaustive detail how to grow cotton. The process starts with soil preparation: fields were ploughed in early winter, ideally to a depth of 33 to 40 centimetres – more than China's light ploughs could manage.[44] Two weeks before planting, organic fertilizer was spread out in the fields and ploughed under in a second, shallow ploughing, and fields were harrowed in a crisscross pattern. Seeds were hand-selected and prepared for sowing by rolling them in wood ash (a natural fungicide) or pesticide. Farmers were told to determine germination rates by sprouting seeds in warm water, and to adjust seed density accordingly. Seeds were sown with seed drills or by hand, in rows 50 to 70 centimetres apart. They were thinned repeatedly, each time eliminating the weakest seedlings, until a final plant distance of 30 to 40 centimetres was achieved. Any gaps in the rows would be closed by transplanting.[45]

The guidelines prescribed repeated hoeing – the more frequent, the better. Hoeing removes weeds, prevents the formation of a soil crust, and ensures that water, fertilizer, and air reach the roots. It started before seedlings emerged and was repeated every ten days or so for the duration of the growing season. The first rounds of hoeing were shallow, no more than a scraping of the soil. As the plants grew, hoeing gave way to hilling: soil in between the rows was scooped up with the hoe and pushed against the plants, creating ridges that grew higher with each turn. Hilling helped root formation and increased soil temperature, while the resulting trenches between the rows facilitated irrigation. When the cotton bolls began to set, deep hoeing was once again replaced by shallow scraping, so as not to harm the roots, which now grew closer to the surface. The guidelines recommended ten to 15 rounds of hoeing in a 30-week growing season, although this level was rarely achieved.[46] Hoeing was combined with irrigation and fertilisation. Fields were hoed after irrigation and after heavy rainfall to allow water to sink to the roots. Droughts, which were common in the summer season, called for manual watering: men, women, and children were mobilised to carry water to the fields and apply it directly to the roots. The guidelines recommended reliance on an or-

---

44 Agronomic Research Institute of Xinxiang, Henan province, *Cotton* (Zhengzhou: Henan Renmin Chubanshe, 1974) (河南省新乡地区农业科学研究所, 棉花), 33.

45 Agronomic Research Institute, *Cotton*, 54; Ji Junmian, *Handbook of Cotton Cultivation* (Beijing: Zhonghua Shuju, 1951) (季君勉, 种棉手册), 25.

46 Agronomic Research Institute, *Cotton:* 57–8; Ji Junmian, *Handbook of Cotton Cultivation:* 26; Zhao Lunyi, *Growing Drought-Resistant Cotton* (Shanghai: Xinnong chubanshe, 1952) (赵倫彝, 抗旱植棉法), 26–28.

ganic base fertilizer, supplemented with top dressings of synthetic fertilizer, applied manually and at frequent intervals.[47]

In contrast to cotton growers elsewhere in the world, Chinese farmers meticulously pruned and shaped their plants, in order to remove excess foliage and direct all nutrients to the bolls. When the first buds appeared in June, leaves and side shoots were removed from the lower parts of the stem, a process known as "stripping the pant legs." Next, non-fruiting branches and sucker shoots were removed. In late July, plants were topped, i.e., the central shoot was snipped off to encourage lateral growth. Some guidelines also recommended breaking off the tips of fruiting branches above the last bud, to ensure that all nutrients went to the buds, and pinching off side shoots growing in the axils between branch and stem. Late in the season, excess leaves were removed to expose ripening bolls to sunshine. Properly pruned cotton plants had a straight stem and 10 to 20 fruit-bearing branches, growing at a right or acute angle to the stem. Branches of neighbouring plants should meet over the rows without crowding out each other.[48]

Cotton attracts a large variety of insect pests such as the bollworm, the pink cotton worm, the red spider, and the cutworm, as well as many fungal and bacterial infections.[49] Lindane and dichlorodiphenyltrichloroethane (DDT) became available in the 1950s and were used wherever available. However, pesticides were in short supply and could not kill bugs hidden under leaves or larvae in the boll. Cotton-growing teams therefore relied heavily on manual pest removal. Infected leaves and branches were cut off, eggs were stripped off the plant, and bugs were shaken into basins filled with soap water, brushed with tobacco juice, or speared with sharpened chopsticks.[50]

As Sigrid Schmalzer has argued in her work on China's green revolution, the techniques introduced under the collectives had the potential to both skill and de-skill rural people. On the one hand, the embodied and experiential knowledge of the individual farmer was to some extent replaced by written codes that prescribed a fixed sequence of actions. On the other, the newly introduced techniques were often complex and required careful attention and good judgement.[51] The shortage of modern inputs meant that skilled manual work was not replaced by the quick fixes of industrial agriculture. Pesticides, for examples, were sometimes

47 Zhao Lunyi, *Growing Drought-Resistant Cotton*, 29.
48 Agronomic Research Institute, *Cotton*, 58–62; Ji Junmian, *Handbook of Cotton Cultivation:* 29; Zhao Lunyi, *Growing Drought-Resistant Cotton*, 30–31.
49 Agronomic Research Institute, *Cotton*, 81–134; Li Huaiyin, *Village China under Socialism and Reform:* 187–189.
50 Agronomic Research Institute, *Cotton*, 128–129.
51 Schmalzer, *Red Revolution, Green Revolution*, 25, 125–128.

sprayed, but often applied manually – not because of environmental concerns but because this ensured a better use of a scarce resource.

One feature that collective-era farming technologies have in common is their labour intensity, compared not only with earlier Chinese practise but also the rest of the world. Handbooks and guidelines were at pains to present their techniques as in line with tradition, but records from the Republican years suggest much lower labour inputs. Experimental farms in the 1940s applied ten labour days per *mu* of cotton land: four days of hoeing, two days of watering, two days of topping and pruning, and one day each of bug removal and manuring.[52] A 1963 survey found that collective farmers worked 35 to 40 days per *mu* on unirrigated land; the figure for irrigated land must have been higher, around 45 days per *mu*.[53] It seems, then, that labour input in the collective fields was three or four times higher than on pre-1949 experimental farms – which must have practised more intensive cultivation than the average peasant farm. Labour input in China was high also by international standards. Repeated hoeing ("chopping") was practised in the United States South before mechanisation, but much of the work was done with mule-drawn sweeps, using ploughs that pushed soil from the middle of the row to the beds on both sides. Topping and pruning were known but not widely practised in the United States' South.[54] Some Egyptian growers pruned their plants but the practise was not generally followed, and I have found no evidence of cotton being pruned in Brazil, South Asia, or Central Asia.[55]

Cotton Picking

The changes discussed so far were modifications of traditional practises. Developments in cotton picking went further: the aim was to teach women farmers a way of picking that would improve fibre quality and minimise spoilage and theft. Industrial processing requires careful and timely picking. Cotton should be picked

---

52 Li Guozhen, *Shaanxi's Cotton Industry* (Wugong: National Northwest Agricultural College, 1947) (李国桢，陕西棉业，武功国立西北农学院), 203.

53 Wu Yongxiang, "An evaluation of the economic efficiency of growing cotton on dry land in Wugong county," *Jingji Yanjiu* 10 (1963) (吴永祥, "武功县旱地植棉经济效果砰价", 经济研究), 34.

54 Joyce E. Chaplin, "Creating a Cotton South in Georgia and South Carolina, 1760–1815," *The Journal of Southern History* 57, 2 (1991): 171–200, states that topping and suckering were common in the Old South. Twentieth-century handbooks mention it but advise against it. See Harry Bates Brown, *Cotton: History, Species, Varieties, Morphology, Breeding, Culture, Diseases, Marketing, and Uses* (New York: McGraw-Hill, 1938), 302.

55 Moritz Schanz, *Cotton in Egypt and the Anglo-Egyptian Sudan* (Manchester: Taylor, Garnett, Evans & Co, 1913), 66.

immediately after the seed capsule has opened; if picked too early, the boll (the clump of cotton wool) may not separate neatly from the shell and fibres may be thin, moist, and likely to deteriorate. If, on the other hand, cotton is left in the field too long, fibres may be blown off by the wind, taken by birds and rodents, or exposed to rain and frost. Since capsules open over a period of ten weeks, pickers must go through the fields again and again – the more frequently, the higher the yield and the better the quality. Cotton must be extracted neatly, separating the boll from the capsule in one swift movement, and put to dry in the sun as soon as possible. Pickers must resist the temptation to increase weight by adding dirt, twigs, leaves, or water, and of course they must not pocket cotton for themselves.

Traditionally, farmers in China practised this kind of "clean" picking only in mid-season, during warm autumn days when bolls ripened quickly and separated easily from the shells. In the early and late season, they twisted off entire capsules, dried them at home, and removed the fibres in the comfort of their homes. The advantage of this method was that pickers could harvest ripe and unripe burrs together, reducing the number of pickings from about 12 per season to just four or five. This, however, meant that much cotton was picked before or after the moment of maturity. This was of no great concern to rural people who did not care about the cotton's colour and could spin yarn from short and mildewed fibres, but it greatly reduced its use for processing and hence its value for the state.

Changing the way cotton was picked had been a central concern for Republican reformers, who found that up to 50 percent of "twisted" cotton was discoloured, while cotton that was picked clean was whiter, longer, stronger, and fetched much higher prices.[56] To the chagrin of the planners, twisting persisted long into the collective years, despite attempts to educate farmers about the advantages of the new method. The case against traditional picking methods was laid out in a 1955 Women's Federation document. Clean picking, women were told, resulted in higher quality, which was important for state industry. Women may believe that twisting saved time, but this was a misconception: if one added the hours spent extracting fibres from the capsules, twisting was actually slower than clean picking. Moreover, fibre extraction took place at night, resulting in women "burning lamp oil and their eyes" (*aoyou aoyan*) in tedious labour. Wouldn't it be better, the Federation asked, if women used their evenings to attend night school or village meetings?[57]

The same Women's Federation document contains detailed instructions on how to stand and move in the fields. The key was posture: one had to remain

---

56 Li Guozhen, *Shaanxi's Cotton Industry*, 133–136.
57 Xingping County Archives, 4–1–25 (1955–09–16): 55–56.

bent double as long as possible and move through the fields in a low crouch. Pickers were told not to fear being slow but to fear straightening their back. One should use both hands; if cotton was ripe and detached from the capsules easily, both hands moved separately; if not, one hand grasped the capsule while the other pulled out the cotton. Hands should be in constant motion; half-opened capsules should be passed by, and bolls that did not detach at first try should be left for the next round of picking. Hands and eyes should work in unison, with the eyes always one step ahead of the hands.[58] Pickers were equipped with partitioned sacks so that they could separate mildewed, yellowed, or otherwise substandard cotton from white cotton. They were told to practise "three cleans" and "five separates" while picking: cotton should be free of dirt, leaves, and stems; and fibres from different fields should be picked, dried, stored, ginned, and sold separately, to avoid the mixing of seeds.[59]

Documents from the collective years treat continued twisting as a sign of opposition to state policies. Labour shortages during the Leap forced many teams to pick in this fast and labour-saving way. The Women's Federation, however, argued that labour shortages were just a pretext: the real reason was rightist thinking and lazy acceptance of poor work habits.[60] Another document described the competition between clean picking and twisting as an instance of the two-line struggle between socialism and capitalism.[61] This heated language suggest that the conflict was not primarily about work efficiency or product quality (although it was this, too) but about controlling the harvest. Planners sought to reorganise work in ways that not only increased total yield but, crucially, increased the state's share of the harvest. The way to do this was to get the cotton out of the villages and into guarded depots as soon as possible, ideally within days of the harvest. As long as cotton remained in the villages, it was vulnerable – not only to mice, insects, and fungal infections but also to a peasant population suffering from a severe textile shortage and therefore likely to steal any cotton they could lay their hands on. Clean picking was preferred because cotton could be moved to depots within forty-eight hours and remained in constant view of collective and state leaders as it moved from fields to drying grounds to packing stations. Traditional twisting left the cotton in the village for much longer periods and thus created op-

---

58 Xingping County Archives, 4–1–80 (1960–11–16): 58–59.
59 Xingping County Archives, 4–1–25 (1955–09–16): 56; 4–1–45 (1957, no date): 90–91.
60 Shaanxi Provincial Archives, 178–1–217 (1959–11–17): 26.
61 Xianyang Municipal Archives, 056–1–0093 (1963–09–09): 2.

portunities for theft, especially if the seed capsules were stored and dried in rural homes rather than in collective storerooms, as was often the case.[62]

One way to think about the politics of picking is to see it as a struggle over wages. In pre-industrial settings, workers often had customary rights to scraps: wood chips from the shipyard, coal from the mine, slops from the kitchen. If wages are inflexible, the struggle for fair pay focuses on these forms of in-kind remuneration. Employers insist that workers provide their own tools, bring oil and coal to heat and light the workplace, pay for spoiled goods and broken implements. Workers, on the other hand, claim a customary right to take home scraps and cuttings and fight fines for late or shoddy work.[63] In the case of collective farming, people who had seen a huge increase in their workload but little improvement in their living standards felt justified in keeping some of the harvest for themselves. Pickers stuffed cotton in their shirts and pants, sent their children out at night to take cotton from the fields, or engaged in late-season gleaning, following the customary rule that cotton still standing in the fields after a certain date could be taken by the village poor, with the stalks to be used as fuel and the remaining cotton to be used for padding. Some collectives tacitly connived in this by leaving cotton in the fields until the autumn rains and then distributing the spoiled stalks to households.

From the perspective of planners and agronomists, clean picking, repeated hoeing, and intensive pruning were best practises – "best" in the sense that they produced higher yields and increased sales to the state. Yet as with all such practises, the question is best for whom? State planners did not regard rural labour as a cost; they treated it as a free, inexhaustible resource. Their concern was to feed the urban cotton mills and safeguard accumulation, and they were willing to prescribe cultivation methods that doubled or tripled rural workloads, even if the yield increase was small. At the same time, administrators viewed the rural workforce as akin to the bollworm, the greenfly, and the fusarium wilt: a predator who would devour the crop if given half a chance. Precautions against theft were built into field management regimes that detailed not only how often the crop was to be watered, pruned, and weeded, but also ensured that workers were not left unsupervised, that members of picking teams checked up on one another, and that crops remained in full view of collective leaders while they ripened in the fields. The simplification of the landscape into a grid of equally sized rectangles, crisscrossed by roads and canals, may have been motivated pri-

---

62 Xingping County Archives, 04–01–25 (1955–04–21): 55–6; Shaanxi Provincial Archives, 178–1–316 (1962–09–18): 16.

63 John Rule, *The Labouring Classes in Early Industrial England, 1750–1850* (London: Longman, 1986), 116–119.

marily by "high modernist" beliefs, but it also facilitated labour supervision in the fields.

The Levers of Control: State and the Rural Workforce

How are we to think of China's rural workforce: as a peasantry rooted in the land and working in traditional ways for its share of the harvest, or as a semi-proletariat, working for wages under the supervision of bureaucratic managers? The answer depends largely on two factors: did rural people own and control the means of production? And were they able to evade, subvert, or resist orders coming from above? Formally, all land in China was owned by the people as a whole, but farmland was *de facto* managed by the lowest level of the three-tiered collective structure, the Agricultural Production Team. Other productive assets – sheds, stables, ploughs and other farm tools, and draft animals – were also owned and controlled by the teams. Large and expensive equipment such as tractors, small power stations, and small factories were owned and operated by brigades or communes. Households owned the tools they needed to farm their private plots, but no draft animals or heavy tools. Pigs, poultry, and other small animals were for the most part privately owned. Depending on time and place, households were subject to sales and production quotas for meat and eggs or allowed to keep them for private use or sale. Residential housing was private property although the land on which it was built belonged to the team. Most teams reserved about five percent of their farmland for private plots, assigned to members on a per capita basis. These plots were meant to be used as kitchen gardens but in Guanzhong at least, people grew grain on them to supplement their scarce collective rations.

While land was owned by the collectives, its use was subject to several levels of state planning. At the most basic level, planners set procurement quotas for grain, cotton, and other products. To ensure that these quotas were met, they also prescribed how much of the land was to be allocated to which crops and set yield targets.[64] Quotas were set through top-down negotiations: the central government in Beijing negotiated quotas with the provinces, which then passed on more detailed quotas to prefectures, which in turn negotiated with counties. County governments then assigned quotas to communes, which passed them on to brigades and production teams. At each level, units might try to negotiate a reduction

---

64 Marc Blecher and Wang Shaoguang, "The Political Economy of Cropping in Maoist and Dengist China: Hebei Province and Shulu County, 1949–90," *The China Quarterly* 137 (1994): 63–98.

of their burden, but since the overall quota had to be met, a reduction for one team or brigade only meant an added burden for other units at the same level. Peer pressure ensured that quota reductions were rare and limited in scope.[65] Under-reporting was common, as each level of the hierarchy sought to keep a share of the harvest for themselves, either to barter it for needed inputs or to distribute it to their members. Higher levels expected this to happen and factored it in when they set their targets.

The state's leverage over collectives, and the collectives' leverage over their members, depended largely on their ability to withhold crucial resources. Collectives could legally convert their harvest into cash only by selling it to the state, and legally acquire gasoline, pesticides, and fertilizer only from state agencies. Most collectives sought to build up resources that reduced their dependence on the higher levels: they opened up unregistered land, underreported and hid their harvests, and engaged in black-market trading, sometimes for profit, more commonly to obtain the scarce inputs that they needed in order to meet the state's procurement quotas. These strategies, however, were risky for collective leaders, and could at best supplement the inputs supplied by the state. Similarly, house-holds with non-collective income from private plots, small side-lines, or from some village commons that were better equipped to resist pressures from team leaders. Non-collective income typically amounted to one-third to one-half of household income, but it took the form of cash (or, for example, firewood, reeds, and mushrooms from the village commons), not of grain.[66] For their grain income, people depended on the collective, and this alone ensured that they turned out for work.

The household registration system, formalised in 1960, made it all but impossible for rural people to leave their place of birth (or place of marriage, in the case of women who married into another village). People were tied to their place of reg-istration so closely that it could be said with equal justification that they belonged to the land as much as the land belonged to them. In one example (a village that has now been swallowed up by metropolitan Shenzhen), rural men obtained urban household registration at a rate of 228 per million in a given year; the rate for women was 28 per million.[67] Village membership was for life and, in fact, hereditary: people growing up under the collectives expected their children and grandchildren to be living in the same community. This meant, on the one hand, secure tenure: short of sending them to a labour camp, a team could not

---

65 Oi, *State and Peasant in Contemporary China*, 57–62.
66 *Materials on the Agrarian Economy*, 524–525.
67 Sulamith H. Potter, "The Position of Peasants in Modern China's Social Order," *Modern China* 9, 4 (1985): 495.

get rid of unwanted members. On the other hand, it meant that villagers were deprived of the exit option – migration to the city or to some distant border region – that had traditionally allowed them to express their discontent. Lifelong team membership is perhaps best seen as a form of local citizenship, a right to livelihood and participation in the team but not beyond.

Chinese rural workers were unfree in the specific sense that they were tied to a community and a place, and thus also to a workplace that they could not leave. They were subject to the discretionary power of team leaders, who were also neighbours and often relatives. This power was not, as a rule, despotic: team leaders used harsh coercive measures against class enemies (a small part of the population, usually less than five percent of a team) but rarely against ordinary members. What drove people to work was hunger: while work point grain was not the only source of cash and calories, other supplies – basic grain rations, private plots, and side-line incomes – were calibrated to be insufficient: people needed work point grain in order to survive. Members of rural collectives were thus free not to work in the same way as the early factory proletariat, namely in the sense that they were free to choose between work and starvation. People remained on the land, in physical possession of the means of production. However, their subsistence no longer came directly from the land: most food grain now took the form of a wage, determined in a complicated bureaucratic process.

Experientially, work under the collectives came to resemble factory work. It was performed collectively, under the supervision of leaders, regulated by clocks and gongs. Labour effort was measured, albeit imperfectly, and rewards were calibrated to the work performed. These changes were not necessarily unwelcome: women in particular remembered work in the fields as filled with song and laughter, in sharp contrast to work that kept them at home, in domestic isolation.[68] Low capital intensity in agriculture ensured that farm work remained manual and highly skilled. In fact, many rural people, especially young women, learned new skills, and the state tried, with considerable success, to inculcate habits of scientific experimentation. At the same time, rural people's scope for decision-making was radically reduced. Farmers no longer chose what to grow; instead, they grew the crops demanded by the state – be it high-yield rice, wheat, corn, or cotton – even if these were not suited to local conditions or local palates and required immense amounts of extra work. Moreover, they grew these crops in prescribed ways, following schedules developed in research institutes and experimental farms and disseminated through the agricultural extension system. To use the language of the introduction to this essay, agricultural work became heteronomous: it

---

68 Gao Xiaoxian, "Silver Flower Contest," 604–605.

was controlled – albeit remotely, through a multi-tiered bureaucracy – by state managers whose interest in output and procurement maximation overrode rural people's interest in a secure and self-determined life.

Ju Li

4 Facing the Market and Fighting without Union: Labour Resistance History of Chinese State Workers

Introduction

Traditional labour studies, largely based on the prototypical experience of the Western working class, tend to implicitly regard the existence of independent or-ganisations like unions as an essential condition for an effective – or true – labour movement. An absence of unionisation is often taken as a sign of inadequacy or backwardness that would block or has actually already blocked the development of a real labour movement in many less developed parts of the world. Such a pre-sumption, as rightly criticised by Marcel van der Linden and other global labour scholars,[1] tends to ignore a much more complicated, richer, and sometimes more dynamic and strategic, though not necessarily more efficient, labour resis-tance history. Rather than slotting into a supposedly universal but rigorous mould, grassroots labour movements can adopt various kinds of vigorous, creative, pragmatic, or regressive forms, always arising as a specific response to particular historical contexts and conditions. As Frederic Cooper argues, "labor movements were more than automatic responses to becoming a proletarian, but were rooted in specific patterns of affiliation and strategies of mobilisation and alliance-build-ing."[2]

Moving beyond the stories of formal unions, this essay aims to provide an al-ternative narrative of the history of labour resistance in one particular state-owned-enterprise in China, which, to preserve its anonymity, is referred to here under the pseudonym Nanfang Steel. Although workers at Nanfang Steel lacked the opportunities to organise any legal and formal unions, they nevertheless re-sponded to and resisted against the steady emergence of new capitalist labour re-lations not just on the shop floor but also in their daily life, by manoeuvring through the existent system in rather pragmatic and shifting ways. This essay traces and compares the changing mode and efficiency of labour resistance move-

---

1 Marcel van der Linden, *Workers of the World: Essays Toward a Global Labor History* (Leiden and Boston: Brill, 2008), 9.
2 Frederick Cooper, *Decolonization and African Society: The Labor Question in French and British Africa* (Cambridge: Cambridge University Press, 1996), 116.

https://doi.org/10.1515/9783111086552-005

ments as adopted by two generations of workers at different historical moments following the market reforms between the 1980s and the mid-2010s. Informed by the political opportunity structure framework developed by Sidney Tarrow and others,[3] I investigate how the changing political opportunities and constraints faced by workers in different historical periods affected the processes, strategies, and outcomes of their contentious collective actions. I follow Tarrow's definition of political opportunity structure as the "consistent – but not necessarily formal or permanent – dimensions of the political struggle that encourage people to engage in contentious politics."[4] The key insight behind this concept is that contentious politics are always context-dependent.[5] This means that contentious politics emerge and develop in response to changes in political opportunities and constraints, with participants employing their known "repertoires of contention."[6]

Located in a mountainous area within the province of Sichuan, Nanfang Steel was an immense state-owned enterprise that had been developed as one of thousands of "Third Front" enterprises during the Third Front Construction era in the 1960s. The subsequent Cultural Revolution disrupted the construction and production process to a large extent, while, at the same time, producing a relatively militant working class armed with a strong socialist ideology and rhetoric, as well as an enclosed industrial community secluded from its rural surroundings. The cautious market reforms introduced in the 1980s shifted the focus from class struggle to production and slowly engendered a paternalistic factory regime with a general improvement in workers' living standards to create a prosperous community. During its heyday of the late 1980s and early 1990s, Nanfang Steel was one of the biggest taxpayers in Sichuan province, employing around 30,000 workers. Between the mid-1990s and the early 2000s, a variety of radical market-oriented means – mergers, partial privatisation, downsizing, burden alleviation, large-scale lay-offs, and so on – were imposed on Nanfang Steel. These programmes brought tremen-

---

3 Among many others, see Peter K. Eisinger, "The Conditions of Protest Behavior in American Cities," *American Political Science Review* 67, 1 (1973): 11–28; Doug McAdam, Sidney Tarrow, and Charles Tilly, "Dynamics of Contention," *Social Movement Studies* 2, 1 (2003): 99–102; Charles Tilly and Sidney Tarrow *Contentious Politics* (Oxford University Press, 2006); Sidney Tarrow, *Power in Movement: Social Movements and Contentious Politics* (Cambridge: Cambridge University Press, 2011); David S. Meyer and Suzanne Staggenborg, "Movements, Countermovements, and the Structure of Political Opportunity," *American Journal of Sociology* 101, 6 (1996): 1,628–60; David S. Meyer and Debra C. Minkoff, "Conceptualizing Political Opportunity," *Social Forces* 82, 4 (2004): 1,457–1,492.
4 Tarrow, *Power in Movement*, 32.
5 David S. Meyer, "Protest and Political Opportunities," *Annual Review of Sociology* 30 (2004): 125–145.
6 Tarrow, *Power in Movement*, 2.

dous destruction and chaos to the factory. The final preservation of the factory afterward, largely for the sake of social stability, failed to revitalise it, dragging it instead into a painful process of slow death, with a streamlined despotic factory regime on the shop floor, a pauperised working class, and a disintegrated factory community.

What we witness here is the epitome of the eventually victorious establishment of capitalist labour relations in the workplace, evolving from its more cautious and hesitant early stages to the more determined later years. Throughout these different periods, Nanfang Steel workers managed to employ various forms of contentious collective action, from protests, through strategically manoeuvring official ideology, to desperate militant confrontation and more hidden forms of resistance. While they were never able to organise any kind of formal union, Nanfang Steel workers nevertheless found their own ways to express their voices and fight for their interests, successfully or not.

All the interviews and oral testimonies were collected during my five field trips to Nanfang Steel between 2007 and 2013, as well as an additional trip in 2016. Altogether, I conducted more than 60 interviews, including with retired workers, currently employed workers, and cadres. All interviews were recorded with the subjects' permission and later transcribed and translated.

Compromise and Consent: Responding to Budding Capitalist Labour Relations

Following the so-called cage and bird policy, which insists that a State-Owned Enterprise (SOE) is a bird with its wings untied that could only fly within the "big cage" of a socialist state-owned economy,[7] early market reforms in the 1980s were cautious and ideologically bound. Two trends were seen during this period, in Nanfang Steel as well as in other SOEs. On the one hand, decentralisation and profit retention, which were the two major aims of early SOE reform, provided more money and autonomy for the factory to develop a more prosperous industrial community while also raising the living standards of ordinary workers. Meanwhile, outside the factory-supply network, a consumer market slowly emerged, largely due to earlier agricultural reforms, as the cautious growth of non-state economic sectors outside the command economy began to provide state workers with alternative employment opportunities, although they were still perceived as subop-

---

7 Wu, Xiaobo, *The Turbulent Thirty Years* (Beijing: CITIC Press, 2008), 67 (吴晓波，激荡三十年，中信出版社, 2008).

timal choices at the time. By weakening workers' structural dependence upon the regime, these developments helped to create a more hegemonic "bureaucratic paternalistic" labour regime at Nanfang Steel.[8] On the other hand, by the second half of the 1980s, the central government had begun to endorse a series of reforms that sought to give factory managers more authority, as well as introduce more flexible labour policies.[9] Power, thus, came to be increasingly concentrated in the hands of factory managers, and the income gap (relating to wages, bonuses, and distribution of homes) between workers, but especially between workers and managers, widened in more and more dramatic ways.[10] Nevertheless, the ideological "cage" of the socialist social contract between the state and state workers was largely preserved in this period: the tenure labour system remained intact; management did not acquire any new power over workers based on threats of firing or laying-off; and tentative efforts by the government in the 1980s to introduce a more flexible labour system were largely ineffective.

These two trends represented a particular political opportunity structure for workers at Nanfang Steel, which was employed in various ways by different generations of workers with their distinct repertoires of contention. While the retired workers, who still harboured vivid memories of the more militant working-class traditions that emerged during the Cultural Revolution, had launched quite a few successful contentious collective actions during the 1980s, contemporary workers, who were more directly influenced by carrot and stick policies, were largely compliant and even cooperative.

Fearless Pensioners: "We Are Still the Biggest Brother"

By the time of the market reforms at Nanfang Steel, most of its pioneering workers had either already retired or were entering retirement. This generation of workers had spent most of their working lives in the Maoist era and thus had the most vivid

---

8 Li, Ju, *Enduring Change: The Labor and Social History of One Third-Front Industrial Complex in China from the 1960s to the Present* (Boston and Berlin: Walter de Gruyter, 2019).

9 Jeanne L. Wilson, "The People's Republic of China," in *Trade Unions in Communist States*, edited by Alex Pravda and Blair A. Ruble (Boston: Allen and Unwin, 1986), 233; Leung, Wing-yue, *Smashing the Inn Rice-Pot: Workers and Unions in China's Market Socialism* (Hong Kong: Asia Monitor Resource Centre, 1988), 99.

10 Jackie Sheehan, *Chinese Workers: A New History* (London: Routledge, 2002), 197–198; Anita Chan, "Revolution or Corporatism? Workers and Trade Unions in post-Mao China," *The Australian Journal of Chinese Affairs* 29 (1993): 40; Andrew G. Walder, "Workers, Managers and the State: The Reform Era and the Political Crisis of 1989," *China Quarterly* 127 (1991): 479.

memories of a socialist past – especially the Cultural Revolution (1967–1969) with its high ideology discourse and radical anti-bureaucracy and mass rebellion movements – as a lived historical alternative to the current society. As a result, when market reforms got underway, they immediately sensed the change and the implicit detrimental effects upon workers and took action unhesitatingly.

Cuiye is a retired worker activist in his eighties. He was dubbed an "old revolutionary" by other workers because of his adamant hold on socialist ideology and his never-hesitant readiness to put up a fight against the cadres. Bold but also shrewd, he was one of the core figures among these pensioners and played a crucial role in almost every collective action. In one of his interviews, he narrated one particularly vivid and bold story about a victorious fight he and his comrade-pensioners had pitted against the cadres at Nanfang Steel during the 1980s:

> That was in 1983 or 1984. I had already retired. I was not convinced by the behaviour of the cadres ... Their only concerns then were production; they didn't care for workers' welfare, and they did not implement the mass line [....] So I posted small posters everywhere. These small posters were copies of a government document about anti-corruption.

Many of the other retirees referred to the years 1982 to 1983 as the real turning point in Nanfang Steel's history. Such feeling is justified not only by factory documents and reports from the time but also the factory's official daily newspaper, *Nanfang Steel News*, which, from 1982 onward, saw content such as fulfilling production quotas, increasing enterprise autonomy, strengthening labour discipline, wage raising, and bonus distribution replace previous topics of politics and class struggle. Moreover, it was during 1983 that the management of Nanfang Steel was restructured in response to the state's call for a younger and more educated leadership in SOEs. For the first time in Nanfang Steel's history, intellectuals with college degrees – rather than senior workers – made up the main body of its management. That some crucial changes began to occur around this period was keenly perceived by the retired workers. Cuiye's complaint, for example, about cadres caring more for production than workers' welfare and not implementing the mass line could be understood against this background. Even though he was caught and taken to the security department for putting up the posters in protest, he boasted to me that he feared nothing:

> The department chief there asked me why I posted the small posters. I replied to him that it was my freedom and right to put them up. The chief said that what I was doing was destroying the production. I told him that was rubbish. Then, after only five minutes, all the other retired workers heard about this incident. They soon gathered and surrounded the security department building. When the chief saw so many people, he became afraid. He begged me to go home. He said, 'We did something wrong, so we apologize to you. Please go home.' I said,

'Arresting people without reason is illegal. So now you have to tell me what illegal things I did. Or pasting small posters for anti-corruption is illegal? Is that your logic?' I did not leave. I stayed in their office, and all the retired workers stayed outside to support me. I was afraid of nothing (*laugh*) [...] I know how to deal with these bureaucrats. I am not afraid of them at all. There were so many people behind me.

"There were so many people behind me" – that was the greatest strength behind Cuiye's fearless and cunning behaviour. It was also the reason that the cadres were so ready to cave in. Such mass solidarity within this generation of workers arose from many factors, including their shared working-class identity that had been formed largely by the socialist state's policies, their shared working and living experiences, and the communal public spaces they occupied. Most had come to Nanfang Steel during the earliest period of the Third Front construction and had spent their lives together in this factory community. Before retirement, they had worked together; after retirement, they shopped at the same markets, exercised in the same parks, and played cards or *Mahjong* in the same teahouses. My interviews show that while these pensioners never formed any kind of organisation with an administrative or functional structure in the strict sense, they were nevertheless able to act in quite effective and prompt ways. They distributed information at markets, in teahouses, and in parks; sometimes, when there was something really important, notes would be posted on public notice boards in different residential areas calling for a meeting; at other times, urgent issues would be communicated by telephone. In this way, information could be distributed very quickly and, most of the time, the pensioners responded promptly. And this is exactly what happened in Cuiye's triumphant declaration that within five minutes of his arrest, his loyal comrades had appeared to back him up. These sorts of "dense informal social networks and rich, historically deep, subcultures of resistance to outside claims" described by Scott[11] have also been observed by other scholars in Chinese SOEs, especially during the 1980s when their industrial communities were steadily growing. They all point to the strong bargaining power over management that workers obtained from such dense informal social ties.[12]

Another victorious resistance organised by the pensioners during this period, as repeatedly recounted to me during the interviews, involved a protest against the distribution of homes in 1986. That year, Nanfang Steel had built two residential

---

11 James Scott, "Everyday Forms of Resistance," *Copenhagen Papers* 4 (1989): 52.
12 Bian, Yanjie, "Bringing Strong Ties Back In: Indirect Ties, Network Bridges, and Job Searches In China," *American Sociological Review* 62, 3 (1997): 366–385; Tang, Wenfang, and William L. Parish, *Chinese Urban Life Under Reform: The Changing Social Contract* (Cambridge: Cambridge University Press, 2000), 131–132.

apartment buildings with larger living areas than normal. The initial plan was for these larger residential apartments to be assigned to the cadres. However, when the pensioners heard this news, they immediately gathered to surround the administration building. Cuiye recounted the event:

> We had about seven hundred pensioners surrounding the administration building. The enterprise said that these flats were for the cadres. We asked why? There were still so many workers who didn't have decent places to live. Why the cadres? What kind of contributions did the cadres make? Who contributed more to the enterprise and the country: the workers or cadres? Without workers, your cadres were just rubbish! We told them that the working class was still the greatest; the working class was still the biggest brother; and your *dang guan de* (cadres) were as small as ants. We told them that if they dared to give these flats to the cadres, we would smash their offices. I said that at that time. I said, you could try to see who was more fearless, you or us. They became scared. Later, the factory decided to assign all these flats to the pensioners as we asked in the beginning. We told them that these flats had to be given to the pensioners because they were becoming old and they should enjoy their old age, according to our socialist country's policies.

During the second half of the 1980s, under the more and more explicitly developmental and reforming agenda, the intellectual cadres now unquestionably consolidated their power over workers not only in the production process but also within the redistribution sphere. In both legal and illegal ways, more and more benefits ended up in managers' pockets. Managerial privileges – or even the corruption that had been temporarily suppressed by the harsh political movements during the Maoist era – quickly re-emerged as power and structural change within the Chinese industrial field became prevalent and inevitable. On the other hand, slogans like "the working class is the biggest brother" were not yet being openly challenged, not even by the managers, and the pride that was taken in being a socialist worker was still cherished by this generation. The fearless image of the working class that had been portrayed by the socialist state and strengthened during the rebellious era of the Cultural Revolution persisted among these pensioners.[13] In addition, they had so little to lose: they had already retired, so any promises or threats surrounding job tenure no longer applied to them, and, with their pensions guaranteed by the state, they felt that no real harm could be inflicted on them. Therefore, they could confidently claim that it was still the working class, not the managers, who created wealth for the country, and they fought. Once again, management yielded to their demands.

---

13 Anita Chan, "Revolution or Corporatism": 50; Sheehan, *Chinese Workers:* 143.

Compliant Workers: Manufacturing Consent in a Golden Age

My research finds that, during the 1980s, no collective protest ever took place among the younger workers who then made up the labour force, although different kinds of everyday resistance could be argued to have widely occurred. Obviously, the two trends described above – a paternalistic factory regime accompanied by improved living standards and an emerging flexible labour management system – were more effective as a carrot and stick for current workers rather than those who had already retired.

For one thing, at least before 1992, SOEs in China were still socio-political communities, with the top managers expected to serve as community leaders with responsibility not only for production and financial performance, but also for enhancing employees' income and delivering a wide range of employee welfare benefits and services. According to Andrew Walder, managers in the 1980s who failed to deliver higher bonuses and new housing units or to upgrade the quality of meal services would be faced constantly with low-grade problems such as absenteeism, breakdowns, tardiness, and high rates of lost and wasted materials.[14] Walder also believed that a kind of collusion existed between managers and workers during this period, both of whom had an interest in retaining the highest level of incentive funds from the state and distributing it relatively equally.[15] Having not developed a real "market sense" that might have heightened cost-sensitivity, managers chose to encourage worker cooperation by maximising bonuses and other benefits, while minimising contention and conflicts by not making quotas too tight, distributing rewards relatively equally, and maintaining a less-than-ironclad link between output and pay.[16] In any case, incentive funds were drawn from retained profits according to proportions set by the higher-level authorities through negotiation and involved, therefore, virtually no cost for management. This tacit alignment between managers and workers benefited both sides. From a comprehensive study of 20 large and medium Chinese SOEs in the 1980s, Granick asserts that managers' decision-making was mostly guided by a desire to maximise the average welfare of factory employees rather than seeking a profit.[17] My research shows very similar processes also in place at Nanfang Steel during this period, so

---

14 Andrew Walder, "Factory and Manager in an Era of Reform," *The China Quarterly* 118 (1989): 242–264.

15 Andrew Walder, "Wage Reform and the Web of Factory Interests," *The China Quarterly* 109 (1987): 22–41.

16 Walder, "Wage Reform": 22–41.

17 David Granick, *Chinese State Enterprise: A Regional Property Rights Analysis* (Chicago: University of Chicago Press, 1990).

much so that many workers at the time, at least on reflection, regarded this decade as the golden age of the factory.

Meanwhile, the introduction of a more flexible labour management system, no matter how ineffective and reluctant at this early stage, did send some unsettling signals to workers. For example, the contract labour system introduced in 1986, while it did not change the status of existing permanent workers, applied to any newly recruited workers. Calls by the state in 1988 to cut down on "redundant" workers in order to deal with widespread "over-manning" may not, in practise, have resulted in workers being fired, but it did place some workers on reduced wages. These tendencies served to make workers recoil for fear of potential penalties, such as wage/bonus deductions, or even dismissal under the more flexible labour policies aimed at labour activists. So, at least ostensibly, they kept quiet.

In general, during this early stage of market reforms, a paternalistic labour regime was established at Nanfang Steel that largely relied on consent and compromise rather than coercion to guarantee a smooth production process and a stable industrial community. [18] Different generations of workers, equipped with various "repertoires of contention", responded to developments in distinct ways. Meanwhile, though still cautious and ideology-bound, these tendencies nevertheless slowly but effectively relegated an earlier revolutionary era to a remote and irretrievable past, and paved the way for the more radical market-oriented restructuring that was to come.

Defeated: Confronting the Brave New World in Desperation

In the mid-1990s, responding to the central state's determination to push market reforms further and deeper, a variety of radical restructuring policies, including mergers, downsizing, burden alleviation, large-scale layoffs, and so on, were suddenly imposed by the state on Nanfang Steel. Instead of revitalising the factory, however, these programmes dragged Nanfang Steel into a situation of chronic financial loss and decline. Since then, it has entered into a decades-long lingering demise involving a particular process of erosive deindustrialisation: half of its workers were laid off while those remaining worked under a transformed, alienated, and despotic factory regime and earned an average wage far below that of Sichuan province generally. The once fully functioning, consolidated, and prosper-

---

18 See Michael Burawoy, *Manufacturing Consent: Changes in the Labor Process under Monopoly Capitalism* (Chicago: University of Chicago Press, 1982).

ous industrial community supported by the factory declined irreversibly into a working-class slum, with its old comprehensive welfare system shattered and all attendant institutions (hospitals, schools, recreation centres, housing systems, and many others) degraded or abandoned. Worst of all, the threat of bankruptcy hangs ever-present in the air. What happened at Nanfang Steel is a vivid illustration of the degradation of SOE workers under attack by the overwhelmingly triumphant establishment of capitalist labour relations nationwide.

The total abandonment of workers by the state created a particular political opportunity structure that left Nanfang Steel workers with almost no resources to count on. They were simply left alone. Out of desperation, a group of pensioners launched the largest, longest, and most militant protest ever seen in Nanfang Steel's history. Ultimately, they were defeated as the current workers, anguished by entangled feelings such as anger, shame, and powerlessness, silently adopted the double-edged "weapons of the weak."[19] The formation of a subaltern group was complete.

Pensioners: Finally Defeated "Not With a Bang But a Whimper"

For most of the pensioners, this neoliberal blow was unexpected, bewildering, and shocking.[20] The radical restructuring agenda happened so dramatically and swiftly that it left most pensioners and their families in semi- or outright poverty, particularly as their retired wages had increased only very slowly over the previous years and remained extremely low relative to ever-rising living costs. Worse, most of their children and even grandchildren still worked in the factory and were constantly threatened with layoffs, an increasingly hazardous working environment, and low wages. Resentments accumulated as time passed.

In 2002, when the enterprise decided to cut off subsidies for all pensioners as part of its "burden-alleviation" programme, it triggered the largest, longest, and most militant and desperate protest in Nanfang Steel's history. On the very day that the decision document was dispatched, the pensioners set up a workers' committee composed of elected representatives and got organised. In contrast to a formal union as a relatively stable institution, this workers' committee was temporary, improvised, informal, and, according to state policy, illegal, hence having to be

---

19 James C. Scott, *Weapons of the Weak* (New Haven, CT: Yale university Press, 1987).
20 The section title quotes T.S. Eliot, *The Hollow Men* (Cambridge, MA: Harvard University Press, 1925).

hidden. But the "dense informal social networks"[21] behind it made it highly efficient in terms of taking action. The next day, several thousand pensioners besieged the administrative building of the factory. With no immediate response forthcoming, the angry retirees broke in and partially occupied the building. All of the grievances and anger, along with the sense of having been betrayed and abandoned, that had accumulated over the years of radical reforms finally erupted. The retirees told me that they were doing this not for just a small amount of money, but for their "backbones": "we can't swallow the resentment anymore; we can't let them do whatever they want." The siege and occupation lasted for nearly half a year under organised leadership. As time passed, the atmosphere grew tense; the protest swelled in size and escalated until, in May 2002, the administration finally called for an urgent meeting in the factory's grand auditorium. The meeting was intended to facilitate a dialogue between the protesters and the highest levels of management. However, it ended in great chaos and violence. Laoyin, a former official union chairman, was still able to recount the event in great detail many years later:

> That day was a nightmare for me. We were in the auditorium. The police cars stayed outside in case we needed to escape... Before the meeting even had a chance to start, these old people simply pushed forward and rushed up to the stage. We all thought they were going to beat us. We were so frightened that we ran away immediately. Other managers ran from the shortcut behind the auditorium. I ran to the police car outside the auditorium. When the workers found out that all other managers had already run away except me in the police car, they were so angry that they surrounded the car and even lifted it up. I sat inside, shaking, watching the never-ending flow of people rushing forward, their waving fists, and their fingers pointing to my nose from behind the closed car window and cursing me [....] I would never blame these pensioners. Everybody needs to survive. I just wished that I could do more for them, but I didn't have such power. What kind of cadres we were in these money-losing SOEs!

Similar to Bartha's observations of Hungarian state workers, who blamed everything except the system for their negative experiences during the post-socialist transformation,[22] the indignation of the Nanfang Steel workers was directed at the managers, who were condemned as "betrayers of the enterprise" and thus scapegoated for the failed market reforms at Nanfang Steel. Many pensioners told me that Nanfang Steel's problems had nothing to do with the command economy or the market economy, but was due entirely to the corruption of managers.

---

21 Scott, "Everyday Forms of Resistance": 52.
22 Eszter Bartha, "Workers after the workers' state: Ethnography of Change in an Ex-socialist Model Factory," *Eszmelet* 62 (Summer 2004), http://www.eszmelet.hu/en/en-bartha_eszter-workers-after-the-workers-state-ethnograp/, accessed 10 January 2023.

Significantly, despite the militancy and fierce protests of the retirees, despite the feelings of guilt and intense illegitimacy among many high-level managers, and despite the relatively small amount of money involved, the enterprise refused to cave in. Even though it adopted a policy of restraint by "swallowing all the beating and scolding from the workers and never calling and fighting back," the fundamental yet implicit principle was "moving on." Burden alleviation was a state policy, and the enterprise itself in any case was on the brink of bankruptcy.

Meanwhile, by that time, the socialist social contract had already been abandoned; socialist ideology and the image of a workers' state had become so obsolete that it was being openly mocked as a utopia at best or implicitly yet meaningfully connected with a totalitarian past by mainstream liberal intellectuals. The image of workers as fearless and proud proletarians who created national wealth had long been replaced by "backward" and "inefficient" "lazy bones" both in the mass media as well as in many intellectual works as a way of legitimising the large-scale bankruptcy of the SOEs and the layoffs of state workers.[23] "Working class is nobody" was the widespread self-mockery expressed by those I interviewed. There is no doubt that the pensioners were well aware of this. The degradation and marginalisation of the working class infuriated them and was the crucial reason for their militancy,[24] but it was also the social reality that they were now facing. So, although the resistant pensioners still drew upon the political discourses of class, Maoism, and socialist ideology to ground their claims – much as Ching Kwan Lee also observed in her rust-belt factory pensioners' cases[25] – as time passed, these claims began to sound increasingly feeble and anachronistic, no matter how desperate and militant the pensioners' fighting stance was.

Nevertheless, the pensioners' resistance persisted into 2004. The enterprise refused to compromise, and no progress was really made regarding the original pension subsidies. The pensioners and the enterprise seemed to have reached a deadlock. Then, in May of that year, an incident occurred that would put an immediate stop to any large-scale demonstrations. As a senior manager was getting onto a bus, an angry retiree came up behind him and forcefully dragged him off. The senior manager fell and broke his rib, and the former worker was arrested, put in jail, and sentenced to two years. Nevertheless, resistance continued tenaciously and the workers' committees decided to change their strategies. First, they sent representatives to Beijing to appeal directly to the central state, in the hope that the cen-

---

23 Li, Ju, "From 'Master' to 'Loser': Changing Working-Class Cultural Identity in Contemporary China," *International Labor and Working-Class History* 88 (2015): 190–208.
24 William Hurst and Kevin J. O'Brien, "China's Contentious Pensioners," *The China Quarterly* 170 (2002): 345–360.
25 Lee, Ching Kwan. *Against the Law* (Berkeley: University of California Press, 2007).

tral state would care more about their predicament than the "corrupt" local governments. They were ignored, and Beijing simply retransmitted the case back to the local level, which left the protesters back at square one.

Next, the committee decided to turn to the law. China had passed its first National Labour Law in 1994. By 1999, "ruling the country by law" was formally incorporated into Article 5 of the Constitution and has since become part of the official lexicon now widely adopted in government, legislature, and party reports. This more rational state ruled by law was meant to replace the obsolete image of the workers' state; and the new social contract based on law was meant to replace the old one based on ideology. Having lost their old weapons taken from the previous social contract, the pensioners finally decided to take up this new arsenal of law, suspiciously but hopefully. In 2004, the committee collected money from the pensioners and hired a lawyer to sue Nanfang Steel. They lost the case since the court decided that the enterprise had the right to deduct its own welfare programme. Immediately afterward, in October 2004, Nanfang Steel issued a public notice through its newspaper and TV channel, declaring a victory and also claiming that, from now on, the enterprise would no longer respond to any such related issues. Resistance seemed finally to be dying down. Two years later, in 2006, the committee made one last effort. They collected more money from the pensioners and hired another lawyer, who vowed to fight for their interests. After taking the money, however, this so-called lawyer simply disappeared into the sunset.

This incident served as the final blow. The largest and most militant labour protest in the history of Nanfang Steel came to an end amid a great sense of embarrassment and inadequacy. The failure proved fatal, not just because many participants were becoming exhausted with the unceasing frustrations, but also with the ease with which they had been cheated. The situation forced most of them, even the most active organisers, to realise their weak, helpless, obsolete, and vulnerable position in a quickly changing world that they were finding increasingly incomprehensible. Without the support of the socialist social contract, their formal knowledge and experiences – their known repertoire of contention – were simply irrelevant and anachronistic. They were no longer the experienced old revolutionaries; but rather the gullible, naïve, and stupid old fellows in a market society full of traps and deception. For many pensioners, this was a cruel awakening. It defeated the movement once and for all, by declaring and formalising their final abjection and exclusion from the historical stage.

Weapons of the Weak: Everyday Resistance of Workers

In her global narrative of labour unrest over the past 130 years, Beverly Silver identifies two types of labour unrest: Marx-type and Polanyi-type. Marxist unrest mainly refers to workers' struggles against capitalist exploitation in production. Polanyian unrest, by contrast, refers to the backlash resistance from those workers who had benefited from but have been "unmade" by established social compacts.[26] Both forms were absent among the currently employed workers at Nanfang Steel. In fact, despite being faced with continuously degenerating social status and deteriorating living and working conditions since the 1990s, the workers never once organised any form of collective resistance. Instead, they were, at least ostensibly, acquiescent and resigned. However, it would be cursory to conclude that these workers were merely passive victims who tamely submitted to the oppressive external power/order and fatefully accepted an uncontrollable destiny. My ethnographic research reveals that many workers harboured great resentment, and even hatred, mostly against the management, and tactically expressed these feelings in more surreptitious, spontaneous, and individualised ways. That is to say, Nanfang Steel workers employed their "weapons of the weak" in ways quite similar to those of the Malaysian peasants in James Scott's study[27]: ways that include ostensible conformity, backstage rumours and curses, and shop floor non-confrontational resistance.

On the shop floor, according to my observations, workers rarely confronted their direct managers, the section chiefs. Usually, workers were obedient, with a small number appearing deferential or even adulatory, and most others, passively compliant. The reasons for their compliance and resignation were quite simple: a fear of losing their jobs and a clear recognition of their disposability. Zhangyong, a steel worker in his early thirties, explained this in his own words:

> Who needs our workers? Now there are so many peasant workers rushing into the cities. There is nobody to do the job? Just go to the labour market and yell, 'I have some jobs here, want to come?' People will surely rush to you like a swarm of bees. So our workers are just nobody.

Greater competition from peasant migrant workers in the labour market was of course just one among many other reasons that workers feared losing their job. The sudden change in state policy, the broken social contract between the state

---

26 Beverly Silver, *Forces of Labor: Workers' Movements and Globalization since 1870* (Cambridge: Cambridge University Press, 2003).
27 Scott, *Weapons of the Weak.*

and workers, the arbitrary power of management, and the increasingly alienating and deskilling labour process on the shop floor; all these changes had forced workers to realise their powerlessness and disposability. In the late 1990s, an unprecedented large-scale lay-off, under the radical restructuring agenda of "downsizing for efficiency," was imposed on Nanfang Steel, leaving half of the workforce suddenly unemployed. Even though massive layoffs like this ceased in 2002, the fear of losing their job still haunted the minds of those who remained in work.

The hope of finding a suitable job outside Nanfang Steel was also dim. If pitted against the large labour reserve army of rural migrant workers and other workers who had been laid-off from bankrupted SOEs, as well as fresh college graduates, these workers in their thirties and forties, many of whom possessed only manual or limited skills, would be at a severe disadvantage. For example, in the second half of the 1990s, when the Nanfang Steel market reform was in its most turbulent phase – workshops were being closed; workers were being either laid-off or sent on long, unpaid vacations; and the enterprise continued to delay payday – many workers I interviewed took advantage of this period to try their luck in the outside world. Some went to work in the township and village enterprises (TVEs), others in the private enterprises, but always as manual workers. Most concluded their outside journey by returning to Nanfang Steel at the end of the radical marketisation phase, when some production returned to normal in the early 2000s. The then highly unregulated outside labour market illustrated by many scholars[28] did not bring the better life promised by the free market; instead, it further strengthened the subjugation of workers, locked them into the most disadvantaged positions within the labour market, and excluded them from it to a certain extent. In this sense, the preservation of Nanfang Steel may indeed have saved the Nanfang Steel workers from a fate of joining the millions upon millions of dislocated labourers in the export-oriented globalised sweatshops in the south, or simply becoming unemployed. But it also created a permanent possible threat, constantly reminding the workers of the fragility of their jobs and how easily and sometimes arbitrarily these could be taken away. Seen in this light, the workers' compliance was far from a reflection of their backwardness or cowardice; it was self-protective and pragmatic in the face of a threat of job deprivation. As Scott puts it, "his effort and his achievement, in one sense, have been to swallow his anger lest it endanger his livelihood."[29] But it was a very hard thing to swallow for many workers and, indeed, always accompanied by humiliation, resentment, and even hatred.

---

28 Anita Chan, *China's Workers Under Assault: Exploitation and Abuse in a Globalizing Economy* (London: Routledge, 2016).
29 Scott, *Weapons of the Weak*, 279.

Almost every worker I interviewed harboured a strong sense of resentment and indignation toward the factory's management. This found expression in phrases such as "those people are not human" or "they are merely ghosts." During an interview with Dayong, a steel worker in his early thirties, he spent one-third of his time cursing the managers at Nanfang Steel. When he talked about a case of theft that had happened in his workshop two years ago, he angrily attributed the incident to the managers:

> You know, what had been stolen were tons of Ni plates. That was a lot. How could the common workers steal them out? … We all believe that those *dang guan de* did some tricks with the accounting books. When the Ni plates were claimed to be ordered from outside and then stolen, our workshop was on temporary shutdown. So who knows? … When the cops talked to us, we all told them to investigate the case thoroughly, find out the thief (thieves), and shoot him (them) to death.

He emphasised the point that the managers should be shot to death at least three times. And he was not alone; in fact, it seemed that resentment was hiding in every worker's heart. During my time at Nanfang Steel, whenever the workers gathered, management corruption was always one of the most popular topics: who had embezzled a huge amount of money (the amount of which was always ridiculously high and, most likely, exaggerated); who had just bought another apartment in the city or a luxurious car; who had sent his/her kid to an expensive private boarding school; and so on. And the stories usually ended with curses, such as "these bloodsuckers will die as dogs" or "they should be shot to death."

Besides the backstage insults and rumours about management, the workers also strategically channelled their resentment and grievances in various negative ways on the shop floor. While absenteeism, tardiness, and resistance to discipline had been partially suppressed by strict financial penalties in recent years, foot-dragging and indifference had become the most prevalent forms of daily resistance. Almost all the workers I interviewed described their work as "muddling around in the workplace." When faced with strict labour controls at the production site, many workers adopted strategies of apathy and indifference, characterised by apparent resignation, rooted in a strong sense of powerlessness, but accompanied by feelings of cynicism and suppressed resentment. Abin, a mechanic in his thirties, put it in this way:

> Before, when we were maintaining the equipment, we tried our best. If there was damage here, we would think that maybe there was damage there. So we did a total check and fixed everything; now if there is damage on this spot, the manager would say, 'You have to fix this in five minutes, otherwise…' When we bring apart the equipment, we might realize that the real reason for the damage on this spot is actually caused by problems from someplace else. But the manager doesn't know this. He might just say, 'Quick, replace this with a

new one.' Our workers then say nothing too. We just do what he tells us and replace the bad hardware. After several hours, uh-oh, the equipment is out of order again. The manager doesn't know what happened and becomes disturbed a lot. And our workers don't say a word.

In this way, the workers expressed their indifference and even disdain toward their managers. By remaining aloof, watching the machine break down again and again, and revelling in their managers' inability to do anything, workers exacted revenge in their particular way. In an environment where grievances and a sense of resentment had to be oppressed, workers turned to their own labour and skill as the weapon of last resort by withholding or hiding them from their oppressors, the managers. This low-profile technique avoided outright defiance of their managers but endowed the workers with a secret power to counterbalance, even if only to a small degree, the arbitrary and dominant power of management.

Meanwhile, the amount of pilferage increased dramatically, according to the superintendent in the security department of Nanfang Steel when I was there in 2013. The workers I interviewed also admitted to me that stealing valuable alloys or other materials from the enterprise was very common behaviour. One worker estimated that about one-third of workers were involved in various kinds of theft. Even though theft would be strictly penalised if discovered – with the guilty worker fired or even jailed – many still chose to take the risk. To some extent, such deeds were justified and tolerated by many workers as a desperate strategy for survival: as one worker angrily put it, "how much did we put in and how much did we get? How could we workers survive with several hundred yuan per month in this society?" Besides poverty as a rationale, theft was definitely one form of resistance performed by workers against corrupt managers and bureaucrats, as illustrated by a common saying among workers: "people at the top steal big; people in the middle steal middle; workers at the bottom steal small." The hidden inference here was that when compared with the large amount of money that corrupt managers embezzled from the factory, petty theft by the workers essentially amounted to nothing. Many workers also acknowledged that they would look the other way if they happened to catch somebody in the act.

All these forms of everyday resistance adopted by Nanfang Steel workers under the camouflage of ostensible conformity were actually the only means left for these workers to express their strong sense of deprivation and inadequacy, without seriously jeopardising their and their family's survival. Such actions were spontaneous, yet rational. However, as weapons of the weak, these were also a two-edged sword.

Needless to say, superficial compliance as a veil for actual non-cooperation greatly damaged the production process on the shop floor. To some extent, it almost crippled the whole production process, doomed Nanfang Steel to its chronic losses, and rendered the reforms at Nanfang Steel a complete failure. But, if all these forms of everyday resistance were eating away at the regime in a persistent yet imperceptible way, as Scott argued, what kind of consequences did they have for the workers – the performers of this resistance? At the most obvious level, everyday forms of resistance did offer a safer outlet for workers to express their frustrations and grievances; to a certain extent, they also curtailed managers' controlling powers on the shop floor; and presumably, the government sensed the subdued but desperate signals, which contributed to measures that helped to delay their final unemployment. Yet beyond all these, my ethnographic research also reveals a more hidden effect of these particular forms of resistance on workers: their psychologically detrimental effect. That is to say, everyday resistance, expressed as it is in passive and negative ways, actually went against the moralities generally held by most Nanfang Steel workers, and resulted in distancing them from their work, shattering their sense of honour and pride, and, in turn, strengthening their feelings of inadequacy and powerlessness.

Even though they had been exposed to the emerging money worship and utilitarianism that has been wholeheartedly embraced by the middle and upper classes in contemporary Chinese capitalist society, many workers I met at Nanfang Steel still held fast to some basic moral principles inherited from the older working-class generations, learnt from their school education, and possessed as part of human nature. Honesty, righteousness, and industriousness still constituted the ethical framework through which workers could claim their dignity and pride. Yet, the spontaneous forms of everyday resistance adopted by the workers ran counter to these virtues.

To illustrate this argument, consider again the description given by Abin of workers apathetically looking on while both machines and managers fall into disorder. Although such inaction served as a form of revenge against their managers, there was also a paradox hidden in this strategy: in order to resist against management, the workers had to take an antagonistic approach to their own jobs. That meant restraining themselves from experiencing the fulfilment and pride they could have earned from their labour, for example, through successful problem-solving in this case, instead of remaining aloof and hostile, not only to their managers, but also in relation to their own labour. A similar process of self-estrangement and antagonism could also be found in foot-dragging. It forced workers to doubt further the meaning of their work and, sometimes, their own right to continued employment. As many workers told me half-jokingly: "We really should be laid off." When I asked Abin if he felt satisfied acting in such a way, he shook his head bitterly, and said: "No, I feel sad. It is just ridiculous." Abin started at Nanfang Steel in the early 1980s. He had been renowned across the factory for his exquisite skills and been recognised many times as a model worker in the 1980s and early 1990s. Now, almost in his fifties, he asked me if there might be any opportunity for him to migrate to the United States as a "coolie."

A more acute paradox for workers lay in the pilferage that went beyond self-estrangement and actually challenged many workers' moral baselines. Even though many of the interviewees were eager to defend other workers' pilfering, almost everyone would add: "But I would not do those kinds of things." It was always other people, not they, who stole. Such efforts to distance themselves from such behaviour did not necessarily come from their distrust toward me for fear of being reported, since a strong sense of trust had been established between us while I was in the field; it was more likely to come from the deep shame they felt about it. It brought humiliation and disgrace. Even though they, themselves, claimed not to be involved, they knew by instinct how easily and conveniently the image of the whole working class, like any subordinate social group, could be stereotyped and stained by such deeds, even if performed only by some. In other words, these strategies of resistance could be argued to have deprived workers of the pride and even legitimacy that could have been derived from clearly claiming their rights and proudly confronting management.

Such everyday strategies, combined with other dilemmas, also brought pain – a feeling that originated in more than poverty or a deteriorating social status, but also in a sense of powerlessness and having no way out. As described by Richard Sennett and Jonathan Cobb, it is "the feeling of not getting anywhere despite ones' efforts, the feeling of vulnerability in contrasting oneself to others at a higher social level, the buried sense of inadequacy that one resents oneself for feeling."[30] Often, when the pain became unbearable, workers chose to numb themselves in different ways. For example, gambling and playing *Mahjong* were the most popular forms of entertainment among Nanfang Steel workers and managers, which they would engage in everywhere from teahouses, *Mahjong* houses, parks, people's homes, to the night-duty rooms of the workshop. Job insecurity, the depressing future of the factory, the anxieties of survival or making money, feelings of humiliation or illegitimacy; all of these brought people to the gambling table. At least by cheering or contesting every small gain or loss, they could escape from their unhappy reality, even if only briefly. When I asked Xiaoxia, a steelworker in his early thirties, why he spent so much time at the *Mahjong* table, he smiled shyly: "you have nothing to do here. Playing *Mahjong* makes me happy; otherwise, I might go crazy." Pausing for a while, he added uneasily: "I am hopeless." Dali, a

---

30 Richard Sennett and Jonathan Cobb, *The Hidden Injuries of Class* (New York: W.W. Norton & Company, 1972), 58.

worker in his late forties, shrewdly pointed out: "Gambling is one way to numb us. Everybody plays *Mahjong* because we don't have any inner resources to support ourselves."

What we can see from the descriptions above is that none of the forms of resistance enacted by the current workers at Nanfang Steel – cursing, apathy, foot dragging, irresponsibility, pilferage, gambling, and so on – empowered them. Instead, they constantly contradicted and challenged their previously strongly held moral values, which, in turn, only strengthened their sense of inadequacy. When I asked the workers whether they would fight back if Nanfang Steel went bankrupt, almost all of them gave a similar reply: that they would just leave and find another job somewhere else.

This strong feeling of inadequacy was also reinforced by workers' simultaneous yet contradictory experiences of the external macro changes and the internal micro changes within the factory. They saw in the mass media and witnessed for themselves a rapidly prospering country with dazzling skyscrapers, grand projects, luxurious commodities, and newly affluent people with seemingly unlimited money. But simultaneously, they watched themselves sinking into desperation and poverty, and their community sliding into an incessant decline. In other words, they were experiencing the transformation as a process of abjection, as defined by James Ferguson as "a process of being thrown aside, expelled, or discarded"[31] from the track of development, progress, and modernity that China now claims. Such highly contrasting and contradictory experiences bewildered and frustrated many workers, as Xiaozhang, a worker in his mid-thirties lamented:

> No matter how this enterprise or this country changes, we workers work as before, but now with so little pay.... People like us couldn't understand the stuff about the reform, but we could feel the pain in the grassroots enterprise.

Even if they sensed a change in the attitude of the state toward the working class, workers couldn't confidently blame the state or the system since it was this that was leading the country out of its status as a poor and underdeveloped third-world country previously suppressed by the West and granting a nationalistic pride to the Chinese people as members of an emerging global superpower. As a result, they focused their ire on management (and sometimes themselves) for their marginalisation and abjection, directed their resentment and hatred there, and fought silently, yet at a great cost.

---

31 James Ferguson, *Expectations of Modernity: Myths and Meanings of Urban Life on the Zambian Copperbelt* (Berkeley: University of California Press, 1999), 236.

What we witness here, then, is an eventual and total defeat of the state working class, both former and current workers, as they encounter the sweeping neoliberal reform agenda and the full establishment of the dis-embedded capitalist labour relationship. Workers in China did resist. But, as I have illustrated, they were largely able to do so only within a highly pressurised and constrained space, and the forms of resistance taken had to be circumvented, veiled, distorted, and sometimes even go against their morality and nature, which, in turn, alienated, disempowered, and subordinated the workers themselves. Even for the pensioners, who had no material interests to lose since their pensions were guaranteed and hence could afford to take militant action, when faced with a systematically unequal power structure, failure was inevitable.

Once, when I was talking with several workers in their break room, one leaned over to me and asked: "You come from the United States, so can you tell me, are the workers there happier than us?" The others looked at me eagerly for an answer. I hesitated, and replied that I couldn't speak on their behalf, but maybe not. They all laughed, and the worker continued: "So can they afford houses? Dare they go to hospital when they are sick? Do they worry about tuition fee for their kids?" When I told them that the working class in the United States has their own big problems, they laughed bitterly, yet sounded half-relieved, and one remarked: "So, workers everywhere are the same: small."

Conclusion

By tracing the collective actions of two different generations of state workers in one state-owned enterprise in China when faced with the demise of an old ideology together with all its imaginations and the slow but determined establishment of capitalist labour relations in their working and living space, this study has provided an alternative labour history without the conventional tool of independent unions. Manoeuvring through their resources at hand, constrained by the contextualised political opportunity structure at distinct historical moments, workers picked up their available tools and took action in their own carefully calculated and highly pragmatic ways. It is also by no means just a supplementary story to the mainstream history of union-centred labour resistance; it is instead an example of a much wider, deeper, and more complicated picture of labourers' rebellious activities when wronged.

Meanwhile, the eventually triumphant establishment of capitalist labour relations and the final defeat of the working class demonstrate less the inefficiency of non-unionised resistance than the intrinsically unequal power structure of our current capitalist system of production. Mainstream labour study scholars, especially those from the school of comparative studies of advanced capitalism, tend to assume that the working class, by organising unions, developing modes of collective representation and collective bargaining, and initiating demonstrations, strikes, or any other forms of collective resistance, would eventually develop an equally counter-balanced power against capital (private or state). Building on the idea of labour as a social partner within a triadic relation of power, these scholars argue that workers should be able to negotiate and bargain equally and constantly with the other two social partners – capitalists and the state.[32] However, such argument blurs the systematic and structurally unequal power relations between different social actors, while assuming the existence of a counterbalanced and hence democratic labour bargaining mechanism found in advanced capitalist countries. Yet, this illusion has already been smashed by the advent of dis-embedded capitalism, whereby unions and collective bargains suddenly became emaciated and ordinary workers quickly lost what fragile fruit they had arduously achieved through hundreds of years of struggle and sacrifice. These harsh realities only throw into sharp relief the oppressive nature of the system itself as well as the vulnerability and limitations of struggle of subordinated groups, with or without independent unions; workers everywhere are indeed the same: small.

---

32 See, for example, Wilhelm Eberwein, Jochen Tholen, and Joachim Schuster, *The Europeanisation of Industrial Relations: National and European Processes in Germany, UK, Italy and France* (Aldershot: Ashgate, 2002); Wolfgang Streeck, *Industrial Relations in West Germany: A Case Study of the Car Industry* (Portsmouth: Heinemann Educational Books, 1984); Wolfgang Streeck, "Skills and the Limits of Neo-Liberalism: The Enterprise of the Future as a Place of Learning," *Work, Employment, and Society* 1, 3 (1989): 281–308; Chris Tilly and Charles Tilly, *Work under Capitalism* (Boulder, CO: Westview Press, 1998).

Görkem Akgöz

5 Between State Feminism and Work Intensification: Gendered Labour Control Regimes in Turkish Textile and Tobacco Industries

On a winter's night in 1938, a Turkish bureaucrat was driving on the new "straight as a rope" road stretching from the train station to the recently opened state textile factory in Kayseri, a small town in Central Anatolia. He almost felt as if he was travelling through time; each passing kilometre took him further away from the lethargy of the underdeveloped Empire and toward the contemporary dynamism of the Republic. As he left behind the old town, which was "getting ready to sleep in the eternal depth of darkness and silence," he felt pity for its "poverty and senility" and focused his gaze on the factory buildings that extended before his eyes "wide as a city in itself … under a flood of lights," filling the flat-lying plain with mechanical sounds and radiating "youth and national energy." Resembling a starry sky, the largest state industrial investment of interwar Turkey lured him in and filled his heart with national pride and a sense of duty. But something he learnt from the factory director would spoil this picture-perfect scenery. Only 10 percent of the factory workforce was female; the factory had failed to attract the group of workers that the Turkish industrialisation drive needed the most. Why, he asked, as he approached his destination; why were the heroic Turkish women, who had fought and worked side by side with men first in the Independence War and then in the Republican revolutions, running from their national duty at the factory? [1]

The bureaucrat's enthusiasm for industrialisation in interwar Turkey was fuelled by a recent shift in economic policy. After 1929, the devastating effects of capitalism's global crisis had forced the problem of underdevelopment and its possible cures firmly onto the agenda of Kemalist politicians and economists. In the aftermath of the Great Depression, the young Turkish state jumped on the bandwagon of economic nationalism, an ideology that arose in reaction to the reigning liberal doctrines of the previous half-century in East-Central Europe, South America, and the Middle East. Economic nationalism combined an intense dislike of foreign cap-

---

1 Sahir Üzel, "Kayseri Fabrikası Günde 40,000 Metro İş Çıkarıyor," *Cumhuriyet* (11 May 1936); Endüstri Hayatımızda İnkişaf (three part article), *Erciyes Halkevi Dergisi* (March, April, and June 1938).

https://doi.org/10.1515/9783111086552-006

ital with protectionism, autarky, and industrialism.[2] The first three of these four elements had already been strong in the 1920s. In 1932, the decades-long oscillation between the two developmental models of agriculture and industry was finally resolved in favour of the latter, and Turkey made the first industrial planning attempt by a developing country outside the Soviet Union.[3] Factory production doubled between 1929 and 1938, and the share of industry in the Turkish gross national product increased from 10.8 percent between 1925 and 1929 to 17.8 percent between 1933 and 1941.[4] In political terms, industrialisation policy was presented as key to the national reconstruction strategy and was thus connected closely to the ideological core of authoritarian Kemalist nationalism. Repressive state actions and policies, such as the outlawing of strikes and class-based organisations, weighed down on industrial workers by severely constraining their repertoire of available protest options.

Two historically female-dominated industries expanded in the 1930s and 1940s. The first had a direct connection to planned industrialisation. Underlined by a sense of urgency and speed, the initial Five-Year Plan focused on manufacturing previously imported simple consumer goods for which internal markets and local raw materials existed. Because textiles were a major import item and the textile industry was lighter and more labour intensive, heavy investment was secured to establish a domestic textile industry.[5] Private investment in the textile industry also benefited from the industrialisation policy of the 1930s and expanded rapidly in the postwar period. The Turkish industrialisation drive focused on a second industry with a historically high concentration of women. After more than 40 years of foreign control, the Republican state monopolised the tobacco industry in 1925. The focus of this essay is the women working in these two industries, whose employment was marked by visible gender discrimination.

---

2 Jan Kofman, "How to Define Economic Nationalism: A Critical Review of Some Old and New Standpoints," in *Economic Nationalism in East-Central Europe and South America 1918–1939*, edited by Henryk Szlajfer (Geneva: Droz, 1990), 52.

3 Gunnar Myrdal, *Asian Drama: An Inquiry into the Poverty of Nations* (New York: Pantheon Books, 1972), 248–249; Korkut Boratav, "Kemalist Economic Policies and Étatism," in *Atatürk: Founder of a Modern State*, edited by Ali Kazancıgil and Ergun Özbudun (London: C. Hurst & Company, 1981), 175; Charles Issawi, "De-industrialization and Re-industrialization in the Middle East Since 1800," *International Journal of Middle Eastern Studies* 12, 4 (1980): 474.

4 A.H. Hanson, *Public Enterprise and Economic Development* (London: Routledge, 1959), 124; Faruk Birtek, "The Rise and Fall of Etatism in Turkey, 1932–1950: The Uncertain Road in the Restructuring of a Semiperipheral Economy," *Review (Fernand Braudel Center)* 8, 1 (1985): 410.

5 Percentages calculated using the data in Şevket Süreyya Aydemir, *İkinci Adam*, vol. 1 (Istanbul: Remzi Kitabevi, 1984), 414–415.

Industrial production in the 1930s and 1940s was bottlenecked by poor efficiency and low productivity on the one hand and labour instability on the other. Throughout this period, a permanent and skilled industrial labour force was conspicuously lacking and high rates of labour turnover were of great concern to industrialists. Since workers changed jobs easily and frequently, market pressures played a decisive role in shaping the state's and employers' strategies and practises of labour recruitment and control. Added to these pressures was a low supply of female industrial labour, which is central to the development of light manufacturing industries. The Turkish state's and employers' efforts to expand the female factory workforce is evident in state documents, expert reports, and the print media. These efforts largely failed until the mid-1950s when private investment and rural-urban migration gained momentum. Between 1927 and 1943, the number of industrial workers increased by 87 percent from 147,128 to 275,083. The share of women in the industrial workforce increased from 25.6 to 29 percent.[6]

I contend that throughout this industrialisation drive, a new ideology of women's work was articulated, which would shape state, employer, and trade union policies in subsequent decades. Through a set of labour market and shop floor discourses, this new ideology constituted the basis for a specific female industrial labour control regime combining a new set of external labour discourses with older forms of shop floor labour control. In its unwillingness to address women's problems at work or to enhance protections for their work-based rights, this new ideology failed to bring women to the shop floor. I build my argument on two premises: (1) the production of state and cultural discourses plays an important part in the constitution of labour control regimes; and (2) labour control regimes not only exploit, but also reconstruct, gender difference through daily interactions on the shop floor. The first part of this essay focuses mainly on state actions relating to industrial female labour. I analyze the development of state and cultural discourses on industrial development and women's industrial labour and their effect on protective legislation in interwar Turkey. In the second part, I adopt an experience-near level of analysis to document women's experience of factory work.

---

6 Ahmet Makal, "Türkiye'de Erken Cumhuriyet Döneminde Kadın Emeği," *Çalışma ve Toplum* 2, 25 (2010): 21–24.

Visible Modernity: Factory Women and the Large Factory

In 1930s Turkey, the image of the large factory ignited a national structure of feeling: a relief from the burden of a dark, underdeveloped past and an enthusiasm for rapid change in the name of modernisation.[7] The factory – both its physical shell as well as its internal organisation – represented modernity in the imagery of the Republican elites, who saw the secular and modern industrial buildings and their surroundings as a way out of tradition-bound Ottoman architecture and backwardness. Foreign visitors referred to the slender smoking chimneys of modern factories as "Atatürk's minarets"; for the local elites these were "the chimneys of civilisation rising in all corners of the homeland."[8] Together with a nationalised and expanded railway network, factories were state instruments to transform the disparate post-imperial land into an integrated national unit and disseminate the new ideas of the Republic to the periphery. As much as an economic policy, industrialisation was a "civilizing mission" tied in with the larger Kemalist project of nation-building and modernisation.[9]

While the factory acquired a potent social imagery in interwar Turkey that was cast in both economic and cultural terms, another equally (or possibly even more) powerful signifier of modernity was gaining ground. The secular Republic represented nothing short of an all-out attack on existing social institutions concerning the status of women, making their legal and social status the banner of Kemalist development narratives.[10] A central feature of the nascent state's self-

---

7 Raymond Williams, *Marxism and Literature* (Oxford and New York: Oxford University Press, 1977), 131.

8 Max Weston Thornburg, Graham Spry and George Soule, *Turkey: An Economic Appraisal* (New York: The Twentieth Century Fund, 1949), 105–106; Selim Cavid, "Fabrikalarımız: Izmit Kağıt Fabrikası," *İktisadi Yürüyüş* 6 (1940).

9 Sibel Bozdoğan, "Industrial Architecture and Nation-building in Turkey: A Historical Overview", in *Workplaces: The Transformation of Places of Production – Industrialization and the Built Environment in the Islamic World*, edited by Mohammad al-Asad (Istanbul: Istanbul University Press by the cooperation with the Aga Khan Award For Architecture, 2010), 27; Catherine Alexander, "The Factory: Fabricating the State," *Journal of Material Culture* 5, 2 (2000): 180.

10 Yeşim Arat, "From Emancipation to Liberation: The Changing Role of Women in Turkey's Public Realm," *Journal of International Affairs* 54, 1 (2000): 107–123; Yeşim Arat, "Nation Building and Feminism in Early Republican Turkey," in *Turkey's Engagement with Modernity: Conflict and Change in the Twentieth Century*, edited by Celia Kerslake, Kerem Öktem, and Philip Robins (London: Palgrave Macmillan, 2010), 39; Deniz Kandiyoti, "Emancipated but Unliberated? Reflections on the Turkish Case," *Feminist Studies* 13, 2 (1987): 317–338; Deniz Kandiyoti, "The End of Empire: Islam, Nationalism and Women in Turkey," in *Women, Islam and the State*, edited by Deniz Kandiyoti (Philadel-

identification was to distance itself from its Ottoman legacy. References to a remote and mythical past glorified as a golden age were common currency within Turkish intellectual circles of the period, with women at the forefront of this glorification.[11] In her 1930 *Turkey Faces West* treatise published in the United States, Halide Edib, the prominent national heroine who played an active role in the War of Independence, called for Turkish culture to be "cleans[ed]" of "foreign" elements. The inferior position of women was a result of the Byzantine and Persian as well as Islamic influences; the "genuine" nomadic culture of Anatolia "would delight the soul of the western feminist in some respects [...] [because] women are on an equal footing with men in every respect."[12] This narrative lost none of its appeal among middle-class women and men alike in the coming decades. By the end of the 1940s, a female author writing for a middle-class feminist newspaper portrayed the Republican regime as a morning full of light and joyful excitement for women who had just awoken from a centuries-old suffocating night. By recognising women's right to work, the Republic had saved women from the dishonor of being mere toys for men.[13] The condemnation of certain aspects of Ottoman patriarchy, associated mainly with religious bigotry, became part of official state ideology, making celebratory images of women in public life central to the iconography of the new regime. A series of legal reforms concerning women's legal and civil status were undertaken in the 1920s and 1930s. These included the replacement of the Islamic civil code with the Swiss secular code, the abolition of polygamy, the recognition of women's right to vote, and the launch of a nationwide campaign for girls' education.[14]

Comparisons between the gendered oppression women suffered under Ottoman imperial rule and their emancipation in the Republic filled the pages of the mainstream media and fuelled state and middle-class intellectual discourses.

---

phia: Temple University Press, 1991), 22–47; Binnaz Toprak, "Emancipated But Unliberated Women in Turkey: The Impact of Islam," in *Women, Family and Social Change in Turkey*, edited by Ferhunde Özbay (Bangkok: UNESCO, 1990), 39–50; Jenny B. White, "State Feminism, Modernization, and the Turkish Republican Woman," *NWSA Journal* 15, 3 (2003): 145–159.

11 Mary Motassian, "Ideologies of Delayed Industrialization: Some Tensions and Ambiguities," *Economic Development and Cultural Change* 6, 3 (1958): 223–224.

12 Halide Edib Adıvar, *Turkey Faces West: A Turkish View of Recent Changes and Their Origin* (New Haven: Yale University Press, 1930), 6.

13 Şükûfe Nihal, "Cumhuriyette Kadın," *Kadın Gazetesi* (17 October 1947).

14 Until the 1980s, these reforms had been presented as a set of top-down policies enacted by an enlightened leader, resulting in amnesia about women's struggles in the late Empire and the early Republic. Feminists increasingly problematised this historiography by bringing women's writing and organising to the forefront. See, for example: Serpil Çakır, *Osmanlı Kadın Hareketi* (Istanbul: Metis Yayınları, 1993), and Yaprak Zihnioğlu, *Kadınsız İnkılap* (Istanbul: Metis Yayınları, 2003).

These comparisons celebrated the Republican present as a historical moment: when women in Turkey first encountered modernity through their entry into modern forms of labour, including factory work. The mixed-gender industrial workspaces and recreational facilities significantly reinforced the Republic's secularisation agenda and strengthened its claim to a new positioning of the state vis-à-vis women. As key spaces for a modern and secular state in the making, factories seemed to be a sort of Westernised cultural representation of the world with women at the forefront.

Two types of state discourses regarding women's industrial employment emerged in the narrative space created by the claim to a clean slate in the 1930s. The first insisted that women's factory work was unprecedented, while the second built its case on the claim of a significant improvement in women's conditions of industrial work. The argument based on novelty was, of course, unfounded. Ottoman women were present and visible in the expanding domain of the factory as a result of the Empire's integration into the world economy from the mid-nineteenth century onward. Similar to historical trends in western Europe, female industrial employment resulted from the transfer of home production to factories in the Ottoman Empire, making textiles one of the two industries where female labour was widely used.[15] Tobacco was the other traditionally female industry. Women would take up industrial jobs in other sectors with time, but still more than 90 percent of women labourers worked in either the textile or food industry.[16] An estimate based on scattered evidence from 1908 gives the total number of industrial workers in the Empire as 250,000, with women making up between 70,000 and 75,000.[17] According to the 1913 to 1915 Industrial Census, which covered

---

15 Sabahaddin Zaim, *Istanbul Mensucat Sanayiinin Bünyesi ve Ücretler* (Istanbul: Istanbul Üniversitesi İktisat Fakültesi, 1956), 134.

16 Gündüz Ökçün, *Osmanlı Sanayi 1913–1915 İstatistikleri*, (Istanbul: Hil Yayın, 1984); Donald Quataert, "Women Households and Textile Manufacturing 1800–1914," in *The Modern Middle East*, edited by Albert Hourani, Philip S. Khoury and Mary C. Wilson (London: I.B. Tauris, 1993), 255–270; Donald Quataert, "The Workers of Salonica," in *The Workers and the Working Class in the Ottoman Empire and Turkish Republic, 1839–1950*, edited by Donald Quataert and Erik Jan Zürcher (London and New York: Tauris Academic Studies in Association with the International Institute of Social history, Amsterdam, 1995), 66; Donald Quataert, "The Social History of Labor in the Ottoman Empire," in *The Social History of Labor in the Middle East*, edited by Ellis Jay Goldberg (Boulder, CO: Westview Press, 1996), 27; Halil İnalcık, *Economic and Social History of the Ottoman Empire: 1300–1914* (Cambridge: Cambridge University Press, 1997), 902; Can Nacar, "*Labour Activism* and the *State* in the Ottoman Tobacco Industry," *International Journal of Middle East Studies* 46, 3 (2014): 533–551; Lütfü Erişçi, *Türkiye'de İşçi Sınıfının Tarihi* (Istanbul: Kutulmuş Basımevi, 1951), 7.

17 Şehmus Güzel, "Tanzimat'tan Cumhuriyet'e Toplumsal Değişim ve Kadın," *Tanzimat'tan Cumhuriyet'e Türkiye Ansiklopedisi* 3–4, (1985): 870.

the main industrial centers within the later Republican borders, one out of three industrial workers was female.[18]

In terms of the ethno-religious composition of the female industrial workforce, Muslim women comprised a small part. In 1891, the *Régie Française des Tabacs* factory in Istanbul, known as the Cibali Factory, employed four hundred men and boys, and 1,500 women, the majority of whom were Jewish and the rest Greek and Armenian. "Of course," noted an American publication, "there is not a single Turkish woman among the employees.[19] By 1914, there were Muslim women at the factory, working in separate all-female rooms.[20] In 1912, in response to the reports of sexual abuse in tobacco workshops in Aydın, "the local government stipulated that women tobacco workers were to be hired only with the permission of their guardians, employed in separate rooms, and paid their wages by female accountants."[21] As late as 1915, Turkish workers made up only 15 percent of the industrial workforce.[22] But a dramatic change in the demographic composition of the population was already underway. In the first two decades of the twentieth century, much of the Ottoman industrial labour force was removed through deportation and emigration, pulling Muslim women to the shop floor. With the onset of the war, the number of Muslim women further increased.[23] In 1917, 5000 out of 8000 workers at the Feshane Factory were women and children. "[This is] a complete revolution," wrote the editor of *Frankfurter Zeitung* upon seeing men and women working together at this factory, "caused by the necessities of the war."[24]

---

18 Ahmet Makal, "Erken Cumhuriyet Döneminde Kadın": 18.

19 "The Central Tobacco Factory in Constantinople," *Scientific American Supplement* 31, 783 (1891): 12,508.

20 "The Ottoman Tobacco Industry," *Journal of the Society of Arts* 42 (1894): 733–734.

21 Can Nacar, "*Labour Activism*": 537.

22 G. Bie Ravndal (compiled by), "Turkey: An Economic Handbook" (unpublished, 1924): 347; Records of the Department of State Relating to Internal Affairs of Turkey, Economic Matters, (2 June 1910–17 December;1929), Decimal File 867.50, NARA, https://go.gale.com/ps/retrieve.do?tabID= Manuscripts&resultListType=RESULT_LIST&searchResultsType=SingleTab&searchType=Ad vancedSearchForm&currentPosition=1&docId=GALE%7CSC5111519615&docType=Manuscript&sort= Relevance&contentSegment=GDSC221&prodId=GDSC&contentSet=GALE%7CSC5111519615&search Id=R11&userGroupName=cumhurb&inPS=true&ps=1&cp=1, accessed 1 May 2020.

23 A.J. Sussitzki, "Ethnic Division of Labour," in *The Economic History of the Middle East (1800– 1914)*, edited by Charles Issawi (Chicago and London: The University of Chicago Press, 1966), 120.

24 Alexander Giesen, "National, Economic and Cultural Work in the New Turkey," (5 December 1917); Records of the Department of State Relating to Internal Affairs of Turkey, Economic Matters, (2 June 1910–17 December 1929), Decimal File 867.50, NARA, https://go.gale.com/ps/retrieve.do?tabID= Manuscripts&resultListType=RESULT_LIST&searchResultsType=SingleTab&searchType=Ad vancedSearchForm&currentPosition=1&docId=GALE%7CSC5111519615&docType=Manuscript&sort=

The demographic change suggests an increasing presence of Muslim women on the shop floor, especially after the 1923 population exchange with Greece, which resulted in the loss of not only an important source of cheap labour but also of artisanal skills particularly in urban areas.[25] Industrial statistics from the 1930s and 1940s do not break down the ethnicity of workers. However, given the demographic change explained above and women's increasing presence in the public sphere under Kemalist modernism, it would be safe to argue that the majority of women in factories in the 1940s were Muslim.

Fig. 1: Cibali Factory Workers, 1923 (National Library of Turkey, Courtesy of Sinan Çetin)

This is true of the majority of women in the labour market. Industrial policymakers recognised the changing ethno-religious composition of the reserve army of female labour and the requirement for extra-industrial interventions into the labour market that it created. Being well aware that the labour market is a mental, cul-

Relevance&contentSegment=GDSC221&prodId=GDSC&contentSet=GALE%7CSC5111519615&search Id=R11&userGroupName=cumhurb&inPS=true&ps=1&cp=1, accessed 1 May 2020.
25 Çağlar Keyder, *State and Class in Turkey: A Study in Capitalist Development* (London: Verso, 1987), 104; Erik Jan Zürcher, *Turkey: A Modern History* (London: I. B. Tauris, 1998), 172.

tural, and social as well as an economic space,[26] industrial policymakers and middle-class intellectuals underlined two points: Turkish women 'could' work at factories ('the right to work') and Turkish women 'should' work at factories ('the duty to work'). To overcome the religious bigotry that they believed kept women at home, and to appeal to women's nationalist sentiment, their efforts focused on making factory work socially acceptable and communicating effectively "the high ideal of the factory" and the notion of women's factory work as patriotic service.[27]

On the shop floor, however, things were a lot messier than they were portrayed in the realm of high ideals. In the labour market of the 1930s, the greatest difficulty lay in recruiting women to the newly established factories near small Anatolian towns. Historically, the imperial capital and its hinterland, as well as cities in West Anatolia such as Izmir and Bursa, constituted the industrial heartland of the country; women's factory work was concentrated in these regions. These concentrated urbanisation and industrialisation patterns remained intact throughout the 1930s and 1940s.[28] In 1938 – five years after state-led industrialisation had begun and after large factories had been constructed outside these industrial heartlands – the Marmara and Aegean regions were still home to 71.1 percent of all industry (the figure was even higher for the textile sector). Istanbul, Izmir, and Bursa were the three industrial centres where women workers were concentrated; in 1943, almost 70 percent of factory women worked in Istanbul and Izmir.[29]

Left to their own means, new factories struggled to secure the labour force they needed. For the women living in the hinterlands of the newly established factories, factory work was completely alien. The first stage of female labour control was thus the process of bringing women to these factories. The availability of a specific group of workers in the social space of the labour market is determined by, among other things, the social construction of the group's identity. During her

---

26 Karin Hausen, "Wirtschaften mit der Geschlechterordnung. Ein Essay," in *Geschlechterhierarchie und Arbeitsteilung. Zur Geschichte ungleicher Erwerbschancen von Männern und Frauen*, edited by Karin Hausen (Göttingen: Vandenhoeck & Ruprecht, 1993), 58.

27 Sait Kesler, "Sanayi İnkişaf Ettikçe İşverenin Katlanacağı Külfetler," *Türk İşçisi* (31 May 1947); İffet Halim Oruz, "Ekonomi Alanında Kadınlığımıza Düşen Görev," *Kadın Gazetesi* (19 December 1949); Üzel, "40,000 Metro İş Çıkarıyor," 1936.

28 Frederic C. Shorter, "Turkish Population in the Great Depression," *New Perspectives on Turkey* 23 (2000): 111–112.

29 Ökçün, *Osmanlı Sanayi 1913–1915 İstatistikleri*, 14; "Sanayi Hayatı: Fabrikalar Hakkında Bir İstatistik," *Haber-Akşam Postası* (25 January 1934); Erdal Yavuz, "The State of the Industrial Workforce, 1923–40," in *Workers and the Working Class in the Ottoman Empire and the Turkish Republic*, edited by Donald Quataert and Erik Jan Zürcher (London: Tauris Academic Studies, 1995), 97–98; "Sanayi İstatistiği," *Haber-Akşam Postası* (31 January 1934); Makal, "Erken Cumhuriyet Döneminde Kadın": 26.

visit to the Kayseri Factory shortly before it entered operation in 1935, the exiled German writer and reporter Lilo Linke noted a managerial strategy developed in response to local community characteristics to manipulate that social construction. Linke toured the country and found Kayseri to be the most conservative. Women were "shocked at the very idea of working side by side with men though they were living in dire poverty and could well do with a few piasters." To break women's resistance to factory work, the ambitious factory director devised the strategy of employing girls "while they were too young to be spoilt by their mothers" and familiarise them with the mixed-gender world of the factory. A number of girls were already enlisted during the construction phase, and they were kept "in a kind of kindergarten," where they played. They were a little older than twelve, Linke was told, but looked younger, "like half-starved mice." The factory director compared their living conditions to the homes they came from and revealed his plans for the girls once the factory started operating:

> [They lived in] Dirty hovels where they had neither air nor light and worked from morning to night. Here they'll be properly looked after. I'll get two forewomen from Russia to train and mother them. They'll have decent meals, the sports grounds as a playing-field, clean dresses and a doctor to watch over their health. You won't be able to recognize them two years hence.[30]

We will come to the prevalence of young labour in the coming pages. But let us now turn to the second discourse on Ottoman women's industrial labour in interwar Turkey and the ways in which it functioned as an external labour control strategy.

Women's Factory Work and Protective Legislation

If the claim to novelty concerning women's industrial work strengthened the notion of their right to work, a second set of discourses strengthened the idea of women's work as national service. In early Republican Turkey, if, and when, Ottoman women's industrial labour was acknowledged, it was depicted as women's suffering under the control of foreign capital and management. While the denial of

---

30 Lilo Linke, *Allah Dethroned: A Journey Through Modern Turkey* (London: Constable and Co Ltd, 1937), 312. Turkey had close connections with the Soviet Union during the first phase of state-led industrialisation. The first Five-Year Plan was prepared with the help of Soviet experts and was partially financed by the Soviet Union. Soviet industrial experts aided the construction and operation of the textile factories, and Turkish engineers and workers went to the Soviet Union for training.

women's industrial employment prior to the Republic was based on the narrative of women's emancipation from religious bigotry, comparisons between Ottoman and Turkish women's factory work emphasised the nation's emancipation from colonial capitalism. Reflecting a strong sense of national pride, depictions of women's presence on the shop floor often drew comparisons with the "dark, old times" (see Figure 2). Similar to other cases of gendered nation-building, the female body invoked a site of both suffering and endurance in these narratives, as seen in this description of women's conditions of work in the Ottoman factories by a medical doctor in the journal of the Ministry of Labour:

> The factory whistles were blown before sunrise to call the workers in [he uses *amele*, a degrading term for worker]. The woman worker came out of her warm bed, left her home behind unattended, packed her daily food, which was only cheese and olives [a powerful symbol of poverty in Turkish culture], and rushed to the factory. At sunset, she came back home exhausted and weary. Her nails fell off because she had to put them in boiling water, her body was exhausted after the twelve-hour working day, but she could not find anybody to listen even if she complained. The war changed everything … In the past, women working at these alleged factories that were managed by foreigners, left their young kids to their neighbours and the older ones on the street. Today, for example working mothers at the Cibali Tobacco Factory leave their children to the care of a doctor and nanny in a clean nursery next to the factory [....] The colonialist minded [non-Turkish employers] did not treat [women] workers humanely.[31]

The doctor was correct on the absence of protective legislation for factory women in the Empire. Ottoman women worked long hours (ten to fifteen hours a day) for a fraction of men's wages under unhealthy conditions and without childcare benefits.[32] But how different from this were women's conditions of work in the 1930s really?

Although factory women attracted considerable public attention in the 1930s, information on their conditions of work is almost non-existent in state-produced documents. What limited evidence is available suggests that the view of factory women in state discourse contradicts the actualities of their factory experience. In a rare autobiography of a worker from the period, tobacco worker and, later, trade unionist Zehra Kosova portrays the grim reality of industrial work. She de-

---

31 Dr. Osman Şevki Uludağ, "İş ve İşçi," *Çalışma Vekaleti* 1 (1945); Şehmus Güzel, "Toplumsal Değişim ve Kadın": 870.
32 Laurence S. Moore, "Sanayi Yaşamının Bazı Yönleri," in *İstanbul 1920*, edited by Clarence Richard Johnson, translated by Sönmez Taner (İstanbul: Tarih Vakfı Yurt Yayınları, 1995); Charles Issawi, *The Economic History of Turkey, 1800–1914* (The University of Chicago Press: Chicago, 1980), 313; Donald Quataert, *Sanayi Devrimi Çağında Osmanlı İmalat Sektörü*, translated by Tansel Güney (İstanbul: İletişim Yayınları, 1999), 88, 227, 230, 305–306.

DÜN: Korkunç ve umacı şeklinde çalışan kadınlarımız... ·

BUGUN: En müsait şartlar altında çalışıyorlar.

Fig. 2: "Yesterday: Our women working in a frightening and ogre-like manner. Today: They work under most favourable conditions." (Hürbilek, January 15, 1949)

tails the dire precariousness caused by the seasonal demand in tobacco labour, extremely low pay, the dreadful housing, and the hazardous working conditions of tobacco workers, especially women, as was seen in the high numbers of miscarriages.[33] Occasional coverage of women's conditions of work in the mainstream press points at factory girls working in hot, humid, and dusty workshops for ten to fifteen hours a day, constituting the main victims of tuberculosis, and there are also reports of hundreds of women and children seeking jobs at small textile factories in the industrial centers to work twelve hours a day for very low wages.[34] Nazlı, the main protagonist of the prominent journalist and political activist Suat Derviş's 1936 social realist novel *This is the Novel of Things That Actually Happen*, dreads working in unbearable heat fourteen hours a day, in a cramped workshop off a dusty alleyway behind the Golden Horn area of Istanbul. Terrified of the long commute to the factory, which Kosova also describes in bleak detail, Nazlı compares her shaking body and knocking knees to those of Jesus while carrying the cross on his way to his crucifixion.[35]

The first legislation protecting women workers had actually been adopted as part of the 1930 Public Health Law (*Umumi Hıfzıssıhha Kanunu*), which predated the above accounts. This raises three points. First, despite the growing presence

---

33 Zehra Kosova, *Ben İşçiyim* (Istanbul: İletişim, 1996).
34 "Bursa'da Kızlar Günde Kaç Saat İş Görürler?," *Son Posta* (23 September 1930); "Sanayi Hayatımızda Amelenin Vaziyeti," *Cumhuriyet* (19 January 1932).
35 Suat Derviş, *Bu Roman Olan Şeylerin Romanıdır* (Istanbul: İthaki, 2018), 33.

of women on the shop floor, legislation specific to their labour came quite late. In the early industrialised countries, the debate on the social value of protective legislation had already taken off in the 1890s through a series of international congresses and national investigations on working women and children.[36] Second, protection for factory women was stipulated in public health legislation and not in labour legislation because of the delay in the Turkish state's enactment of a labour code. It took the government numerous failed attempts, each of which revealed the burgeoning intra-ruling elite fissures concerning labour protection and workers' political rights. Fifteen years after the first attempt, which was made by the government of the Grand National Assembly during the Independence War in 1921, the parliament finally managed to enact a labour code. This was a strikingly long period for a regime that impressed both its own citizens and the international community with the speed of its superstructural and legislative reforms. Third, because public health legislation as a whole strongly conveyed Republican anxieties over population growth, its protective measures for women workers resided in their capacity to give birth.[37] Clauses of the 1930 law relating to women workers were limited to prohibiting women's employment three weeks before and three weeks after childbirth (for jobs potentially dangerous for the mother and the fetus, this period was three months prior to birth) and granting women the right to two lactation breaks of thirty minutes during the work day in the first six months following the delivery.[38] In any event, because there was no labour inspectorate mechanism, application of these stipulations largely failed.[39]

Meanwhile, the debate surrounding a labour code was escalating. In spring 1936, Suat Derviş penned a series of worker portraits in order to demonstrate

---

36 Alice Kessler-Harris, Jane Lewis, and Ulla Wikander, "Introduction," in *Protecting Women: Labor Legislation in Europe, the United States, and Australia, 1880–1920*, edited by Ulla Wikander, Alice Kessler-Harris, and Jane Lewis (Urbana and Chicago: University of Illinois Press, 1995), 7.
37 The Republican state faced a serious population problem due to consecutive wars, forced migrations, epidemics, and high infant mortality, which had reduced the population in the Republican territories from 16 million in 1913 to 13 million in 1923. The state sought to bolster its birth rate and population growth by pursuing aggressive pronatalist policies. In 1926, the Turkish Criminal Law banned abortion, while four years later importing, producing, and selling contraceptives became illegal. An amendment to the Penal Code effectively forbid family-planning education. See Cem Behar, "Osmanlı İmparatorluğu'nun ve Türkiye'nin Nüfusu 1500–1927," *Historical Statistics Series* 2 (Ankara: State Institute of Statistics, 1996): 65; Shorter, "Turkish Population": 114.
38 "Umumi Hıfzıssıhha Kanunu," *Resmi Gazete* (6 May 1930).
39 Cahit Talas, *Türkiye'nin Açıklamalı Sosyal Politika Tarihi* (Istanbul: Bilgi Yayınevi, 1992); Nadir Özbek, *Cumhuriyet Türkiyesi'nde Sosyal Güvenlik ve Sosyal Politikalar* (Istanbul: Tarih Vakfı, 2006), 88–89.

the urgency of the legislation. Walking in the poor neighbourhoods of Istanbul, Derviş was struck by the despair on the faces of children left to their own devices on the streets by their mothers who were searching for casual employment in the factories. The majority of these women were either widows or their husbands were too sick to work. She met Ayşe, a skilled lace worker who had had a work accident and had been laid off by her head foreman, only to be replaced by younger women ready to work for one quarter of her wage. Hacer, a carpet weaver since the age of six, had also suffered a work accident that left her with one leg shorter than the other, and found herself in dire poverty after the carpet factory closed down. Refia, a widow with three children, was fired from the Cibali Factory after falling sick because of the tobacco dust. She lived with her ageing mother and two sisters, who were also unemployed because they had to leave a textile factory due to the violent behaviour of their employer's son. Another unnamed woman from the Cibali Factory had to leave her job to look after her severely burnt toddler. She also had to take care of her in-laws while her husband was on military service. Reduced to utter poverty, she asked Derviş the question that preoccupied the minds of all the poor working mothers: "Us, women workers, what should we do when our children are sick? If I work, my child will die. If I don't work, we will all starve to death."[40]

Two months after Derviş ended her series, the Labour Code, modelled on the 1927 fascist Italian legislation and defined as a "law of the regime" that would "wipe out the erroneous roads leading to class consciousness" by the Minister of Internal Affairs, was finally enacted on 12 June 1936.[41] The code covered enterprises employing at least ten workers and remained in force until 1967. Protective legislation continued to reside in women's primary roles as childbearers and child rearers, with the code prohibiting underground and underwater employment of women at any age (and of men under eighteen) as well as women's nighttime employment, and retaining the ban on women's employment in the three weeks before and three weeks after childbirth. An important change, however, was the obligation for employers to pay half wages during maternity leave, and they were also banned from terminating their employment contract while they were on maternity leave. With regard to the minimum working age and regulation of the workday, the law did not differentiate between men and women. The minimum working age was set at 12 and the working week was limited to 48 hours (eight hours a day

---

40 Suat Derviş, "Günü Gününe Yaşayanlarımız," *Cumhuriyet* (8 April 1936; 12 April 1936; 14 April 1936; 15 April 1936; 17 April 1936). My sincere thanks to Aslı Odman for sharing this material with me.
41 Quoted in Kurthan Fişek, *Türkiye'de Kapitalizmin Gelişimi ve İşçi Sınıfı* (Istanbul: Doğan Yayınevi, 1969), 72.

for workers under 16). Last but not least, the law provided for a bylaw specifying the types of jobs that were forbidden and the conditions of work for pregnant and nursing women, as well as the construction of crèches and rooms for nursing in the workplace. Although the deadline for this bylaw was six months after the code's implementation, which was in June 1937, it was delayed by sixteen years to 1953. But before it could even be enacted, another piece of legislation stripped women of the little protection they had acquired thus far.[42]

Within three years of implementation of the Labour Code, war exigencies led to the suspension of its protective measures. Although the country remained out of the conflict, the full mobilisation for a possible war massively eliminated men from the labour force, with estimates ranging from a million to one and a half million.[43] A year into the war, the Turkish government suspended the application of protective labour measures under the powers conferred upon it by the National Protection Act. This meant overriding the regulations on working hours and enforcing compulsory work and overtime, as well as prohibiting workers from leaving employment. Limitations on the employment of women and children over twelve years old were also lifted, causing an increase in the share of girls among working children.[44] By 1943, girls made up 42 percent of child workers (more than 45 percent in the twelve-to-sixteen age group), while women and girls together made up 29 percent of the entire industrial workforce.[45]

The immediate postwar period witnessed the extension of the Turkish state's regulatory powers over the labour market, including a gradual institutionalisation and extension of social insurance schemes, the first of which was the 1945 Work Accidents, Occupational Diseases and Maternity Insurance Bill. Maternity insurance secured women workers' right to partially paid leave and legislated for a birth and breastfeeding allowance for women workers and male workers' wives. The number of women benefiting from maternity insurance increased more than tenfold in the first four years of its implementation, reaching 26,000 in

---

42 The law also required the enactment of a bylaw defining heavy and dangerous jobs and regulating conditions of women's and children's employment in these within the same period of six months. The enactment of this bylaw had to wait until 1948. Ahmet Makal, "Erken Cumhuriyet Döneminde Kadın": 33.

43 Şevket Pamuk, "Turkey: 1918–1945," in *A History of Middle East Economies in the Twentieth Century*, edited by Roger Owen and Şevket Pamuk (Cambridge, Mass.: Harvard University Press, 1999), 24; Erik Jan Zürcher, *Turkey: A Modern History* (London and New York: I. B. Tauris., 1993), 207.

44 Lütfü Erişçi, *Türkiye'de İşçi Sınıfının*, 25.

45 Ahmet Makal, "65. Yılında Milli Korunma Kanunu, Çalışma İlişkileri ve İş Mükellefiyeti Üzerine Bir İnceleme," *Toplum ve Bilim* 102 (2005): 8; Ahmet Makal, "Erken Cumhuriyet Döneminde Kadın": 24.

1949. Of these, only between 10 to 15 percent were actually women workers; the wives of industrial male workers were the main beneficiaries.[46]

What was happening on the shop floor as the state expanded its regulatory powers through legislation? In 1947, a decade after the implementation of the Labour Code, a parliamentary inspection report on 60 factories detailed the conditions of women workers. In both state and private factories, the inspectors noted widespread employment of girls under 12 and the common practise of falsifying their age, reminding us of Linke's 1935 observations on the girls at the Kayseri Factory. In the coming pages, the reader will find firsthand testimonies of this practise. In some factories, girls between nine and 12 years of age were given heavy jobs, worked 10 or even 12 hours a day, and seemed to be "at the complete mercy of their foreman."[47] Tuberculosis was still a big threat for women working in unhealthy conditions, and voices from the shop floor confirmed this. A male worker angrily interrupted the calm conversation between a journalist and a pale-faced, troubled-looking young woman at the state tobacco factory in Istanbul, claiming that only a handful of tobacco workers would pass a proper tuberculosis examination. Terrible working conditions and malnutrition due to low wages scared workers from having children, he continued, resorting to a metaphor of murder: "Getting married was my first murder. Should I have children and commit a second one?"[48]

But what about the women workers who "committed that crime"? In a rare example of criticism published in the journal of the Ministry of Labour, an author admitted that, in terms of childcare, women workers were left to their own means. When working-class houses were uninhabitable due to cold or when it was no longer possible to ask for help from neighbors, working mothers had to bring their children to the dirty and humid factories where they worked.[49] The 1947 parliamentary report expanded on these general comments with details of childcare provision in state and private factories. Considerable variation existed among state factories: while some did not provide any childcare facilities, others had crèches, albeit with extremely limited capacities. The crèche of the state-owned leather factory in Istanbul, for example, had a capacity of 25 children even though

---

46 *İşçi Sigortaları Kurumunun 1953 Yılı Çalışma Raporu ve Bilançosu* (Ankara: İşçi Sigortaları Kurumu, 1954), 11–17.
47 "T.B.M.M. Çalışma Komisyonu Üyesi Milletvekillerinin 15.7.1947–12.9.1947 Tarihleri Arasındaki Araştırma Gezilerine İlişkin Raporları," Republic of Turkey Prime Ministry General Directory of State Archives, 490.01/728.495.5: 20–7, 30–6, 68, 24/1.
48 "2000 Kişinin Kaynaştığı Yer," *Türk İşçisi* (18 January 1947).
49 M. Şevki Yazman, "Kadın İşçilerin Çocuklarının Bakımı Meselesi," *Çalışma Vekaleti Dergisi* 13 (1946): 42.

women made up one quarter of the entire thirteen-hundred-strong workforce. The situation was comparable at the state glassware factory in Istanbul, as well as the state cotton textile factories in Istanbul and Nazilli. At Defterdar, the oldest state textile factory in the country, where seven hundred women worked, there was no crèche. The paper factory in Izmit, the artificial silk factory in Gemlik, and the textile factories in Hereke and Bursa did not have crèches either. An exception was the Cibali Tobacco Factory in Istanbul, where 75 percent of the workforce was female. The crèche facilities at this factory were described as "perfect" by the inspectors.[50] But workers knew very well that the limited capacity meant that the crèche was only for those women who had no one to leave their children to. One of these women, Ahter, favourably mentioned the breakfast, lunch, and fruit juice her two children received daily at the crèche: "How else could a woman worker like myself give her children such food?"[51] In Samsun, however, women tobacco workers employed by the same tobacco monopoly administration had to leave their children alone most of the time.[52] Childcare provision at private factories was even worse. Only a few had crèches, and these were often in a terrible, unsanitary state. In 1946, the newly established Ministry of Labour set increasing female industrial labour as one of its primary goals and calculated that in Istanbul alone 18 crèches were needed to accommodate the needs of 46,358 women workers.[53] In 1960, there were only thirty-three nursing rooms and thirty-two crèches registered in the whole of Turkey, and the number of children attending these was under three thousand.[54] In the mid-1950s, a contemporary sociologist attributed the below-average rate of female industrial employment to the lack of childcare provision.[55] From the perspective of women workers, the situation was clear: "There was a labour law, but who cared really?"[56]

---

50 "T.B.M.M. Çalışma Komisyonu Üyesi Milletvekillerinin," 22, 25–27, 30, 68.
51 "2000 Kişinin Kaynaştığı Yer," 1947. Already a problem in the 1930s, working-class malnutrition was aggravated during the war years. In 1942, the director of the Istanbul Tobacco Warehouses told the story of crying women when the factory began serving lunch and their deep gratitude to "the father state" (*Devlet baba*). İsmet Alkan, "İnhisarlar: Istanbul Depolar Grubu," *İktisadi Yürüyüş* 66–67 (1942): 58.
52 Ahmet Makal, "Erken Cumhuriyet Döneminde Kadın": 32.
53 *Çalışma Bakanlığı İlk Yılı ve İlk Hedefleri: Beş Yıllık İş Programının Esasları* (Ankara: Çalışma Bakanlığı Yayınları, 1946), 85–88.
54 İsmail Akçay, "Sosyal Hayatta Annenin ve Çocuğun Himayesi," *Çalışma Vekaleti Dergisi* 4 (1960): 5.
55 Sabahaddin Zaim, *Istanbul mensucat sanayiinin bünyesi ve ücretler (Istanbul: Istanbul Üniversitesi İktisat Fakültesi, 1956)*, 134–138.
56 Zehra Kosova, *Ben İşçiyim*, 57.

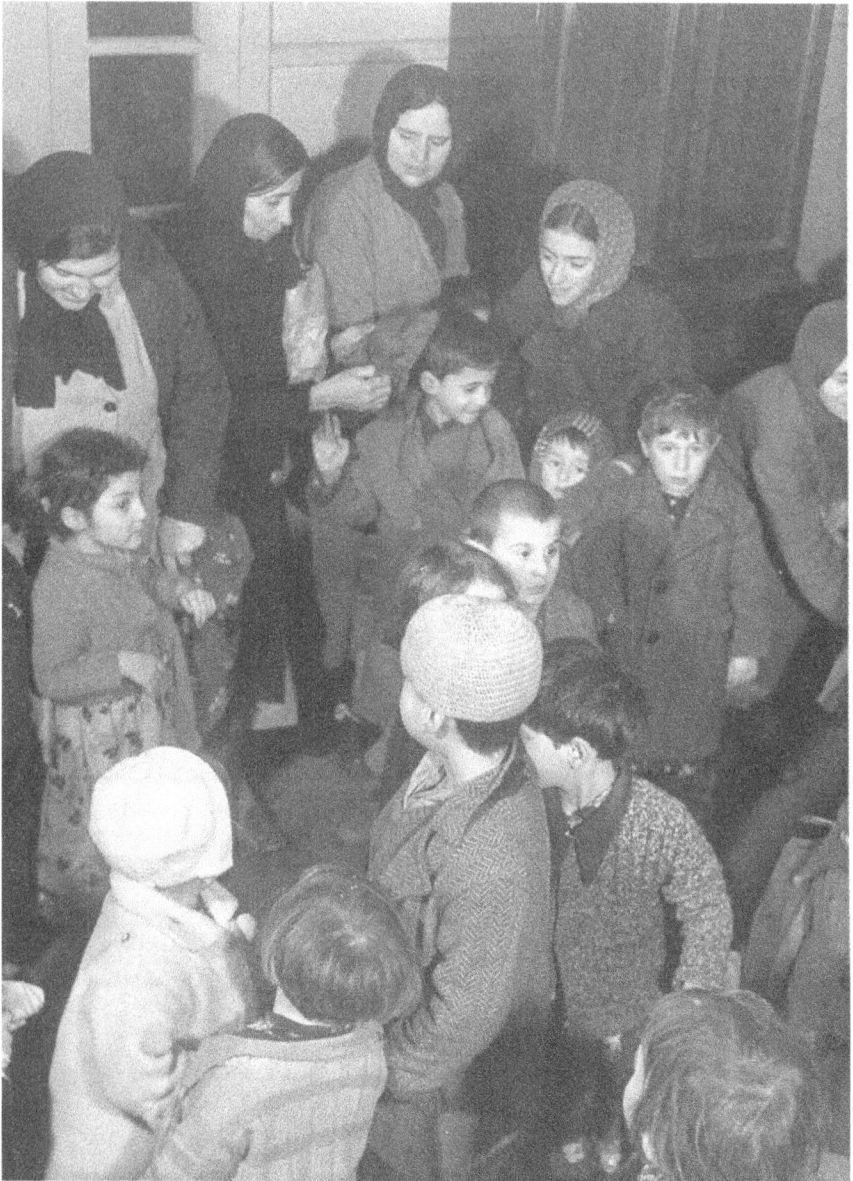

Fig. 3: Women workers picking their children up at the factory daycare facility at Cibali, c.1940. (Margaret Bourke-White/The LIFE Picture Collection/Shutterstock)

Behind the late timing, limited scope, and partial implementation of the protective legislation lay two significant differences compared with earlier, turn-of-the-century legislation in Europe and North America. First, protective legislation for factory women historically preceded the recognition of women's political rights, and developed within the context of public debates among industrialists with an interest in opening the labour market, social reformers with an interest in the moral and physical wellbeing of working-class women, and early feminists with an interest in women's social and political rights.[57] In Turkey, women gained the right to vote only four years after the earliest protective legislation. The Republican regime managed to erase the memory of the early feminist movement, and co-opted its agenda into the larger Kemalist modernisation discourse, while the repressive class politics further crippled the emergence of a public debate on women's work. Instead of a social question, the category of factory women was treated as a source of secular national identity and a civilisational premise of the ideal Republican woman. The hegemonic capacity of Kemalist nationalism and state feminism engulfed considerations of factory women's conditions of work and rendered protective legislation the product of a "humanitarian perspective" and a paternalist gift from a regime designated as the "protector of women."[58] A female author powerfully summarised middle-class women's faith in the regime: "In revolutionary Turkey, where women were given the right to vote without having to ask for it, they will surely be given the worth of their labour in accordance with the peculiarities of their nature."[59]

The second important difference between this wave of Turkish protective legislation and its previous incarnations concerns the scope of the law. The three major areas of protective legislation have historically been hours, wages, and reproduction.[60] In the Turkish case, the rhetoric of national economic development and state feminism pushed women's material conditions of industrial work to the margins. Identifying the problem as one of bigotry and the weight of traditions, industrial policymakers ignored the structural determinants of women's inferior position in the labour market. Legislative emphasis was placed on protecting women as potential or actual mothers and on notions of what was considered appropriate work for women, affirming and extending the gendered division of labour at the social level. Dominated by such concerns, policymaking related to women and work failed to support women or accommodate their needs, such as through equal pay for comparable work, job security in case of pregnancy and childbirth, protection against sexual discrimination and harassment in the workplace, and adequate assistance for childcare. The political subordination of labour

---

57 Alice Kessler-Harris et al, "Introduction", 13.
58 Kadri Kemal Kop, "Yakın Tarihimizde İş ve İşçi Meseleleri," *Çalışma Vekaleti Dergisi* (1945): 69.
59 Fahamet Gökel, "İş Hayatında Kadın," *Çalışma Vekaleti Dergisi* 3 (1946): 68.
60 Alice Kessler-Harris et al., "Introduction", 6.

to the rhetoric of a populist and nationalist development agenda expanded the state's room for maneuver to facilitate capital accumulation in this period, and it was women workers who paid the highest price.[61]

In the first part of this essay, I have covered the external control of women's labour through state and intellectual discourses and legislation. In what follows, I move from the "politics of production" to the "politics in production," and extend my analytical lens to the workplace to analyze the way gender is built into the material fabric of work on the Turkish shop floors of the 1930s and 1940s.[62]

Gendered Labour Control on the Shop Floor

If one side of the Janus face of Turkish industrialisation as it developed in the 1930s and 1940s entailed nationalist pride and propaganda, the other side involved anxieties over problems of poor efficiency and low productivity. No matter how noble the social and national goals behind industrialisation are, an engineering journal by the end of the 1940s warned that they would not be enough to achieve industrial efficiency; industry could only rise on the shoulders of a trained cadre of all levels operating on the basis of rational organisation.[63] This was exactly what the state elite had in mind when they called for the adoption of a "new industrial mentality" in the early 1930s, that is, a combination of rational work and patriotic labour.[64] Industrial policymakers carefully followed the developments in both Europe (especially Germany) and the Soviet Union, and sought the help of foreign experts in order to reorganise production and implement scientific methods of labour control.[65] In the 1940s, local industrial experts joined the chorus emphasising the primacy of administrative rationality and scientific labour control in solving the problem of low productivity.

---

61 Michael Burawoy, "The Colour of Class Revisited: Four Decades of Postcolonialism in Zambia," *Journal of Southern African Studies* 40, 5 (2014): 973.

62 Michael Burawoy, *The Politics of Production: Factory Regimes Under Capitalism and Socialism* (London: Verso, 1985).

63 Abdülkadir Gözen, "Bizde Devletçilik ve Devlet Endüstrisi," *Feshane Mensucat Meslek Dergisi* 1 (1949): 11.

64 Bilsay Kuruç, *Belgelerle Türkiye İktisat Politikası, 1933–1935*, vol. 2 (Ankara: Ankara Üniversitesi Yayınları, 1993), 269; "Başvekil Hz. Sümer Bank Fabrikalarını Tetkik Ettiler," *Cumhuriyet* (22 November 1933); "Yeni Daireleri Dün Açıldı," *Haber-Akşam Postası* (14 August 1934).

65 I have written on the activities of these foreign experts here: "Experts, Exiles, and Textiles: German 'Rationalisierung' on the 1930s Turkish Shop Floor," *International Review of Social History* 66, 2 (2021): 179–216.

But their suggestions seemed to fall on deaf ears. There was a strong appearance of a formal administrative organisation of factories based on a set of objective and legitimate rules to restrict the discretion of any individual participant. But the actual operating activities were decoupled from this formal bureaucratic structure. The information I gathered from inspection reports, workers' files, interviews with workers, and the press coverage of state factories starkly contradicts the "ceremonial façade," namely the image of highly institutionalised, rationalised, and seemingly impersonal prescriptions on which organisational practise is based.[66] The failure to adopt bureaucratic and technical forms of control was to a large extent compensated for by disciplinary measures and pressure from the foreman. The factory was run by the iron hand and arbitrary justice of the foreman, who continued to be the prime regulator of the work effort on the shop floor using the "drive system," involving close supervision, abuse, profanity, and threats in order to maintain or increase effort.[67] Because this disciplinary system centered on workers' gendered bodies, the foreman's authority had a specific meaning for women workers. In this section, I analyze its most prominent aspects.

To industrial experts, low productivity was to a large extent a reflection of weak management starting from the point of recruitment. The foreman had considerable power over recruitment and promotion decisions, even in state factories with a personnel department. As late as 1945, the foreman's control over employment began at the factory gates, where job seekers waited to be selected.[68] Among these were also underage girls. Cazibe, for example, remembers the foreman refusing to recruit her because she was only 11 when she first joined the crowd of job seekers. Advised by the foreman to falsify her age, she fetched her father and ran to the birth registration office, where she left officially two years older.[69] Having heard from her older sisters how things worked at the factory, 11-year-old Meryem took matters into her own hands and borrowed a pair of high heel shoes from a neighbor to elevate her appearance in front of the factory gate.[70]

Once they made it to the factory, women were under the complete control of the foreman responsible for their work group. Because they had to address them-

---

66 John W. Meyer and Brian Rowan, "Institutionalized Organizations: Formal Structure as Myth and Ceremony," *American Journal of Sociology* 83, 2 (1977): 341–343.

67 Sanford M. Jacoby, *Employing Bureaucracy: Managers, Unions, and the Transformation of Work in the 20th Century* (London: Routledge, 1985), 17.

68 "Sümerbank İşletmelerinde İşletmede İnsan ve İşçi Meseleleri 1945 Yılı Umumi Murakebe Heyeti Raporu," Archival Collection of the Republic of Turkey Prime Ministry Supreme Audit Board. Amb. /Db. No: K.A./255.07.02.01.7462, 17; Sebahat Yürekli, interview by author, online, 15 June 2019.

69 Cazibe Doğan, interview by author, 5 June 2019.

70 Ayten Durukan Günüvar (Zarife's daughter born in 1965), interview by author, 5 June 2019.

Fig. 4: Spinning girls Zarife (on the right) and Nuriye in the late 1940s donning dresses made of cloth manufactured at the state factory where they worked in Ereğli (Courtesy of Ayten Durukan Günüvar).

selves to him for all sorts of problems and requests, "management" was basically akin to the foreman for women workers. Cazibe explained: "To reach the factory manager was like reaching the top of a snowy mountain." She recalled the one time she was summoned by the department chief. She shivered with fear and could only go to his office after her foreman ordered her to do so. They saw the head foreman twice a day, in the mornings and the evenings; throughout the day they worked under the close supervision of what they called the "loom foreman."[71] That is, when they could work of course. Frequent conflicts between the foremen and women on the piece rate were reported in 1934 because the latter often spent the entire day waiting to be assigned work at the factories.[72] On the job, women were frequently punished by the foreman for lateness, absenteeism, and poor performance. My analysis of workers' files in a state factory demonstrates that although they did not even make up one quarter of the sample, women received more than 35 percent of all fines.

---

[71] Cazibe Doğan, interview by author, 5 June 2019; Muazzez Atalay, interview by author, 4 June 2019.

[72] "Fabrikalarda Çalışan Kadınlar," *Haber-Akşam Postası*, 15 March 1934.

There was also physical violence on the shop floor. Because she had to take care of a sick family member, Emine skipped work one day. When she showed up on the shop floor the following day, her foreman, accompanied by the head foreman, angrily questioned her and then raised his hand to hit her, only to be stopped by the head foreman. In a rare case of protest by a woman, an angry Emine reported the attempted beating to a newspaper that covered industrial disputes: "I am an honorable married woman and a mother," Emine protested, "I come to work to earn a living for my children, not to be beaten by the foreman. Even if I make a mistake, the worst the foreman can do is to fine me, not beat me."[73] Two points arise from Emine's story, and the first concerns the timing. The incident happened in 1955, that is, eight years after the trade union movement began. Considerable changes regarding working-class politics had happened during that time, with women, as well as men, increasingly using the space opened up by the postwar political climate.[74] Second, Emine's protest rests on a combination of her critique of the foreman's discrete power and her strategical use of the hegemonic capacity of the maternal ideology; two strong trends in the worlds of factory women that were carried over into the 1950s.

Male workers also attempted to wield the moral authority derived from patriarchal values over women. The patriarchal basis of social relations on the shop floor was even more pronounced for women whose male family members also worked in the same factory. In 1942, textile worker Mehmet petitioned to warn the director against his wife, Kesire, who also used to work at the same factory before she "robbed his house and ran away." Enraged to hear that she had requested to be rehired at the factory, Mehmet strongly protested that "this woman … would spread immorality [to the factory]." The management's reaction was first to check with Kesire's ex-foreman to make sure that she had not committed any "mistakes" while on the job, and then inspect her police certificate of good conduct, which also covered moral offenses. Kesire's story demonstrates that labour control policies were finely tuned to local cultural values, and women workers were under close surveillance with regard to their gender and familial roles.

Because all of the managerial, and almost all of the supervisory, staff was male, the shop floor environment of the 1930s and 1940s was highly gendered and male-controlled. Where groups of women were employed together, a male overlooker would have to be in charge of them, maintaining the traditional author-

---

73 "Gece Postası Gazetesi Yazı İşleri Müdürlüğü Yüksek Makamına," 10 July 1955, Kemal Sülker Papers, folder no. 402, International Institute of Social History, Amsterdam.
74 I have written on working-class politics in the first years of the trade union movement in "Citizens on the Shop Floor: Negotiating Class, Citizenship and National Identity in a Turkish State Factory," *Labor History* 61, 1 (2020): 24–35.

ity relationship between women and men. In the workshops where women and men worked together, such as the weavery, the women's subsidiary role was clear in their job titles such as "weaver helper." Skill requirements and training for jobs was organised in such a way that, when they worked with machines, women had to have male overseers to repair and adjust machines. The industrial workplace was one defined by a rigid male-dominated hierarchy, where women were concentrated in the lowest job ranks and supervised by male workers in their daily activities on the shop floor.

Fig. 5: The spinnery of the Feshane Factory, 1940s to 1950s (Taha Toros Archive, Marmara University)

As a general rule, the shortage of skilled labour and the absence of any evaluation of skills meant that task assignment was random – with an important exception: the gendered segregation of jobs. A weaver described the gender composition of the textile workforce in the 1940s as follows:

> There were a lot of women; a lot in the spinnery, not that many in the weavery, only a few, [but] the spinners were mostly women. In the dressing [department] there were no women, [they were] all men. In the warp [department] there were women, I mean those who bring

the thread back when it is broken, and you tie it to the warp beam, and it keeps going again. Later it got automatic, it stopped when it [the thread] broke, and you find the tip and tie it.[75]

A comparison of spinning and weaving workshops by a German industrial expert offers a glimpse into how such stereotyping worked on the Turkish shop floor in the 1930s. Spinning is much easier than operating weaving looms, the expert wrote. In fact, it was so easy that virtually anybody could master it. More to the point, if spinning were to be mechanised, all preparation work would be done automatically, which would leave no room for mistakes. The only skill needed would then be to tie the ends of the broken yarn as quickly as possible and with the minimum loss of material. Apart from that, the productivity of the spinning workshop depended on the availability and quality of raw material, the quality of the spinning machines, the spindle gauge, and the technical knowledge of the managing engineer. Echoing the dominant gender stereotyping of jobs in Germany, he concluded that since the task required no intellect, women – or better still, girls – should be employed in the spinning shop. By contrast, he claimed, both the quality of cloth and productivity depended on the weaver's skill.[76] Unsurprisingly, therefore, weaving in Turkish textile factories was almost exclusively a job for men.

The writings of this and other industrial experts were a response to the rising anxiety over low industrial productivity. A unanimously agreed-upon bottleneck of production was the high labour cost of production. Although labour was poorly remunerated, its low productivity pushed up production costs. In an industrial context with an unskilled, cheap, and unorganised labour force, the two possible solutions to this problem were the recruitment of even cheaper labour or the intensification of the work rhythm. Both of these concerned the female factory hands directly.

Incentive Wages and Work Intensification

Behind the demand for female industrial labour in interwar Turkey, there was what now seems to be a blindingly apparent proposition that strongly resonates

---

75 Asım Kocabaş, interview by author, 3 August 2009.

76 Mary Nolan, *Visions of Modernity: American Business and the Modernization of Germany* (Oxford: Oxford University Press, 1994), 96; Max von der Porten, "Kayseri Fabrikası İplik ve Dokuma Daireleri Hakkında," Archival Collection of the Republic of Turkey Prime Ministry Supreme Audit Board, Amb. /Db. No: K.A./255.07.02.01.06.1114.

Fig. 6: Spinners at the Bakırköy Factory, 1950s. (Kemal Sülker Collection, International Institute of Social History, Amsterdam)

with patterns of gender-based job segration elsewhere in the world.[77] In the Turkish context, however, this proposition has not been explicitly articulated and its significance for class formation has not been adequately acknowledged. The motivation was to profit more intensely from socio-culturally acceptable low female wages and from the gendered notion of women's suitability as cheap, docile, more dexterous labourers for labour intensive work. During his 1934 symbolically loaded visit to a renovated Ottoman textile factory, the prime minister openly referred to the oft-cited "nimble female fingers" and the "refined female taste" tropes to explain why female labour lay at the center of the Turkish industrialisation

---

[77] Anne Phillips and Barbara Taylor, "Sex and Skill: Notes towards a Feminist Economics," *Feminist Review* 6 (1980): 79–88; Diane Elson and Ruth Pearson, "Nimble Fingers Make Cheap Workers: An Analysis of Women's Employment in Third World Export Manufacturing," *Feminist Review* 7 (1981): 87–107; Diane Elson, "Nimble Fingers and Other Fables," in *Of Common Cloth: Women in the Global Textile Industry*, edited by Wendy Enloe and Cynthia Chapkis (Amsterdam: Transnational Institute, 1986), 5–14; Miriam Glucksmann, "In a Class of Their Own? Women Workers in the New Industries in Inter-War Britain," *Feminist Review* 24, 1 (1986): 7–37; Sylvia Chant and Cathy Mcilwaine, "Gender and Export Manufacturing in the Philippines: Continuity and Change in Female Employment?" *Gender, Place and Culture* 2, 2 (1995): 147–176.

drive.[78] A convergence of racist and sexist stereotypes underpinned this highly familiar trope since, in the Turkish case, it was not only their sex but also their ethnicity that endowed the emancipated Turkish women with these qualities.

Women were thus drawn into industrial labour while at the same time finding themselves restricted to particular kinds of work assumed to be apt for their "natural qualities." In the rare cases where they exceeded these restrictions, tension on the shop floor soared. In 1936, a fuming textile machine operator, Celal, told of the sequence of events that had led to his firing:

> They laid us off saying business went down, and then hired women ready to work for cheaper wages. I was a machine operator, and I earnt well. Machines are a good thing you know because women cannot operate them. I was thus confident. But just as they go and try everything, women also operate machines these days. One day I saw this woman in the workshop and fearing that she would replace me, I messed with the machine. But she was smart like the devil; she knew more about the machine than I do! She screwed the nails and all, fixed all the parts. I also know about electricity, so I messed with that as well. And she fixed that too! There was no job for me after that.[79]

The confrontation between Celal and the "devilishly smart" woman worker undermines an important source of women's subordination on the shop floor: men's monopolisation of the knowledge of the machinery.[80] But this was not the only thing Celal was angry at women for. According to his reasoning, by agreeing to work for less, women brought the wages down, forcing men to work for "women's wages." Of course, one man's meat is another's poison; what made Celal angry was a positive, but not good enough, trend in the eyes of the industrial policymakers. In 1945, inspectors compared the percentage of women in Turkey's state textile industry with a number of countries including the Soviet Union and Japan and found that the rate of 25 percent was at best half that of other countries. For example, in Italy, women made up more than 77 percent of the textile workforce, which, they claimed, was one of the reasons why Italy, a cotton-importing country, was exporting cheap cotton yarn to Turkey, a cotton-growing country.[81] The following year, a booklet published to document the first year's activities of the Ministry of Labour referred to employers' preferences for "cheap and dexterious female hands" as the reason behind the threefold increase in the number of factory women in Istanbul. Women who were "trying to get out of poverty" had become "a factor of production" and they did not seem to want to leave employment,

---

78 Bilsay Kuruç, *İktisat Politikası*, vol. 2, 227.
79 Suat Derviş, "Günü Gününe Yaşayanlarımız," (13 April 1936).
80 Cynthia Cockburn, "The Material of Male Power," *Feminist Review* 9 (1981): 41–58, 44.
81 "İşletmede İnsan": 8–9.

the publication reported.[82] Wage figures from various shop floors showed that women earned between forty and 60 percent of men's wages.[83] By the end of the 1940s, employers were on the hunt for more female factory hands. According to a private employer, men were flocking into textile factories due to a lack of investment in heavy industry. As a result of the difficulty in finding working girls, men were employed in "jobs that men cannot do" or would be unproductive at.[84]

What kind of discourses were at play that kept women's wages low despite the persistent demand for their labour? The discussion among industrial experts and managers on incentive wages provides a window into understanding how female wages were suppressed. Criticism over the lack of a consistent wage policy in state factories emerged as early as 1936 and continued into the 1940s. Expert after expert pointed out that the absence of a clear and accessible system of remuneration hindered the formation of a stable labour force.[85] A contemporary sociologist put it succinctly in 1954 that "until very recently" wage levels at state factories were de-

---

82 "Çalışma Hayatımızda Çocuklu Kadınlar ve Kreş İhtiyacı," *Çalışma Bakanlığı: İlk Yılı ve İlk Hedefleri* (Ankara: T.C. Çalışma Bakanlığı Yayınları, 1946), 85–88.

83 "Santral Mensucat Fabrikası İşçi ve İşverenleriyle Bir Röportaj," *Hürbilek* (13 November 1948); Ahmet Makal, "Erken Cumhuriyet Döneminde Kadın": 29.

84 "Santral Mensucat."

85 Bereznitsky, *Kayseri Bez Fabrikası Hakkında*, Archival Collection of the Republic of Turkey Prime Ministry Supreme Audit Board. Amb. /Db. No: K.A./ 255.07.02.01.06.1224; "Sümerbank Birleşik Pamuk İpliği ve Dokuma Fabrikaları Müessesesi 1939 Yılı Umumi Murakebe Heyeti Raporu," in *Sümerbank 1939 senesi faaliyet ve hesap devresine ait İdare Meclisi raporu, bilanço, kar ve zarar hesabı,* Archival Collection of the Republic of Turkey Prime Ministry Supreme Audit Board. Amb. /Db. No: K.A./ 255.07.02.01.06.3227, 37–9; Hösli, *Ereğli Bez Fabrikası Hakkında Rapor,* Archival Collection of the Republic of Turkey Prime Ministry Supreme Audit Board. Amb. /Db. No: K.A./ 255.07.02.01.06. 1099; *Hösli,* Nazilli Bez Fabrikası Hakkında, Archival Collection of the Republic of Turkey Prime Ministry Supreme Audit Board. Amb. /Db. No: K.A./ 255.07.02.01.06.1226; Hösli, *Merinos Fabrikası Hakkında,* Archival Collection of the Republic of Turkey Prime Ministry Supreme Audit Board. Amb. /Db. No: K.A./ 255.07.02.01.06.1117; "Sümerbank 1942 Senesi Faaliyet ve Hesap Devresine Ait İdare Meclisi Raporu, Bilanço, Kar ve Zarar Hesabı," in *Sümerbank 1942 Yılı Umumi Murakebe Heyeti Raporu,* Archival Collection of the Republic of Turkey Prime Ministry Supreme Audit Board. Amb. /Db. No: K.A./ 230.1/338.4, 23; Sümerbank Genel Müdürlük Yüksek Katına, "Fabrikalarımızın 1945 Senesi Faaliyetleri, Neticeleri ve Tahlilleri," 9 February 1946, Republic of Turkey Prime Ministry General Directory of State Archives, 730 05 01 EK 1–11 16–111, 31; Sabahaddin Zaim, "Türkiye Mensucat Sanayiinde Ücretler," *Sosyal Siyaset Konferansları, Sekizinci Kitap* (1956): 37–38; "Sümerbank İplik ve Dokuma Fabrikaları Müessesesi 1948 Yılı Raporu," *Sümerbank 1948 Senesi Faaliyet ve Hesap Devresine Ait İdare Meclisi Raporu, Bilanço, Kar ve Zarar Hesabı,* Archival Collection of the Republic of Turkey Prime Ministry Supreme Audit Board. Amb. /Db. No: K.A./ 255.07.02.01.06.3272: 33–34.

termined on the basis of "social justice and moral deliberation."[86] A major factor that played into these deliberations was women's duration of employment.

If the prevailing assumption about women's work was that it did not require any specific skills, the second was that women were transient workers. Setting aside the accuracy of these claims for a moment, let us focus on how this assumption plays out in labour control practises. The assumption that women are transient workers due to marriage has been prevalent across time and space, and feminist research has questioned this as an overstatement since the late 1970s.[87] The circulation of the image of factory women as temporary workers aids managerial control by reproducing the image of women as marginal labour. The idea that women belong primarily and eventually to the private sphere positions women as a ready source of secondary labour willing to accept jobs with little or no career prospects. It thus reproduces the primacy of women workers' gender identity over their work identity. Low wages, long hours, and little or no prospects for advancement are, in turn, the effects of this assumption.[88]

What limited evidence exists in the Turkish case does not support the claim that female work was intrinsically more unstable. A comparison of turnover rates at the weavery, where the majority of workers were male, and the spinnery, where the majority of workers were female, in a state textile factory suggests a much lower turnover rate for women in 1943.[89] Two years later, factory inspectors broke down the turnover rate in state textile factories by several categories, including sex, and found that women's turnover rate was proportionate to their percentage in the workforce.[90] Supporting evidence for this came in later reports, which attributed labour turnover and productivity problems to extremely low per-

---

86 Ziyaeddin Fahri Fındıkoğlu, "Türkiye'de Sinai Sosyoloji Araştırmaları 1-Defterdar Fabrikası," *Feshane Mensucat Meslek Dergisi* 2, 12 (1954): 393.

87 Judy Lown, "Not So Much a Factory, More a Form of Patriarchy: Gender and Class During Industrialisation," in *Gender, Class, and Work*, edited by Eva Gamarnikow, David H.J. Morgan, June Purvis, and Daphne E. Taylorson (London: Heinemann, 1983), 28–45; Anna Pollert, "Women, Gender Relations and Wage Labour," in., Gamarnikow, et al., eds, *Gender, Class, and Work* , 96–114; Aihwa Ong, "The Gender and Labor Politics of Postmodernity," *Annual Review of Antropology* 20 (1991): 279–309; Sally Alexander, Anna Davin, and Eve Hostettler, "Labouring Women: A Reply to Eric Hobsbawm," *History Workshop* 8 (1979): 174–182.

88 Louise A. Tilly, "Gender and Jobs in Early Twentieth-Century French Industry," *International Labour and Working-Class History* 43 (1993): 31–47; Ong, "Gender and Labor Politics": 287; Paul Thompson, *The Nature of Work: An Introduction to Debates on the Labour Process* (London: Palgrave, 1993), 180–209; Alice Kessler-Harris, *Out to Work: A History of Wage-Earning Women in the United States* (New York: Oxford University Press, 1983), 301.

89 Hösli, *Nazilli*, 8.

90 "İşletmede İnsan": 14–18.

centages of women in the industrial workforce compared with other late industrialising economies such as Greece and Italy. The solution lay in recruiting more women, the inspectors claimed.[91]

Accompanying the image of women as transient workers was the assumption surrounding women's motive to work, which came up in the discussions on wage payment systems. Believing that most employment and labour relations problems could be solved through a properly devised incentive wage, industrial experts pressed for its wider and better use. The high level of mechanisation, the lack of an effective labour movement, and the primacy of hard and attentive work for high productivity, they argued, created the perfect conditions for the successful implementation of a piece-rate wage system.[92] The method was simple enough to be understood by "the simplest of the workers," an expert with experience in the American textile industry added, but there was one group of workers who would not have an interest in this payment system: the girls, "because they are obliged to give their earnings away to their families anyway."[93] The private employer, who we heard complaining of men's unproductivity at women's jobs in the above pages, similarly claimed that girls were not that productive either "because they are forced to work by their families."[94]

Restricted to expert reports in the 1930s, the question of why women work at factories spilled over to the trade union and middle-class feminist press in the late 1940s as the postwar years witnessed the emergence of a broader consumer culture that increasingly shaped work and leisure.[95] With the proliferation of the media image of the frivolous factory girl, the management of female desire for consumption emerged as a powerful tool in the social regulation of femininity on the shop floor. The issue of where young factory girls spent their earnings was commonly discussed in terms of two sets of questions: morality and the national economy. Portraits of young women on the shop floor oscillated between the image of the adolescent girl orphaned or with sick parents and dragged into paid work during household exigencies and the image of the irresponsible and selfish factory girl making superfluous consumption choices that were damaging to their families and

---

91 "Sümerbank İplik ve Dokuma Fabrikaları Müessesesi 1948 Yılı Raporu": 30–31.
92 Max Von der Porten, "Feshane ve Hereke Fabrikaları Tetkiklerine Dair," Register K.A./ 255.07.02.01.06.1285 (1936); Hösli, Bakırköy Bez Fabrikası Hakkında Rapor, Archival Collection of the Republic of Turkey Prime Ministry Supreme Audit Board. Amb. /Db. No: K.A./ 255.07.02.01.06. 1241 255.07.02.01.06.1241.
93 Klopfer, Sümerbank Memur ve Amelelerine Prim ve İkramiye Esasları, Archival Collection of the Republic of Turkey Prime Ministry Supreme Audit Board. Amb. /Db. No: K.A./ 255.07.02.01.06.1263.
94 "Santral Mensucat Fabrikası," Hürbilek.
95 Kessler-Harris, Out to Work, 303.

the nation. While external discourses on working women coded normative categories of gender and labour, concerns for the chastity and femininity of factory women strengtened the foreman's grip on the shop floor. The foreman strictly regulated women workers' physical appearances, including their hairstyle, makeup, and clothes. Muazzez remembers being forced to wear a black headscarf by her foreman: "He was very strict, he did not like us paying attention to our appearance," she lamented, "for example, he did not allow us to wear silk stockings, we had to wear thick, black stockings, blue overalls and wooden slippers at work, we were not allowed to keep our shoes on."[96]

The strict discipline over women's bodily appearance was accompanied by a close monitoring of their work effort, which is easily detectable in another popular trope of factory women. In the postwar period, there was widespread use of mechanistic metaphors to depict the industrial female body in both trade union publications and the middle-class feminist press where notions of female "efficiency" and "productivity" were articulated on an unprecedented scale. In most of these depictions, female work intensification is associated with the utilisation of so-called feminine characteristics, and women's high productivity is cited as a natural product of their female qualities such as diligence and endurance for fast, monotonous work. Dazzled by the work speed in the all-female workshops of the tobacco, cigarette box, and textile factories, middle-class observers were proud to witness "the patience and the endurance of the Turkish women worker."[97]

Contrary to male experts and employers' claims about the unsuitability of incentive wages for young women workers, scattered evidence suggests that women liked the piece-rate system, and the foremen used this against them. When there were problems with product quality, Muazzez remembers, the foreman made them work on daily wages. Between 1944 and 1949, Şükriye quit the textile factory where she worked three times, and each time she returned, she asked to change her department from maintenance, where she was paid an hourly wage, to another department where a piece-rate was implemented.[98] Young girls working at cigarette box and liqueur factories proudly showed off the golden bracelets they had bought with their piece-rate earnings.[99]

---

96 Muazzez Atalay, interview by the author, 4 June 2019.
97 Paşabahçe Rakı Fabrikasında," *Türk İşçisi*, (4 January 1947); "Cibali Kutu Fabrikasında: Makineden Üstün Randıman Veren İşçiler," *Türk İşçisi*, (30 August 1947); Selahattin Güngör, "Bir Yün-İplik İmalathanesini Gezdim," *Türk İşçisi*, (1 November 1947); Muzaffer Daysal, "Kutu Fabrikasının 1200 Canlı Makinesi Arasında Bir Gün", *Hürbilek*, (2 February 1949).
98 Personnel file of Şükriye Ürer (Demir).
99 "Cibali Kutu Fabrikasında: Makineden Üstün Randıman Veren İşçiler," *Türk İşçisi*, (30 August 1947).

Despite the fascination of their contemporaries with women's machine-like bodily movements, the majority of the women in tobacco and cigarette manufacturing did not tend machines. In tobacco manufacturing, for example, they remained in traditional sex-typed occupations such as the separation and sorting of tobacco leaves. The mechanisation of tasks undertaken by men, however, increased their pace of work directly, while indirectly increasing the pressure on women performing manual tasks. A similar trend was observable in the cotton textile industry, which suffered from yarn shortages in the 1930s. When the automation of the weaving looms exacerbated problems of production integration between the spinnery and weavery in textile factories, women spinners had to work day and night to supply enough yarn for the weavers.[100] Zarife acquired a nickname in this process: Because she moved so fast behind the loom, her shop floor name was "young goat." Exhausted from work, she and her fellow workers got often caught sleeping in the bathroom and were scolded by their foremen. When she arrived at home, Zarife often could not eat due to exhaustion; sleep was all she wanted. Sleep deprivation and exhaustion were especially hard during the night shift, Cazibe remembers.[101] In 1943, a foreign expert called the operation of state textile factories "the anxiety to increase production," and defined it as a combination of a lack of scientific labour control and a managerial mentality of getting the most out of the workers and the machines.[102]

Things were no better for tobacco women. In the 1930s, a change in the method of tobacco processing further aggrevated women's health on the shop floor. A form of processing known as "tonga" gradually displaced more labour intensive methods of classifying leaves in multiple categories and placing them accordingly in boxes. In the tonga method, tobacco leaves of different qualities were placed together in the same bale, speeding up the labour process at the expense of damaging the quality of the final product.[103] Zehra Kosova noted the increase in miscar-

---

100 Hösli, *Bakırköy*, 6; "Sümerbank Birleşik Pamuk İpliği ve Dokuma Fabrikaları Müessesesi 1940 Yılı Raporu," in *Sümerbank 1940 Senesi Faaliyet ve Hesap Devresine Ait İdare Meclisi Raporu, Bilanço, Kar ve Zarar Hesabı*, Archival Collection of the Republic of Turkey Prime Ministry Supreme Audit Board. Amb. /Db. No: K.A./ 255.07.02.01.06.3231, 17, 25; Selim Cavid, "İpekiş Yünlü Mensucat Fabrikası İstihsal Kapasitesini Bulamıyor," *İktisadi Yürüyüş* 4 (1940): 16; Kemal H. Karpat, *Turkey's Politics: The Transition to a Multi-Party System* (New Jersey: Princeton University Press, 2016), 90; Sümerbank Genel Müdürlük Yüksek Katına, "Fabrikalarımızın," 12.
101 Ayten Günüvar, interview by author, 5 June 2019; Cazibe Doğan, interview by author, 5 June 2019.
102 Hösli, *Bakırköy*, 19.
103 Juan Carmona Zabala, "State Expansion and Economic Integration: A Transnational History of Oriental Tobacco in Greece and Germany (1880–1941)," (unpublished doctoral dissertation, University of California at San Diego, 2018), 232–235.

riages among tobacco women after the introduction of the tonga method.[104] At a 1951 trade union meeting of tobacco workers in Istanbul, a male unionist claimed women working with this method "writhed in agony."[105] As did the women textile workers. After long years of working at the heavy looms, women suffered from a variety of health problems. Instead of assigning these skilled workers lighter jobs, male managers laid them off because they could not keep up with the pace of production.[106] On the Turkish shop floors of the 1930s and 1940s, patriarchy and capitalism interconnected to ensure that productivity through work intensification and male authority bolstered each other.

Conclusion

Although the persistent sexual division of labour on the shop floor and its economic functions is a constant across all industrial contexts, the combination of workplace and extra-workplace mechanisms through which it is established and perpetuated are context specific. The indestructability of the socioproductive hierarchy on the shop floor across time and space can be explained by reference to the particular class and gender configurations in specific historical settings. The simultaneous processes of secular state-building and industrialisation in the 1930s and 1940s gave a peculiar character to that configuration in the Turkish case.

In the context of rising interwar economic nationalism, the young Turkish state adopted a policy of industrialisation based on light and labour intensive manufacturing. From its onset, this wave of industrialisation was characterised by interrelated problems of labour productivity and instability on the one hand, and low levels of female employment on the other. The state, with the help of middle-class intellectuals, resorted to a set of cultural discourses that built on nationalism, secularism, and citizenship identity to increase female industrial labour participation. But these efforts proved largely ineffective.

In a climate where more was asked of women in the workforce, instead of enacting and effectively enforcing protective legislation for women's wage work and improving women's conditions of industrial work on the shop floor, the state appealed to a narrative of women's citizenship rights and duties related to work. Two sets of discourses based on women's role in the national development effort effectively obscured their conditions of work on and off the shop floor: The glori-

---

104 Zehra Kosova, *Ben İşçiyim*, 57–58.
105 "Tütün El İşçilerinin Sezon Davası Artık Halledilmelidir," *İşçi Hakkı*, (12 July 1951).
106 Hasene Ilgaz, "Hastalık ve Analık Sigortası: Çalışan İşçiyi Hasta Olmadan Önce İşverenin Koruması Gerekir," *Kadın Gazetesi*, (26 December 1949).

fication of women's right to industrial work as a consequence of their emancipation from the Ottoman patriarchy, and their duty to work as an opportunity for patriotic service. These state discourses have influenced popular thinking and have been encoded into state policies.

In this context of repressive industrialisation and nation-building, laws protecting women workers had less to do with the public debate on women's work, as was the case with earlier legislation outside of Turkey. In the absence of pressure from an independent feminist movement and a trade union movement until the late 1940s, the Turkish state did not effectively enhance the protection of women workers. Protection for factory women was restricted to maternity-related issues without the establishment of childcare provision, which lies at the very heart of the inequalities in the employment market. Other significant issues such as wages, protection at work, and equal opportunities were completely excluded from the legal domain. Still, this minimal and half-enforced protective legislation was successfully presented as a bestowment on factory women.

Although appeals to state feminism and patriotism failed to "lure" women into the factories, poverty brought them to the shop floor. And what awaited them there was far from the celebratory images that filled the pages of the mainstream press in the 1930s and the trade union and women's press in the second half of the 1940s. While factory women served as motifs of social, economic, and cultural change, not much changed for them on the shop floor. The gendered order of labour and its hierarchically interpreted differences remained intact as women's industrial employment followed the historically well-known structures of production with gendered valorisation of wages and skill and a moral disciplining of working women's bodies that made use of the sexual divisions within society. Low wages, harassment under gendered disciplinary regimes, unhealthy conditions, punishment for minor infractions, and work intensification conspired to make the factories a living hell for women.

Women suffered from a lack of a voice to resist these gender-specific forms of labour control that emerged in the nationally specific social structure of accumulation. The combination of a state feminist discourse and work intensification under the authority of the foreman enabled employers to get high levels of productivity from their female workers with little resistance. Reinforcing each other, these two forces created a passive female labour force employed in jobs that required rapid performance of repetitive tasks. Thus, in this essay, women workers appear acted upon rather than the actors. But this would change in later years, with the smoldering undercurrent of women's discontent on the shop floor rising to the surface, as we have seen in Emine's story. The first signs of women challenging the socioproductive hierarchy at work were not seen until the 1950s, when women began to question wage inequity, and thereby challenge the gendered hierarchies of power that treated their factory work as marginal and appropriate to their gender role. In the industrial disputes of the 1960s and 1970s, women demonstrated considerable militancy and determination. That history still waits to be written and given the urgency and relevance of gender discrimination at work in contemporary Turkey it needs to be written soon.

Christian Strümpell

6 The Politics of and in (Re-)Production in an Eastern Indian Company Town

Steel and Labour in Independent India

Throughout the twentieth century, the Indian steel industry was considered of utmost national importance, economically, politically, and socially. Since its beginnings in the early twentieth century, the Mumbai-based capitalist, Tata, and the large steel enterprise he had built in Jamshedpur were closely connected to the independence movement.[1] The three public sector steel plants built by the government of India in the 1950s were cornerstones for nation-building after the country's independence in 1947.[2] They were supposed to buttress India's hard-won political independence by granting the country economic autarchy from advanced industrialised countries. Another purpose was to integrate the country's mineral-rich – yet backward – internal peripheries in central eastern India into the emerging national economy, and, by locating the three steel plants across three different union states, to boost a regionally balanced development. They were, in the words of India's first prime minister, Jawaharlal Nehru, the "temples of modern India."[3]

These large steel plants were also supposed to set the standards for the relation between (state) capital and labour in India. In the first half of the twentieth century, Tata workers had successfully fought for security of employment, maximum working hours, minimum wages, paid holidays, pensions, and the right to union representation, which made it the national archetype of a formally employed workforce.[4] The three post-independence public sector steel plants, like other public sector industries, were also expected to act as model employers, providing the same standards as Tata from the outset. It was hoped that this benevolence would contribute to the larger ideological mission of Nehruvian nation-

---

1 Vinay Bahl, *The Making of the Indian Working Class. A Case of the Tata Iron and Steel Company, 1880–1946* (New Delhi: Sage, 1995); Andrew Sanchez, *Criminal Capital. Violence, Corruption and Class in Industrial India* (New Delhi: Routledge, 2016).

2 Srirupa Roy, *Beyond Belief: India and the Politics of Postcolonial Nationalism* (Durham: Duke University Press, 2007), 133–137; Sunil Khilnani, *The Idea of India* (London: Penguin Books, 2003 [1997]), 61–106.

3 Khilnani, *The Idea of India*; Jonathan Parry and Christian Strümpell, "On the Desecration of Nehru's 'Temples': Bhilai and Rourkela Compared," *Economic and Political Weekly* 43, 19 (2008): 47–57.

4 Sanchez, *Criminal Capital*, 17.

https://doi.org/10.1515/9783111086552-007

building. Public sector workforces were to become "producer patriots," relentlessly working to – quite literally – build the nation,[5] not only by moulding steel, but also socially, by becoming truly modern, secular, and socialistic Indians.

Since the internal peripheries were relatively sparsely populated and the local residents had little industrial experience, the labour that was required to build and run the steel plants had to be largely drawn from elsewhere in India. The steel workforces were thus heterogeneous. By working together in a modern steel factory, as well as living together in the modern townships that were built on the green field sites alongside the plants, and all under the guidance of a benevolent state employer, public sector steel workers and their families would inevitably transcend their "primordial" identities of ethnicity, religion, and caste. As such, they would not only form secular, modern "mini Indias," but also represent a model for the nation at large.[6]

Behind the benevolence of these public sector industries also lay hard-nosed motivations. These industries had to attract workers to their remote locations and turn them into a stable workforce. Furthermore, as key industries, they formed neuralgic points for the state's developmentalist ambitions. The state was interested in co-opting workers, all the more so since a wave of strikes in the aftermath of World War Two had shown that labour was able to seriously flex its muscle.[7] The fear of a radicalisation of industrial workers was widespread among politicians, bureaucrats, and capitalists.[8] To avert working-class unity, they also encouraged the affiliation of trade unions to different, rival parties; and to avert a direct confrontation between employers and workers, the state made arbitration compulsory and appeared itself as a third principal party in all disputes.[9] Over time, the legal and political measures greatly succeeded in dividing labour

---

5 Satish Deshpande, "Imagined Economies. Styles of Nation-Building in Twentieth Century India," *Journal of Arts and Ideas* 25–26 (1993): 25; see also Roy, *Beyond Belief*, 147.

6 Roy, *Beyond Belief*, 155.

7 Ravi Ahuja, "Das Ähnliche speist den Unterschied: Die globale Wohlfahrtsdebatte und die Erzeugung 'informeller Arbeit' im Indien des 20. Jahrhunderts," in *Arbeit in globaler Perspektive. Facetten informeller Beschäftigung*, edited by Hans-Jürgen Burchardt, Stefan Peters, and Nico Weinmann (Frankfurt and New York: Campus, 2013), 132; Vivek Chibber, "From Class Compromise to Class Accommodation: Labor's Incorporation into the Indian Political Economy," in *Social Movements and Poverty in India, edited by* Mary Katzenstein and Raka Ray *(Rowman* and Littlefield Publishers, 2005), 38–39.

8 Chibber, "From Class Compromise to Class Accommodation": 38–39; Ahuja, "Das Ähnliche speist den Unterschied": 132; Jan Breman, "The Formal Sector: An Introductory Review," in *The Worlds of Indian Industrial Labour*, edited by Jonathan P. Parry, Jan Breman, and Karin Kapadia (New Delhi: Sage Publications, 1999), 30–31.

9 Breman, "The Formal Sector," 31.

along the lines of formal and informal employment.[10] As has also been amply documented, the liberalisation of the Indian economy – slowly and by stealth since the early 1970s, and officially and faster since the 1990s – gave rise to a shift among formal sector undertakings. While they relied on supplementary informal labour in the 1970s and 1980s, since the 1990s they increasingly employed informal labour to replace the formal workforce.[11]

This essay discusses how this politics of production, that is, the intervention of third actors external to the relation of conflict and cooperation between (state) capital and labour within an economic undertaking, impinges on the politics in production, that is, these very relations between capital and labour in a given undertaking.[12] I focus on one of the three post-independence public sector steel plants, the steel plant in the town Rourkela where I have conducted ethnographic research intermittently between 2004 and 2014, lived among and talked continuously and extensively to steel plant workers, unionists and executives, as well as other inhabitants.[13] The Rourkela Steel Plant is one of India's biggest steel plants, employing 15,000 executives and workers (as of 2014) and producing annually around four million tonnes of steel, particularly special silicon steels, pipes, and flats. The town of Rourkela is a provincial industrial town of 550,000 inhabitants situated in a far-off corner of the eastern Indian state of Odisha. Rourkela was selected as the site for the steel plant because the surrounding region offered abundant reserves in iron ore and other essential minerals, water, and – thanks a newly constructed nearby large dam – an electricity supply. It was also already connected by rail to India's major industrial centres in Kolkata and Mumbai. A further reason was that Odisha in 1954 was among India's poorest states and in need of development. This was even more the case in the Rourkela region, which was primarily inhabited by various "tribal" or Adivasi communities engaged in subsistence agriculture and whom the upper-caste elite considered particularly backward.

---

10 See Jonathan Parry, "Company and Contract Labour in a Central Indian Steel Plant," *Economy and Society* 42, 3 (2013): 348–374.

11 See Parry, "Company and Contract Labour in a Central Indian Steel Plant": 348–374; Christian Strümpell, "The Politics of Dispossession in an Odishan Steel Town," *Contributions to Indian Sociology (n.s.)* 48, 1 (2014): 45–72; Sanchez, *Criminal Capital.*

12 See the introductory and concluding chapters in this volume.

13 My ethnographic research in Rourkela extended over roughly 32 months conducted in intervals between 2004 and 2014. I gratefully acknowledge the support of the German Research Council (DFG), the Max-Planck-Institute for Social Anthropology, Halle, Germany, and the research centre Work and Human Lifecycle in Global History at Humboldt University Berlin. I am also deeply indebted to Marcel van der Linden and Nicole Mayer-Ahuja for their insightful comments on earlier drafts of this article, and to Rajat Singh, Zoober Ahmed and Ganesh Hembram for their invaluable research assistance. The usual disclaimers apply.

In what follows, I show that the relations between (state) capital and labour that evolved in RSP revolved as much around labour recruitment as around labour processes, and that, in both instances, ethnic and caste identifications played a major role in how these relations were experienced, contested, and negotiated. I also demonstrate that it was the highly ethnicised project of regional state formation being pursued by the regional elite in Odisha that was driving this dynamic, which can be seen even more decisively in the late 1960s, when Odisha gained substantial powers with regard to labour recruitment to and labour representation in RSP. Shortly after, however, RSP began to rely increasingly on precariously employed contract workers, and slowly but zealously cut the number of relatively well remunerated and securely employed company workers – by natural attrition rather than by retrenchment. During more recent decades, especially in the wake of India's transition to economic (neo)liberalisation in the 1990s, employment status replaced ethnicity and caste as the major fault line between workers at RSP. This fault line was not only economic, but increasingly also social and – apart from one historical moment in the early 1990s – also political. It was at this moment that the first generation of company workers, who were close to retirement, perceived casualisation as a threat to the reproduction of their class position. Thus, the politics of and in production relates, I argue, to what could be termed the politics of and in social reproduction.

The RSP Workforce, 1950s to the 1980s

Construction work on RSP started in 1956, and the first departments were commissioned from early 1959 onward. During the construction period, RSP employed only a relatively small number of executive and non-executive staff for essential services such as the supply of water. In April 1959, RSP had a workforce of 2,630.[14] By 1965, when the first wave of recruitment had slackened, it counted 25,000.

Although women made up a relatively large part of the temporarily employed workforce involved in the construction of RSP, those recruited to run it were almost exclusively male, thus revealing the narrowly gendered notion of the "modern industrial worker".[15] The workforce was also very heterogeneous in terms of caste and ethnicity. Contrary to expectations, this heterogeneity was not transcended by their working together at RSP. Rather, caste and ethnic difference was exa-

---

14 Jan B. Sperling, *Rourkela. Sozio-ökonomische Probleme eines Entwicklungsprojekts* (Bonn: Eichholz Verlag. 1963).
15 RSP employed women only as office staff, as teachers in company schools and as doctors and nurses in the company hospital.

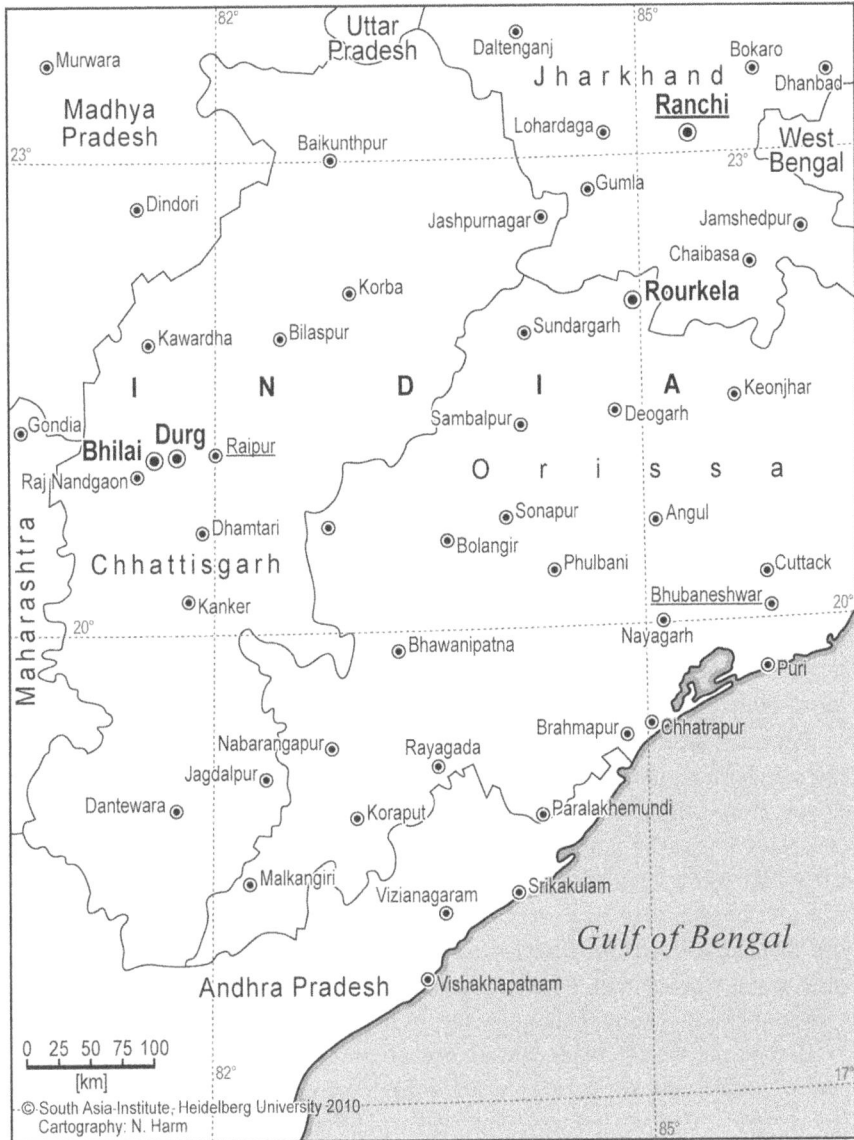

Fig. 1: Rourkela in Odisha (until 2010 spelt Orissa) and Eastern India
Source: The map was produced by Nils Harm, cartographer at the South Asia Institute Heidelberg, who kindly gave the permission to reproduce it here free of cost.]

cerbated, especially among the first generation of workers, who were recruited in the late 1950s and early 1960s and began to enter retirement in the early 1990s.

This can be attributed to the way ethnicity and caste defined a worker's position in the company. Clerks were largely Malayalam, from the southern Indian state of Kerala, skilled operators were Punjabi, Bengali, or Bihari, while the semi- and unskilled workers under their supervision had an Odia and Adivasi background. This ethnic clustering of (blue- and white-collar) workers in the formal set up of RSP contradicted the official Nehruvian vision of public sector steel plants. However, as interlocutors in Rourkela explained, it came about because of the discretionary powers enjoyed by departmental heads at the time in labour recruitment. RSP only acquired a personnel department in 1963,[16] and until then, departmental executives would have the final say in employment selection. Executives used these discretionary powers regardless of workers' ethnic and caste belonging, at least in theory. Executives were predominantly from other Indian states and are reported to have preferred their co-ethnics, especially for supervisory posts, hiring Odia and Adivasi only as unskilled underlings.

RSP executives were in a position to choose how to distribute jobs because there was no scarcity of labour in Rourkela. The surrounding region had until then been relatively sparsely populated, but soon after construction started thousands flocked to Rourkela from near and far. By 1961, their numbers stood at 76,000.[17] As soon as construction work ended and construction companies retrenched workers, the number of applicants far exceeded the number of jobs available at RSP.

Once at RSP, workers depended on the goodwill of RSP executives to retain their jobs because they were initially only employed on a temporary basis. For skilled operator positions, either workers would be hired temporarily from the Tata steel plant in nearby Jamshedpur or trainees would be recruited to be trained at the Tata plant or on the job at RSP. For unskilled posts, RSP took on workers on a muster roll, that is, as casual workers with the prospect of regularisation once they proved capable of performing their job. Whether they were deemed capable or not was again at the discretion of departmental executives. This was one important tool that granted them the means to discipline workers, at least initially.

Despite the discretionary powers executives enjoyed with regard to employment, at least some workers were not entirely powerless in the process, too. In 1959, several hundred trainees who had completed their training at the Tata steel plant organised a strike to press for their promised yet – in their eyes arbi-

---

16 Kshetra M. Sahoo, *Industrial Democracy* (New Delhi: Deep & Deep Publishers, 1989), 105–106.
17 Sperling, *Rourkela*, 22.

trarily – delayed regularisation, with the higher pay this would bring.[18] The trainees organised the strike autonomously, but they soon gained the support of the Rourkela Workers Union (RWU), a small union affiliated with the trade union wing of the Socialist Unity Centre of India, a small revolutionary left party that was already active among construction workers in Rourkela. The state and RSP management were both anxious to prevent this or any other "red flag" union from gaining a foothold among the workforce, and the police came down heavily on the strikers and the unionists, baton-charging and arresting many of them.[19] Another union, the Hindustan Steel Workers Association, which was affiliated with the Indian National Trade Union Congress (INTUC), the umbrella trade union organisation of the Congress, i.e. the party ruling at the national level and in the state Odisha then, sensed its chance to establish itself in Rourkela and stepped in then. It took the view that if skilled operators were to take up influential positions at RSP, organising them would also generate influence for their union. It was thanks to its connections with the Congress, my interlocutors had no doubt, that INTUC succeeded in negotiating the regularisation of the trainees. This meant that workers could circumvent the discretionary powers of management in the recruitment process if they had the backing of powerful state actors.

Over time, the state began to intervene more actively in the recruitment process at RSP. In 1961, the government of the state Odisha set up an employment exchange in Rourkela, where RSP was expected to source candidates for vacancies. In the early years, recruitment through departmental channels nevertheless remained the rule. In 1968, however, the national government made it mandatory for public sector undertakings to channel recruitments for non-executive posts through employment exchanges.[20] Employment exchanges fell under the jurisdiction of regional states, not of the central state. Hence, this amendment effectively granted the regional states control over the recruitment process. In the case of RSP, this had profound consequences because the state of Odisha had a keen interest in distributing the privileged employment offered by RSP to the "sons of the soil." Public sector industries were supposed to promote regional as well as national de-

---

18 In 1958, the daily wages of muster roll workers increased from 1.50 to 2.00 rupees (see Arun K. Patnaik, "Formation of the Working Class. A Study of the Labour Force of the Rourkela Steel Plant," Ph.D. thesis, Jawaharlal Nehru University, 1990, 158). That was actually the same amount that unskilled contract workers earned on RSP's construction sites. Supervisory RSP workers, by contrast, were entitled to a monthly wage of 250 rupees (see Pravat K. Mohanty, *Collective Bargaining in the Steel Industry* [Delhi: Discovery, 1988], 185).

19 See Patnaik, *Formation of the Working Class*, 200.

20 Myron Weiner, *Sons of the Soil: Migration and Ethnic Conflict in India* (Princeton, NJ: Princeton University Press, 1978), 339.

velopment. As part of that goal, the local population was expected to be integrated into the workforce. The state of Odisha used this argument to complain about the overrepresentation of foreigners in the RSP workforce, while RSP management countered that the locals' industrial skills were too low to recruit any more. Elder interlocutors in Rourkela agreed that in the first decade, roughly one-third of RSP workers were locals, both Odia and Adivasi, with two-thirds coming from other states. However, the central government's amendments to the formal recruitment process in 1968 granted the Odisha state government the means to pursue its nativist agenda at RSP. State government officers *sub rosa* instructed staff at the Rourkela employment exchange, several unionists and executives told me, to see that jobs at RSP went to locals, and they used ethnic, rather than territorial identifications to define who was a local and who was not. Jobseekers who had been brought up in Rourkela during the 1960s but were not ethnically Odia, for example as sons of RSP workers, would be screened out by staff at the Rourkela exchange.

In the same period, RSP expanded old departments, such as the blast furnaces, to increase steel production from one to 1.8 million tonnes per annum, and opened new mills, such as special pipe plants, to grow its portfolio. For these departments, RSP recruited workers in large numbers. The RSP workforce once again ballooned, from 25,000 in 1966 to 37,000 in 1974. The queues of applicants for the new jobs at RSP were long. Although, by then, a viable ancillary industry, mostly in the private sector, had developed in Rourkela, the jobs they offered were no match for RSP in terms of wages, fringe benefits, and security of employment. In 1972, the monthly wage for an unskilled worker in any of the private industries on Rourkela's industrial estate would not exceed seventy-five rupees, as unionists active on the estate then told me. At RSP, by contrast, the monthly wage for unskilled workers stood at 125 rupees in 1965, rising to 240 rupees in 1970, and 393 rupees in 1975.[21] Similar wage disparities also applied to skilled workers. However, the Odia officers at the Rourkela employment exchange saw to it that the large majority of the new, much-coveted RSP jobs went to Odia – both unskilled workers but also, since many more Odia had undergone industrial training by then, skilled workers.[22] As a result, the makeup of the RSP workforce became increasingly Odia.

This drive to preferentially distribute the relatively privileged public sector jobs at RSP among the supposed autochthons had its roots in the strong nativist sentiments prevailing in Odisha at the time. These sentiments date back to late-nineteenth-century colonialism, when self-declared Odia nationalists demanded

---

21 Mohanty, *Collective Bargaining in the Steel Industry:* 187–198.
22 The small census I conducted in 2008 on one work group in an electrical resistance welding pipe plant that opened in the late 1960s shows that the 23 workers are almost exclusively Odia, thus confirming this widespread assumption.

the amalgamation of all Odia-speaking tracts into a separate political entity within British India. These tracts were scattered across the British-Indian territories of the Bengal and Madras Presidencies, the Central Provinces, and a few small kingdoms under indirect British rule. Odia nationalists claimed that Odia-speaking minorities in these British-Indian territories were marginalised by the Bengali, Telugu, or Hindi-speaking majorities, that members of these "intermediary ruling races" monopolised positions in the lower rungs of the colonial administration open to Indians educated in colonial institutions, and that they were driving Odia landlords off their land.[23] As this suggests, Odia nationalism was promoted primarily by a frustrated local elite of landlords and a small urban-educated intelligentsia. This elite finally succeeded, and Odisha was granted regional statehood, initially in 1936 during the last years of colonial rule, over the densely populated, fertile eastern lowlands on the coast where the state capital and most other urban and religious centres were located. Later, in 1948, shortly after India's independence, Odisha state was widened to encompass the relatively sparsely populated, forested hilly uplands, where Rourkela is situated. However, the Odia elite continued to see itself as disadvantaged at the hands of other Indians with more leverage over the central government and its funds.[24] RSP was supposed to turn the tide, but it only revived this sense of unfulfilled entitlement, when Bengali and other Indians acquired a dominant position in India's icon of industrial modernity on Odisha's soil. Asserting the interests of the "Odia nation" in Rourkela by laying claim to RSP jobs was deemed to be of paramount importance.

The Odia elite, of course, saw its own interests as congruent with those of the Odia nation, and it claimed jobs not only for manual workers but also for itself. Odia officers did come to occupy several important executive posts at RSP, such as head of the personnel department who had considerable discretionary powers over the workforce for example with regard to postings, promotions, and disciplinary action. The regional state thus not only formally appropriated some of the management's discretionary powers over labour recruitment, but it also began to informally take control of some of the institutions "that organize, transform or repress struggles over relations in production and relations of production at the level of the enterprise" – what Michael Burawoy calls the "internal state."[25] As is generally the case, at RSP, too, the internal state formed a sphere that is relatively autonomous from the "external state," but, as a public sector undertaking,

---

23 Frederick. G. Bailey, *The Need for Enemies: A Bestiary of Political Forms* (Ithaca: Cornell University Press, 1998), 32.
24 Bailey, *The Need for Enemies*, 31.
25 Michael Burawoy, *Manufacturing Consent. Changes in the Labor Process under Monopoly Capitalism* (Chicago: University of Chicago Press, 1979), 116–117.

this autonomy was naturally more compromised than in a private company in India or elsewhere, and the regional state took advantage of this.

RSP Workers, Unions, and the State, 1950s to the 1980s

During the first decades, RSP workers engaged in several collective actions that transcended rank and skill, as well as ethnicity and caste. In 1957, during the construction phase, 17,000 construction workers went on strike for retrenchment benefits that had been withheld by the private companies contracted by RSP. The strike was organised jointly by the far-left RWU and the Rourkela Mazdoor Sabha ("Rourkela Workers' Council"), a union affiliated with an all-India trade union umbrella organisation close to the moderately left Praja Socialist Party.[26] The majority of the strikers were unskilled workers from Odia and Adivasi backgrounds, but some belonged to other ethnic groups and castes, and the unionists were primarily Bengali. Similarly, the trainees striking for their regularisation in 1959 were largely, but not exclusively, Bengali. In the early 1960s, when RSP had started operating, workers from different departments engaged in several strikes, again often organised or co-organised by communist and socialist unions. They went on strike for a variety of reasons, most notably to press for the actual implementation of existing labour laws, or to call for the reinstatement of workmates who had been dismissed for their leftist union activities. In late 1966, the whole of the RSP workforce went on a major three-week strike to demand payment of the annual bonus. As these strikes show, workers and their unions had to press RSP management to grant them the benefits that were supposed to come with formal public sector employment, and they often succeeded.

However, such moments of relative working-class unity are only part of the picture, and a more exceptional one at that. In fact, already during the construction years, relations between Odia (and Adivasi) workers and workers from other backgrounds, particularly Bengali, Punjabi, and Madrasi, were tense, and frequently turned violent. At the root of the violence lay the stark inequalities between the relatively well paid, securely employed skilled construction workers who had come to Rourkela from other parts of India and the unskilled Odia and Adivasi workers who identified as locals. As mentioned above, these inequalities resurfaced at RSP, as did the tensions. Odia and Adivasi tended to find themselves posted in the ranks of unskilled workers under supervision of Bengali, Punjabi, Bihari, or south Indian

---

26 The all-India trade union umbrella organisation was the Hind Mazdoor Sabha.

operators, foremen, and executives. The former considered the authority of their supervisors arbitrary, and this was indeed often the case, given that the tasks and competencies of different grades of workers were yet to be formally defined. Knowing that executives would usually have the same regional ethnic background, workers in higher, supervisory grades often felt free to offload their work onto subordinate unskilled ethnic Others. Some of these subordinates had already gained industrial experience elsewhere and alleged that shop floor hierarchies were less a matter of skill than of shared ethnic ties. To add insult to injury, Odia and Adivasi workers also felt culturally ridiculed, as the retired workers I met in Rourkela recalled with a palpable sense of anger, for example, for their clumsy ways of speaking Hindi or Bengali, which served then as RSP's shop floor language rather than Odia or any of the Adivasi languages.

As Burawoy argues in his classic 1970s study on a Chicago machine shop, consciousness brought into factory settings from outside, such as ethnicity, may continue to shape workers' attitudes at work, but it only shapes their activities when it is reproduced in the specificities of a particular labour process.[27] The oral histories I gathered in my talks with elder or already retired RSP workers, unionists and executives do not reveal enough of the nitty-gritty of the everyday labour process to seriously probe whether or to what extent that is true for RSP. However, they clearly show that ethnic identifications in conjunction with differences in rank and skill began to tinge union politics and would be exacerbated by subsequent union rivalries. The Congress had a keen interest in establishing its own INTUC union in such a vital and prestigious industry, and in gathering the majority of workers behind it. All registered unions are legally allowed to represent workers, but only the union with the majority of members among the unionised workers of an undertaking, the so-called recognised union, is entitled to represent the workforce as a whole in collective bargaining with management.[28] After INTUC's success in the trainees' strike, many workers did go on to join their local branch, and the state government's labour department declared INTUC the RSP's recognised union in 1964. However, everybody I talked to in Rourkela agreed that most RSP workers joined INTUC for strategic reasons whereas, in fact, they preferred the RMS (especially after management and the state had successfully warded off the red flag RWU). As long-term Congress supporters in Rourkela also told me, INTUC union leaders sent from the headquarters in Delhi, as well as those dispatched from Jamshedpur to Rourkela, quickly gathered a coterie of

---

27 Burawoy, *Manufacturing Consent*, 140–157, 215.
28 The legal framework is the Industrial Disputes Act that applies to industrial relations in RSP, but not to organised sector industries in other states such as Madhya Pradesh.

loyal skilled operators and exhibited an extraordinary degree of arrogance toward all other workers. Whenever a conflict arose between workers and management, they usually advised workers to abide by management orders, arguing that RSP was a public sector undertaking of national importance. In protest against the high-handedness and alleged corruption among INTUC leaders, a local Congress stalwart founded a rival faction, which especially attracted unskilled workers, who were predominantly Adivasi and Odia. Many of these workers were quick to strike an Odia nationalist tone in their allegations concerning INTUC leaders and the skilled operators around them, who tended to be from Punjab, Bengal, Bihar, or southern India.

Most RSP workers actually preferred the RMS leaders, my interlocutors in Rourkela emphasised regardless of political affiliation and ethnic background, because they were cut from very different cloth to their INTUC rivals. They lived frugally, freely rubbed shoulders with all kinds of workers, and they were more militant in their approach to management, organising slow-downs and strikes when negotiations stalled. They aimed to organise workers from different ranks, skill, ethnicity, and caste. When the RMS was founded in Rourkela in 1956, its leading activists were Adivasi, Bihari, as well as Odia, and later a few Bengali also joined. Nevertheless, the union had its strongest support base among the unskilled Odia workers, which tinged its rivalry with INTUC with ethnic sentiments. The ethnic identification of the RMS also intensified over the years. In the late 1960s, RMS office bearers, from the shop floor to the plant level, were overwhelmingly Odia. This was at a time when ever more Odia were entering the RSP workforce thanks to the influence of the state government on recruitment. Of course, I came across several Odia interlocutors who had been working at RSP during the 1960s and 1970s and who accused the RMS of letting them down on one or several occasions. However, Bengali, Bihari, and Punjabi RSP workers of that time tended to unequivocally dismiss the RMS as an Odia union. When it came to support in conflicts with management or among workers, or regarding promotions, the allocation of remunerative overtime work, or the allotments of accommodation in the township, the RMS were seen as always backing their own people first, who were almost all Odia.

The political re-orientation of the RMS toward Odia nationalism was significant because it was accompanied by changes in its political status. In 1967, the Congress was voted out in several Indian states.[29] In Odisha, it was replaced by a coalition of a regional party and a Congress split-off faction committed to asserting Odia interests in Rourkela more firmly than its predecessor. The new government

---

[29] Ramachandra Guha, *India after Gandhi: The History of the World's Largest Democracy* (New York: Harper Collins, 2007), 417–144.

also relied on external support from the Praja Socialist Party, with which the RMS was closely affiliated. Ahead of the elections, a new general secretary took charge of the RMS and also contested the elections as the Socialist Party's candidate in the Rourkela constituency. He won and became one of the government's main confidants on Rourkela affairs. Thanks to these newly gained political connections to the state of Odisha, the RMS replaced INTUC as RSP's recognised union. It is the state government's labour department that verifies which union holds the majority of membership among a company's unionised workforce based on a sample of only two percent of the unionised workforce, and hence qualifies as its recognised union. Hence, it was taken for granted in Rourkela that political backing by the state government was critical for a union to turn the process to its favour.

This new political standing was accompanied by a new attitude to labour politics. As RMS veterans and retired managers explained to me, the new union leaders abandoned the militancy of their predecessors, choosing instead to follow a "responsible" approach focusing on negotiations with management. These negotiations did not include crucial issues such as pay scales, because these were set for all public sector steel plants by the wage board in the capital, New Delhi. Umbrella trade union associations were represented on the board, but the recognised unions of each steel plant had only a limited say.[30] Veteran RMS interlocutors, however, liked to boast about the successes reaped by the strategy. When, in the late 1960s, the RSP industrial engineering department conducted large-scale job evaluations across almost all departments, the RMS successfully lobbied for the involvement of union representatives. RMS veterans I was still able to meet in the early 2000s claimed that this resulted in the sanctioning of more posts in many departments, and often also in a higher grading of workers, which, in turn, meant higher wages. RMS unionists also prided themselves in management having agreed, at their behest, to install or to revive several bipartite committees at plant and department level for safety, grievances, production, and township welfare and amenities,[31] and that this greatly increased industrial democracy at RSP. However, the union representatives to the committees were nominated by the recognised union, rather than being elected by the workforce, and, under the critical gaze of the local employment exchange, newly sanctioned jobs primarily went to Odia applicants. The RMS's successes thus cemented its position, resulting in a *de facto* strengthening of Odia dominance at RSP.

---

30 The wage board consists of management representatives from each steel plant on one side and representatives of the federal trade union umbrella organisations plus one representative from the recognised union in each steel plant on the other. It was replaced by the Joint Wage Negotiation Committee in 1970, but it remained a bipartite body consisting of the same kinds of representatives.
31 Sahoo, *Industrial Democracy*, 169–192.

In many important regards, the RMS managed to curtail the discretionary powers of management. However, achieving this position of power relied on patronage from the regional state. In the process, it became enmeshed in the state's nativist political agenda and, consequently, effectively curtailed management's power more to the benefit of the nativist faction of the workforce than others. The Odia nationalism of the recognised union also attracted many workers identifying as Odia because it offered space to manoeuvre, first into RSP employment and, once in place, in conflicts between management and labour as well as among workers – in RSP's politics in production. And this was only thanks to changes in the politics of production during the late 1960s that afforded the state of Odisha greater scope to intervene at RSP and thus to set the (nativist) tone that the politics in production would take.

Adivasi Workers, 1950s to the 1980s

For obvious reasons, the changes described above in the politics of and in production restricted the room for manoeuvre of workers from other ethnic backgrounds, for example, Bengali workers, who often enjoyed good relations with co-ethnics in supervisory positions. Worse was the situation for Adivasi workers, however, who were also employed in large numbers at RSP. They either came from Rourkela and the surrounding villages or had migrated from adjacent districts. They saw themselves as the true locals, many of whom had indeed lost their small landholdings to the urban-industrial complex.[32] Upper-caste interlocutors usually assumed Adivasi to be uneducated and wild (*jungli*), and to drink excessively and eat all kinds of impure meats. They referred to these tribal characteristics also routinely when explaining to me what made Adivasis ideal manual labourers.

This upper-caste view of Adivasi-ness closely resembles colonial perceptions of the alleged distinctiveness of Adivasis, "aboriginals," or "tribals," which made them the perfect "coolie nation" to withstand the harsh working conditions in the Assam tea plantations.[33] In Rourkela, the same stereotypes saw RSP personnel managers assign Adivasis to RSP's iron and steel zone or to its "hot shops," the coke ovens, blast furnaces, and the steel melting shop where fumes, dust, and heat made working conditions extremely hazardous. The mill zone, by contrast, where steel ingots are rolled into sheets and welded into pipes, offered a much better working envi-

---

32 Strümpell, "The politics of dispossession."
33 See Prabhu Mohapatra, "Coolies and Colliers: A Study of the Agrarian Context of Labour Migration from Chota Nagpur, 1880–1920," *Studies in History* 1, 2 (1985): 247–303; Nitin Varma, *Coolies for Capitalism. Assam Tea and the Making of Coolie Labour* (Berlin: De Gruyter, 2016).

ronment. Adivasis rarely found themselves posted here, and, if at all, only for one the few heavy unskilled jobs, usually as slingers lifting pipes. Although upper-caste RSP executives, workers, and unionists legitimated these allocations along the labour process with reference to the low levels of schooling and technical training among Adivasis, even the few who were better qualified ended up toiling in the hot shops. Furthermore, retired RSP executives reported that few of the RSP workers recruited in the 1950s and 1960s had any vocational training; most had not even completed school and were usually illiterate. Adivasis, then, were not exceptional in their lack of formal education and technical skills. What set them apart was their lack of connection to those with discretionary powers, be it RSP executives or state representatives.

Adivasis, in many ways, aimed to resist the harsh control and exploitation they experienced at RSP. They did so temporally through absenteeism, which was said to have been particularly high among the Adivasi workers. RSP, like other public sector steel plants,[34] adopted a rather liberal approach in response to this practise, which may occasionally have led to sanctions but rarely to dismissal. The Adivasis contested the very notion of Adivasi-ness propagated by upper-caste executives as well as their co-workers and unionists.[35] The Adivasi workers I spoke to emphasised that it was their hard work that kept the whole plant running; they were the ones working in RSP's "mother departments," where the steel is actually produced.

The pride they took in their work did not mean that they were unaware of the extent of their exploitation. Not only were they posted in the hot shops, but they also had to do all the heavy and hazardous work there. Many of their upper-caste co-workers did little more than boss them around in cahoots with the upper-caste executives. Most upper-caste workers and executives were involved in this, irrespective of their ethnic background. However, my Adivasi interlocutors were unanimous in the view that Odia who had positions in or good relations with the RMS were particularly exploitative and particularly work-shy. The union, thus, offered no remedy for the Adivasi workers and quickly alienated them, if they had ever even felt that they belonged. Many joined a new union, the Ispat Shramik Sangh ("Steel Workers' Union"; ISS), which had been founded by a handful of educated, white-collar Adivasis together with some Odia from western Odisha. The ISS raised the banner for the exploited tribal worker, but it instantly gained support also from other workers who felt antagonised by the RMS, the Bengali, Punjabi, or other out-of-state migrants. Although Odia workers enjoyed strength in numbers

---

34 See Jonathan Parry in collaboration with Ajay T.G., *Classes of Labour: Work and Life in a Central Indian Steel Town* (New Delhi: Social Science Press, 2020), 244–247.
35 Christian Strümpell, "Struggles about Class and Adivasi-ness in an Eastern Indian Steel Plant," *Modern Asian Studies.* 56, 5 (2022): 1691–1714.

after the amendment of the recruitment process, elder unionists, workers, and executives estimate that almost half of the workforce was still non-Odia. Given its widespread support among many different constituencies of workers, the ISS was convinced that it held the majority among unionised RSP workers and demanded a new verification process. However, unlike the RMS, or, rather, like the RMS in the early 1960s, the ISS lacked political backing. It was unaffiliated with any of the major trade union umbrella organisations, maintaining only close political links with a small regional tribal party. Unsurprisingly, the state's labour department confirmed that the RMS still held the majority. Without any hope of gaining recognition, the union fell apart.

This episode again highlights the extent to which the regional state and its nativist agenda moulded the politics in production at RSP. It also reveals that the nativist agenda was primarily concerned with the upper-caste factions among the supposed autochthon workers but not with the lower-caste Adivasis among them. Thus, unimpeded by the external state, the particular position of Adivasi RSP workers in the labour process indeed reinforces their Adivasiness. In this instance, however, the labour process also enjoys only relative autonomy from what happens outside the factory, if not from the external state then from wider society.[36] The labour process at RSP reinforces the Adivasiness of the Adivasi workers because the executives with the discretionary powers to assign workers to their positions within it are predominantly upper-caste, who, conveniently, draw on widespread upper-caste prejudices against Adivasis in the process.

The fact that RSP engulfed much of the urban space in Rourkela also relativised the autonomy of the labour process from the town and neighbourhoods. As mentioned at the beginning, RSP built a full-fledged company township alongside the steel plant to accommodate the whole workforce and their families. Initially reckoning with a workforce of 15,000 plus 5,000 service providers, each a family of five, RSP planned a township with twenty thousand company quarters (and bungalows for executives) for 100,000 inhabitants. Given the rural backwater that the Rourkela region was at the time, a township like this was essential to attract and retain a stable workforce. Yet, just like the steel plant, the township was also supposed to form a mini-India whose heterogeneous inhabitants would transcend divisions of caste, regional ethnicity, and religion, to become model citizens, or producer-patriots. Thus, the township – and the steel towns in general – involved what could be termed a politics of reproduction. It also formed the groundwork for a politics *in* reproduction, for relations of conflict and cooperation between the company and its workforce in the context of local urban life. It was hoped that the dif-

---

36 See Burawoy, *Manufacturing Consent*, 152.

ferent township sectors would bring together executives and workers from all caste, ethnic, and religious backgrounds. In connivance with the RSP township department tasked with allotting company quarters, they became, rather, neighbourhoods of co-ethnics. What developed was not a melting pot, but a conglomeration of ethnic clusters.[37] Furthermore, already by the mid-1960s, the township had become too small to accommodate the entire workforce. Those who did not live in the township were predominantly RSP's Adivasi workers. Instead, they put up in the unplanned slums and labour colonies that interspersed the township sectors or had developed in the surrounding area, many of which had grown out of the small local villages that had not given way to the industrial-urban complex. As argued elsewhere,[38] in the slums they often had bigger houses than those offered to similarly low ranking RSP workers in the township, where women could often continue working small garden plots. Furthermore, in the slums they all could avoid the surveillance of and humiliation by snooty upper-caste neighbours, at least off work. Thus, experiences in the productive sphere of the factory are reflected in the (semi-autonomous) reproductive sphere in town.

Company and Contract Workers at RSP, 1970s to the 1990s

Since the late 1960s, roughly at the same time as when wages in the public sector really took off,[39] RSP management returned, as it had done for the plant's construction, to employing contract workers in large numbers. In the late 1960s, RSP employed 4,000 contract workers. By 1987, their numbers stood at ten thousand.[40] RSP did not employ them directly, but through chains of privately operating labour contractors and subcontractors. This meant that, unlike regular company workers, they did not enjoy legally sanctioned employment security, union representation, and standards of working conditions.[41] Contract workers were therefore cheaper and politically weaker than company workers. In contrast to RSP company work-

---

37 See Rajkishore Meher, *Stealing the Environment. Social and Ecological Effects of Industrialization in Rourkela* (New Delhi: Manohar, 2004), 139.

38 Christian Strümpell, "Precarious Labor and Precarious Livelihoods in an Indian Company Town," in *Industrial Labor on the Margins of Capitalism. Precarity, Class, and the Neoliberal Subject*, edited by Chris Hann and Jonathan Parry (New York: Berghahn, 2018), 146.

39 See above; Mohanty, *Collective Bargaining:* 187–198.

40 Nirmal Sengupta, *Contract Labour in the Steel Region: Rourkela* (Rourkela: Asian Workers Development Institute [mimeo], 1983), 51.

41 See Parry, "Company and Contract Labour"; Parry, *Classes of Labour,* 61–70.

ers, contract workers could be hired and fired at will, and, depending on their skill and gender, they would earn effectively between one-third and one-fifth of the amount earned by a regular worker.

While the company workforce was almost entirely male, women made up around one-third of the contract workforce. Since contract workers did not enjoy any security of employment, they faced greater difficulties in organising and confronting their employers. According to received local wisdom, management considered it less troublesome to employ contract workers for the most hazardous and strenuous tasks, for example cleaning and repair work in the hot shops, than to persuade or pressurise the regular public sector workers to do them. With this new category of worker, management built up a new 'frontier of control' at RSP. This frontier of control rested on the different employment relations enforced by management. Caste nevertheless exacerbated the control that management and contractors were able to exert on these workers. The contract workers would primarily be Adivasis from the wider region and from Rourkela's slums and labour colonies,[42] where also Adivasi RSP company workers lived, and the subordination they faced because of their caste in wider society imbued the power of capital over this category of labour with an additional edge.[43]

Yet, despite their precarious and temporary employment status, many were employed actually on a rather continuous basis. Sengupta states that one-third of the 144 contract workers he interviewed in the early 1980s worked for more than five years at RSP.[44] During my research in the 2000s, I also came across many who had worked at RSP for years or decades with only minor interruptions. Many contract workers were often also deployed in various departments, not in just one, as was usually the case for company workers. They frequently emphasised in our talks how they have seen the whole plant and therefore understand the production process at RSP much better than company workers. Even if that may be an exaggeration in an attempt to counter the disrespect harboured toward them by many company workers, many contract workers will certainly have acquired a considerable amount of informal knowledge about production processes at RSP despite their temporary and precarious employment. Given the importance

---

42 See Gail Omvedt, "Steel Workers, Contract Labourers and Adivasis," *Economic and Political Weekly* 16, 30 (1981): 1227–1229; Sengupta, *Contract Labour in the Steel Region*, 75.

43 See Jens Lerche and Alpa Shah, "Conjugated Oppression within Contemporary Capitalism: Class, Caste, Tribe and Agrarian Change in India," *The Journal of Peasant Studies* 45, 5–6 (2018): 927–949.

44 Sengupta, *Contract Labour in the Steel Region*, 112.

of such knowledge for efficiently operating production processes,[45] it is plausible that the stability of at least a core group of contract workers is the reason why RSP was able to outsource so many jobs to them. It is also plausible, I suggest, that it was the urban structures that had developed in Rourkela that helped to secure this stability of the contract workforce.

Public and formal sector industries across India had also begun to casualise labour around this time.[46] This shift is in line with a more general approach of the Government of India to liberalise the economy by stealth, to relax its licensing guidelines for the private sector, to restrain government expenditure, and to crush strikes seeking to opposing it.[47] The aim of this policy shift was to curb a grave economic crisis that was displaying staggering inflation rates triggered by, among other things, the 1971 Bangladesh Liberation War and the 1973 international oil shock crisis.[48] The remedies to overcome the crisis – cuts in public expenditure and curtailing formal employment – converged with wider global trends that took centre-stage in the third quarter of the twentieth century.[49] Obviously, the company is embedded in national and international political and economic structures, not only in wider society.

The restructuration of the Indian public sector has accelerated over the last 40 years. In the early 1990s, the Indian government began to break away even more decisively from the Nehruvian developmental paradigm. In 1991, a severe balance of payments crisis, which had built up partly due to the Gulf War, dwindling remittance payments from the Gulf, and rising oil prices, forced the Indian government to seek a loan from the International Monetary Fund. The IMF, in return, demanded a sharp reduction in the fiscal deficit and wide-ranging economic reforms coming under the header of economic liberalisation, such as devaluing the rupee, cutting tariffs levels, allowing for foreign direct investment up to 51 percent, slashing

---

45 Nicole Mayer-Ahuja, "Die Globalität unsicherer Arbeit als konzeptionelle Provokation: Zum Zusammenhang zwischen Informalität im Globalen Süden und Prekarität im Globalen Norden," *Geschichte und Gesellschaft* 43, 2 (2017): 288.

46 See Parry, *Classes of Labour:* 21–23; Patnaik, *The Formation of the Working Class:* 57–59; Sanchez, *Criminal Capital.*

47 Baldev Raj Nayar, *Globalization and Nationalism: The Changing Balance in India's Economic Policy, 1950–2000* (New Delhi: SAGE Publications, 2004 [2001]), 114–115.

48 Nayar, *Globalization and Nationalism*, 112.

49 Mayer-Ahuja, "Globalität unsicherer Arbeit"; Jan Breman and Marcel van der Linden, "Informalizing the Economy: The Return of the Social Question at a Global Level," *Development and Change* 45, 5 (2014): 920–940; see also Jonathan Parry, "Introduction: Precarity, Class, and the Neoliberal Subject", in *Industrial Labor on the Margins of Capitalism. Precarity, Class, and the Neoliberal Subject*, edited by Chris Hann and Jonathan Parry (New York: Berghahn, 2018), 1–38; David Harvey, *The New Imperialism* (Oxford; New York: Oxford University Press, 2003), 137–182.

tax rates, and drastically reducing the number of industries reserved for the public sector.[50] In the wake of these reforms, the remaining public sector undertakings also underwent structural adjustment. A few flagship companies were earmarked to be turned into competitive global players, and among them was the Steel Authority of India Ltd. (SAIL), the holding company of the central government to which RSP belonged.[51] A central part of this adjustment was a drastic reduction in the regular workforce, and its partial replacement with contract workers. The security of employment enjoyed by regular workers prevented management from achieving such a large-scale reduction of the workforce by retrenchment. Instead, it offered voluntary retirement schemes. Even more substantially, it used natural attrition as a chance to reduce the workforce. In the late 1980s and early 1990s, the first generation of RSP workers reached the age of superannuation at 58, and RSP recruited a smaller number of workers to replace them.

The major unions tried to resist these moves, but only in a rather lukewarm fashion, as unionists from the small, far-left RWU emphasised. In order to reduce the number of vacancies, RSP's management aimed to introduce a multi-skilling scheme, which allowed it to merge different jobs into new ones, such as fitter-cum-welder-cum-mechanic-cum-technician. The RMS accepted this on the condition of a cluster promotion scheme, which would guarantee workers a promotion every four years. They thought this was one of the most pressing concerns of RSP workers and were surprised at the opposition they received. RSP workers had long resented the RMS as a high-handed and corrupt "caretaker" union that was less concerned about their interests than about its cosy relationship with RSP's management. These resentments came to be increasingly shared by workers irrespective of ethnic identifications.

The cluster-promotion and multi-skilling scheme was a bone of contention for such a large number of company workers, elder unionists and workers told me, because the resulting curtailment of vacancies also curtailed the chances of their grown-up children being able to follow in their footsteps. Disillusioned by the RMS in numbers across all ethnic-cum-caste divides RSP workers quickly started rallying behind a new union, the Rourkela Shramik Sangh ("Rourkela Workers' Organisation," RSS) that an RSP clerk had just formed. That clerk had gained local fame for a case he had filed for the regularisation of RSP contract workers and for his determination to withstand pressure by RSP management and the RMS to withdraw it. In 1994, the Indian supreme court indeed obliged RSP to employ as regular

---

50 See Nayar, *Globalization and Nationalism*, 129–150; Daniel Münster and Christian Strümpell, "The Anthropology of Neoliberal India: An Introduction," *Contributions to Indian Sociology (n.s.)* 48, 1 (2014): 1–16.
51 See Strümpell, "The Politics of Dispossession."

company workers 4,500 of its contract labour force[52] and in 1995, the RSS also replaced the RMS as RSP's recognised union. The links the RSP clerk-cum-unionist had established with the Congress, which had returned to power in Odisha in 1995, too, helped him to succeed in both struggles. However, equally crucial was the overwhelming combined support he received from RSP's contract workers and company workers. The episode reveals that the politics in production evolving at RSP in the late 1980s and early 1990s – at the moment of generational change – was also driven by concerns about the reproduction of class positions, and that these concerns drew company workers closer to the contract workers' struggle for regularisation – not by design, but in a *de facto* manner.

Production and Reproduction in Rourkela since the 2000s

Ultimately, the new union also failed to prevent manpower cuts at RSP. Some said this was because of its affiliation with the Congress that was driving the neoliberal reforms and also because since the 1990s courts in neoliberal India in general were more unsympathetic to trade union claimants than before. Since the early 1990s, employment figures have dropped incessantly. In 1989, there were 39,000 company workers. When I started my ethnographic research in Rourkela in 2004, that figure was already down to 22,000, and by the time of my last extended visit in 2014, it had fallen even further to 15,000. Meanwhile, the number of contract workers at RSP had risen to 15,000.

As had been the case earlier, the large majority of contract workers were Adivasis, either from Rourkela itself or the wider region of northern Odisha and southern Jharkhand. Company workers were, apart from a few exceptions, all Odia and Adivasis. The Odisha state administration continued to control the recruitment process so that most migrant workers from other states had little chance of getting any of the few posts that would open up at RSP. Some found employment in the small numbers of local private sector industries or went into self-employment, for example as shopkeepers, but many also left Rourkela after their father's retirement. Of the newly recruited workers, upper-caste Odia once again dominated the mill zone while the lower-caste Adivasi were concentrated in the iron and

---

52 Christian Strümpell, "Law Against Displacement: The Juridification of Tribal Protest in Rourkela, Orissa", in *Law Against the State: Ethnographic Forays into Law's Transformations*, edited by Julia Eckert, Brian Donahoe, Christian Strümpell, and Zerrin Özlem Biner (Cambridge: Cambridge University Press, 2012), 211–213.

steel zone. The new Adivasi RSP company workers took the same pride in working in the "mother departments" as the earlier generation had. They also continued to emphasise that they were the only ones who could work there, not the notoriously work-shy Odia. It became clear in our conversations that they still did not feel truly respected and, in fact, were often repudiated by their Odia co-workers as well as executives, and that they distrusted the Odia on the shop floor and beyond. However, they were equally emphatic that the upper-caste Odia would no longer dare to openly reprimand them or boss them around. Furthermore, they put equal emphasis on the fact that, in contrast to the earlier generation of Adivasi RSP workers, and in contrast to the continuing stereotyping of Adivasis, they were educated, having completed school plus vocational training or college.

Higher levels of education were one of the main differences in the social profiles of the first and second generation of RSP workers. In the mid-1980s, completion of the tenth grade of school became the minimum qualification for RSP company workers, and RSP only considered applicants who had completed additional vocational training or a diploma. Managers claimed that technical modernisation and the more sophisticated, computerised production processes demanded a better-trained workforce. As the large presence of contract workers already shows, however, technological upgrading of production processes did not render unskilled tasks – for which such training was not required – obsolete. The gulf between contract and company workers remained wide. In 2008, a contract worker earned a monthly net wage of three thousand rupees, while a regular worker would take home no less than 15,000 rupees. Manpower cuts entailed stricter control of the attendance and performance of company workers, but defaulters still rarely faced dismissal. The contract workers I talked to often complained that "our sweat never dries but they [the company workers] sit around eating air" (idling around). Furthermore, the remit of company workers was often limited to the supervision and control of contract workers. Although the Adivasi company workers claimed that they were capable of working hard, it was the also largely Adivasi contract workers who actually did most of the real hard work. This shows that it is nowadays not so much caste that determines one's power on the RSP shop floor, but employment status.

This is reflected in the politics in production at RSP. Although Adivasi company workers claimed that they neither trusted nor cared to mingle with their Odia co-workers, they also did not fraternise with their fellow Adivasi contract workers. Many had little respect for the contract workers, who they characterised as uneducated, and accused them of drinking too much and never thinking about the morrow by saving money and educating their children. This is because they are Adivasis, as the upper-caste Odia RSP workers insinuate, or it is because they are from the labour class, as the Adivasi RSP workers insist. Regardless of caste background,

RSP company workers unanimously considered these contract workers unfit for and undeserving of regular employment. That is a far cry from the late 1980s and early 1990s, when we saw RSP company workers supporting the struggle of contract workers for regularisation.

As argued elsewhere,[53] the increasing economic and political divide between the two kinds of workers was entrenched by a more decisive gap between them in the sphere of reproduction, not only production. By the 2000s, the Adivasi RSP company workers were also living in the spacious company township, no longer in the slums surrounding it. The workforce had shrunk to such an extent that the township could accommodate the entire workforce. Adivasi company workers also moved into the township, in an effort to buttress their claims to belong to the local middle-class, to be educated, diligent and sober, in the face of widespread upper-caste prejudice.

Reproduction also played a major role in the realignment of boundaries of caste and class in space. The Adivasi company workers who had been recruited to RSP since the 1990s unanimously stated that the education of their children, as well as their future employment prospects, were the main reasons for moving into the township. They were in their late thirties and early forties, usually married and with children of school age. The money and time that they spent on their children's education would usually be something that only a local middle class or RSP company worker could afford – not a contract worker. Most of the RSP company workers, whether Odia or Adivasi, also seemed confident that if their children did well at school and college they would be sufficiently well equipped to compete successfully for the employment opportunities in the private sector that India's economic liberalisation was opening up elsewhere in the country. Consequently, they were more concerned about their children's education than about the lack of employment prospects in the public sector. This contrast with the situation in the late 1980s and early 1990s suggests, I argue, that wider questions of social reproduction are crucial for understanding the politics in production at RSP at different historical junctures.

Conclusion: The Politics in and of Production and Reproduction

The politics of production heavily impinges on the politics in production at RSP. That the state plays a central role also in the internal workings of a public sector

---

53 Strümpell, "Struggles about Class and Adivasi-ness."

undertaking is of course not entirely surprising. What is more important is that RSP, from the outset, provoked conflicts of interest between various levels of the state. Weiner has argued that the Nehruvian project of industrial modernisation suffered from an inherent contradiction between the attempt to turn public sector industries into mini-Indias and creating Indian producer patriots, while at the same time distributing them across different union states as a means of fostering regional development.[54] This required these industries to simultaneously employ an ethnically diverse workforce while also focusing on locals. Since they indeed offered privileged employment conditions, competition for jobs was fierce, and locals would cite the purported regional development agenda as a means to get an upper hand in the competition. This led to the question of who should count as "local." In Rourkela, the state of Odisha made it unremittingly clear that local belonging was not to be defined territorially, but rather ethnically, by being an Odia or, to a lesser degree, an Adivasi.[55] The result was ethnic clashes around access to RSP, and ethnic conflicts on the shop floor that were further entrenched by ethnicised union politics.

It is important to note that Nehru's model of state-led industrialisation does not inevitably provoke such a politics in production. In his work on Bhilai, the town of RSP's sister concern in Odisha's neighbouring state of Chhattisgarh, Parry emphasises that local Chhattisgarhi compete with migrants from other states over jobs at the Bhilai Steel Plant.[56] In Bhilai, however, a lid has so far been kept on ethnic tensions because the locals who found employment at the steel plant also internalised the Nehruvian culture that is lived in the plant and the township. Such a culture was able to thrive in Bhilai, because in Chhattisgarh state (part of Madhya Pradesh until 2000) the government never felt compelled to reserve the coveted jobs at the plant for sons of the soil or to interfere otherwise in its politics in production. A self-conscious sense of a singular identity barely prevailed in the state, and nobody gave much thought to creating one.[57]

At RSP, ethnic and caste conflicts among the workforce attenuated only with the advent of India's economic liberalisation at the turn of the 1990s. The increased casualisation of the most hazardous and menial jobs rendered the ethnic or caste background of workers less decisive for their position in the labour process than their employment status with the company. Furthermore, since the scope for regular employment at RSP was greatly reduced with the recruitment of the new (and

---

54 Weiner, *Sons of the Soil.*
55 See Christian Strümpell, "Social Citizenship and Ethnicity Around a Public Sector Steel Plant in Orissa, India," *Citizenship Studies* 15, 3–4 (2011): 485–498.
56 Parry, *Classes of Labour,* 623–624.
57 Parry and Strümpell, "On the Desecration of Nehru's Temples": 56.

smaller) workforce in the 1990s, there was not much left to gain for the state of Odisha by distributing these few jobs to the sons of the soil. Consequently, the conflict of interest between the regional state and RSP's management waned, as did its influence on the politics in production. The reduced importance of ethnicity and caste also fostered a more class-based politics among RSP workers. At the turn of the 1990s, company workers across these primordial differences switched their allegiance to a new union that seemed capable of taking on the management, and in the process also allied with the precarious contract workers fighting for their regularisation at RSP. By the time of my ethnographic research in Rourkela, however, not much was left of this moment of solidarity, and the better-off, middle-class RSP company workers had already sought to distance themselves from the contract workers.

I have argued that these changes in the politics in production point to important differences in the sphere of reproduction at these two junctures. At the turn of the 1990s, retiring company workers saw the reduction in RSP's company workforce as a threat to their sons' employment prospects and hence to the reproduction of their class position. Fifteen years later, most company workers were in their forties, years away from retirement. They saw their children's future in the private sector, and were more concerned about giving them an education that would grant them access to formal employment there, rather than about declining prospects in the public sector. Whether their attitude will change again, perhaps at some point in the future if the expected career prospects for their children fail to materialise, remains to be seen. It also remains to be seen what effects this will have on their politics. However, what I hope to have shown is that concerns about social reproduction are also crucial in shaping the way RSP workers – and, I suggest, also workers in general – view and act within the relations between labour with capital, both at the level of the enterprise and in wider society.

Toby Boraman

7 Destructuring the Dis-assembly Line: The Reversal of Power Relations in the Aotearoa/New Zealand Meat Processing Industry

Assembly-line workers were frequently at the forefront of the major wave of work-place conflict that occurred in high-income countries during the long 1970s.[1] They subsequently bore much of the burden of de-industrialisation, automation, neoliberal de-regulation, and globalisation in the long 1980s.[2] Meat processing workers suffered from such a fate, as a wave of plant closures rippled around the world from Argentina to Australia, the United States, Aotearoa/New Zealand, and beyond.[3] Aotearoa/New Zealand presents an almost classic example of these global transformations, although with some local twists, as shall be highlighted in the case study presented in this essay – briefly set within a global backdrop – of startling reversals in power relations in that industry during the 1970s and 1980s.

Meat processing was the most strike-prone industry in Aotearoa/New Zealand throughout the 1970s and 1980s. It accounted for 50 to 60 percent of workers involved, as well as working days not worked, in all industrial stoppages nationally during the long 1970s.[4] Most accounts – from employer, government, academic, and labour union sources – concur that a kind of low-intensity war between management and meatworkers (dubbed "meatpackers" in the United States) occurred dur-

---

1 Beverly Silver, *Forces of Labor: Workers' Movements and Globalization Since 1870* (New York: Cambridge University Press, 2003); and Sjaak van der Velden *et al.*, eds., *Strikes Around the World: Case Studies of 15 Countries 1968–2005* (Amsterdam: Aksant, 2007).

2 Although de-industrialisation began in some countries earlier than others. See, for example, Steven High, *Industrial Sunset: The Making of North America's Rust Belt 1969–1984* (Toronto: University of Toronto Press, 2003).

3 By meat processing, I mean the entirety of the industry, not just one aspect of it such as meat-packing. For the Argentinean, United States, and Australian experiences, see, among others, Paul Lewis, *The Crisis of Argentine Capitalism* (Chapel Hill: University of North Carolina, 1990); Roger Horowitz, *"Negro and White Unite and Fight!": A Social History of Industrial Unionism in Meatpacking, 1930–1990* (Urbana: University of Illinois Press, 1997); and Patrick O'Leary and Peter Sheldon, *Employer Power and Weakness: How Local and Global Factors have Shaped Australia's Meat Industry and its Industrial Relations* (Ballarat: Victorian Universities Regional Network Press, 2012).

4 Toby Boraman, "Indigeneity, Dissent, and Solidarity: Māori and Strikes in the Meat Industry in Aotearoa New Zealand During the Long 1970s," *International Review of Social History* 64, 1 (2019): 4.

https://doi.org/10.1515/9783111086552-008

ing this period in numerous plants.[5] While their wide-ranging resistance was typical of other rebellious factory workers globally,[6] Aotearoa/New Zealand meatworkers diverged significantly from the typical Eurocentric Fordist worker because the workforce was precarious (work was seasonal, and seasons sometimes only lasted three to four months a year) and disproportionately indigenous.[7]

During the long 1980s, an astonishing inversion in social relations occurred in the meat industry. Employers gained the upper hand by thoroughly restructuring the industry in order to render it more profitable. They closed most older abattoirs and as good as cut the workforce in half, while also constructing new, highly automated slaughterhouses, in which they re-asserted their "right to manage" the work process. Widespread resistance to this "destructuring" (as restructuring was labelled by some unionists) resulted, but was eventually overcome.[8] After the early 1990s, the extent of strikes in the industry dropped precipitously.

In this essay, I will contrast two powerful theories that help explain these transformations. The first is a broadly socialist perspective that roughly corresponds to the above summary. It argues that restructuring was a counterattack by capital to the rise of combative grassroots class struggles during the long 1970s, as such workers' dissent began to squeeze profits. Many support this thesis, in various forms, including Beverly Silver, the Italian autonomist Marxists (such as Antonio Negri), and David Harvey.[9] The second is the "strategic choice" school of employment relations, which emphasises the role of the state, global and local markets, and especially the choices of employers, in propelling restructuring.[10]

---

5 See, for example, Department of Labour, *Work Stoppages in the Meat Freezing Industry Part II* (Wellington: DOL, 1973); John McCrystal, *A Long Season: The Centennial History of AFFCO New Zealand* (Wellington: Kukupa Press, 2004); Roger Middlemass, "A Report on Industrial Relations at the Co-operative Wholesale Society's Longburn Freezing Works" (n.d.), New Zealand Meat Workers' Union Aotearoa branch files; and Don Turkington, *Industrial Conflict: A Study of Three New Zealand Industries* (Wellington: Methuen, 1976).

6 See, among others, Aaron Brenner et al., eds., *Rebel Rank and File: Labor Militancy and Revolt from Below during the Long 1970s* (London: Verso, 2010); and Colin Crouch and Alessandro Pizzorno, eds., *The Resurgence of Class Struggle in Western Europe Since 1968* (New York: Holmes & Meier, 1978).

7 Toby Boraman, "Indigeneity, Dissent, and Solidarity": 1–35.

8 For example: Jim Knox, the President of the New Zealand Federation of Labour, used the term. *FOL Bulletin* 22 (September 1980): 6.

9 See David Harvey, *A Brief History of Neoliberalism* (Oxford: Oxford University Press, 2005); Antonio Negri, *Revolution Retrieved: Selected Writings on Marx, Keynes, Capitalist Crisis and New Social Subjects 1967–1983* (London: Red Notes, 1988); and Silver, *Forces of Labor.*

10 Bruce Curtis, "New Zealand's Meat Board, Markets and the Killing Season: A Twentieth-Century Labour History of Unintended Consequences," *Labour History* 114 (2018): 93–112; O'Leary and Shel-

Both approaches have strengths and weaknesses. A history-from-below focus on shop floor relations, as with the autonomists, can over-emphasise the local at the expense of the global, when conflict in the meat industry in Aotearoa/New Zealand was also heavily shaped by the deeply scarring global recessions of the 1970s and the loss of that country's major export market due to the United Kingdom joining the European Economic Community (EEC) in 1973. Highlighting workers' resistance can also overlook the profound effects of how the state de-regulated the meat industry and eliminated agricultural subsidies in the 1980s. Conversely, focusing on the strategies of employers and the state, and the role of markets, can be too institutional, impersonal, and top-down. Such a structuralist analysis can marginalise labour unions' and workers' agency, as well as neglect the labour process and everyday social relations on the shop floor, such as the "blood and guts" nature of meat processing work on the Fordist "dis-assembly line" (where animals were progressively dismembered after they were slaughtered).

This essay proceeds by outlining the extent of workplace conflict in the meat processing industry in the 1970s, including its many causes. It then explores briefly two subjects that are frequently neglected in traditional studies of factory workers and their social relations with employers: the role of informal social bonds (including the influence of indigenous Māori meatworkers in developing workplace families) in workers' dissent; and second, the relatively extensive magnitude of workers' and unions' control over the work process in the long 1970s. Next it examines capital's restructuring of the industry during the long 1980s in the aim of regaining control and suppressing strikes. Finally, it surveys the changing role of the state in, first, both inadvertently enabling and explicitly constraining conflict in the industry in the 1970s, and, then, facilitating capital's restructuring of the industry during the 1980s. Overall this essay attempts to intertwine structure and agency, and the local and global, in order to help fathom the complexities of the shifting frontiers of control in abattoirs. I realise these ambitious aims cannot be adequately explored due to lack of space. Consequently, some topics have been excluded, including relations between supervisors and workers on the killing floor, relations between companies (transnational and local), and how meat capital was globalised during this era.[11]

---

don, *Employer Power and Weakness;* and "Strategic Choices and Unintended Consequences: Employer Militancy in Victoria's Meat Industry, 1986–93," *Labour History* 95 (2008): 223–242.

11 For an overview of United States meat processing firms and their global ties, see Gouveia Lourdes, "Global Strategies and Local Linkages: The Case of the U.S. Meatpacking Industry," in *From Columbus to ConAgra: The Globalization of Food and Agriculture*, edited by Alessandro Bonanno et al. (Lawrence: University of Kansas Press, 1994), 125–148.

The Dis-assembly Line and Workplace Conflict in the 1970s

Based on categories developed by Erik Olin Wright, Beverly Silver provides a helpful framework for discussing sources of workers' power. Associational power results from the collective organisation of workers (such as unions), while structural power is the power that accrues from the position of workers in the economy. She further sub-divides structural power into marketplace bargaining power, which results from "tight labor markets," and workplace bargaining power, which accrues from the strategic location of workers.[12] Such a framework lacks discussion of institutional power (power derived from the institutions and resources of the state), informal sources of workers' power, and sources of employer power.[13] Nonetheless it can be usefully applied to the meat industry in Aotearoa/New Zealand.

In the long 1970s, workers and unions in the meat industry possessed a relatively high degree of associational and structural power. Importantly, meatworkers were located at the heart of Aotearoa/New Zealand's agro-export economy. They were internationally significant too. Despite its small size, Aotearoa/New Zealand was by far the largest worldwide sheep meat exporter during the 1970s, accounting for just over half of global mutton and lamb exports during that decade.[14] Furthermore, strong, "militant" unions developed in the meat industry. They generally adopted tactics of collective direct action to gain better pay and conditions (although strategies differed locally and regionally, as will be discussed). Near full employment, achieved until about the mid-1970s due to the long boom and expansionary Keynesian government policies, greatly increased workers' marketplace bargaining power, as did recurrent shortages of labour during peaks in the killing season.

Workplace bargaining power was also high due to how the labour process was organised in slaughterhouses. In 1977, Kerr Inkson claimed being inside an Aotearoa/New Zealand slaughterhouse was "like a premonition of hell":

---

12 Luca Perrone, Erik Olin Wright, and Larry J. Griffin, "Positional Power, Strikes and Wages," *American Sociological Review* 49, 3 (1984): 412–426; Silver, *Forces of Labor*, 13–16; and Erik Olin Wright, "Working-Class Power, Capitalist-Class Interests, and Class Compromise," *American Journal of Sociology* 105, 4 (2000): 957–1002.

13 Silver does not see state power as a separate form of power, but as something that has influenced both associational and structural power. Silver, *Forces of Labor*, 14–15.

14 N. Blyth, *A Review of the World Sheepmeat Market: Australia, New Zealand and Argentina* (Lincoln: Agricultural Economics Research Unit, 1981), 25, 40.

Machines clack and shouts echo eerily from the metal rafters; steam hisses and melts into the damp air; blood spurts and spatters across clinically white garments; animal carcasses swinging on their hooks roll slowly past, throats cut, heads dangling grotesquely, while the men sever and slash with their razor-sharp knives.[15]

Work was highly monotonous, arduous, obnoxious, and hazardous. After the animals were killed, they were hung on a moving "chain" – or dis-assembly line. Different specialised departments of workers then progressively dismembered those carcasses as they travelled past, working like "macabre surgeons."[16] Because every step of the dis-assembly process was dependent on every other step, workers and unions could easily disrupt it. If just one butcher experienced difficulties, the entire chain could grind to a halt. This would then have flow-on effects in stopping work in the other departments that carried out further processing of animal carcasses (such as the boning, trimming, and packing departments), and their by-products, such as entrails, organs, blood, tallow, manure, wool, and hides. As such, work throughout the plant could eventually cease. As meatworker Helen Mulrennan said, while the job was "tedious" and "menial," workers knew they possessed strategic power through their unions.[17]

Much of the intense dissent in the meat industry was related to the "blood and guts" nature of meat processing work. "Blood and guts" was a commonly used term to capture the unpleasant nature of such work, as blood gushed profusely from the animals after workers cut them open and extracted their guts and other organs. Indeed, many meatworkers saw it as a revolt against a "soul destroying" job.[18] For example, "a butcher on the chain must carry out the same operation over and over again, 7 and half times a minute, 450 times an hour, 3600 times per day, day after day" of "endless mindless meaningless work."[19] Roger Middlemass, a meatworker who later became a union official for the New Zealand Meat Work-

---

15 Kerr Inkson, "The Man on the Dis-assembly Line: New Zealand Freezing Workers," *Australian and New Zealand Journal of Sociology* 13, 1 (1977): 2.

16 Kerr Inkson, "New Zealand's Troubled Meat Industry", *Employee Relations* 2, 1 (1980): 12. For the "dis-assembly" labour process, see Inkson, "The Man on the Dis-Assembly Line"; Kerr Inkson and Peter Cammock, "Labour Process Theory and the Chain System in the New Zealand Meatworks," *New Zealand Journal of Industrial Relations* 9, 3 (1984): 149–160; and Don Turkington, *Industrial Conflict*.

17 Helen Mulrennan, Interview with author, Auckland, 18 December 2013.

18 Department of Labour, *Work Stoppages in the Meat Freezing Industry*; A. J. Geare, "The Problem of Industrial Unrest: Theories into the Causes of Local Strikes in a New Zealand Meat Freezing Works," *Journal of Industrial Relations* 14, 1 (1972): 13–22; Inkson and Cammock, "Labour Process Theory"; and Don Turkington, *Industrial Conflict*, 85.

19 Kerr Inkson, "So What's Wrong With Being a Freezing Worker?" *New Zealand Listener* (7 August 1976), 24.

ers' Union (NZMWU), remembers work was "very physical. Much more physical than now [....] Your hands would play up and you'd cut yourself and everyone cut themselves at some stage or other 'cause the knives were really sharp."[20] He has also asserted working conditions were poor as work was highly insecure, noisy, and temperatures varied between extremes of heat (up to fifty-five degrees Celsius, presumably on the chain in summer) or cold (down to minus twenty-nine degrees Celsius, presumably in the freezers).[21]

Overall, the causes of disputes in the 1970s were multifaceted. They were not just related to workers' associational and structural power, or the interdependent and unpleasant nature of work. They were a product of numerous disputes over wages, working conditions, seasonality (strikes were more common nearer to the end of a season, when unions possessed more bargaining power), how animals were perishable, the generally high level of (informal and formal) shop floor organisation and solidarity among workers, varied and changeable union and management attitudes and practices, as well as being shaped by the wider economic, political, and social context.[22] The literature which examines these causes – whether influenced by labour process theory or industrial psychology – overlooks a major historical cause: as John Kelly argues, strike waves often occur during transitional phases from economic upswing to downswing (and vice versa), as established patterns of class relations are ruptured. Simply put, meatworkers expected the rise in real wages that occurred under the post-WWII long boom to continue in the 1970s, and they rebelled when their living standards began to decline.[23] That is, the economic context of transition from boom to recession (and associated high inflation) was a key factor in the high levels of stoppages in the industry.

Workers' disobedience ranged from everyday or informal resistance to hundreds of formal local and national stoppages.[24] The stark difference between government and employers' statistical records of stoppages (see Table 7.1) stemmed

---

20 Roger Middlemass, Interview with author, Palmerston North, 2 October 2013.

21 Middlemass interviewed in "Korero [Talk] from the Works," *Roadrunner* (March 1975): 10.

22 For overviews of the substantial debate about these causes, see Kerr Inkson, "Organisational Behaviour: A Review of the New Zealand Research," *New Zealand Journal of Psychology* 16, 1 (1987): 12–13; and Don Turkington, *Industrial Conflict*, 41–139.

23 Although Kelly also recognises the influence of generational change, the balance of class power – the extent of worker mobilization, and state, and employer counter-mobilisation (and employer unity) – in the global strike wave of 1968 to 1974. John Kelly, *Rethinking Industrial Relations: Mobilisation, Collectivism and Long Waves* (London: Routledge, 1998), 98–102.

24 See Toby Boraman, "Wildcat Homers, Gamifying Work, and Workplace-whānau in the Meat Industry: Re-examining the Subversiveness of Informal Workers' Resistance," *Journal of Labor and Society* 20, 4 (2017): 467–485.

largely from how government figures under-reported the level of stoppages, as government officials themselves admitted. For example, government officers informally excluded stoppages of less than half a day's duration while employers did not, and thus the latter's figures captured to some extent the remarkable number of short-lived strikes which arose on the shop floor. Yet the New Zealand Freezing/ Meat Companies' Association figures were themselves inflated by how they often recorded strikes in each plant separately, and thus substantially over-counted regional and national stoppages,[25] and how they often counted factory-wide union meetings held during company time as strikes (which the government did not).

Table 7.1: Industrial stoppages in the Aotearoa/New Zealand meat processing industry, 1967 to 1991

Year	Number of stoppages		Working days not worked		Workers involved	
	Govt. figures	Meat employer figures	Govt. figures	Meat employer figures	Govt. figures	Meat employer figures
1967	31	No data	50,433	No data	13,556	No data
1968	49	No data	79,702	No data	23,493	No data
1969	37	No data	69,551	No data	22,040	No data
1970	91	1058	109,633	117,959	45,333	207,545
1971	75	893	43,449	68,027	34,208	201,361
1972	68	793	81,258	91,096	35,449	173,292
1973	107	No data	145,552	No data	74,708	No data
1974	72	No data	92,899	No data	35,145	No data
1975	69	No data	99,932	No data	31,424	No data
1976	118	No data	227,296	No data	102,821	No data
1977	199	No data	176,766	No data	80,791	No data
1978	155	No data	172,405	No data	108,065	No data
1979	182	No data	143,822	No data	78,361	No data
1980	138	No data	150,026	No data	59,698	No data
1981	88	No data	128,341	No data	37,455	No data

---

25 Toby Boraman, "Merging Politics with Economics: Non-industrial and Political Work Stoppage Statistics in New Zealand during the Long 1970s," *New Zealand Journal of Employment Relations* 41, 1 (2016): 66.

Table 7.1: Industrial stoppages in the Aotearoa/New Zealand meat processing industry, 1967 to 1991 (Continued)

Year	Number of stoppages		Working days not worked		Workers involved	
	Govt. figures	Meat employer figures	Govt. figures	Meat employer figures	Govt. figures	Meat employer figures
1982	96	1025	220,400	345,183	88,689	356,374
1983	68	920	141,542	183,800	60,005	310,480
1984	62	1103	219,116	271,320	63,462	379,530
1985	63	1183	217,734	320,761	59,101	502,942
1986	13	No data	1,007,597	8,508,949	47,046	991,159
1987	No data	No data	No data	579,226	No data	140,495
1988	19	No data	134,287	No data	12,867	No data
1989	No data	No data	No data	No data	No data	No data
1990	21	No data	217,872	No data	13,686	No data
1991	6	No data	20,530	No data	14,155	No data

Notes for government statistics: The figures for export slaughterhouses and non-export abattoirs have been combined. Figures exclude non-industrial stoppages up to 1983, and stoppages that accrued less than 10 working days not worked.

Sources: For government figures, Department of Labour (DOL), *Industrial Stoppages/Work Stoppages* Annual Reports, 1972–1985; *New Zealand Yearbook* 1967–1991; *N.Z. Monthly Abstract of Statistics* 1975; and Don Turkington, *Industrial Conflict*, 18–22. For employers' statistics, *Auckland Star* (15 November 1971); Department of Labour, "Discussion Paper on the Adequacy of Current Stoppage Statistics," Research and Planning Division of the Department of Labour, 1976, R20442084, Archives New Zealand, Wellington; and New Zealand Freezing Companies' Association/New Zealand Meat Industry Association annual reports 1982/1983 to 1987/1988.

Solidarity, Informal Resistance, Workplace-*Whānau*, and Divisions within the Workplace

Silver's discussion of associational power focusses on formal collective organisations, such as unions and political parties, rather than informal shop floor forms of collective organisation. Here an autonomist Marxist understanding is useful, in that it emphasises how workers' everyday experiences can cause dissent.

They argue that a new class composition emerged amongst the working class under Fordism in the 1960s and 1970s. That is, they maintain the working-class re-made itself – in response to Fordist working conditions – to become more unified (despite becoming more diverse, as migrants and women entered workplaces in greater numbers) and rebellious against work.[26] Viewed from this optic, the Ao-tearoa/New Zealand case is an important instance of a class composition that was substantively influenced by indigenous workers and later women workers, rather than the traditionally white male blue-collar worker. Forty to 50 percent of meatworkers were Māori, almost none of whom were managers.[27]

In reaction to the alienating, mind-numbingly repetitive, and brutal nature of slaughterhouse work, meatworkers frequently attempted to make work more fun, social, and bearable. This humanisation of work contributed to many attempts to control the labour process, as shall be discussed below, and also produced substantive informal resistance. Such insubordination was characterised by high levels of absenteeism, theft, turnover, indiscipline, tardiness, and playing around on the job.[28] For example, James Robb remembers at the Tōmoana slaughterhouse in the late 1970s that:

> The absenteeism was huge sometimes. They [management] would knock off [shut down] half a chain on Friday just because there were so many people who would just leave at lunchtime and go to the pub and not come back. It was kind of so obvious, and it would happen towards the end of the season, too. By that time they'd [workers had] got a bit more money in their pocket, and also just getting more and more tired and worn out and needing a holiday.[29]

Due to the strong associational power of workers and unions, practices such as cooking kidneys or tongues in knife sterilisers and then eating them during breaks – technically instances of theft – were difficult for management to control. According to Robb, so long as supervisors did not catch workers placing the meat in the sterilisers, they could not be prosecuted for theft. They needed "hard evidence" otherwise workers would strike to re-instate their colleague.[30]

---

26 See Antonio Negri, *Revolution Retrieved;* and Steve Wright, *Storming Heaven: Class Composition and Struggle in Italian Autonomist Marxism* (London: Pluto, 2002), 176–196.
27 Toby Boraman, "Indigeneity, Dissent and Solidarity": 8. A small minority of meatworkers were transnational migrants from Sāmoa, Tonga, the Cook Islands, and elsewhere. Far from being passive workers, these Polynesian migrant workers tended to be concentrated in several strike-prone plants.
28 See Toby Boraman, "Wildcat Homers" for a broader overview of the humanisation of work and informal resistance.
29 James Robb, Interview with author, Auckland, 10 October 2013.
30 James Robb, *The Chain* (Wellington: Steele Roberts, 2012), 36–37.

Furthermore, joking around on the job – such as workers flicking pieces of meat at each other, or at supervisors – was part of a larger, seemingly constant, "industrial game," whereby workers sought relief from the monotony of work including finding seemingly minor issues to disrupt work.[31] To some extent, meatworkers' practised *Eigensinn* – a concept developed by Alf Lüdtke which may be described as "putting up with political power to the degree that one must, while pursuing one's own ends to the degree that one can"[32] – in their everyday indiscipline. However, this disobedience was frequently far more conspicuous during the turbulent long 1970s rather than occupying a "kind of middle ground between compliance and non-compliance or accommodation and resistance."[33] While everyday resistance has often been dismissed as an inherently individualistic and harmless method of coping with work, it was also sometimes collectively organised and overall led to more lost production and profits than formal resistance.[34]

In many meatworks – a common term for slaughterhouses in Australasia – this process of humanising work was strongly influenced by indigenous workers. Indeed, a seemingly unique aspect of meatworkers' unrest in Aotearoa/New Zealand in the long 1970s, relative to other high-income countries, was the central role indigenous workers played within it. Māori played a significant role not only in meatworkers' generally strong and democratic unions, but also in creating and maintaining the filial-like relations that existed amongst workers on the killing floor. Melissa Williams has termed these connections "workplace-*whānau*." *Whānau* means extended family, and in this context, workplace-*whānau* refers to how Māori created extended family-like relations between themselves and other workers, regardless of whether they were white/*Pākehā*, Sāmoan, Tongan, male, female, and so on.[35] In a workplace-*whānau*, everyone in a work group or worksite (excluding supervisors and other managers) was ideally treated like an extended family member, with the strong reciprocal bonds and mutual obligations this generally entails in Māori society. Māori meatworkers commonly reported that a "one big family" atmosphere existed among workers in many plants. Many multigenerational (nuclear and extended) family members and friends from the local

---

31 Don Turkington, *Industrial Conflict*, 85. See also Toby Boraman, "Wildcat Homers."
32 John Eidson, *Compulsion, Compliance, or Eigensinn? Examining Theories of Power in an East German Field Site* (Halle/Saale: Max Planck Institute, 2003), 1. See also Alf Lüdtke, ed., *History of Everyday Life: Reconstructing Historical Experiences and Ways of Life* (Princeton: Princeton University Press, 1995).
33 Eidson, *Compulsion, Compliance, or Eigensinn?*, 4.
34 See Boraman, "Wildcat Homers."
35 Melissa Matutina Williams, *Panguru and the City, Kāinga Tahi, Kāinga Rua: An Urban Migration History* (Wellington: Bridget Williams Books, 2015), 183.

neighbourhood worked alongside each other in meatworks, and thus to many it represented "a home away from home."[36] By uniting with fellow workers, the aim was to transform "often physically demanding, monotonous, and impersonal workplaces into bearable, sometimes fun, and culturally familiar spaces of community engagement."[37] Workplace-*whānau* thus could be interpreted as being created by Māori to self-manage, to a degree, work spaces and rhythms according to their general cultural norms. They also became a pillar for workers' dissent.

Nevertheless, this culture that developed in many plants was influenced by a multiplicity of other factors. The homogenising, cooperative, and collective nature of Fordist dis-assembly line work, in which hundreds and sometimes thousands of workers worked interdependently together, meant it was easier to develop social bonds. Meatworkers' unions also developed strong traditions of solidarity and struggle. As they gained some degree of control over re-hiring (as discussed below) it meant that workers could work at the same plant year after year and build lasting social connections, despite the seasonal nature of the work.[38]

Such solidarity was never universal, however. Indeed, substantial geographical, gender, ethnic, occupational, social, and political tensions existed within the meat processing workforce, as well as antagonism between many union officials and rank-and-file workers. For example, workplace-*whānau* were often highly masculine and sexist. In 1979, around 92 percent of meatworkers were men.[39] Camaraderie was often based on a tough-guy culture of males drinking alcohol and playing sport together outside of work. As many men were seen as being "married to their jobs," they neglected their partners and children. Dalvanius Prime, a Māori musician who formerly worked at the Pātea meatworks with his father, noted:

> [A] man is there [at the Pātea slaughterhouse] all day punching skins and comes home and has no time for his wife and family. He goes off to the pub with his mates. We never saw our father until the weekend and that was the case for most people here.[40]

Women inside the meatworks, including Māori women, were confined to smaller, by-product departments that were poorly paid and experienced the most unpleasant working conditions, such as working within the offal and manure departments. Most employers, male workers, and some union branches were initially op-

---

36 Boraman, "Indigeneity, Dissent and Solidarity."
37 Williams, *Panguru and the City*, 190.
38 See Boraman, "Indigeneity, Dissent and Solidarity"; and Ross Webb, "'The camaraderie and the whakawhanaungatanga': Work, Culture and Community in the New Zealand Freezing Works, 1970s and 1980s," *New Zealand Journal of History* 53, 2 (2019): 83–105.
39 Boraman, "Indigeneity, Dissent and Solidarity": 23.
40 Quoted in *Daily News*, (18 August 2001).

posed to allowing women to secure jobs in better-paid occupational departments. White and Māori women alike began challenging this exclusion from the mid- to late 1970s onward. After they eventually overcame this occupational segregation, women often became prominent in the strikes of the 1980s against restructuring and those that secured union recognition in several newly automated plants in the 1980s.[41]

Fig. 1: Whatu Brown, Charlie Christie, Egypt Lambert, Coogie and Hemi Rapaea at Tōmoana slaughterhouse, c.1980s.
Source: https://numawaruwire.wordpress.com/tag/tomoana/#jp-carousel-213'

Solidarity was also not rigidly unchangeable geographically. Indeed, the incidence of strikes was spatially highly uneven. For example, just five abattoirs (out of a national total of 37) between 1967 and 1973 were responsible for 55.7 percent of all days not worked due to stoppages across the industry.[42] Research is limited as to the causes of these disparities, although the available evidence suggests a combina-

---

41 See Boraman, "Indigeneity, Dissent and Solidarity": 22–23, 29–30; John Leckie, "Women in Industrial Action: Some Female Profiles in a Redundancy Strike in Vestey's New Zealand Meat Works, 1988," *Labour History* 61 (1991): 88–100; and Cybele Locke, *Workers in the Margins* (Wellington: Bridget Williams Books, 2012), 63–66.
42 Don Turkington, *Industrial Conflict*, 42–43.

tion of factors was at play. Some large, urban slaughterhouses experienced higher rates of unrest, but not all urban plants.[43] Meatworker unionists often argued management practices at certain meatworks caused stoppages, such as modifying the production process due to hygiene regulations without proper consultation, or being authoritarian and uncommunicative.[44] In contrast, the New Zealand Meat Industry Employers' Association argued that frequent conflict arose at some slaughterhouses due to the decentralised way the two major meatworkers' unions – namely, the smaller Auckland and Tōmoana Freezing Workers' Union (ATFWU), which served the upper North Island, and the larger NZMWU, which covered the rest of the country – were organised. Considerable autonomy for local branches meant that some plants were free to develop militancy.[45] Overall, it is clear that strong enmities developed between management and unions at certain plants, and between certain companies and workers.

Workers' Control of Work

During the long 1970s, a major revival in workers' control of work occurred in many high-income countries. The forms that this workers' self-management took ranged from everyday job control to outright workplace occupations.[46] Likewise, in the Aotearoa/New Zealand meat industry, job control – both informal and formal – was endemic, although sit-ins were infrequent. Workers and unions endeavoured to control working conditions (including work speed, numbers of workers employed in various specialised occupations, temperatures, and health and safety measures). For example, workers in some occupational departments organised unofficial breaks so that a few workers could rest while others performed their tasks for them. Employers alleged that the overall tendency towards workers' control was a consequence of the precarity of meat processing work, as "workers have shown a tendency to resist employment for short periods in each year only, and

---

43 Department of Labour, *Work Stoppages in the Meat Freezing Industry*, 10–13; and Don Turkington, *Industrial Conflict*, 112–118.
44 Boraman, "Indigeneity, Dissent and Solidarity": 12; and "Papers handed in by Mr McNulty – Sec. of NZ Meat Processors, Packers, Preservers, Freezing Works and Related Trades Union on 13.8. 1973," Commission of Inquiry into the Meat Industry, R18523367, Archives New Zealand, Wellington.
45 New Zealand Meat Industry Employers' Association, "Submissions on Industrial Relations," Commission of Inquiry into the Meat Industry, 1973: 14, R18523264, Archives New Zealand, Wellington.
46 See, for example, Immanuel Ness and Dario Azzellini, eds., *Ours to Master and to Own: Workers' Councils from the Commune to the Present* (Chicago: Haymarket Books, 2011), 284–355.

various labour restrictive practices have grown up over the years in an effort by the workers to extend the period of their employment in each season,"[47] yet it was also a consequence of trying to make dangerous and tiring working conditions safer, less arduous, and more humane, as well as to make workplaces more democratic.

The most important forms of workers' self-management (or, perhaps, self-regulation) were, first, attempts to control hiring and firing and, second, efforts to control the rhythms of production. McNulty, the secretary of the NZMWU, claimed that a seniority system – which represented a degree of union-run hiring and firing – existed "in varying degrees" in every meatworks.[48] Despite how employers generally tolerated these local systems, they resisted attempts to have seniority written into the national award for the industry (which set legal minimum national standards for employment through the state's system of compulsory arbitration and collective bargaining). Seniority rankings ensured that unionists who had been employed the previous season were guaranteed an offer of work at the beginning of the new killing season. Seniority also assured that the workers employed earliest at the start of the season were the last to be laid off at season's end (this seasonal seniority system differed from the uninterrupted seniority system that existed in large United States meatpacking plants which operated throughout the year). Nevertheless, unions had less influence over firing than they did hiring, as employers ritually laid off workers as the season wound down at the end of summer. For Ken Findlay and Ben Matthews, two Māori meatworkers who became NZMWU officials, this precarity was a major driver of meatworkers' militancy. Matthews argued that meatworkers experienced unsettling and wide-ranging job, life, and family insecurity, and Findlay argued that when meatworkers were annually fired, they "were reminded *very* forcefully that you were a commodity meant to be used and dumped. And there is no sentiment [....] Every year they do the same thing."[49] However, workers also sometimes attempted to "refuse the sack" during the season, especially sackings (firings) for alleged insubordination, minor restruc-

---

47 New Zealand Freezing Companies' Association, "Submissions," Commission of Inquiry into the Meat Industry, 1973, Part XIII: 2, R18523275, Archives New Zealand, Wellington.
48 Frank McNulty, *The Freezing Workers' Case: Union Submissions to the Meat Industry Inquiry* (Christchurch: New Zealand Monthly Review Society, 1974), 26.
49 Ken Findlay, Interview with author, Wellington, 21 January 2014 (emphasis in original); and Ben Matthews, "Submissions – by B. Matthews on behalf of 1. The general public and 2. Nga Tamatoa," (1973): 39–40. R18523343, Archives New Zealand, Wellington. While meat processing was precarious work, this precarity differed from that often found in the informal sector in low and mid-income countries, as meat processing work was still highly regulated by unions, the state and management, and was highly regimented assembly-line work.

turing, and theft, as alluded to earlier. Strikes to reinstate colleagues were some-times successful – as in the case of forty-eight butchers who were dismissed after undertaking an alleged illegal strike in Dunedin in 1967 but were reinstated after the local NZMWU branch banned loading out export meat from the plant.[50]

Union control of production included negotiated maximum production line speeds with employers, and especially the tally system. Maximum tallies specified the quantity of livestock that butchers would slaughter daily. This was fixed at around 3,200 to 3,600 sheep per dis-assembly line. The tally also set out the mini-mum numbers of workers to be employed on each chain. Employers bitterly com-plained that the tally restricted output, as they claimed most butchers finished work, on average, half an hour early after they had attained their tally. They esti-mated that the tally system lost them around seven percent of annual production (or precisely 3,363,292 lambs not killed), yet lamented that they were unable to break this "restrictive practice" due to butchers being pieceworkers.[51] Unions es-tablished tallies so as to iron out daily fluctuations in workload, either through working too little or too much. While some employers viewed tallies as a lengthy go-slow that restricted production, work was far from slow despite the tally. The mechanised line speed was rigidly set so workers had to process an animal about every eight seconds to achieve the tally; to comply with EEC and United States hygiene regulations, which required butchers to dip their knives in a steri-liser for every animal, Robb remembers, *"every single second of your labour was taken."*[52]

Furthermore, in order to increase production, management subverted the tally through either building new assembly lines,[53] hiring more workers on the chain after negotiating local agreements with union branches, or through offering sub-stantive performance payments to meatworkers (which were also negotiated by union branches and management via local agreements). Piecework agreements were commonplace – especially for strategically placed butchers at the start of the dis-assembly line – in the 1970s and 1980s. Other workers in follow-on depart-ments were consequently forced to work harder for no extra pay. Hence these hourly-paid workers increasingly went on strike in order to gain performance pay for themselves in the 1970s, and to maintain pay relativity with butchers.

The extent of union and workers' control – and resistance – began to alarm some employers during the 1970s. For example, Alan Hellaby – the managing direc-tor of the Shortland meatworks, a militant Auckland slaughterhouse – said that in

---

50 *New Zealand Meat Worker* 5 (1968): 19, 21.
51 New Zealand Freezing Companies' Association, "Submissions," part XIII: 9–10.
52 James Robb, email to author, 9 March 2020, emphasis in original.
53 Bruce Curtis, "New Zealand's Meat Board": 104.

the 1970s "we [management] started to really lose control within the plants...And it became very, very difficult to manage."[54] He also asserted that the balance of power had massively shifted towards unions from the late 1960s onwards, particularly in large industries with monotonous work where many employers were "feeling that they have lost their rights to manage."[55] However, Kerr Inkson has argued that meat industry management still largely shaped "the pattern of activity in a works" despite such claims that they felt helpless to control the widespread conflict that was then rife in the industry.[56] This indicates that perhaps a major diminution of managerial control occurred in the long 1970s rather than a complete forfeit of that control.

Capital, Management and Restructuring

Patrick O'Leary and Peter Sheldon argue that the Australasian meat industry employment relations literature has largely focused on the labour process and workers, and has thereby neglected the role of employers. Employers, they claim, possessed multiple sources of power, especially the power derived from their ownership and control of capital. They also derived power through the use of their organisational structure (which enforced rules and regulations), and their control of technology and the labour process. Some of these sources of power were contested, as discussed above.[57]

The industry comprised many different companies: British transnationals (including Vestey's, Borthwicks, and the Cooperative Wholesale Society) and local companies (which were often run as farmers' cooperatives) alike. Michael Barry argues that these companies became splintered during the 1970s in their responses to considerable wage demands:

> Frustration followed frustration as individual members made concessions that union officials worked hard to turn into new industry benchmarks. Employer disunity gave the unions considerable scope to improve their members' conditions by pursuing direct action in contradiction to the industry's formal disputes procedures.[58]

---

54 Alan Hellaby interviewed in *The Black Singlet Legacy*, directed by Tainui Stephens (Auckland, Television New Zealand, 1991 [video documentary]).
55 Alan Hellaby, "The Changing Balance of Power in New Zealand Industry," *New Zealand Journal of Industrial Relations* 2, 2 (1977): 43.
56 Kerr Inkson, "New Zealand's Troubled Meat Industry," *Employee Relations* 2, 1 (1980): 14.
57 Patrick O'Leary and Peter Sheldon, *Employer Power and Weakness*, 3–5.
58 Michael Barry, "A Bone of Contention: Managerial Initiative vs Employer Association Regulation of the New Zealand Meat Industry, 1960–75," *Labour History* 84 (2003): 84.

As strikes became endemic in some plants, and profits fell across the industry over a five-year period up to the late 1970s, the New Zealand Freezing Companies' Association noted that many employers had adopted a strategy of "get[ting] closer to senior Union leaders" in order to lessen the problem of unrest and to introduce new technology.[59] This only succeeded in a few plants, and as costs mounted by the late 1970s, a consensus emerged among employers that drastic restructuring and downsizing was necessary to restore long-term profitability.

Expenses rose due to multiple local and global factors. Fixed-capital expenditure increased dramatically. Companies had to expand their processing capacities because livestock numbers increased to historic highs, largely due to generous government farm subsidies. EEC and other countries' hygiene regulations required meat companies to spend hundreds of millions of dollars to modernise plants and machinery.[60] Transport and production costs rapidly rose due to global recessions, oil crises, and high inflation. Labour unrest increased wage costs in a labour-intensive industry. Yet given the aforementioned weighty surge in other costs, it was seemingly not – contrary to some theories such as autonomist Marxism – the primary cause of the profit squeeze that afflicted the industry.

Concurrently, income became more limited and variable due to several global factors. The most important of these was the profound effect of the United Kingdom joining the EEC in 1973. Britain was by far the largest market for Aotearoa/New Zealand meat, and its alignment with the EEC terminated the guaranteed market for Aotearoa/New Zealand lamb and mutton. As EEC quotas shrank the amount of meat that could be exported to the United Kingdom, companies were forced to sell meat in other markets such as Japan, North America, and Iran. Furthermore, as global competition in the export sheep meat market increased, and over-production began to occur, prices for sheep meat declined.

During the 1980s, employers became belligerent and united in their approach to employment relations. Employer militancy was emboldened after the government de-regulated the industry in 1980.[61] The way companies restructured the meat industry mirrored that which occurred in the United States during the 1980s.[62] In both countries, de-industrialisation was designed to maximise profita-

---

59 New Zealand Freezing Companies' Association, *5th Annual Report 1978/79*, Wellington: n.d.: 4, 8.
60 New Zealand Freezing Companies' Association, *7th Annual Report 1980/81*: 8 and *8th Annual Report 1981/2*: 1.
61 De-regulation also increased competition between companies, and contributed to several company mergers and takeovers, yet employers were united in their militancy towards unions.
62 For the United States case, see Kathleen Stanley, "Industrial and Labor Market Transformation in the U.S. Meatpacking Industry," in *The Global Restructuring of Agro-Food Systems*, edited by Philip McMichael (Ithaca: Cornell University Press, 1994), 129–144. A major difference between the

bility and to minimise labour unrest. For example, companies closed large, outdated plants in urban areas, throwing thousands of workers out of work, while opening smaller yet more automated plants in rural areas situated on cheaper land. These rural meatworks were located closer to stock and in areas without strong union traditions (indeed, several were opened as anti-union plants). In the Aotearoa/New Zealand case, by 1998, companies had closed 29 plants and opened forty-three new ones after de-regulation commenced in 1980. Despite the establishment of these new slaughterhouses, the workforce was nearly cut in half, declining from 34,000 in 1981/82 to about 18,000 in 1999.[63] While productive output rose due to greater automation and the introduction of shift work, wages were slashed, either under threats of closure, or when new meatworks were established. In some non-unionised new plants, temporary work agencies employed workers on daily contracts.[64] A pro-management history of the industry that praised this restructuring soberly noted that unionists thought working conditions in the new automated slaughterhouses were "brutal."[65]

Evidence is patchy as to the impacts of restructuring on the killing floor. What evidence is available suggests that management concertedly attempted to re-assert its alleged right to manage the factory floor in the late 1980s and 1990s. For example, in new plants in the late 1980s, highly disciplinary measures were instituted so as to curb informal and formal resistance, as well as workers' control and autonomy.[66] According to Bruce Curtis, the tally system remained an industry standard until at least 1996.[67] With sped-up production, accident rates increased. To Findlay, abolishing the tally system was inherently dangerous as "those tallies are worked out by bloody thousands of people getting mutilated over a long period of time!" He remembers that in one anti-union plant during the late 1990s some workers experienced "most *horrific* injuries. People with a bolt going through their fucking bodies."[68]

An alleged shift away from Fordism to flexible work arrangements occurred through restructuring, although there are few case studies about these practices,

---

United States and Aotearoa/New Zealand was that United States employers depended upon significant numbers of migrants – especially Latinos – to work in the newly established plants.

63 Boraman, "Wildcat Homers": 479; Department of Statistics, *Census of Manufacturing 1981/82*, (Wellington: Dept. of Statistics, n.d.), 12; and *The Cutting Edge*, unnumbered, n.d. (c. 1998): 4.

64 Council of Trade Unions, *Under Pressure: A Detailed Report into Insecure Work in New Zealand* (Wellington: CTU, 2013), 31.

65 Mick Calder and Janet Tyson, *Meat Acts: The New Zealand Meat Industry 1972–1997* (Wellington: Meat New Zealand, 1999), 290.

66 Boraman, "Wildcat Homers": 479–480.

67 Curtis, "New Zealand's Meat Board": 104.

68 Ken Findlay, Interview with author.

which makes it difficult to make industry-wide generalisations.[69] However, from the evidence available, it appears that the work process was transformed in several plants through instituting job rotation and multi-skilling (although the dis-assembly line work process is still largely Fordist), teamwork (and the renaming of supervisors as "team leaders"), total customer service and total quality management. Although at one plant, these new work arrangements only applied to twenty percent of the workforce.[70] While a flatter management structure was adopted in several plants, which gave teams some autonomy from strict disciplinarian supervision, overall these work processes and management styles attempted to nullify dissent through a more indirect form of managerial control, as workers were encouraged to cooperate and completely identify with management and their goals at every step of the production process, and thus become more agreeable to austerity such as wage cuts.[71] This "new regime of discipline," as Curtis calls it, was underpinned by local branches of unions at several plants, wherein union delegates (who were also appointed as team leaders) became the central figures in the everyday disciplining of workers to ensure quality control and avoid "lost" production.[72] Mick Calder and Janet Tyson argue that these management processes were successful in reducing strikes and absenteeism in the 1990s.[73]

Rationalising attempted to reduce meatworkers' structural and associational power. Workers' marketplace bargaining power was undermined by greatly increasing mass unemployment in the 1980s. Meatworkers' workplace bargaining power was reduced, as sheep farming became less strategically important in the Aotearoa/New Zealand economy (sheep farmers often became cattle (dairy) farmers after the 1980s, as dairy farming was a more profitable and less unionised industry). Their associational power was somewhat shattered, as unions were marginalised, and informal bonds seemingly fractured. Conversely, employers utilised various strategies to increase their productivity and profitability (and overcome resistance), including spatial fixes (such as moving meatworks to rural areas) and technological fixes (such as introducing greater automation, and developing larger

---

69 See, for example, Bruce Curtis, "Producers, Processors and Markets: A Study of the Export Meat Industry in New Zealand," Ph.D. thesis, University of Canterbury, 1996; and Alan Foster, "Workplace Reform and Weddels Staff," M.A. thesis, Massey University, 1995.

70 Martin Perry et al., *Reform at Work: Workplace change and the new industrial order* (Auckland: Longman Paul, 1995), 95.

71 For example, after total customer service and teamwork was introduced in 1993 at Tōmoana meatworks, wages were cut by 13 percent and 120 jobs were lost. In 1994, Tōmoana was then closed. Foster, "Workplace Reform and Weddels Staff": 100–102.

72 Curtis, "Producers, Processors and Markets": 264–272. He uses the term "new regime of discipline" on page 268.

73 Calder and Tyson, *Meat Acts*, 290.

sheep breeds and more productive grasses). In other words, the autonomist Marxist thesis that class struggle produced multiple innovations for capital seems validated, although these innovations were not just a reaction to that antagonism.

These immense transformations did not occur without stern opposition, however. Strikes became longer, more defensive, and intense as unions attempted to retain jobs and conditions in the 1980s. This is illustrated in Table 7.1, which shows a major spike occurred during the 1980s in working days not worked due to stoppages. In contrast, the majority of 1970s stoppages were short-lived localised conflicts that generally aimed to maintain or further living standards.[74]

Many of these clashes – both local and national – were focused on workers gaining redundancy payments, as few redundancy provisions were provided in the national award. Strikes were often unsuccessful in that they resulted in concessions to employers or only blunted the extent of wage or job cuts. Divisions and tensions between and within unions meant that resistance was fractured. As plants closed, and unemployment grew, morale among workers and unions gradually waned. This was a drawn-out process, however, as wages and conditions were still retained in some plants in the 1990s.

In comparison with the United States, resistance to restructuring seems to have been more widespread. The militant social unionism of the United Packinghouse Workers of America became diluted through successive mergers with larger, yet more moderate, unions in 1968 and 1979. As a result, national opposition to meat industry restructuring in the United States was limited in scope, especially under the "controlled retreat" strategy of the United Food and Commercial Workers of America in the 1980s. Several meatpackers' local unions opposed wage cuts or closures on their own in direct conflict with their national union, as occurred during the defeat of the seminal Hormel meatworkers' strike in Austin, Minnesota in 1985 to 1986.[75]

In contrast, while much opposition to restructuring was also localised in Aotearoa/New Zealand, both major unions supported plant-based strikes against it (through, for example, organising national collections or levies for local strike funds). They also mounted nationwide opposition. The most important instance of this was the tumultuous national strike against restructuring in 1986, which represented the largest dispute in the country since 1951 in terms of working days not worked (according to government statistics, about one million working days were

---

74 However, some lengthy and national disputes occurred in the 1970s, and many localised disputes occurred in the 1980s. Further, many disputes were not simply about wages in the 1970s and restructuring in the 1980s, but also about working conditions, dismissals, and so on.

75 See Peter Rachleff, *Hard-Pressed in the Heartland: The Hormel Strike and the Future of the Labor Movement* (Boston: South End Press, 1999).

not worked in the industry in 1986; see Table 7.1). Employers viewed the strike as a stellar victory as it allowed them to introduce new technology and work methods in the national award or "master agreement."[76] The strike was hampered by divisions between the NZMWU and the ATFWU, as the former returned to work after six weeks, and the latter held out for eight weeks. This mistrust between the unions hindered other major national strikes against closures. For example, when the ATFWU went on strike to demand that the closed Southdown plant re-open in 1980, a stoppage that succeeded in re-opening the slaughterhouse temporarily, NZMWU members voted against joining their strike. Conversely in 1982 when the NZMWU struck in a redundancy dispute after the Petone plant closed, the ATFWU offered to only undertake a symbolic two-day strike, but the conflict was settled before the Auckland union's sympathy stoppage ensued.

Divisions also existed within unions. For example, the NZMWU's East Coast regional North Island branch adopted a conciliatory attitude towards restructuring. Employers exploited these divisions as it meant they could introduce new technology and work methods more easily in some plants and regions, and thus place pressure on other regions that attempted to oppose them. Hence conditions were gradually eroded. Overall, opposition to restructuring was unable to stem employers' militancy. Stoppages in the broader category of manufacturing (which meat processing was presumably included within) fell dramatically after 1991 (separate strike statistics in the meat industry were not kept after 1991 and are thus not included in Table 7.1).

The Influence of the State: From the Keynesian Class Compromise to the Neoliberal Disciplining of Labour

This section shall endeavour to briefly examine the considerable impacts of state regulation and de-regulation of the meat industry and employment relations. Perhaps the state's influence in employment relations may be called "institutional power," that is, power derived from state institutions and resources. Under the Keynesian policy framework of widespread state regulation (which existed in Aotearoa/New Zealand from 1935 to 1984), it would seem the state largely enabled union power and limited employers' power. Indeed, full employment, near compulsory unionism, and compulsory centralised wage bargaining increased unions'

---

76 New Zealand Meat Industry Association, *Annual Report 1985/86*: 7.

structural and associational power significantly. Furthermore, Curtis has importantly argued that the New Zealand Meat Producers' Board, a statutory body which regulated the meat processing industry (which he argues represented the collective interests of farmers),

> unintentionally and indirectly empowered meatworkers and their unions. This empowerment was instituted despite farmers and the Board being inherently hostile towards labour organization [....] The Board used its statutory powers to limit the scale and scope of meat companies and, by limiting their powers in the product markets of central concern to farmers, made these companies commensurately weak in labour markets.[77]

Substantial evidence supports this argument: the Meat Board only authorised a limited number of companies to operate in the market until de-regulation in 1980; it issued few licenses for companies to construct new plants; and it restricted the number of foreign companies operating in the country.

Yet these claims, however essential, neglect the wider picture beyond the Meat Board's regulation of the industry. In general, the state played a contradictory role in social relations in the meat industry under Keynesianism – it both enabled and constrained (or attempted to constrain) union and workers' power. This reflects how the Keynesian compact was an uneasy class compromise between capital, the state, and labour, rather than a one-sided arrangement that (intentionally or unintentionally) empowered labour.[78]

After the Arbitration Court issued a nil wage order (a general wage increase of zero percent for all workers covered by the state's arbitration system) in 1968, effectively a wage cut given inflation, militant unions – including the meatworkers – lost faith in the state's employment relations system of compulsory arbitration and centralised wage settlement. Meatworkers' unions banned all meat exports until the nil wage order was abandoned and wages were nationally increased by five percent.[79] Afterward they increasingly utilised localised strikes in order to gain incentive payments over and above the national award set by the Arbitration Court. This direct action was often much to the annoyance of employers. For example, the New Zealand Freezing Companies' Association complained that unions routinely disregarded or by-passed the dispute procedures set out in the national award and ignored the requirement under the Industrial Relations Act 1973 to give two weeks' notice for strike action in essential industries.[80]

---

77 Curtis, "New Zealand's Meat Board": 93.

78 See Bruce Jesson, *Fragments of Labour: The Story Behind the Labour Government* (Auckland: Penguin, 1989), 9; and Wright, "Working-Class Power."

79 Boraman, "Revisiting the Local and Global Upheavals of 1968," *Counterfutures* 6 (2018): 45.

80 New Zealand Freezing Companies' Association, *7th Annual Report 1980/81*: 5.

In the 1970s and 1980s, wage increases were often seen by the state as the primary cause of the rampant inflation of the time. Consequently, successive leftist and conservative governments attempted to curb strike activity, limit wage increases, and decry militant unionism. Meatworkers' unions were commonly portrayed as wrecking the national interest for their own selfish gain. Jonathon Boston argues that Aotearoa/New Zealand was subject to a higher degree of governmental wage restraints from the early 1970s to the mid-1980s than any other country in the Organisation for Economic Co-operation and Development.[81]

As Bert Roth noted, the state's increasingly strict restrictions on strikes had no deterrent effect; instead, they increased strike activity in response.[82] Meatworkers' unions generally possessed enough strategic clout during the 1970s to simply ignore state-mandated dispute resolution procedures and curbs on striking. Extensive wage controls, including lengthy wage freezes in 1976 to 1977 and 1982 to 1984, further inflamed meatworkers' dissent during an inflationary era when living standards declined for most.[83] Meatworkers claimed substantive pay increases after wage controls were lifted. Conversely employers and the government seemed reluctant to risk a major national confrontation in a key export industry in the 1970s. When a conservative government attempted this in 1978, after 192 meatworkers were convicted for undertaking an alleged illegal strike at the Ocean Beach abattoir, the government was forced to back down. They withdrew their court case after the NZMWU threatened national action in response.[84]

A relatively harsh version of neoliberalism was introduced during the 1980s and 1990s in Aotearoa/New Zealand, which greatly swung the balance of power in favour of employers.[85] After the 1980 de-regulation of the meat industry, the Meat Board no longer restricted the construction of new abattoirs, or limited the number of companies that could enter the industry. Yet this liberalisation was done within an overall Keynesian framework; neoliberalism as a comprehen-

---

81 Jonathan Boston, *Incomes Policy in New Zealand 1968–1984* (Wellington, Victoria University Press, 1984), 77.

82 Bert Roth, "The History of New Zealand Industrial Legislation," *New Zealand Monthly Review* 186 (1977): 4–9.

83 Governments were able to pass regulations – similar to executive orders in the United States – that froze wages under various acts, such as the Economic Stabilisation Act 1948. Due to the concentration of state power in the executive under Aotearoa/New Zealand's British-modelled parliamentary system, governments could issue such orders in an unimpeded fashion.

84 Pat Walsh, "The Saga of Ocean Beach: A Cautionary Tale," in *New Zealand Industrial Relations in the Late 1970s: Three Cases*, edited by Pat Walsh and Raymond Harbridge (Wellington: Industrial Relations Centre, 1983), 33, 38–40.

85 See Jane Kelsey, *The New Zealand Experiment: A World Model for Structural Adjustment?* (Auckland: Auckland University Press, 1997).

sive policy regime was rolled out later in 1984 by a formerly social democratic Labour Party. In 1985, the Labour government phased out all subsidies to pastoral farming. Subsequently, sheep numbers declined from a peak of 70 million in 1982 to almost 49 million in 1995 as many farms closed, slaughterhouses were shut down en masse, and rural regions experienced a depression.[86]

Far from being laissez-faire in employment relations, Gérard Duménil and Dominique Lévy argue that neoliberalism in practice tends to produce greater liberty for capital while endeavouring to discipline and control labour.[87] While under neoliberalism, governments abandoned interventionist wage restraints, they intervened in a more fundamental way by altering the underlying legislative framework to be largely in favour of employers. For example, the Labour Relations Act 1987 forced unions to choose between plant-based local agreements with employers or the national award. According to Cybele Locke, employers utilised that law "to destroy all second-tier [local] bargaining agreements and significantly reduce wages and conditions in the national award."[88] Pay was also severely cut by employers terminating some of the aforementioned local piecework agreements that many meatworkers primarily depended on for their pay, and sometimes negotiating new local agreements which were more favourable to employers.

That law was a minor change when compared with the Employment Contracts Act (ECA) 1991, which represented the biggest overhaul to the state's employment relations system in a hundred years. Introduced by a neoliberal National Party government, it ended the state's system of compulsory centralised wage bargaining (including the meatworkers' national award) that had existed since 1894. The ECA imposed voluntary unionism and encouraged individual contracts between workers and employers rather than collective agreements between unions and employers. Consequently, it sharply diminished workers' structural and associational power.[89] However, as Calder and Tyson note, the ECA in some respects "clarified and codified what was already underway," in that employers had already managed

---

86 Hugh Stringleman and Robert Peden, "Sheep farming – Importance of the sheep industry," *Te Ara – the Encyclopedia of New Zealand*, http://www.TeAra.govt.nz/en/interactive/16621/sheep-numbers-in-new-zealand-1851-2014, accessed 23 March 2020.

87 Gérard Duménil and Dominique Lévy, "The Neoliberal (Counter-)Revolution," in *Neoliberalism: A Critical Reader*, edited by Alfredo Saad-Filho and Deborah Johnston (London: Pluto, 2005), 10.

88 Cybele Locke, *Workers in the Margins*, 156.

89 Marjorie Jerrard, "Meat Industry Unions, Industry Restructuring, and Employment Relations Change in New Zealand and Australia," *New Zealand Journal of Employment Relations* 31, 1 (2006): 37–59.

to undermine the national award by introducing favourable plant-based agreements.[90]

Furthermore, the ECA outlawed almost all localised skirmishes that were common in the meat industry, as it made all strikes illegal outside official bargaining periods and except for major health and safety issues. Yet in contrast to the 1970s and much of the 1980s, unions were not in a position to challenge these disciplinary leg-irons. As Findlay noted, under the pressures of restructuring and recession the old macho belief that meatworkers were "big enough, and strong enough, and ugly enough to take on employers and win on their own" was now anachronistic.[91] Indeed, meatworkers' unions began to shift away from militancy by about the late 1980s and early 1990s, as was evident in how they only offered symbolic, short-lived opposition to the ECA.[92]

Conclusions

Curtis has importantly argued that a site-bound labour process approach to power relations between employers and workers is "blind to the range of actors, motivations and actions outside the workplace" including the impacts of global value chains and global and local markets, as well as the influence of the state.[93] Conversely, a focus on the role of employers, markets, and the state – as with the strategic choice approach of Curtis and others – is too top-down. It marginalises workers' and unions' agency. History-from-below captures well localised killing floor relations between workers and management, including the "blood and guts" and precarious nature of meat processing work, the everyday battle for control over work, and the overall influence of workers' and unions' informal and formal sources of power (including indigeneity and masculinity).

The widespread workers' revolt that occurred in the meat industry in the long 1970s was shaped both from below, as exemplified in extensive informal resistance and innumerable localised short stoppages, and from above by global factors such as the oil shock recessions and associated inflationary surge. The structural and associational power of unions and workers, and their informal and formal control of work, reached a peak during this time. Employers and the state were often

---

90 Calder and Tyson, *Meat Acts*, 288.
91 Ken Findlay interviewed in *Socialist Action*, 10 February 1984.
92 Ellen Dannin, *Working Free: The Origins and Impact of New Zealand's Employment Contracts Act* (Auckland: Auckland Univ. Press, 1997), 146; and Sarah Heal, "The struggle for and against the Employment Contracts Act, 1987–1991," M.A. thesis, University of Otago, 1995, 97, 132.
93 Curtis, "New Zealand's Meat Board": 97.

forced into defensive positions, despite many attempts from both to shackle wage increases and strikes.

In contrast, management re-asserted its right to manage work by thoroughly restructuring the industry in the 1980s. A primary aim of rationalising was to stamp out the subversive industrial game that prevailed in many slaughterhouses. Employers aimed to break up the subversive multi-ethnic bonds that existed among many workers and to shatter the power of unions, and their forms of control ("restrictive practices") over work. This restructuring was a reaction to global and local transformations that undermined profitability. "Destructuring" was enabled by the state de-regulating the industry and abandoning its centralised employment relations system, both of which startlingly diminished the power of unions. Overall, structure and agency (from both below on the slaughterhouse floor and above via union, employers, and state officials), and the local and global, were all fundamentally entangled in the extraordinary transformations that occurred in the meat industry during the 1970s and 1980s.

Nevertheless, restructuring was not simply a case of capital and the state working meticulously together against workers and unions. The state caused a massive slump in the industry when it ceased pastoral subsidies. Furthermore, the 1980s was not simply a period of utter employer and state dominance; restructuring was massively contested by unions, as evident in numerous national and local strikes. Gradually, however, employers gained the upper hand as unemployment rose and factory closures mounted. Despite how the level of workers' dissent has plunged markedly since the early 1990s, it is not all quiet on the workplace front in the meat industry today, given underlying dissatisfaction with the more precarious and exploitative relations that today exist in the industry.[94]

---

94 For example, the NZMWU's "jobs that count" campaign against precarity and a more contemporary round of meat industry restructuring resulted in lengthy lockouts in 2012 and 2015 to 2016 at several slaughterhouses. (The ATFWU became a regional branch of the NZMU in 2005.)

Sabine Rutar

8 Resistance and Regulation on the Self-managed Shop Floor in Yugoslavia

Introduction

In the 1960s and 1970s, the Yugoslav "third way," perched somewhere between Western-style capitalisms and Soviet-style planned economies, generated considerable fascination and hope, not least among Western European intellectuals. Heteronomy has a specific meaning in an authoritarian society such as Yugoslavia's under Tito, and the self-management system introduced workers' participation on other levels than just the ideological-rhetorical plane. Because of these ambivalences, an inquiry into participatory practises and its (further) potential yields interesting questions. How did the Titoist ideological construct play out on the shop floor? By what means was the social contract maintained? How was consent manufactured?[1] In laying out structural and locally contingent issues alike, this chapter focuses on Yugoslavia's largest shipbuilding centre, situated in the northeastern Adriatic city of Rijeka.

A good starting point for exploring the ambivalences of resistance and regulation is Wolfgang Höpken's monograph *Socialism and Pluralism in Yugoslavia*, published in 1984.[2] Apart from being a brilliant analysis, Höpken's study has the advantage of having been written in the final years when self-management functioned as a valid – if waning – model in Yugoslavia. At the end of the 1970s and the beginning of the 1980s, Höpken surveyed three decades of self-management as idea and as practise, but he studied the phenomenon before the 1990s wars of Yugoslav dissolution. Höpken thus worked before the imposition of the posthumous interpretive grid that would dominate analyses of Tito's state for many years after its demise. Scholars, deeply affected by events, struggled to regard objectively something that had been compromised and subject to an inevitably ethnicised gaze.[3] Yugoslavia has also tended to be treated as a twentieth-century state experiment whose failure had been foreordained from its inception in 1918, almost as if state-building had proceeded knowing full well that it was ulti-

---

1 Michael Burawoy, *Manufacturing Consent. Changes in the Labor Process under Monopoly Capitalism* (Chicago: University of Chicago Press, 1979).
2 Wolfgang Höpken, *Sozialismus und Pluralismus in Jugoslawien* (Munich: Oldenbourg, 1984).
3 Boris Previšić and Svjetlan Lacko Vidulić, eds., *Traumata der Transition. Erfahrung und Reflexion des jugoslawischen Zerfalls* (Tübingen: A. Francke, 2015).

https://doi.org/10.1515/9783111086552-009

mately doomed.[4] In this interpretative (and emotionally strained) context, certain scholars linked the self-management model causally to the outbreak of war.[5]

Socialism, Pluralism and Labour: A Potentiality

In *Socialism and Pluralism in Yugoslavia*, Höpken takes the Yugoslav experiment of direct democracy seriously and dissects it with great analytical depth. He was interested in determining whether socialism and pluralism are compatible "theoretical organisational models of industrialised societies." He found that there was potential for pluralist development in the Yugoslav model, albeit temporarily, in the period between the mid-1960s and the early 1970s: "In spite of some disillusionment, Yugoslavia has been not only a challenge to the socialist states of the Eastern bloc, it time and again has influenced also the discussions on democracy and participation in societies with a parliamentary setup."[6]

In recent years, the labour and company history of socialist Yugoslavia has seen a small revival, focusing mostly on companies and/or industries during the turbulent second half of the 1980s and during the sociopolitical transformations in the wake of state socialism's demise.[7] Scholars' interest in exploring how the

---

4 Goran Musić, "The Self-Managing Factory after Tito. The Crisis of Yugoslav Socialism on the Shop Floor," ([Ph.D. Thesis] Ph.D. Thesis, European University Institute, Florence, 2016), 13–24, gives a good overview of this scholarly production. For the book he shortened this particular section, Goran Musić, *Making and Breaking the Yugoslav Working Class. The Story of Two Self-Managed Factories* (Budapest, New York: CEU Press, 2021), 4–9.

5 Aleksandar Jakir, "Workers' Self-Management in Tito's Yugoslavia Revisited", *Mitteilungsblatt des Instituts für soziale Bewegungen* 33 (2005): 137–155. Jakir has renewed this assessment recently, see Aleksandar Jakir and Anita Lunić, "What Were the Outcomes of the Self-Managed Economy in Socialist Yugoslavia?" in *Cultures of Economy in South-Eastern Europe. Spotlights and Perspectives*, edited by Jurij Murasov, Davor Beganović, and Andrea Lešić (Bielefeld: transcript, 2020), 79–96.

6 Wolfgang Höpken, *Sozialismus und Pluralismus*, 17. All translations are mine.

7 Goran Musić, *Making and Breaking the Yugoslav Working Class*; Rory Archer and Goran Musić, "When Workers' Self-Management Met Neoliberalism. Positive Receptions of Market Reforms among Blue-Collar Workers in Late Yugoslav Socialism," in *Labor in State-Socialist Europe, 1945–1989. Contributions to a History of Work*, edited by Marsha Siefert (Budapest: CEU Press, 2020), 395–418; Tanja Petrović, "Fish Canning Industry and the Rhythm of Social Life in the Northeastern Adriatic," *Narodna Umjetnost* 57, 1 (2020): 33–49; Chiara Bonfiglioli, *Women and Industry in the Balkans. The Rise and Fall of the Yugoslav Textile Sector* (London: I. B. Tauris 2019); Ulf Brunnbauer and Andrew Hodges, "The Long Hand of Workers' Ownership. Performing Transformation in the Uljanik Shipyard in Yugoslavia/Croatia: 1970–2018," *International Journal of Maritime History* 31, 4 (2019): 860–878; Stefano Petrungaro, "Ethics of Work and Discipline in Transition: Uljanik in Late and Post-Socialism," *Review of Croatian History* 15, 1 (2019): 191–213; Anna Calori and Kathrin

post-Yugoslav societies coped (for better and for worse) has thus recently connected to the work of historians studying the events leading up to and following the systemic changes of 1989/1990.[8]

Fewer scholars have focused on the 1960s and 1970s, a time when Yugoslav self-management functioned as an international model.[9] Notably, and extending beyond the Yugoslav case, there are intellectual connections between those decades and current reflections on alternative (capitalist) socioeconomic organisation. For example, a few years ago the French historian Pierre Rosanvallon published a widely acclaimed "extended theory of democracy applicable to practices of government" in which he looks (predominantly) to France's and Great Britain's respective pasts to unearth tools that might be used to forge a consolidated democratic future.[10] Significantly in the context of this chapter, Rosanvallon started his career in the 1970s working on *autogestion*,[11] "utopian capitalism,"[12] and connections between *autogestion* and parliamentary democracy.[13] As Johanna Bockman has recently put it, such linkages are difficult to detect today, as "the capitalist

Jurkat, "'I'm Both a Worker and a Shareholder.' Workers' Narratives and Property Transformations in Postsocialist Bosnia-Herzegovina and Serbia," *Südosteuropa. Journal of Politics and Society* 65, 4 (2017): 654–678; Rory Archer and Goran Musić, "Approaching the Socialist Factory and Its Workforce. Considerations from Fieldwork in (Former) Yugoslavia," *Labor History* 58, 1 (2017): 44–66; Ivan Rajković, "Struggles for Moral Ground. Problems with Work and Legitimacy in a Serbian Industrial Town," Ph.D. thesis, University of Manchester, 2015.

8 Philipp Ther, *Die neue Ordnung auf dem alten Kontinent. Eine Geschichte des neoliberalen Europa* (Berlin: Suhrkamp, 2014); Frank Bösch, *Zeitenwende 1979. Als die Welt von heute begann* (Munich: C.H. Beck, 2019).

9 Sabine Rutar, "Labor Protest in the Italian-Yugoslav Border Region During the Cold War. Action, Control, Legitimacy, Self-Management," in *Labor in State-Socialist Europe*, Siefert, 373–394; Sabine Rutar, "Containing Conflict and Enforcing Consent in Titoist Yugoslavia. The 1970 Dockworkers' Strike in Koper (Slovenia)," *European History Quarterly* 45, 2 (2015): 275–294; Ulrike Schult, *Zwischen Stechuhr und Selbstverwaltung. Eine Mikrogeschichte sozialer Konflikte in der jugoslawischen Fahrzeugindustrie 1965–1985* (Berlin: Lit, 2017); Igor Stanić, "'Jedan od najtežih dana u Uljaniku!' Štrajk u brodogradilištu *Uljanik* 1967. Godine," *Problemi sjevernog Jadrana* 15 (2016): 73–95; Igor Stanić, "Što pokazuje praksa? Primjer funkcioniranja samoupravljanja u brodogradilištu Uljanik 1961.–1968. godine," *Časopis za suvremenu povijest* 46, 3 (2014): 453–474.

10 Pierre Rosanvallon, *Die gute Regierung* (Hamburg: Hamburger Edition, 2016), 27 and on. The French original (*Le bon gouvernement*) was published in 2015.

11 Pierre Rosanvallon, *L'âge de l'autogestion ou la politique au poste de commandement* (Paris: Ed. du Seuil, 1976).

12 Pierre Rosanvallon, *Le capitalisme utopique. Critique de l'idéologie économique* (Paris: Ed. du Seuil, 1979).

13 Pierre Rosanvallon, "'Autogestion' oder parlamentarische Demokratie?" in *Demokratischer Sozialismus für Industriegesellschaften*, edited by Gesine Schwan (Cologne: Europäische Verlagsanstalt, 1979), 52–63.

counterrevolution against the twentieth-century socialist revolutions has been so powerful that it has obscured this past."[14]

Indeed, it is analytically useful to avoid treating state socialism *en bloc*. Pavel Kolář has convincingly shown how after Stalin's death in 1953, a "post-Stalinist discourse of ambiguity" emerged in the East European societies, which maintained "the bipolar worldview of socialism vs. capitalism," albeit in a "post-Stalinist confused and ambivalent" manner. He also chronologically distinguished post-Stalinism from sclerotic late socialism, thereby implying that assessments of these three phases could legitimately yield differing conclusions.[15] Yugoslavia's path was conditioned by its split away from the Soviet Union in 1948. However, post-Stalinist politics in the Soviet Union led to a rapprochement between the two countries. Yugoslavia, acting in between the ideological blocs, remained part and parcel of the larger Cold War story.[16]

Wolfgang Höpken anticipated Kolář's temporal subdivision. Kolář writes that it was the narrative "link between the plots of 'class' and 'nation'" that fostered the "post-Stalinist discourse of ambiguity and ambivalence," thereby generating "both stabilizing and also pluralizing effects."[17] Some 30 years earlier, Höpken had written that "the idea of a connection between socialism and pluralism" could be understood as a "historical and theoretical negation of Stalinism, that is of its persisting structural leftovers."[18] In place of Stalin's mass terror there was "a broad and finely graded system of institutionalized control," which nonetheless implied that open repression could be reactivated at any moment.[19] Social conflict came to be tolerated due to "the necessity to increase [economic] effectivity." The post-Stalinist societies began to resort to politics that sought legitimation and cohesion rather than merely control and, in economic terms, to a more con-

---

14 Johanna Bockman, "The Struggle over Structural Adjustment. Socialist Revolution versus Capitalist Counterrevolution in Yugoslavia and the World," in *Economic Knowledge in Socialism, 1945–1989*, edited by Till Düppe and Ivan Boldyrev (Durham and London: Duke University Press, 2019), 254. In a similar vein, see Sabine Rutar, "Betriebliche Selbstverwaltung zwischen den Blöcken – und danach? Das jugoslawische Modell in Rückschau und Perspektive", in *Erfahrungs- und Handlungsräume. Gesellschaftlicher Wandel in Südosteuropa seit dem 19. Jahrhundert zwischen dem Lokalen und Globalen*, edited by Heike Karge, Ulf Brunnbauer, and Claudia Weber (Munich: De Gruyter, 2017), 118–135.

15 Pavel Kolář, *Der Poststalinismus. Ideologie und Utopie einer Epoche* (Cologne: Böhlau, 2016), 213, 226.

16 On the Tito–Stalin split, see Jeronim Perović, "The Tito–Stalin Split: A Reassessment in Light of New Evidence," *Journal of Cold War Studies* 9, 2 (2007): 32–63.

17 Kolář, *Der Poststalinismus*, 176.

18 Höpken, *Sozialismus und Pluralismus*, 42.

19 Höpken, *Sozialismus und Pluralismus*, 26.

sumerist approach. Both Höpken and Kolář point out how mechanisms of author-itative discourse are not some idiosyncrasy of state socialist systems, found as they are in "western and eastern systems" alike (Höpken),[20] under Margaret Thatcher or Helmut Kohl as well as in post-socialist neoliberal contexts (Kolář).[21]

Conceptually, Höpken linked pluralism to the parliamentary constitutional state, that is, to fundamental rights of liberty as well as legitimacy, judicial impar-tiality, the requirement of fairness, and competition among autonomous political forces, especially political parties.[22] Titoist Yugoslavia, obviously, cannot be so clas-sified. To test his hypothesis of pluralist potential, Höpken formulated the mini-mum requirements characteristic of ideal pluralism: heterogeneity in the forma-tion of political objectives was something that needed to be acknowledged; interests had to be articulated autonomously; dissent and conflict had to be legit-imate; extended participatory opportunities had to exist in all societal realms; and the relation between the single elements of the political system had to be based on equal standing and independence. He confirmed that, in principle, pluralism and socialism were compatible, "for instance in the sense of a socialist market econo-my." One of his several analytical fields consisted of the numerous work stoppages and strikes that in Yugoslavia were "a continually occurring, de facto recognised and [...] practically never sanctioned phenomenon," studied so that "they can be assessed as an effectively institutionalised means of direct articulation of interests and thus as a pluralistic systemic element."[23]

Yugoslavia was faced with the "original conflicts of distribution and power [...] inherent to the relation between capital and labour"[24] in line with other (capitalist) evidence of the adaptability of the relationship between state and market and of the role that labour played within this relationship.[25] The Yugoslav half-decade of potential (partial) democratisation occurred during "the peak phase of organ-ized capitalism" from 1945 to 1975, characterised by "the expansion of the welfare state and labour legislation, the cooperation of organised interests and the state, economic politics with increasingly Keynesian approaches, as well as a solid

---

20 Höpken, *Sozialismus und Pluralismus*, 27.
21 Kolář, *Der Poststalinismus*, 325–328.
22 Höpken, *Sozialismus und Pluralismus*, 33 on.
23 Höpken, *Sozialismus und Pluralismus*, 406.
24 Jürgen Kocka, *Geschichte des Kapitalismus* (Munich: C.H. Beck, 2014), 108.
25 Kocka, *Geschichte des Kapitalismus*, 113–123, gives a concise overview of such adaptability.

share of sectors put under state control and state-led master plans." These features made this peak phase an "economically mixed order."[26]

In Yugoslavia, such a "mix" brought forth, at least from 1966 to 1971, "an internal democratisation and a sectoral pluralism within [...] monistic systemic structures." The potential to expand democratisation was palpable in the frank and elaborate discussions about the merits and the flaws of the self-management model. First and foremost, however, frequent work stoppages indicated the existence of a potential for further democratisation.[27]

Evolving Self-management

Tito's state was complex. Competing interests vied with each other between and within the federated republics, as they did on the local level. Seeking to contain such competition, the ideological framework was permanently under construction and juggled huge structural ambivalences: "Yugoslavia was [...] in several respects a much more 'ideologized' state than other socialist systems in Eastern Europe. Like nowhere else society here experienced a permanent, almost manic change of the institutional order of the system, driven by the ideological imperative of the idea of a self-managed society."[28] At its core were the discrepancies among ideological scripts, technocratic normativities, market requirements, managerial efforts, and the room to manoeuvre allotted to the "heroes of labour," the industrial workers.

After Stalin's expulsion of Yugoslavia from the Council for Mutual Economic Assistance (Comecon) in 1948, self-management became the central means of distinguishing Yugoslavia from the Soviet mode of economic planning. In Yugoslavia's search for new allies, it proved useful for consolidating Yugoslavia's linkage to the West.[29] In 1950, the Basic Law on Management of State Economic Enterprises and Higher Economic Associations by the Work Collectives (*Osnovni zakon o upravljan-*

---

26 Kocka, *Geschichte des Kapitalismus*, 116; a seminal study is Johanna Bockman, *Markets in the Name of Socialism. The Left-Wing Origins of Neoliberalism* (Stanford, CA: Stanford University Press, 2011).

27 Höpken, *Sozialismus und Pluralismus*, 406–409, quote 407.

28 Wolfgang Höpken, "'Durchherrschte Freiheit'. Wie 'autoritär' (oder wie 'liberal') war Titos Jugoslawien?," in *Jugoslawien in den 1960er Jahren. Auf dem Weg zu einem (a)normalen Staat?*, edited by Hannes Grandits and Holm Sundhaussen (Wiesbaden: Harrassowitz, 2013), 54–55.

29 Vladimir Unkovski-Korica, "Worker's Councils in the Service of the Market. New Archival Evidence on the Origins of Self–Management in Yugoslavia 1948–1950," *Europe–Asia Studies* 66, 1 (2014): 108–134.

ju državnim privrednim poduzećima i višim privrednim udruženjima od strane rad-nih kolektiva) was introduced. Defining the company as a sovereign body, it distinguished "governance" from "administration." The basic governing body was the workers' council, founded on the ideological premise that workers possessed the politically induced right to participate in the running of their enterprises. The administrative structure, by contrast, consisted of salaried personnel chosen on merit in compliance with the market and the technological demands of production – the management. The Yugoslav trade union federation's task was to monitor social standards and facilitate the implementation of self-management. Interestingly, the union, during the first decade and a half of self-management, often acted in favour of market reforms, and was thus not quite the typical "party's conveyor belt."[30]

Management was answerable to both the workers' council and the local party functionaries. The director and his administrative board ran the company, but the business plan had to be authorised by workers' representatives, who were elected annually and could hold office for up to two years. While such arrangements were aimed to create a strong bond between a company's workers and its management, the party-state reserved the right to appoint directors. In this way, the goal was to "keep the pluralist development of [...] organisations and institutions within a controllable framework."[31]

The organs of industrial democracy did not extend beyond the factories. The actual power of the workers' councils remained very limited, as the business plan, in these early years, largely depended on state economic policies that were outside the sphere of influence of the individual company. The council's main tasks were to foster work discipline and a spirit of self-sacrifice and to effectively anchor the party among the industrial workers. Igor Stanić has aptly summarised what sociologists and economists, in assessing the system, found mind-boggling about how it was put into practise: the social ground had not been prepared beforehand; the company was chosen to occupy the central organisational level, while the workforce was brought up to its tasks only (very) partially; management was connected to the workers' council and workers' referenda in its decision-making. Company directors had to deal with the decision-making power of the workers, whom they perceived as amateurish; proceedings were complicated, if not ineffi-

---

30 Boris Kidrič, *Sabrana dela*, vol. V (Belgrade: Komunist, 1985), 11–13; also see Vladimir Unkovski-Korica, *The Economic Struggle for Power in Tito's Yugoslavia. From World War II to Non-Alignment* (London: I. B. Tauris, 2016).
31 Höpken, *Sozialismus und Pluralismus*, 405; also see Blagoje Bošković and David Dašić, eds., *Socialist Self-Management in Yugoslavia 1950–1980, Documents* (Belgrade: Socialist Thought and Practice, 1980), 63–73.

cient, and became ever more so as the system evolved into a complex regulatory regime.[32]

The economic reform of 1965, which came to be known as the introduction of "market socialism," was a significant moment. The following year, Yugoslavia joined the General Agreement on Tariffs and Trade (GATT), and the reform delivered the accompanying domestic framework. The dinar was linked to the US dollar and devalued, so that one hundred old dinars were now equal to one new dinar. State-managed investment funds were abolished and the banks took over. This came as a shock to many companies, who were suddenly expected to cope with the conditions of the (international) market. When, in mid-1965, the cost of living increased by 35 percent, many companies reacted with hiring moratoria or even layoffs, or reduced subsidies for canteen lunches or commuting expenses, as well as freezing or cutting pay. Labour fluctuation, closely linked to the lack of skilled personnel, was a complex issue. However, the main factors in play at the time included the market adaptability of a particular industry. Moreover, in the socialist republic of Croatia, of which Rijeka was a part, the unemployment rate peaked at 6.25 percent in 1968, its highest postwar level.[33]

As I have shown elsewhere, many companies had already been operating within the framework of the global market before these reforms, especially those industry sectors hugely dependent on multinational commerce, such as the operators of ports and shipyards. These firms welcomed the official acknowledgement of market affinity offered by the reform as an opportunity to streamline their companies with (now) assertive rigour. In implementing the law, the workers' councils relied heavily on external consultants, which led to the workforce's (further) alienation from the self-management system's organisational bodies. Workers felt overlooked and underinvolved in their enterprises. The reform's economic consequences struck them in immediate and palpable ways, increasing their dissatisfaction. They sought to articulate their discontent via means that ranged from collective visits to trade union and municipal political representatives to work stoppages and strikes. Social conflict was on the horizon.[34] It was in the years following the economic reform that Höpken detected a potential for the political system to be pluralised.

---

32 Stanić, "Što pokazuje praksa?": 457–8 and 471–2.

33 Stanić, "'Jedan od najtežih dana u Uljaniku!'": 73–76; more comprehensively, see Susan Woodward, *Socialist Unemployment. The Political Economy of Yugoslavia, 1945–1990* (Princeton, NJ: Princeton University Press, 1995).

34 Rutar, "Containing Conflict." Stanić, "Što pokazuje praksa?," reaches a similar conclusion for the Uljanik shipyard in Pula.

The Self-managed Shop Floor at the 3. Maj Shipyard

What did the evolution of self-management and its inherent democratic potential look like on the shop floor of Yugoslavia's largest shipbuilding enterprise, situated in the northeastern Adriatic city of Rijeka? In the following, I show how discursive choices depended on different interests and were guided by varying rhetorical enactments of self-management normativities. In a democratic system, this would be understood as pluralism. Yugoslavia, after the events of the so-called Croatian Spring of 1971, chose a different path.

In the interwar years Rijeka's port and shipyard had been under Italian management. The postwar Italo-Yugoslav Peace Treaty of 1947 assigned the city, together with the larger part of Istria and the Kvarner Islands, to the Federal People's Republic of Yugoslavia. A massive population exchange occurred from the war's final stages and peaked after 1947. A large portion of Rijeka's ethnic Italian inhabitants, approximately 80 percent of the city's population, left, the void filled in the years that followed by internal migrants from other parts of Yugoslavia, most of them of Croatian ethnicity and having a rural background.[35]

No matter how massive the change in the city's social texture, its regionally anchored identity held firm, which meant, among other things, that the Cold War border was conspicuously overlooked. Located within a few dozen square kilometres of one another, the ports and shipyards of Trieste and Rijeka, together with the shipyard in Monfalcone, all dated back to imperial Austro-Hungarian times and continued to be viewed as the traditional maritime industries of the northeastern Adriatic. In 1958 they were joined by the newly built port in Koper, Slovenia, established in expressed response to Trieste being "lost" to Italy. With regard to the federal government in Belgrade, Rijeka's managers and political functionaries frequently lamented the neglect of "maritime Yugoslavia" – that is, mainly of Croatia – thereby hinting at a simmering conflict over economic resources between the centre and the republics and/or peripheries.[36]

Rijeka's industrial plants were substantially destroyed in the Second World War, both by Anglo-American bombing and by the retreating German occupiers.[37]

---

35 Pamela Ballinger, "On the Borders of Force. Violence, Refugees, and the Reconfiguration of the Yugoslav and Italian States," *Past and Present* (2011), Supplement 6: 158–176.

36 Dunja Rihtman-Auguštin, "A Croatian Controversy. Mediterranean – Danube – Balkans," *Narodna Umjetnost* 36, 1 (1999): 103–119; Rutar, "Labor Protest."

37 Rajko Samueli Kačić, "Riječka bitka," *Sušačka revija* 49, n.d., http://www.klub-susacana.hr/revija/clanak.asp?Num=49&C=21, accessed 10 January 2023.

In the war's immediate aftermath, the Yugoslav military administration – until 1947, Rijeka, Istria, and the Kvarner Islands were part of a Zone B, while Trieste and its surroundings, as Zone A, were under Anglo-American military administration – focused on re-establishing some kind of everyday life in the midst of the rubble and dysfunctional structures and concentrated as well on efforts directed against those who had (allegedly) committed war crimes.[38] Starting in 1946, the port and the shipyard were re-built. The shipyard initially kept its old name *Cantieri navali del Quarnaro / Kvarnerska brodogradilišta* (Kvarner Shipyards), but in 1948 it was changed to *Poduzeće 3. Maj* (Company 3rd of May) and in 1952 to *Brodogradilište 3. Maj* (Shipyard 3rd of May). The ideological symbolic reference is to 3 May 1945, the day Tito's partisans liberated Rijeka from German occupation.[39]

A huge part of the reconstruction effort was carried out by labour brigades. The work ethic was Stalinist, characterised by shock work, a pace and achievement in excess of norms, and an overall sense of enthusiasm – how genuine or imposed is difficult to determine – in the face of peace and renewed hopes for the future. In 1947, the shipyard was put under the supervision of the Ministry of Defence and an ambitious five-year plan was launched. In 1948, the first professional school for shipbuilders, mechanics, carpenters, and electricians was opened.[40] The lack of skilled labour was partially addressed by the arrival of shipbuilders from Italy, mostly from Monfalcone, who came to Rijeka with the expressed aim of helping build socialist Yugoslavia. After the Tito-Stalin split, however, these workers, who mostly adhered to the Italian Communist Party's support for Stalin, faced harsh suppression, and the majority returned to Italy.[41] When the USSR and other East European countries withdrew their support for Rijeka's industries, the labour brigades were tasked with increasing production in spite of the new status quo.[42]

---

38 Mihael Sobolevski, "Fiume: una storia complessa / Zamršena povijest Rijeke," in *Le vittime di nazionalità italiana a Fiume e dintorni (1939–1947) / Žrtve talijanske nacionalnosti u Rijeci i okolici (1939.–1947.)*, edited by Amleto Ballarini and Mihael Sobolevski (Rome: Ministero per i Beni e le Attività Culturali, Direzione Generale per gli archivi, 2002, 147–193, 163 and passim.

39 Ivan Rogić et al., *'3. Maj.' Složena organizacija udruženog rada brodograđevne industrije Rijeka* (Rijeka: SOUR brodograđevne industrije '3. Maj', 1984), 151.

40 Rogić et al., *'3. Maj.'*, 162.

41 Enrico Miletto, "La speranza e l'illusione. Da Monfalcone alla Jugoslavia di Tito. Il controesodo dei comunisti italiani," *Contemporanea* 22, 1 (2019): 51–78; Marco Puppini, *Costruire un mondo nuovo: un secolo di lotte operaie nel Cantiere di Monfalcone. Storie di uomini, di passioni e di valori* (Gradisca d'Isonzo: Centro Isontino di ricerca e documentazione storica e sociale 'Leopoldo Gasparini', 2008); Andrea Berrini, *Noi siamo la classe operaia: i duemila di Monfalcone* (Milano: Baldini Castoldi Dalai, 2004).

42 Rogić et al., *'3. Maj'*, 163.

In June 1950, self-management was first introduced under the aforementioned Basic Law on the Management of State-Run Economic Enterprises and Higher Economic Associations by Work Collectives. In Yugoslavia, 215 companies – 63 in Croatia and six in Rijeka – were chosen as pioneering self-managed organisations, the Shipyard 3. Maj among them. The first workers' council was formed in September. It would take the better part of the 1950s for the council not to operate in the shadow of the company's centralist and highly hierarchical management. From the beginning, seminars and other types of instructive meetings were organised in an attempt to counteract the lack of competence among council members.[43]

Under this framework, from 1952 onwards, the state monopoly over foreign trade was abolished, as was vertical control of factories by political bodies. Decision-making was moved to the enterprise level. The shipbuilding industry, opened up to the world market, was linked to Yugoslavia's foreign policy goals targeting (post)colonial societies in Africa and Asia, as well as the western hemisphere. As a result of such economic policymaking during the 1950s and 1960s, enterprises did "eventually succumb to the competition logic dominant in global capitalism," because export orientation and consequential market dependency "necessitate a different mode of organizing the workplace and the polity."[44]

In 1953/1954, the political rift over the "Trieste question" was again heightened, quelled only when the London Memorandum of October 1954 brought a *de facto* end to the Free Territory of Trieste and confirmed the contested borderline between the remainder of Zones A and B, thus assigning Trieste to Italy. The state border was only ratified, however, in 1975 through the Treaty of Osimo, within the broader context of the Helsinki Accords.[45] By that time the Italo-Yugoslav border had become one of the most open ideological frontlines of the Cold War. Yugoslavs' shopping excursions to Trieste are as emblematic of those years as the thousands of west European tourists on holiday along Yugoslavia's coast.[46]

After the introduction of self-management in 1950, the Shipyard 3. Maj left the Ministry of Defence and began to operate independently. The ministry's Central Shipbuilding Administration (*Centralna Uprava Brodogradnje*, CUB) was replaced

43 Rogić et al., '*3. Maj.*', 171.
44 Unkovski-Korica, *Economic Struggle for Power*, 231–232.
45 Jože Pirjevec, Borut Klabjan, and Gorazd Bajc, eds., *Osimska meja: jugoslovansko-italijanska pogajanja in razmejitev leta 1975* (Koper: Annales, 2006).
46 Breda Luthar, "Shame, Desire and Longing for the West. A Case Study of Consumption", in *Remembering Utopia. The Culture of Everyday Life in Socialist Yugoslavia*, edited by Breda Luthar and Maruša Pušnik (Washington, DC.: New Academic Publishers, 2010), 341–378; Hannes Grandits and Karin Taylor, eds., *Yugoslavia's Sunny Side: a History of Tourism in Socialism (1950s–1980s)* (Budapest and New York: Central European University Press, 2010).

in 1952 by the newly formed Shipbuilding Industry Association (*Udruženje Brodogradevinske Industrije*) and the Federal Chamber of Commerce (*Savezna Privredna Komora*), which worked to improve professional education, connecting the shipyard with the state authorities and sociopolitical organisations as well as administering the foreign exchange fund and studying the market. The CUB's abolition caused 3. Maj to struggle, its administration suddenly tasked with matters it had never been responsible for. More seriously, the abrupt change in the investment lending regime – with state funds yielding to competitive banking funds – jeopardised plans for the construction of ships.[47]

At the beginning of 1953, social ownership and self-managed manufacturing were written into constitutional law, though conundrums related to their implementation remained unsolved. That same year, 3. Maj presented its first market-oriented business plan. The shipyard embarked upon a frenzy of Taylorist modernising efforts that would last two decades, which included ongoing assessment of the effectiveness of the self-management framework. Massive technological improvements exerted an enormous impact on the workforce, as did the streamlining of production and supply chains and of administrative logistics. In 1954, the shipyard began to forge contracts with western countries, first among them Switzerland and Great Britain. Egypt's nationalisation of the Suez Canal in July 1956 (triggering the Suez Crisis) led to a spike in demand for ships, to which 3. Maj responded through further intensification of production and an increase in its ships' size. Special efforts were made to modernise the welding process. The building of small- and medium-sized tankers had stretched the limits of 3. Maj's capacities. At the time its limited capacities seemed a disadvantage, but this specialisation would prove to be an asset in the mid-1970s, when the age of mammoth tankers came to an end.[48]

In January 1958, the Law on Labour Relations ruled that work collectives, even in huge companies such as 3. Maj, could themselves decide how net revenue was to be distributed. The firm's workers' council reacted by, among other measures adopted, raising pay by almost 11 percent for workers in the production sector, levelling out internally the tariff regulations and income inequalities that had existed. Rewards for special merit were also introduced. In 1961, an economic reform set the rule that companies could oversee only one-third of accumulated revenue. That most prices were still determined by the state brought additional interference into the distribution of net revenue. A vast discrepancy opened up between this unfree domestic economic policy and 3. Maj's expanded position on the world market. What is more, the modernisation efforts had proven to be difficult to imple-

---

47 Rogić et al., '3. Maj', 174–175.
48 Rogić et al., '3. Maj', 185–187.

ment on the shop floor, which increased the gap between what was demanded by the international market and how the company functioned locally. Delays in the delivery chain persisted, as did delays in preparing documentation; varying capacities between certain professions were out of balance, and other organisational problems also hampered performance. The shipyard's management continued to tighten the reins in enforcing the Taylorist measures it had adopted: seeking to contain operating costs, it was unable to raise prices at the necessary pace, and it aimed to significantly shorten construction time without exhausting the workers. Mistakes resulting from poor workmanship needed to be avoided. When, in 1962, the trade union saw more workers elected to the workers' council, the increase was little more than a cosmetic boost to their participatory power, because the workers neither received material compensation for their administrative activities nor could perform them in exchange for their hours working in production-related tasks. Thus, the incentive for participation remained low for blue-collar workers.[49]

In 1963, Jadranbrod was founded, an association that aimed to foster cooperation and standardisation among the Yugoslav shipyards and their subindustries as well as with procurement and storage services. Not until 1968 would 3. Maj join Jadranbrod, however, and it was soon apparent that the cooperative efforts were to little avail. The domestic infrastructure continued to fall short. Meanwhile, further attempts at direct democracy were enacted. In 1963, the shipyard's governing bodies installed professional working units comprising a maximum of 250 workers, bound together in "communities" according to competences (technological, economic, social standards, accounting, legal service, occupational psychology, etc.). Eighty-one work units were organised into 23 such working communities, which in turn were bundled into what were now the shipyard's three main structural pillars: management and production, development and investment, and analysis and planning.[50]

There is insufficient space here to delve deeper into the intricacies of competitiveness for 3. Maj or, for that matter, for any other shipyard. It may suffice to point out that large ships can be built only via massive loans, and without state support these loans could reach 100 percent of financing, ensuring that the repayment phase would last several years. Balancing out operating costs was, therefore, a difficult business. The shipyard's economic health was heavily dependent on its ability to contract loans with favourable interest terms and on actually earning the profits envisioned in its calculations at the beginning of the construction phase. Since 3. Maj, to consolidate its competitiveness, had heavily invested in modernisa-

---

49 Rogić et al., '3. Maj', 216–223.
50 Rogić et al., '3. Maj', 219.

tion, it could not concentrate exclusively on the domestic market, which would have meant not making full use of its production capacities. Exports were the way to go.[51]

Market Socialism

Once the insufficiency of the 1961 reforms became evident, a second reform followed in 1965 introducing what is commonly referred to as "market socialism" and freeing from state governance those aspects of the economy previously under its supervision. Now there could be substantial freedom for capital to circulate. This impetus allowed 3. Maj, at least for a time, to reconcile the contradictions between the conditions on the world market and those at home. Its most successful business year to date was 1966, the year it launched its economic plan for 1966 to 1970, aiming to divide production into 70 percent shipbuilding, 20 percent construction of diesel engines, and 10 percent equipment production and development. Construction deadlines were to be shortened once more by about 30 percent. To achieve this target, parallel construction lines were introduced, the assembly flow was re-arranged, and pre-assembly blocks were established. The overall economic goals were so extensive that, once again, the shipyard's capacities had to be considerably enlarged, making 3. Maj look more like a construction site than a facility for the construction of ships: Larger halls, new cranes, and new devices for drying and painting sheets were introduced, as were new machines for sheet-metal cutting and for the hydraulic bending of sheets, along with a fully automated panel line, stronger engines, reconstructed slipways, a floating production unit for the building of larger ships, and new buildings to house 3. Maj's administration. Situated as it was between the sea and the city centre (and the nearby hills), expansion was impossible and available space had to be optimised. The modernising overhaul, undertaken in cooperation with a newly established Norwegian company called Shipping Research Services, was completed in 1972.[52]

During these years of intense activity, income distribution among the work units, as well as between production workers and administrative staff, remained an ongoing bone of contention. In the latter half of the 1960s, a new generation

---

51 The intricacies involved in maintaining this balance are elaborated in great detail in Rogić et al., '3. Maj', 219 on. Comprehensively covered in Raquel Varela, Hugh Murphy, and Marcel van der Linden, eds., *Shipbuilding and Ship Repair Workers around the World. Case Studies 1950–2010* (Amsterdam: Amsterdam University Press, 2017).
52 "Uspješna plovidba u reformskim vodama," *Brodograditelj* (1 June 1969); Rogić et al., '3. Maj', 234–275.

of both political functionaries and company directors took office. Cadres who had joined after the Second World War often regarded having fought in the partisan war to be their principal mark of merit; now, a genuinely educated elite was taking over. The new directors were eager not only to accelerate the market reforms but also to prioritise socioeconomic matters over the party's decision-making. Ideologically, this economic liberalisation and shift in political control were characterised as the workers finally taking over, which raised hopes for a path toward an improved and sustained standard of living for the working class.[53]

Instead, social cleavages only deepened. In 1968, a constitutional amendment not only returned greater control over the company's revenue (70 percent) to the collective but also gave the workers' council more latitude in whether to invest or increase wages. At the same time, the abandonment of the compulsory membership quota for workers involved in production led the professional and managerial staff, who obviously prioritised investment over wages, to exert greater influence. The situation in the shipyard mirrored general developments in Yugoslavia, as the generational change brought to power a middle class–like professional elite emerging out of the successful postwar modernisation efforts. However, such success had made the ideological straitjacket threadbare: the "heroes of self-managed labour," the workers, had been sidelined when it came to power relations on the shop floor.[54]

Skilled workers continued to be hard to come by. The workforce at 3. Maj was predominantly unskilled, many of its workers recent migrants from the countryside. Ongoing efforts to transform them into fully qualified workers were never sufficient. The measures taken in this regard included professional training, the bestowal of social benefits, as well as offerings related to cultural, sport, and other leisure activities: in sum, the shipyard adopted a comprehensive approach to a lifestyle centred on the workplace. Protective measures against accidents reduced occupational injuries from a staggering 64.5 percent of the workforce in 1952 to 23.8 percent in 1958, and by the 1960s to between 15 and 20 percent, but never any lower. The 1960s saw a substantial economic emigration among the qualified labour force, as salaries in shipyards abroad were higher than those at home. Poor housing provision was an additional factor causing attrition. From

---

53 Jože Prinčić, "Direktorska funkcija v jugoslovanskem socialističnem gospodarskem sistemu," in *Biti director v času socijalizma: med idejami i praksami*, edited by Jurij Fikfak and Jože Prinčić (Ljubljana: Založba ZRC, 2008), 73; Denisson Rusinow, *The Yugoslav Experiment 1948–1974* (Berkeley: University of California Press, 1978), 115.

54 Christopher Prout, *Market Socialism in Yugoslavia* (Oxford: Oxford University Press, 1985), 57; Jim Seroka and Radoš Smiljković, *Political Organizations in Socialist Yugoslavia* (Durham: Duke University Press, 1986), 66.

1966 to 1970, 2,545 workers left the shipyard and 2,792 joined its ranks of workers, representing an exchange of around half the number of total workers. Efforts to counter this churn were only mildly successful. The expressed goal of self-management to strengthen the workforce's loyalty largely failed.[55]

Chronic issues persisted in spite of progress, and this push-pull dynamic seems to have been key to these – relatively prosperous – decades of modernisation and technicisation: Taylorist efforts to rationalise the production process continued apace; the lag effects of domestic infrastructure that collided with the demands of a competitive world market were still evident; trends of labour fluctuation and massive emigration, prompting a huge churn in the workforce, were not halted or reversed; skilled personnel remained lacking, perpetuating a high level of occupational accidents; and, not least, the experiment of direct democracy on the shop floor was sustained yet did not yield a substantiated decrease in inequality.

In the meantime, a Yugoslav culture of work stoppages had been developing since the late 1950s. Importantly, self-management had no built-in provisions to regulate conflict. In the same month (January 1958) that the Law on Labour Relations set out that work collectives would themselves decide how to distribute net revenue, workers in the Trbovlje coal mine in southern Styria, Slovenia, went on strike. By 1969, around 1,750 work stoppages had occurred, most in Croatia and Slovenia but extending throughout the country. Directors sought to convince or manipulate the workers' councils since they could not make decisions without the latter's consent. When workers' councils opted for measures that were perceived as counter to the workforce's interest, workers would simply cease their tasks, often spontaneously and mostly within individual workshops rather than as part of company-wide work stoppages. These, from 1958 onward, spurred the development of considerable discussion among sociologists, economists, and politicians about how they should be dealt with. In most cases, the work stoppages were kept within the confines of the individual factory or facility, the conflicts quelled by giving the workers what they wanted (mostly: higher pay).[56]

Such discussions also unfolded on the local level and incorporated workers' voices. In Rijeka in mid-1968, the daily *Novi List* began to give space to what would become a year-long public debate about why the shipyard was in bad shape and what needed to be done to improve things. In June 1968, several workers at 3. Maj – a carpenter, a metalworker, and an electrician among them – displayed pride and a not uncritical confidence in their self-management, marked by an

---

55 Rogić et al., '3. Maj', 234–275.
56 Neca Jovanov, "Odnos štrajka kao društvenog sukoba i samoupravljanja kao društvenog sistema," *Revija za sociologiju* 3, 1–2 (1973): 27–56, 41 and passim.

ideologically induced, highly moral work ethic. In its eighteenth year, they claimed, self-management had reached a deadlock. The key issues were an overbearing bureaucracy – an "omnipresent if indistinct term of derision in Yugoslav socialism" that "was directly linked to the abuse of power, inhibiting business and contributing to growing social inequalities"[57] – the lagging market conformity of the economy, and widespread low labour discipline. Unemployment and emigration – the vast majority of Yugoslav *gastarbajteri* in the West originated from Croatia – as well as decreasing opportunities for social upward mobility were central concerns, too. The suggested solution, once more, was to grant more power to the company and the workers and to allot less to the functionaries of the federation and the republic. The shipyard workers, indeed, were conscious that they served as a role model for the world: "Everybody looks to us from other countries, both in the East and the West. The workers in France see in our system something to be inspired by. Therefore we must go forward. But also because of ourselves. We will hand over to the federation and the republic whatever it takes. But the economy needs more resources!"[58]

This conscious difference, distinguishing them from their counterparts in capitalist economies, was grounded in the participatory system of self-management. Its success, however, depended on certain preconditions:

> In the West, one product of modernisation is a managerial spirit in business, which transforms the worker into the most common addition to machines in the production process. We must never accept that. Modern management is the new philosophy of the capitalists [....] We cannot accept such management because it is contrary to workers' self-management. However, we must overcome misconceptions which present certain wishful thinking as possibilities. We must replace these with a modernizing path that focuses on capable experts, increased responsibilities for quality as well as efficiency of investment.[59]

Within the framework of Yugoslav self-management, the trade union was to make sure that everybody behaved as they should: "The union is the protector of the working class – in capitalism. In our country, where the working class is in power, the union should protect us against those who are bureaucrats, inside the working class and in society as a whole."[60] In the face of high turnover, high call-in-sick rates, and too many workers simply not showing up for work – one voice in the debate about 3. Maj mentions a staggering nine hundred absentees

---

57 Rory Archer, "'Antibureaucratism' as a Yugoslav Phenomenon. The View from Northwest Croatia," *Nationalities Papers* 47, 4 (2019): 562–580, 565, 568 (and passim).
58 "Jedni su za reformu, drugi su u reformi," *Novi List* (29–30 June 1968).
59 "Modernizacija znači izbor," *Brodograditelj* (15 June 1969).
60 "Jedni su za reformu, drugi su u reformi," *Novi List* (29–30 June 1968).

on one occasion – while other workers had to work overtime, the lack of labour discipline was a core issue: "One could say, there are enough *people* in the enterprise, but too few *workers*."[61]

The discussion was frank and elaborate, no matter whether the daily *Novi List* and the company paper *Brodograditelj* transcribed actual speech or, rather, a synthesised account faithful to the sentiments expressed. These analyses of the situation preceded a fiercely aggressive strike aimed at winning a pay raise, staged in June 1969, word of which even reached, a few months later, the West German weekly *Der Spiegel:* "The port workers in Rijeka armed themselves with a metre-and-a-half-long and four-centimetre thick ropes: they wanted to lynch their bankrupt management. [...] General director Kazimir Jelovica took a beating and fled into the Hotel Bonanija; his colleague Dr. Joško Vukov ran after him and was beaten up in the foyer of the hotel."[62] Such an outrage, the Belgrade Sunday paper *Nedeljne novosti* commented, took the Yugoslav culture of work stoppages to a new qualitative level. While it was not the first strike in Rijeka, "what happened last Monday [on 2 June 1969] had never happened before. Never in the postwar history of strikes in Yugoslavia had anybody chased the bosses through the streets and beaten them up."[63] When almost exactly two years later, in June 1971, such scenes repeated themselves in workers' renewed rioting, the Croatian- and Italian-language local newspapers linked the second escalation to what had happened two years earlier. The *Novi List* wrote that it was "once more a Black Friday" (*opet Crni Petak*) for Rijeka.[64] Two years earlier,

> the sociopolitical organizations had not learned anything about how to deal with such conflicts. It seems as if the trade union and the Party did not exist – the demands of the workers are negotiated in the workers' council. Instead, of course, it was the trade union that would have needed to be the voice of the workers. [...] The air, once more, is full of aggression. Only that this time it counts doubly, because everybody remembers what happened two years ago; the psychological pressure is huge.[65]

The *Novi List* had treated the strike of 1969 as a key event, instead of providing only a few lines of perfunctory reportage and camouflaging the account with ideologised platitudes, as had happened earlier. This sort of expanded coverage was certainly a novelty. Two years later, in 1971, the paper once more reported the events at length. Indeed, before June 1969, never had a strike in Yugoslavia garnered such

---

61 "Jači miris mora," *Novi List* (28–29 December 1968).
62 "Jugoslawien / Streiks: Gehetzte Hasen," *Der Spiegel* (22 September 1969).
63 [no title], *Nedeljne novosti* (8 June 1969).
64 "Crni petak riječke luke," *Novi List* (12–13 June 1971).
65 "Crni petak riječke luke," *Novi List* (12–13 June 1971).

public attention. Earlier work stoppages had sometimes been aggressive, too, but the aggression involved had never gone public; only rumours and word of mouth gave a hint of the adversarial energy in these confrontations. But over time, managers found it increasingly hard to keep such incidents within the confines of their company or even, at the very least, to diminish their scale.[66] In Rijeka, in both 1969 and 1971, the workers marched through the city with red flags and images of President Tito. The local Croatian- and Italian-language newspapers reported that only a small number of men were responsible for the violent escalation, but they reminded their readers that "anything can happen when people fear for their daily bread," thereby hinting at the conflict's existential dimension that was driving the workers to take action.[67] The *Novi List* identified the culprits among the sociopolitical organisations and adopted a more generally exasperated tone: "Had the trade union done its duty, the protest would have remained peaceful. The workers did not only strike because of the bad conditions on their shop floor, but because of the bad conditions in the whole country."[68]

The economic reform of 1965 had triggered – or aggravated – the "conflict between capital and labour" in the shipyard (and elsewhere) since it had opened all doors for an unveiled tightening of the workflow in service of the market. At 3. Maj, the lack of credit security and the necessity for market-conforming planning meant, among other things, that workers were deprived of the subsidies that were of existential importance to them – even more so as massive price rises simultaneously lowered living standards. To be sure, in both Rijeka strikes, the workers' demands were met, which points once more to the ideological conundrum that the work stoppages posed.[69] The solution was sought in procedure. The extended discussions accompanying the work stoppages sought to interpret them as a participatory tool within the system. The "heroes of work" could not be damaged. The cult of labour, especially industrial labour, ensured that workers' articulations of

---

66 Examples of other aggressive labour conflicts are the aforementioned first strike in socialist Yugoslavia, at the Trbovlje coal mine in January 1958, a four-hour strike at the Uljanik shipyard in Pula in September 1967, and a port workers' strike in Koper in March 1970. See Darja Skopec, "Stavka v rudnikih Trbovlje – Hrastnik in Zagorje od 13.1. do 16.1.1958," in *Dokumenti o rudarski stavki v Zasavju leta 1958*, edited by Damjan Hančič and Renato Podbersič (Ljubljana: Ministrstvo za pravosodje Republike Slovenije, 2007), 1–72; Stanić, "'Jedan od najtežih dana u Uljaniku!'": 77–78; Rutar, "Containing Conflict and Enforcing Consent."
67 "Sciopero dei portuali con dimostrazioni di protesta," *La Voce del Popolo*, 3 June 1969; and "Štrajk u riječkoj Luci," *Novi List* (3 June 1969), with similar wording.
68 "Štrajk u riječkoj Luci," *Novi List* (3 June 1969).
69 "Koliko zarađuju brodograditelji," *Brodograditelj* (1 June 1971), illustrates that earnings differed in every Yugoslav shipyard and had risen since 1969. Yet inflation had devoured the rise, if not lowered the net amount.

dissatisfaction were encountered delicately, yet consciously, on a one-by-one basis and mostly without too much noise in the public arena. Yet in Rijeka matters did indeed get loud – which accounted for the perception of a "change in the quality" of strikes as a systemic feature.

The broadcaster Radio Free Europe belonged to those western, United States-led institutions who observed the Yugoslav model benevolently. Yugoslavia was "a friendly state in American eyes."[70] The Munich-based Yugoslav journalist Zdenko Antić, in his report on the Rijeka strike of June 1971, wrote that its handling by the authorities pointed up the freedom of the Yugoslav workers, quite contrary to the situation in Poland, for example, where the year before a strike had been suppressed at the cost of dozens of deaths. The report focused on the "routine negotiations" that were "relatively uneventful" and "business-like." It depicted the strike as a normality rather than as something exceptional, let alone menacing. The riots, with their beaten-up managers and journalists, were left unmentioned. The report hinted at social control and ideological success:

> It appears that Yugoslav political and social elements have finally accepted the strike as an instrument in settling social conflicts. On the other hand, it also seems evident that the workers have learned how to use the strike in order to advance their interests. [...] The latest strike in Rijeka proved the judicious nature of the Yugoslav leadership in acknowledging strikes as being not only legal but also useful.[71]

This learning process, thus, was to be understood as immanent in the system (and explains the passing over of the violence in silence). It was the Yugoslav model of self-management that was teaching workers to successfully work through social conflict, Radio Free Europe suggested. In fact, in Rijeka, the local discussion about the future continued unabated. The company newspaper *Brodograditelj*, a few weeks after the strike of June 1971, called for "a fast solution for the key issues," advocating "a better organization of the shipyard and of the shipbuilding industry comprehensively."[72]

The operative tool that enabled this discussion to be perpetuated in an unabated, procedural manner was the social exclusion of the rioters as well as a program-

---

70 George R. Urban, *Radio Free Europe and the Pursuit of Democracy. My War within the Cold War* (New Haven: Yale University Press, 1997), 133.

71 Zdenko Antić, "Dockers' Strike Successful in Yugoslav Port of Rijeka," Radio Free Europe (16 June 1971) [Electronic record], HU OSA 300–8–3–10618, Records of Radio Free Europe / Radio Liberty Research Institute: Publications Department: Background Reports, Open Society Archives at Central European University, Budapest, accessed 1 September 2020. The toll of the labour protests in the shipyard in Gdańsk, Poland, in December 1970 was close to 100 dead and more than 1,000 injured.

72 "Hitno rješavati ključne zadatke," *Brodograditelj* (1 July 1971).

matic shift away from the work collective towards the "bureaucrats," who were handed all organisational responsibility. The social contract had been broken only by those few who had attacked the managers. In 1969, eight individuals were singled out as being responsible for the violence; each was sentenced to up to two years and ten months in prison. Rhetorically, the strike was positioned as a win-win situation for the workers and the enterprise alike, "as long as the goals of the workers are progressive in their intentions."[73] In other words, "anyone is strongly condemned who, in our socialist self-managing society, uses force and physical revenge to solve their problems, especially when physical revenge targets those who have given their whole life to fight for the rights of the working class, because they themselves originated from it."[74]

The "bureaucrats" were held responsible for the necessity of the strike. They were blamed for directing the workers' council towards the introduction of the regulatory measures that had brought the workers to the brink: cutting basic wages by first 10, then 20 percent, abolishing overtime pay, and halving pay for hours spent idle. The problem was not the strike as such but the inability of the "bureaucrats" within the sociopolitical organisations to identify those individuals who had meant to create havoc. Had the functionaries done their duty, the protest would have remained peaceful.[75] However, while workers during both strikes called for all new regulations to be abolished, what in 1969 had still been easy to argue had come to occupy, in 1971, somewhat more difficult discursive ground.

In 1969, after carefully framing the exclusion of the culprits from the work collective, the party executives addressed the community of "good workers," reminding them of the – commonly fought – war of resistance and liberation against the occupying forces during the Second World War:

> We invite all communists of this city to condemn such acts, and we strongly demand that the security services inform the public about the measures taken against those who threw stigma and shame on the entire working class of Rijeka and the Croatian coast, on this seaside with its peace-loving people who always fought against aggression in order to live in peace and freedom.[76]

When, two years later, three thousand workers went on strike and rioted again, the easier part was to once again fulfil their demands for higher wages. What had become more difficult was the benevolent rhetorical framing, which also had to

---

73 "Štrajk u riječkoj Luci," *Novi List* (3 June 1969).
74 "Štrajk u riječkoj Luci," *Novi List* (3 June 1969).
75 "Štrajk u riječkoj Luci," *Novi List* (3 June 1969).
76 "Štrajk u riječkoj Luci," *Novi List* (3 June 1969).

counter reports that a 15 percent increase in income would scarcely be sufficient given a simultaneous 13 percent cost-of-living increase.[77] The workers might have got their way in narrow terms, but the underlying problem had once again not been solved.

Pluralist Potential Undone

Thus, in the face of workers acting with (increasingly public) aggression toward management due to shrinking living standards and also betrayed promises of participation, how could the long-perpetuated "good worker" trope now continue to be effective? The figure was discursively construed in a way analogous to the theme of "brotherhood and unity among the Yugoslav peoples." The mechanism involved finding culprits to expel from these communities while holding up an increasingly fake collective as an ideal, as well as continuing to regulate – and then over-regulate – societal (and intra-state) relations, which monistically were to bring all digressions back into line with the system. In September 1972, Tito addressed the shipyard workers in Rijeka in a speech which attests to this strategy:

> Why […] are there these work stoppages, this leaving the workplace, these so-called strikes? Primarily because of matters that are not solved, but could be solved very easily, without a strike. One fails to find solutions, until the workers leave their workplace. It happened once here in Rijeka, too. When the workers left their jobs and started demonstrating, then the problem was solved. Without that it had not been possible. There were people among the management and economic experts who thought they could make certain moves in the companies without informing and consulting the workers. Today, this has been overcome; they can no longer do that. The workers must be informed and know what the plan for the company looks like. Managers can make suggestions, but the workers must have their say in all matters.[78]

Between the second huge Rijeka strike of June 1971 and Tito's speech in September 1972 something crucial had happened. Tito and his entourage had purged the political and economic elite of liberal minds and had brought in loyal technocrats to serve in their stead. This change was not primarily due to the workers' actions; rather, it was the result of everything that had piled up over the years, from the student unrest of 1968 to the so-called Croatian Spring, which peaked in 1971 and had seen the Croatian socialist republic's representatives invoke the national

---

77 "Crni petak riječke luke," *Novi List* (12–13 June 1971).
78 Josip Broz Tito, "Riječ radnicima Brodogradilišta '3. Maj,'" in *Tito. Istra – Hrvatsko Primorje – Gorski Kotar*, edited by Ivo Kovačić et al. (Rijeka: Tipograf, 1977), 86.

liberation movement of the Second World War – one of the ideological pillars of the Titoist state – to legitimise the quest for their national aspirations. This could not be tolerated.[79] Tito's words in Rijeka need to be seen in this context: the workers were the "heroes of labour" and a pillar of socialist ideology; they had to be heard; if they harboured discontent and left their workplaces they did so because they had a point and because others, namely the functionaries of the sociopolitical organisations, had done their jobs badly. These others he – Tito – had just removed. Thus, "so-called strikes" were now superfluous.

In reality, the accused "bureaucrats" had been replaced with their successors, newly installed functionaries who handled things even more technocratically. In 1974, the Yugoslav constitution was reformed, becoming one of the world's longest and most complicated documents of the sort. Interestingly, it incorporated several demands put forth by Croatia a few years earlier and brought the competences of the Yugoslav republics and autonomous provinces almost to the level of statehood. The federation became a loosened construct, while the postulate of a "withering away state" remained intact.[80] Another two years later, in November 1976, the Law on Associated Labour (*Zakon o udruženom radu*) was introduced, dubbed the "small constitution" because it added more than 600 articles to the already very long constitution of 1974. The law described in detail the participation of workers in the management of companies. It was an attempt to completely codify shop floor relations. No longer was the company the basic organisation of the economy, but rather the Basic Organisation of Associated Labour (BOAL, *Osnovna organizacija udruženog rada*, OOUR). Each Yugoslav worker now belonged to one of these BOALs, and their role in the production process was meticulously defined. Ideologically, it was still expected that the state would gradually retreat from any intervention in the economy: self-management mechanisms had been worked out to perfection and would ultimately regulate the forces of the market successfully. Now the workers' councils depended on agreement among delegates from each BOAL, and all major decisions concerning shop floor organisation, such as income distribution and capital investments, had to be ratified by the entire work collective. Factory newspapers and bulletins, as well as internal radio stations, were expected to make the relevant information available but an even heightened degree of self-initiative from the workers was required. The Law on Associated Labour

---

79 Darko Dukovski, *Istra i Rijeka u Hrvatskome proljeću* (Zagreb: Alinea, 2007); Tihomir Ponoš, *Na rubu revolucije. Studenti '71* (Zagreb: Profil international, 2007).

80 A good dissection of the Yugoslav state is offered by Dejan Jović, *Yugoslavia. A State that Withered Away* (West Lafayette, IN: Purdue University Press, 2009), especially chapter three, "The Constitutional Debate 1967–1974. Why Did Serbia Accept the Kardelj Concept and the 1974 Constitution?": 95–140.

was, ultimately, to replace the constitution, and the self-managed bodies were to assume responsibility for all tasks previously performed by the state.[81]

As Tito's admonition in Rijeka and the over-regulation of the following years make clear, strikes and work stoppages define the limits of acceptable behaviour in an authoritarian society. The Law on Associated Labour was the culmination of a process begun a decade earlier. Strikes, and even escalations like those in Rijeka, were dealt with in a procedural manner. The elaborate debate about how workers' articulations of discontent could be made an inherent part of the self-management system is testament to the seriousness of the attempts made to improve the system. Autocracy stood in the way of reaching better forms of concrete practise. What ensued was the installation of ever more extensive regulation, and, ultimately, a veritable fragmentation of relations on the shop floor. By the mid-1970s, the liberties of the late 1960s and the possibility of realising democratic potential had been forfeited. As the German doyen of Southeast European studies, the late Holm Sundhaussen, put it: "The problem was not the existing problems but the non-acceptance of any form of political pluralism."[82]

---

81 Dragoljub Đurović, *Das Gesetz über assoziierte Arbeit* (Ljubljana: Dopisna Delavska Univerza, 1977); Tiosav Velimirović et al., *Zakon o udruženom radu* (Belgrade: Privredna štampa, 1976); Jović, *Yugoslavia*, 142–146 ("'Boalization': Associated or Disintegrated Labour?").

82 Holm Sundhaussen, *Jugoslawien und seine Nachfolgestaaten 1943–2011. Eine ungewöhnliche Geschichte des Gewöhnlichen* (Vienna: Böhlau, 2014), 27.

Ravi Ahuja
9 Industrial "Cyclopes" and "Native" Stokers: British Steamshipping and the Attractions of "Racial Management" (c. 1880–1930)

For two generations, comprising the latter half of the nineteenth and the pre-war years of the twentieth century, the steamship epitomised the cutting edge of industrial technology: ever more gigantic steel hulls propelled by enormous batteries of coal-devouring boilers and increasingly powerful steam engines.[1] As early as in the 1860s, Karl Marx had argued that the technological requirements of the propulsion machinery of steamships (as much as of railways) had revolutionised industrial production itself. The machinery and steel hulls of steamers could no longer be built by skilled artisans using preindustrial technologies; instead, their production required "cyclopean machines." As a result, machinery ceased to merely imitate the artisan's work process and large-scale industry began to stand "on its own feet" technologically. Being both a launch pad and a product of this revolutionary "machine system" steamships could be scaled up in ever more monstrous proportions.[2]

Marx ascribed a greater "objectivity" to a production process that depended on these "cyclopean machines" and, conversely, on a decline in the individual labourer's subjective ability to shape the organisation of work.[3] More than a century later, Raphael Samuel found, however, that this transformation had actually been limited and patchy, even in highly advanced industries like shipbuilding.[4] As to steel-

Acknowledgement: This essay presents in condensed form some of the arguments developed more fully in chapters seven to ten of my forthcoming monograph, "The 'Natives' of the S.S. Egypt. Class, Race, and a Shipwreck Inquiry in Late Imperial Britain." I am grateful to Nicole Mayer-Ahuja and Valerie Burton for their comments on earlier drafts. I also thank Karl Müller-Bahlke for his editorial help. The remaining errors are mine.

---

1 Daniel R. Headrick, *The Tentacles of Progress. Technology Transfer in the Age of Imperialism, 1850–1940* (New York and Oxford: Oxford University Press, 1988), 27–30.
2 Karl Marx, *Capital. A Critique of Political Economy. Volume I,* translated by Ben Fowkes (Harmondsworth: Penguin, 1976), 506.
3 Marx, *Capital,* 508.
4 Raphael Samuel, "Workshop of the World: Steam Power and Hand Technology in Mid-Victorian Britain," *History Workshop* 3, 1 (1977): 6–72.

https://doi.org/10.1515/9783111086552-010

hulled steamers, this was even more pronounced once they were launched from the shipyards. An analysis of work processes within the stokeholds and engine rooms shows that the prevalent division of labour here was by no means a direct outgrowth of technology: even though the scope for appropriating (or subjectifying) technology may have been narrower for the individual worker – if compared to earlier ship work – labour processes continued to be mediated by social relations of property and power or, in other words, they were collectively subjectified. As Heide Gerstenberger and Ulrich Welke have argued, excessively steep hierarchies between engineers and firemen were no quasi-natural consequence of technological compulsions; they resulted, to a large extent, from efforts on the part of shipowners to assert an effective "remote control" over the fault-prone engine rooms of their increasingly capital-intensive as well as spatially dispersed fleets. When the artisanal "mechanic" tending to the engines of early steamers was turned into a certified "engineer" over the nineteenth century, this promotion was accompanied by the cultivation of a status difference that set him apart from the bulk of the engine- and boiler-room crew.[5]

Detailed instructions from the P&O Company to their chief engineers thus directed them to "keep proper subordination by not mixing too freely or familiarly" with "those employed in your department." The chief engineer was held fully responsible for preserving "the machinery under his care in the highest possible state of efficiency", for "carry[ing] out the strictest economy" and for "maintain[ing] proper subordination and good feeling amongst those placed under him."[6] Other crew members were to be excluded from the performance of certain 'skilled' work tasks in order to centralise accountability for potentially sensitive technical operations and cut back on costly repairs.[7] As work tasks were separated and circumscribed more narrowly, the firemen saw their ability to adapt the work process to their needs curtailed – though never fully suppressed. 'De-skilling' or, more precisely, a hierarchical segmentation of skills was thus an intended and regulated process.

This intentional, owner-managed division of the workforce along lines of status and skill was not necessarily marked out racially but could be articulated in the language of racial difference. This possibility turned into a reality when Indian so-called "lascars" as well as African, Yemeni, and Chinese ship workers were recruited in large numbers to toil as trimmers and stokers in coal bunkers and boiler

---

5 Heide Gerstenberger and Ulrich Welke, *Vom Wind zum Dampf* (Münster: Westfälisches Dampfboot, 1996), 183–187.
6 NMML, P&O/9/2/1, "Peninsular & Steam Navigation Company: Instructions for Chief Engineers," London, no publisher: 1873: 9.
7 NMML, P&O/9/2/1, "Peninsular,": 22 on.

rooms even beyond the Indo-Pacific rim from the latter half of the nineteenth century onward.[8] The change in the composition of the British steamer workforce went along with a diversification of labour management: shipping lords discovered management-by-'race' as an ideologically irrational but perfectly profitable option.

Working in the Stokehold

If the division between the 'skilled' engineers and 'unskilled' coal trimmers and firemen was a result, to a large extent, of efforts to establish managerial control over the labour process through centralised, remote-controllable structures of accountability, the question remains as to whether coal-bunker and stokehold work afforded merely large quantities of 'raw' muscle-power devoid of any specific quality (or 'skill') acquired either through experience or training. Historians and social scientists have too often been content to accept the epithet 'unskilled' without any serious examination of the actual labour processes in the stokehold,[9] although some insightful analyses do exist that have made use, for example, of detailed accounts of boiler-room work in autobiographical writings.[10] Karl Helbig, for instance, joined the 'black gang' of a German steamer in 1923 and would sign on as a fireman time and again for the next three decades to self-fund his research as an ethnographer, before eventually sitting down to write about his experience of work "at the fires."[11] At the most basic quotidian level, these experiences were shaped by handling rakes, pokers, prickers, brushes, shovels, and tongs – the in-

---

8 Ravi Ahuja, "The Age of the Lascar. South Asian Seafarers in the Times of Imperial Steam Shipping," in *Routledge Handbook of the South Asian Diaspora*, edited by Joya Chatterji and David Washbrook (London: Routledge, 2013), 110–122; Janet Ewald, "Crossers of the Sea: Slaves, Freedmen, and other Migrants in the Northwestern Indian Ocean, c.1750–1914," *American Historical Review* 105, 1 (2000): 84–89.

9 See, for example: Jonathan Hyslop, "'Ghostlike' Seafarers and Sailing Ship Nostalgia: the Figure of the Steamship Lascar in the British Imagination, c. 1880–1960," *Journal for Maritime Research* 16, 2 (2014): 214. For a cliometric account built on similarly shallow conceptions of 'skill,' see Aimee Chin, Chinhui Juhn, and Peter Thompson, "Technical Change and the Demand for Skills during the Second Industrial Revolution: Evidence from the Merchant Marine, 1891–1912," *The Review of Economics and Statistics* 88, 3 (2006): 572–578.

10 Gerstenberger and Welke, *Vom Wind zum Dampf*; Alston Kennerley, "Stoking the Boilers: Firemen and British Merchant Ships, 1850–1950," *International Journal of Maritime History* 20, 1 (2008): 191–220; Richard P. de Kerbrech, *Down amongst the Black Gang. The World and Workplace of RMS Titanic's Stokers* (Stroud: The History Press, 2014); Eric W. Sager, *Ships and Memories. Merchant Seafarers in Canada's Age of Steam* (Vancouver: UBC Press, 1993), 44–53.

11 Karl Helbig, *Seefahrt vor den Feuern: Erinnerungen eines Schiffsheizers* (Hamburg: Hans Georg Prager Verlag, 1987).

struments that firemen continued to use the world over until the end of the age of the steamship in the mid-twentieth century (Figure 9.1).

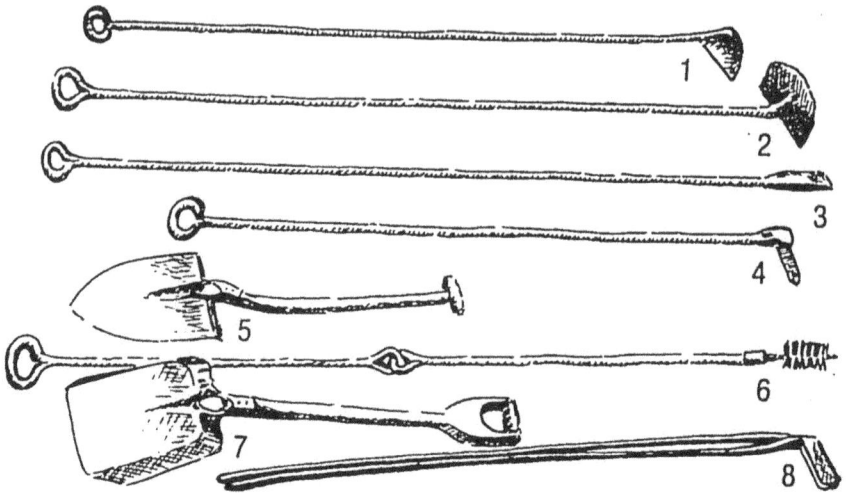

Fig. 1: Firemen's tools. *Source*: Karl Helbig, *Seefahrt vor den Feuern: Erinnerungen eines Schiffsheizers* (Hamburg: Hans Georg Prager Verlag, 1987): 62.

Helbig understood the significance of sketching these simple tools, at a time when engineering manuals saw no reason to waste pages on them – carrying, instead, intricate technical drawings of boilers, triple expansion engines, turbine plants, and winches.[12] De Kerbrech notes that the rake (or "slice bar") used for removing hot coals and clinker from the grates of the furnace was "similar in appearance and construction to a garden hoe."[13] This seemingly rural simplicity is significant in more ways than one for our appreciation of the work processes in the stokehold.

To begin with, it underlines the importance allotted to the extraction of sheer physical energy from human bodies in the organisation of the labour process or, in other words, the low priority afforded to inventing or implementing labour-saving devices. A trimmer was expected to move between 2.4 and four tons of coal on each four-hour watch,[14] running along planks with a shaky wheelbarrow, frequently scorching his shoulders as he squeezed past the searing hot boilers. He also

12 See, for example, John G. Liversidge, *Engine-room Practice: A Handbook for the Royal Navy and Mercantile Marine* (London: Charles Griffin and Co., 1923).

13 de Kerbrech, *Down amongst the Black Gang*, 65.

14 Liversidge, *Engine-room Practice*, 25–27.

needed to break up oversized lumps of coal, while the distances he had to cover grew as the voyage progressed and coal had to be carried from more remote depths of the bunkers. As for firemen, estimates vary greatly,[15] but according to the 1923 edition of Liversidge's engine-room manual, one ship worker could shovel up to 5.6 tons per day in two four-hour watches.[16] In the mid-1890s, several engineers confirmed that a fireman could handle up to five tons of coal per day, though the Manning Committee recommended that the minimum requirement for boiler-room crew (including trimmers and firemen only) should be fixed in proportion to the respective vessel's daily consumption of coal at the rate of one man for every three tons of coal, allowing for a reduction of half a ton in hot climates.[17] In the 1950s, toward the end of the maritime steam age, a technical manual observed likewise that even a sturdy, experienced stoker could manage no more than 3.2 tons of coal in two four-hour watches if he also took proper care of the attendant cleaning tasks.[18] For, apart from stacking coal onto the fire bars, he needed to tear apart large and heavy clinkers, rake them out from the furnaces along with the smoldering ashes, remove scale from within the boilers and soot from the flues, as well as pump out and scrape the bilges. Less frequently, but inescapably, burnt-through bars and grates needed to be replaced with the help of unwieldy, long-armed tongs.[19] Most of these tasks had to be performed in the blazing heat since the boiler pressure, on which the propulsion and the safety of the ship depended, was to be kept up at all times.

In addition, the removal of ashes was a never-ending chore "like a curse from hell," as former engineer and novelist William McFee put it.[20] Depending on fuel quality, the weight of the ashes could amount to as much as one-fifth of that of the

---

15 Compare, for instance, Ronald Hope, *A New History of British Shipping* (London: John Murray Pubs, 1990), 342; Gerstenberger and Welke, *Vom Wind zum Dampf*, 188 and 300 (note 3).

16 Liversidge, *Engine-room Practice*, 25–27.

17 *Report of the Committee Appointed by the Board of Trade to Inquire into the Manning of British Merchant Ships* [hereafter: *MaC*], vol. I: Report (London: Eyre and Spottiswood, 1897), 28 on, 34, 249, 467.

18 Wilhelm Leder, *Schiffsmaschinenkunde. Band I: Schiffsdampfkessel* (Leipzig: Fachbuchverlag Leipzig, 1956), 66.

19 For a detailed analytic account of work process and repair procedures in the stokehold, see Gerstenberger and Welke, *Vom Wind zum Dampf*, 187–92, 204–10. Several graphic descriptions of such work can be found in *MaC*, vol. II: Evidence, and Appendices, London: Eyre and Spottiswood, 1896, see especially 394. See also Alston Kennerley, "Stoking the Boilers": 208–212; de Kerbrech, *Down amongst the Black Gang*, 65–84; John Guthrie, *A History of Marine Engineering* (London: Hutchinson, 1971), 193; Helbig, *Seefahrt vor den Feuern*, 121–124.

20 William McFee, "Oil, and the Hairy Ape," *Fortnightly Review* (May 1932): 567.

burnt coal.[21] To be discharged into the sea, the ashes were hoisted up onto the deck – often in buckets, not always with a hand-winch, and seldom with an ash ejector.[22] This was a laborious duty in itself: each bucket weighed about six kilograms to be heaved up steep iron ladders, sometimes slipping from an exhausted hand and causing severe injuries.[23] The boiler-room crew often found themselves unable to cope with the ashes during their regular working hours and had to let them pile up beside the boilers. On smaller ships, the deck crew would frequently help out and at times even engineers removed their shirts to shovel ashes. More commonly, however, the discharge of ashes and other ancillary tasks compelled the 'black gang' to work overtime either before or after their watch, often adding a further two hours to their two regular four-hour watches, although working days of up to 15 hours were reported in the cases of severe undermanning that were increasingly common toward the end of the nineteenth century.[24]

Ship workers, both on deck and in the stokehold, were furthermore regularly required to perform work in addition to their regular tasks and sometimes even outside of their respective departments: engine rooms, stokeholds, but also freight holds were, for instance, regularly cleaned during so-called "field days" at sea in order to reduce lay days in port.[25] The physical strain of overlong working hours was compounded by inadequate lighting, which occasioned work accidents, and by ubiquitous coal dust, which caused damage to the eyes and the respiratory system.[26] In hot climates, and particularly in the Red Sea, temperatures rose to above 50 degrees Celsius in the ill-ventilated stokeholds.[27] Excessive sweating resulted in painful and debilitating heat cramps – a condition affecting solely the 'black gang' on board.[28] A Special Sanitary Commission set up by the medical jour-

---

21 de Kerbrech, *Down amongst the Black Gang*, 35.

22 Kennerley, "Stoking the Boilers": 198on. See also Frank Bullen, *The Men of the Merchant Service: Being the Polity of the Mercantile Marine for Longshore Readers* (London: Smith, Elder and Co., 1900), 326 on.

23 *MaC*, vol. II: Evidence: 91, 214.

24 *MaC*, vol. II: Evidence: 39, 41, 47, 52f, 57f, 62, 76, 407. Working days in the stokehold of 14 or 15 hours are reported. See *MaC*, vol. II: Evidence: 69, 400, 443. See also Gerstenberger and Welke, *Vom Wind zum Dampf*, 197; Gavin Douglas, *Seamanship for Passengers* (London: John Lehmann, 1949), 17 on.

25 *MaC*, vol. I: Report: 21; *MaC*, vol. II: Evidence: 88, 101 on, 106, 108, 269, 535. See also: Conrad H. Dixon, "Seamen and the Law: An Examination of the Impact of Legislation on the British Merchant Seaman's Lot, 1588–1918," Ph.D. thesis, UCL, 1981), 203; Valerie Burton, "The Work and Home Life of Seafarers with Special Reference to the port of Southampton 1871–1921," Ph.D. thesis, LSE, 1988, 117.

26 *MaC*, vol. II: Evidence: 58, 73, 76.

27 *MaC*, vol. II: Evidence: 63, 396.

28 *MaC*, vol. II: Evidence : 69, 72, 243 on, 735. See also "White Men and Work in the Tropics," *The Lancet* (5 January 1924): 51; "Heat Cramp on Shipboard," *The Lancet* (3 November 1928): 935.

nal *The Lancet* to inquire into sanitation at sea concluded in 1890 that "[s]ix or seven years' constant work as a firemen [sic] on board a steamer seems sufficient to ruin the health of a strong man."[29] The extreme labour intensity of the work process was described by the stoker Thomas Cummings in the following words in his 1896 testimony:

> [Y]ou are continually going round her; as soon as you fire her you have to get your pricker and slicer, and you are always working, continually working, your four hours; you cannot get five minutes to spare out of the four hours. You are working and working very hard all the time.[30]

Even so, in some large vessels, Tayloristic devices such as Kilroy's stoking indicator were installed to further intensify the labour process by sounding a gong at regular intervals.[31] The exploitation of the stokers' vital force was pushed to such extremes that physical fatigue could turn into a mental crisis: the superintendent of Liverpool's Mercantile Marine Office speculated on "a kind of heat insanity" when questioned, in 1902, about the causes for frequent suicides among stokehold crew.[32] Trimmers and firemen were reportedly on average about four times more likely to take their own lives while serving on a steamer than other crew – often by jumping overboard into the open sea. Suicide rates were sufficiently high to raise mild concern in British government circles around the turn of the century and induce them to at least keep track statistically of the phenomenon.[33] The rate of "suicides at work and disappearances at sea" appears to have tailed off only in the 1930s, when oil-fueled ships became more commonplace.[34]

This was, then, a curious combination of cutting-edge technology and a cannibalistic overexploitation of labour power that was almost entirely indifferent to the reproduction of the latter – though only *almost*, as we shall see. The writer and former ship engineer William McFee remembered: "Always in those days it was 'blood for steam.'" He explained:

---

29 "The Lancet Special Sanitary Commission: Report on Sanitation at Sea," *The Lancet* (20 September 1890): 635 on.

30 "The Lancet Special Sanitary Commission": 407.

31 de Kerbrech, *Down amongst the Black Gang*, 67–68.

32 House of Commons Papers, *Report of the Mercantile Marine Committee* [hereafter: *MMC*], vol. II: Minutes of Evidence, London: His Majesty's Stationary Office, 1903: 28.

33 MMC: 28; Kennerley, "Stoking the Boilers": 217–219.

34 Stephen E. Roberts, et al., "Suicides among Seafarers in UK Merchant Shipping, 1919–2005," *Occupational Medicine* 60 (2010): 58.

> The extraordinary feature of the situation, as engines became more efficient, as steam pressures became higher and higher, and as the size, splendour, and speed of ships increased, was that no change seemed possible in the fire-room. [...] [T]he intolerable clumsiness and waste of human effort in the business of stoking seemed to remain forever.[35]

Even though automatic stokers – a technical adaptation of the conveyor belt for the steamship – had been invented around the turn of the century, they were never considered sufficiently reliable or cost-saving. Ash ejectors were recommended in engineering manuals, but failed likewise to establish themselves as the technical standard in merchant shipping and appear to have remained rather fault-prone.[36] If Marx had argued – somewhat too sanguinely as we know today – that the production of steel-hulled steamships had enabled large-scale industry to stand "on its own feet" technologically by generating machines premised on machines,[37] the propulsion of these ships never ceased to harness colossal amounts of muscle energy to shovel and rake, to hand-barrow and bucket.

Skill, Stigma, Segmentation

Even so, the technological simplicity of these tools should not be confused with an absolute redundancy of skill among the workers who used them. Frederick Winslow Taylor's famous formulation that, at least for simple manual work, it was "possible to train an intelligent gorilla so as to become [...] more efficient [...] than any man could be"[38] was an expression of, not more and not less, management objectives that were pursued in practical terms but could never be implemented comprehensively in actual labour processes. Even Taylor's own phrase "intelligent gorilla" contained the admission, as Antonio Gramsci pointed out, that "in any physical work, even the most degraded and mechanical, there exists a minimum of technical qualification, that is, a minimum of creative intellectual activity."[39] If this was true even of Taylor's condescendingly typified Mr Schmidt ("he shall be so stupid and so phlegmatic that he more nearly resembles in his mental make-up the ox than any other type"), who was made to haul 47 tons of pig iron in

---

35 McFee, "Oil, and the Hairy Ape": 566, 568–569.

36 Liversidge, *Engine-room Practice*: 27, 87; Alston Kennerley, "Stoking the Boilers": 198 on; Gerstenberger and Welke, *Vom Wind zum Dampf*, 220 on.

37 Marx, *Capital*, vol. I., 506. But see also Samuel, "Workshop of the World": 41 on.

38 Frederick Winslow Taylor, *The Principles of Scientific Management* (New York/London: Harper & Brothers [1st ed. 1911], 1915), 40.

39 Antonio Gramsci, *Selections from Prison Notebooks*, edited by Q. Hoare and G. Nowell Smith (London: Lawrence & Wishart [1st ed. 1971], 1991), 8.

a working day,[40] the fact that stokers were expected to move 'only' about a tenth of that weight in two watches suggests that there was much more to their job than "shoveling and raking coal" and skills that "could be picked up quite quickly."[41]

Gerstenberger and Welke emphasise that "there is no algorithm for the upkeep of optimal fires."[42] Or, in the less academic but equally perceptive language of a former stoker: "That's one of the hardest things to teach a guy, how to burn coal. You know in burning coal you have to say to a guy 'I'll show you how the job is done, but it's entirely up to your mind how it works and how that fire's going to burn.'"[43] The very absence in maritime engineering manuals of precise descriptions of stoking procedures together with the limited success of attempts to implement Tayloristic work practises in the stokehold indicate an organisational "zone of uncertainty."[44] Attempts to separate decision-making processes from manual labour, as reflected in the rise of the engineer, were largely confined to the technically most sensitive parts of the machinery and focused more on the engine room than on the stokehold. In front of the furnace, the widely varying combustion qualities of different types of coal, as well as the particularities and high susceptibility to failure of the machinery, were among the multiple variables requiring a deep experiential – even sensory – knowledge that defied verbalisation and was, therefore, not recognised as a formally teachable and certifiable 'skill.' Yet such mastery of the intricacies of the work process was crucial to avoid pressure drops, wastage of fuel, damage to the boilers, and risks for the security of the ship: all this required knowledge or, as the old fireman had put it, it was a matter of the mind.

Stokers had to be able to interpret, for instance, the texture of the coal and the colour of the flames as much as the sounds and vibrations of the machinery.[45] Moreover, "[c]onsiderable dexterity is often displayed by the stoker when feeling the moving parts, such as crossheads, crankheads, etc.," observed Liversidge, advising young engineers that they "should also acquire this dexterity." He was quick to add a cautionary note that "considerable care is required in the operation, and

---

40 Taylor, *The Principles*, 59.

41 Hyslop, "'Ghostlike Seafarers'": 214.

42 Gerstenberger and Welke, *Vom Wind zum Dampf*, 196, 188 on.

43 Interview with Len (Smiler) Underhill, former seaman, quoted in Sager, *Ships and Memories*, 47.

44 Gerstenberger and Welke, *Vom Wind zum Dampf*, 195–199. For the notion of organizational "zones of uncertainty," see Michel Crozier and Erhard Friedberg, *Actors and Systems. The Politics of Collective Action* (Chicago and London: Chicago University Press, 1980), 37, 44, and 53.

45 Gerstenberger and Welke, *Vom Wind zum Dampf*, 195–197. See also Kennerley, "Stoking the Boilers": 197–198; Sager, *Ships and Memories*, 47–53. For attempts at Taylorisation, however, see Guthrie, *History of Marine Engineering*, 193 and de Kerbrech, *Down amongst the Black Gang*, 67–70.

many personal injuries have resulted from careless procedure."[46] Such skills, required to keep the ship under steam and the machinery in repair while avoiding wastage of fuel, serious injury, or physical breakdown, were learned on the job and not from manuals or in evening classes: stokehold crew, often in their late teens or early twenties when hired for the first time, toiled as trimmers for some time before they were put in charge of boiler furnaces as firemen.[47] The simplicity and rural appearance of the stoker's tools cannot, therefore, be taken as a proof for the absence of specific industrial skills.

Hence the prevalent labelling of stokehold labour as "unskilled" – or the deprecatory reference to skill as mere "dexterity" – does not indicate an actual absence of mental work, of specialised occupational knowledge, or of ability. Rather, it reflects absent or weak standards of certification and, more than anything else, the low social status assigned to this work. For Liverpool, a major recruitment area for stokers in Britain, it has been shown that 'black gangs,' if compared with deck crew, were recruited from poorer urban districts, with fewer workers having an artisan background and a considerably larger proportion categorised as illiterate.[48] The intensely hierarchical culture of the British merchant marine was the result of a cultivation of status difference: chief engineers were admonished to "keep proper subordination by not mixing too freely" to "always have a watchful eye" over their subordinates, to "[n]ever pass unnoticed an act of willful misconduct," to report on any "refusal to work" and to give "on a man's Discharge" only such character assessments "which he really deserves, and no other."[49]

If the division of labour was much deeper on a steamer than on a sailing vessel and the skill profiles less homogeneous, this went along with (sometimes fictitious but by no means ineffectual) expectations regarding the social profile of the various status groups: if a 'middle-class' background was valorised for deck officers, 'respectable' artisanal or working-class origins were considered desirable for engineers and deck crew,[50] while 'unskilled' employment in the stokehold denoted the lowest rung on the occupational ladder, entailed casual employment pat-

---

46 Liversidge, *Engine-room Practice*, 47.
47 Kennerley, "Stoking the Boilers": 202.
48 Kennerley, "Stoking the Boilers": 213–214. See also de Kerbrech, *Down amongst the Black Gang*, 110.
49 NMML, P&O/9/2/1, "Peninsular & Steam Navigation Company: Instructions for Chief Engineers" (London: 1873): 9–10.
50 Tony Lane, "Neither Officers not Gentlemen," *History Workshop Journal* 19, 1 (1985): 128–143; Valerie Burton, "The Making of a Nineteenth-Century Profession," *Journal of the Canadian Historical Association* 1, 1 (1990): 97–118.

terns, and suggested the likelihood of pauperism and social defectiveness.[51] The work of trimmers and firemen was stigmatised labour, associated both with a lack of social respectability and a propensity for unruliness. Engine-room recruits from British ports were depicted stereotypically as illiterate, violent, and in need of draconian discipline – a stigmatisation that already assumed racist features when catholic Irish immigrants were hired for stokeholds in Liverpool and elsewhere.[52] In 1902, various witnesses to the Mercantile Marine Committee had characterised British firemen as "an endless source of trouble," as unsteady drifters and "bird[s] of passage," as given to drink and thus "often causing serious delay to the vessel," as being prone to "uproarious" indiscipline and devoid of skill, with about 10 per cent of them being "dead-heads" altogether.[53] The "present day fireman is not a sailor; he goes to sea perhaps because he has misbehaved himself in the neighbourhood, and landed himself in gaol once or twice," asserted Henry Radcliffe, a Cardiff shipowner.[54]

Trade union statements of the time correspondingly betray a strong sense of alarm and defensiveness concerning the loss of respectability (or the 'declassment') of the seaman's occupation in general and of the stoker's in particular. In expressing the 'respectable seaman's' struggle for social recognition, the language chosen was often one of exclusion – a combination of idioms of craft and, increasingly, of race rather than a language of class. The *Daily Herald*, a mouthpiece of the British trade unions, lamented in 1912 that "Portsmouth and Plymouth drifters, loafers and criminals fresh from prison cells, Chinese and Lascars, the filthy and diseased wrecks of the five continents are recruited to man British boats, whilst British sailors are left to tramp or starve or rot on land."[55] Across the Atlantic, Andrew Furuseth, the powerful trade-union leader of seamen in the United States, concurred that maritime employment, by not keeping pace with improving labour conditions on shore, had become the domain "of the sewage of the Caucasian race

---

51 Powerful as ideology, these social profiles did not necessarily reflect actual social composition. See Valerie Burton, "Counting Seafarers: The Published Records of the Registry of Merchant Seamen," *Mariners' Mirror* 71, 3 (1985): 316.
52 For an interesting compilation of such stereotypes, see de Kerbrech, *Down amongst the Black Gang*, 108–116. See also W.H. Hood, *The Blight of Insubordination* (London: Spottiswoode and Co., 1903), 20.
53 *MMC*, vol. II: Evidence: 130, 137, 164, 531, 538 on, 543, 548 on, 553, 608.
54 *MMC*, vol. II: Evidence: 477.
55 *The Daily Herald* (2 May 1912): 1.

and of such of the races of Asia as felt that their conditions could be improved by becoming seamen."[56]

As British as well as other shipowners developed a preference for Asian crews (the employment of South Asian 'lascars' on British ships alone doubled between 1886 and 1900), the labour market for seafarers and particularly for stokehold crew came to be stigmatised in increasingly racist terms. Moreover, there were also consequences for the organisation of work on board: the steep command structure of the stokehold was now also underlaid with a racial hierarchy that was more explicit and with a division of labour that was further deepened. This tendency materialised first in the hiring patterns of the shipping concerns with the most privileged access to colonial labour markets: the British India Steam Navigation Company (BISN), which controlled much of the Indian Ocean steamer traffic, and the P&O Company, which plied the transcontinental routes between Asia and Europe, relied on 'lascar' labour extensively from the mid-nineteenth century onward.[57] In the P&O service, Liversidge thus informed aspiring engineers:

> [T]hese greasers and the firemen are all natives. In the stokehold there is a chief fireman or 'serang,' and three leading firemen called 'tindels,' one for each watch. The 'serang' keeps no regular watch in the large ships, but in the smaller ships the 'serang' and two 'tindels' keep the three watches and assist the junior engineer of the watch. The engineer directs the 'tindel' to alter the check valves if the water levels are not kept properly; to avoid confusion the actual adjustment is always performed by one man. [...] The 'tindel' has nothing to do with the feed pumps, which are managed entirely by the engineer. The winchmen employed on the auxiliary machinery are [...] always Europeans.[58]

In effect, the racialisation of recruitment further sharpened hierarchy and skill segmentation. The owner's instructions to the engineers to not mix too freely with the boiler-room crew were even more likely to be followed.

Tramps and Liners

If extreme levels of hierarchy and segmentation were a common trait of labour management on board British steamers, this should not imply that these modes were uniform. Racial segmentation played out, for instance, in different degrees

---

56 Andrew Furuseth, "The Dawn of Another Day", *The American Federationist* 22 (1915): 718. See also Leon Fink, *Sweatshops at the Sea: Merchant Seamen in the World's First Globalized Industry, from 1812 to the Present* (Chapel Hill: University of North Carolina Press, 2011), 106.
57 *MMC*, vol. II: Evidence: 9, 77, 161, 284.
58 Liversidge, *Engine-room Practice*, 32.

and forms, and an explanation of these differences requires a return to the labour process. In navigational terms, a basic technological precondition for the organisation of labour processes on a steam vessel consisted in the simple fact that its maneuverability ceased when the pressure in its boilers dropped. A failure to maintain the pressure while at sea put the ship at risk, as well as the lives of the crew and passengers.[59] Interruptions to the labour process were, therefore, to be avoided at sea under all circumstances. In economic terms, moreover, the higher capital intensity of steamships compared with sailing vessels meant that there was a desire to minimise the time they would lie idle in port, and this was even before the decline of maritime freight rates in the late nineteenth century would further increase the pressure to cut down on demurrage. To sustain work intensity in ports of call and reduce lay days, fluctuations in labour supply on account of land leave, 'failure to join' or 'desertion' needed to be curbed.[60] Moreover, maintenance work could neither be neglected nor taken care of only in port without risking extended and expensive periods of repair. Much of this work, therefore, had to be dealt with at sea, implying a further intensification of work.[61]

The economic compulsion for continuous operation both at sea and in port was somewhat mitigated, however, in the case of so-called tramp steamers, which had longer amortisation periods, delivered goods to one port to take up new cargo for another, and needed more lay days in harbor for this purpose. Their business model implied that shipping companies could afford, in some degree, reduced travel speeds and longer delays. They could operate, therefore, also more easily with underpaid, contractually 'freer,' radically casualised, and consequently highly unstable 'white' crews.[62] As long as proletarian neighborhoods in port cities such as Liverpool or Cardiff supplied an overabundance of poorly paid 'white' (or 'coloured') stokers, these men were generally hired for tramp boiler rooms[63] despite their reputation for drink, for insubordination, and for backing out on contracts – a reputation that was partly an expression of class prejudice and partly, as Tony Lane observed, a reflection of behavioural patterns rooted in a culture of casual employment.[64] As shipmasters of tramp cargo steamers were less pressed for time in port to find replacements for 'white' stokers who signed off or simply disappeared after one voyage (as many did), they were even

59 Bullen, *Men of the Merchant Service*, 308–310.

60 *MMC*, vol. II: Evidence: 77, 98.

61 Gerstenberger and Welke, *Vom Wind zum Dampf*, 190–192; Kennerley, "Stoking the Boilers": 208–210.

62 *MaC*, vol. I: Report: 24 on. See also: *MMC*, vol. II: Evidence: 35, 164, 613.

63 Burton, "Work and Home Life": 70–74.

64 Tony Lane, *Liverpool. City of the Sea*, 2nd ed. (Liverpool: Liverpool University Press, 1997), 59–82.

reported to have encouraged crew to 'desert' with an eye to reducing the wage bill.[65] The particularly harsh practises of undermanning, overlong working hours, and the correspondent super-exploitation of the workforce[66] on board tramp cargo steamers resulted not only in high levels of labour turnover, but also triggered numerous conflicts in the stokehold or, from the perspective of management, raised problems of safety and discipline.[67] Owners may have complained, but, at the end of the day, the system worked sufficiently well. Stokehold labour was considered, as Michael Quinlan puts it, an "expendable resource."[68] Smaller, limited liability shipping companies that engaged in tramp shipping, in particular, had the reputation of "treat[ing] their people," a retired shipmaster alleged in 1894, "as if they were pegs in a machine, and if one peg breaks off they put in another peg."[69]

No loss of time could be allowed, however, in the upper segment of the industry – a segment that was controlled by a cartel of large shipping conglomerates. Their ocean liners required a much heavier initial investment while having shorter periods of usage as they competed perpetually for size as well as speed. For liners, as opposed to tramps, were running on tight and inflexible schedules, which were determined by the needs of passenger and postal services.[70] In 1898, the P&O Company was, for instance, contractually bound to provide a weekly mail steamer service between London and Bombay within 14 and a half days, which meant a reduction in travel time by more than 60 percent over the 23-day journey some 25 years earlier.[71] What this implied in practical terms was set out in Liversidge's variously reprinted engine-room manual:

> A liner steams almost continuously at full speed; stopping for a period of a few hours to coal at ports of call, she steams to her destination, where she may stay from ten to fourteen days. On her return to the home port, after an interval of from one to five weeks, she starts on

---

65 *MMC*, vol. II: Evidence: 164, 281, 526, 532, 608. See also Dixon, "Seamen and the Law": 221 on, 240–244; Lane, *Liverpool*, 75.

66 "The Lancet Special Sanitary Commission," *The Lancet* (20 September 1890): 635 on.

67 *MaC*, vol. I: Report: 6.

68 Michael Quinlan, "Precarious and Hazardous Work: the Health and Safety of Merchant Seamen 1815–1935," *Social History* 38, 3 (2013): 281–307, 305 and on.

69 *MaC*, vol. II: Evidence: 134.

70 S.G. Sturmey, *British Shipping and World Competition* (London: Athlone Press, 1962), 88, 239 on, 249–252.

71 House of Commons, *Report from the Select Committee on Shipping Subsidies: Minutes of Evidence* (hereafter: *SCSS*), (London: H.M.'s Stationery Office, 1901), (statement by Sir Thomas Sutherland) 233.

another voyage. Consequently there is very little time or opportunity for repairs to be made between the terminal ports.[72]

One such schedule was described in more detail:

> The Routine in the P. and O. Service. – The following outline sketch of this routine is given as an example of the general conditions under which a mail steamer is worked. The longest voyage is from London to Sydney, and is about 12,500 miles. [...] The principal ports of call and the lengths of stoppages are as follows: Gibraltar [sic!]; Malta, 8 hours; Brindisi, 14 hours; Port Said, 3 hours; Aden, 6 to 12 hours; Colombo, 18 to 24 hours; King George's Sound, 6 to 8 hours; Adelaide, 12 hours; Melbourne, 36 hours; Sydney, nearly a fortnight. [...] The tubes of the boilers are swept as far as possible, and all fires are cleaned at each port of call. This requires considerable management as steam is required for working the cargo, and it is not advisable to light up the auxiliary boiler for short stoppages.[73]

The port time of a liner was thus measured in hours rather than days, and this tight schedule had implications for the organisation of the labour process both at sea and in port. At sea, the crew had to take care of necessary maintenance and repair work both immediately and in addition to keeping up the pressure required for continuous maximum speed. Postponing tasks for the time in port was not an option. When in port, the boilers could not usually be allowed to cool down, which made cleaning tasks more difficult and required, as Liversidge put it, "considerable management."[74] This was a question of coordinating a variety of work tasks, but also of ensuring the availability of a skilled and experienced workforce – which was, of course, easier if the liner's own crew could be prevented from taking shore leave, from signing off or even backing out of their contract, and if they could be deployed continuously even during the short stays in port.

However, if continuous, uninterrupted operation both at sea and in port was crucial for labour management on steam-powered ocean liners, no single, inescapable solution to this problem arose from either the technology or the economy of the liner. Multiple responses would emerge from processes of social and political contestation and, in the case of British liner companies, at least two alternative strategies appear to have been found. Valerie Burton has shown that liner companies operating from Southampton as their home port sought to regularise the liner workforce by increasing pay and reducing turnover. The average wages of British stokers employed in the liners of Cunard, the American Line, or the White Line appear to have been about 20 percent higher than those paid to firemen serving

---

72 Liversidge, *Engine-room Practice*, 29.
73 Liversidge, *Engine-room Practice*, 30–31.
74 Liversidge, *Engine-room Practice*, 31.

on tramp steamers. To "counter-balance the attractions of wages in the American mercantile marine and ashore in the United States and Canada," the highest wages were paid in the North Atlantic liner service. A typical stoker serving on these British ocean liners was 'white' and English, a family man settled in Southampton or thereabout, and in long-term employment, while Liverpool stokers of often Irish descent were avoided on account of their reputation for carelessness and truculence. Local men were believed to be more likely to remain "with their ships for the duration of the round voyage" and "particular preference was given to men who had sailed with the company before." Labour turnover was much lower on these liners than on tramp steamers and the desertion rate appears to have been negligible.[75] The management strategy chosen by the Southampton-based shipping concerns was thus to preserve skill within the company and increase the average productivity of stokehold crew rather than extend the working day beyond the physical and mental limits of the stokers and accept corresponding fluctuations in skill level and labour supply. If this implied a somewhat larger wage bill, this clearly seemed acceptable.

However, from the mid-nineteenth century onwards, the BISN and P&O companies, controlling much of Indian Ocean shipping and the Euro-Asian liner business respectively, pioneered an approach that was markedly different from that of liner companies plying the North Atlantic from Southampton. They began to replace British crew, and particularly stokers, with Indian seafarers. Even though this process was in full swing long before the Suez Canal was opened in 1869,[76] P&O chairman and managing director, Sir Thomas Sutherland, linked it to this event when questioned by the House of Commons' Shipping Subsidies Committee in 1901. "[W]hen our ships first went through the Suez Canal," he said, "we endeavoured to work them entirely by Europeans, but found it impossible to do so owing to intemperance and insubordination." He conceded that he could "quite believe that a vessel going at a slow rate of speed, and not being tied down to time, might employ Europeans quite as well in the tropics" but insisted that a mail steamer could not do that. On being questioned whether firing was not "as hard on a tramp steamer as it is on a regular liner" he retorted that "a liner, and by that I mean a mail steamer, has to be at each point at a given date, and we found our European crews would not bring us to those given points at those given dates." Sutherland revealed that – despite the much lower pay of Indian sea-

---

75 Burton, "Work and Home Life": 80–101.
76 *MMC*, vol. II: Evidence: 296; see also: Hood, *The Blight of Insubordination*, 13.

farers – about a third of P&O's annual wage bill was being spent on "natives" by the turn of the century.[77]

If British maritime wages had been considerably lower than those, for instance, paid in the United States or Australia even around the turn of the century,[78] the Southampton-based liner companies had to make amends, as we have seen, to increase the productivity of their crews. The BISN and P&O shipping companies, soon followed by others engaged in Asian shipping, instead chose a strategy that avoided larger expenditure on wages. The pay of an Indian seafarer was believed to be between a quarter and a third of that of a British seaman[79] – proportions that would not change substantially up until the 1980s.[80] Since 'lascar' crews were generally much larger, as well as supplemented by a number of 'skilled' European 'able-bodied seamen' and engine-room mechanics, the overall savings on the wage bill were an issue of contention. Havelock Wilson believed savings to come close to 40 percent,[81] shipping industrialists asserted they were nearer to 10 percent and argued that the real economic advantages of 'lascar' employment lay in a reduction of operating costs. [82] Regardless of this divergence of estimates, the fact that hard-nosed British shipping tycoons chose to increase manning scales and employ larger crews does require an explanation in a period when undermanning was the rule in the British merchant marine in response to declining freight rates. And it is at this point that we turn to the issue of management-by-'race.'

Theories of Management-by-'race'

We have seen already how a racial recomposition and segmentation of steamship crews permitted the artificial hierarchies of command to be reinforced even further. But this was only one aspect of 'racial management' – an amalgam of managerial ideologies and practises that assumed shape in the latter half of the nineteenth century and was not confined to British merchant shipping. Elizabeth Esch and David Roediger have shown how United States management experts practised an obscurantist kind of racial algebra seeking to express in equations and tables how the presumably divergent physical and intellectual capacities of human

---

77 *SCSS* (statement by Sir Thomas Sutherland), 252, 254.
78 *MMC*, vol. II: Evidence: 164, 526, 532, 608.
79 *MMC*, vol. II: Evidence: 135, 161.
80 Ravi Ahuja, "Mobility and Containment: The Voyages of South Asian Seamen, c. 1900–1960," *International Review of Social History* 51/Supplement (2006): 112.
81 *MMC*, vol. II: Evidence: 161. See also ibid.: 243.
82 *MMC*, vol. III: Appendix Q, No. 3: 192. See also: *MMC*, vol. II: 532.

'races' could be harnessed and combined most effectively for the benefit of the employer.[83] One particularly influential propagator of such ideas was the mining engineer and future president of the United States, Herbert Hoover, who pronounced that "one white man equals from two to three of the coloured races, even in the simplest forms of mine work" while in "the most highly skilled branches, such as mechanics, the average ratio is as one to seven, or in extreme cases even eleven."[84] If a Chinese worker, as Hoover believed, 'required' only a sixth or even a twelfth of the pay of a 'white' worker, optimizing the racial composition of a workforce was thus a mere matter of balancing racially defined wage costs and productivity rates.[85]

The cultivation of such theories of scientistic racism did not necessarily depend on the hothouse of United States post-slavery society to flourish.[86] Very similar ideas proliferated in Britain's Indian Empire, too. The ability to identify and rate the subcontinent's most valuable 'martial' or 'coolie races' had been held in high esteem as a branch of colonial governance knowledge since the latter half of the nineteenth century.[87] Calculations of how many Indian trimmers and firemen were required to replace one 'European' seaman and speculations about the relative efficiency of 'white' and 'coloured' crews under the divergent climatic conditions of the North Atlantic and the Red Sea had been circulating in British shipping circles for a long time. While some insisted that two Indian seafarers were needed to do the work of one European sailor or fireman, others insisted that three were required, though actual manning scales seemed to suggest that 'mixed crews' with a sizeable 'lascar' component were generally about 50 percent larger than those comprising 'white crew' only.[88] Such rules of thumb could be translated into staffing formulae. Liversidge's engine-room manual presented detailed computations to the effect that a "European" fireman could work between

---

83 Elizabeth Esch and David Roediger, "'One Symptom of Originality': Race and Management of Labor in US History," in *Class, Race and Marxism*, edited by David Roediger (London/New York: Verso, 2017), 138–142.

84 Herbert C. Hoover, *Principles of Mining. Valuation, Organization and Administration* (New York/London: McGraw-Hill, 1909), 163.

85 Esch and Roediger, "One Symptom of Originality": 140 on.

86 Elizabeth Esch and David Roediger, *The Production of Difference: Race and the Management of Labour in U.S. History* (Oxford and New York: Oxford University Press, 2012), 3–16 and on.

87 Heather Streets, *Martial Races. The Military, Race and Masculinity in British Imperial Culture, 1857–1914* (Manchester: Manchester University Press, 2017); Kaushik Ghosh, "A Market for Aboriginality: Primitivism and Race Qualification in the Indentured Labour Market of Colonial India," in *Subaltern Studies X. Writings on South Asian History and Society*, edited by G. Bhadra, G. Prakash, and S. Tharu (New Delhi: Oxford University Press, 1999), 8–48.

88 *MaC*, vol. I: Report: 20, 149, 161.

0.71 and 0.729 tons of coal per hour, depending on the size of the respective liner, while "Natives" would move between 0.378 and 0.417 tons.[89]

The positivistic exactitude of these figures reflects the belief that 'race' possessed an objective, measurable quality or essence, which allowed taxonomic comparison in terms of work capacity and market value. Yet if their tabulations displayed precise data with great confidence, the taxonomers of race found it characteristically hard to maintain coherence in their calculations. The elusive character of 'racial essence' as much as the multiple variables of the labour process foiled attempts to calculate crewing requirements solely according to a ship's total indicative horsepower or fire-grate surface.[90] The very messiness of the data indicates that computational exactitude sat uneasily with the actual work organisation, with a labour process that defied rigid standardisation as it navigated a "zone of uncertainty" contingent upon numerous variables: "There are many minor causes," admitted the Manning Committee, "for making the work to be done below greater or less."[91] By factoring in nebulous notions of 'racial essence,' this mess was further compounded. The proposed exactitude of measurements of racially determined work capacity thus reveals itself as an attempt to rationalise an irrational premise. In the age of capital, ideological unreason fancies the costume of mathematical reason, then and now.

Yet such notions of essential, measurable, and manageable difference between 'races' (or, in a present-day rendering, between nationally defined 'cultures'),[92] have been too persistent in the history of late capitalism to be brushed away on grounds of logical inconsistency alone. For racial (or cultural) essentialism has served not only – in the sphere of social ideology – as a keystone of counter-enlightenment irrationalism. It has also maintained – in the sphere of labour management – some practical utility for employers that needs to be examined and explained. When Indian seafarers came to be employed in ever larger numbers, essentialised racial difference served as a seemingly self-explanatory shorthand and legitimation of racialised labour relations and management procedures.

---

89 Liversidge, *Engine-room Practice*, 25–26.
90 Esch and Roediger, "One Symptom of Originality": 138–142.
91 *MaC*, vol. I: Report: 27. For a pertinent analysis, see Gerstenberger and Welke, *Vom Wind zum Dampf*, 195–197.
92 For a contemporary application of cultural essentialism to the management of 'human resources,' see Geert Hofstede, *Culture's Consequences – Comparing Values, Behaviors, Institutions and Organizations Across Nations*, 2nd ed. (Sage: Thousand Oaks et al., 2001).

Liners and Management-by-'race'

Labour relations of 'lascars' and other 'native seamen' differed substantially from those of 'European' seamen not only regarding wages and other forms of compensation but, even more importantly, in respect of their level of personal subordination. Legally, these differentials were sanctioned, for Indian workers, not merely in divergent contractual conditions, but in a bifurcation of the work contract itself in British imperial maritime law, namely in the creation of a separate category of work contracts for Indian seafarers that were referred to as Lascar (or, Asiatic) Articles of Agreement. Ideologically, the reduced formal freedom of 'lascar' contracts (particularly evident in the severely restricted right to terminate the contract) was justified by ascribing to these seafarers a 'racial essence' that could be harnessed for useful purposes only by specific, skillfully deployed means.[93] If management preferences shaped the labour relations of steamship workers in ways that turned racial stigma into a resource for the fortification of steeply hierarchical labour processes, this tendency was made to appear natural when it was claimed that essential 'racial difference translated organically into contractual difference and, more specifically, into differential entitlements to formal contractual freedom.

Historians have examined the work relations of 'native' seafarers that were forged in increasingly racialised maritime labour markets and have done so from various angles, including the specific forms of legal regulation that combined racialised maritime labour law with harsh and equally racialised immigration restrictions for 'native' seafarers.[94] Under Asiatic Articles, Indian seafarers could be denied shore leave in port while being prevented, by immigration laws, from disembarking in several important shipping destinations that included the United States and Australia.[95] Thus they could be compelled to work continuously even

---

93 OIOC, India Office, E&O, L/E/9/957, 3256 (1926): 3: Brief for the International Labour Conference on Seamen's Articles of Agreement. See also Ravi Ahuja, "Networks of Subordination – Networks of the Subordinated: The Case of South Asian Maritime Labour under British Imperialism c.1890–1947," in *Spaces of Disorder: The Limits of British Colonial Control in South Asia and in the Indian Ocean Region*, edited by Harald Fischer-Tiné and Ashwini Tambe (London: Routledge, 2008), 13 on; Ahuja, "Mobility and Containment": 115–120.

94 See especially Gopalan Balachandran, *Globalizing Labour? Indian Seafarers and World Shipping, c.1870–1945* (Oxford and New York: Oxford University Press, 2012), 58–93, which sums up conveniently the author's important research on these issues; Laura Tabili *'We Ask for British Justice'. Workers and Racial Difference in Late Imperial Britain* (Ithaca, NY: Cornell University Press, 1994), 41–57; Ahuja, "Networks of Subordination"; Ahuja, "Mobility and Containment."

95 OIOC, India Office, E&O (Seamen) L/E/9/974: Shore leave for lascar crews. See also Ahuja, "Mobility and Containment."

in port, while desertion rates were pushed down, contributing substantially to the uninterrupted and punctual performance of liner operations. Crucially, Indian seafarers could not legally terminate their contracts in a port outside India. Accordingly, in the opinion of the superintendent of the Mercantile Marine Office in Liverpool, the fact that "Lascar and other Asiatic seamen" were "not given to going on shore at every port" was one of the reasons why it was "not difficult to understand how they soon were preferred in regular lines"[96] – a view that was frequently repeated before official committees.[97]

These findings remain useful and relevant but address merely one side of the racialisation of steamship labour: they emphasise the labour market rather than the work site, study labour relations rather than the labour process, and examine the sale of labour power, not its extraction. But the liner companies' urge to secure continuous operation and minimise unavoidable interruptions resulted in a racialised organisation of work, particularly in the boiler room – the department where the increase in the employment of Indian seafarers appears to have been most dynamic.[98] It was here that a racialisation of work-time arrangements created more favorable conditions for liner companies. While working hours remained legally unregulated in British merchant shipping in general,[99] informal work-time arrangements – two four-hour shifts per day in the case of stokers – were considered a customary entitlement by European seafarers and, in principle, even by the shipping industry, although overtime and infringement on rest periods were common.[100] The much-quoted and equally informal 'khalasi watch' system, by contrast, explicitly required 'lascars' to be available whenever needed and was officially acknowledged in 1896. [101] In practise, Indian stokers often appear to have been employed in three four-hour watches,[102] though the Government of India reported to the ILO in 1929 that two four-hour watches were customary as much as for 'white' firemen. [103] As with more openly 'unfree' labour relations, working time was not separated from off-time by legal regulation, while customs as well as the conditions for terminating a labour contract were racially defined.

---

96 *MMC*, vol. II: Evidence: 21.
97 *MMC*, vol. II: Evidence: 61; 244, 531; *MaC*, vol. II: Evidence: 581.
98 *MaC*, vol. 1: Report: 19.
99 Dixon, "Seamen and the Law": 203; Burton, "Work and Home Life": 116 on; "Hours of Labour in the Mercantile Marine: Labour Conditions," *International Labour Review* 5, 2 (Feb. 1922): 321 on.
100 *MMC*, vol. II: Evidence: 194. See also Burton, "Work and Home Life": 116 on.
101 *MaC*, vol. I: Report: 20; Hood, *Blight of Subordination*, 48 on; *MMC*, vol. II: Evidence: 200.
102 See, for example, Liversidge, *Engine-room Practice*, 23, 30.
103 International Labour Office, International Labour Conference, Thirteenth Session: *The Regulation of Hours of Work on Board Ship* (Geneva: ILO, 1929): 202–210.

Yet difference was not held up merely by law and custom. 'Native' firemen were bound into an even steeper and, crucially, mediated structure of shipboard hierarchy that reduced (though it did not rule out) direct conflict with the shipmaster or the chief engineer. For the *serangs* and *tindals*, the intermediaries used by British shipping companies to recruit as well as supervise the work of Indian seafarers, functioned as a buffer between the 'white' officers and the 'native' crew.[104] "In a British ship which carries an Indian crew," wrote Amir Haider Khan in his memoirs, "it is a sarang through whom the authorities make man [sic] work for unlimited hours" – whose mediation made, in other words, 'khalasi watches' possible.[105] This hierarchical arrangement countered the egalitarian tendency that had emerged, as Burton argues, among European stokehold crews working "as gangs, organised and disciplined by their own rules."[106] The flip side of the semi-autonomous, flexible, and knowledgeable cooperation of workers that was required to navigate the zone of uncertainty in the boiler room was a potential subversion of the officers' authority, a tendency towards industrial militancy or, in the employers' dictionary, towards 'insubordination.'[107] To supervise this elastic, inherently instable process of cooperation was a laborious management task, which to some extent could be delegated to foremen like the *serangs* and *tindals*. This layer of intermediaries curbed the 'black gang's' autonomy in organising their work while simultaneously reducing the need for – potentially contentious – end-to-end communication along the chain of command. "No leading fireman or engine-room petty officer of an ordinary British steamer can compete," wrote Captain W. H. Hood, "with the engine-room *serang* in keeping control of the black squad."[108] It is not as if relations between 'lascars' and these middlemen were harmonious or free of tension;[109] but the *serangs* possessed means of control over

---

104 For partly differing interpretations of the role of the *serang*, see: Gopalan Balachandran, "Searching for the Sardar: The State, Pre-capitalist Institutions and Human Agency in the Maritime Labour Market, Calcutta, 1880–1935," in *Institutions and Economic Change in South Asia*, edited by Burton Stein and Sanjay Subrahmanyam (Delhi: Oxford University Press, 1996), 206–236; Ahuja, "Networks of Subordination."

105 Amir Haider Khan, *I Break with the Old World* (Part I: Nasik manuscript 1939–1942, typed copy with editorial markings, Pakistan Study Centre, University of Karachi), 225, 228.

106 Burton, "Work and Home Life": 140.

107 Gerstenberger and Welke, *Vom Wind zum Dampf*, 199; Burton, "Work and Home Life": 140. For a typical conflict between an engineer and the "black gang," see: Helbig, *Seefahrt vor den Feuern*, 275–278.

108 Hood, *The Blight of Insubordination*, 50.

109 For a detailed account of shipboard conflicts, see Ravi Ahuja, "A Freedom Still Enmeshed in Servitude: The Unruly 'Lascars' of the SS City of Manila or a Micro-History of the 'Free Labour'

their men that were not available to 'white' officers, including, crucially, systematic indebtedness – a contractual bond that could be reinforced and stabilised by ties of village or kinship networks.[110]

Shipping concerns like the P&O Company favoured continuous family connections among their Indian stokehold crews – their nautical inspector reported with some pride that the 'natives' "stick by the Company. There are men there almost for generations." P&O's "lascars," he added, were "almost an institution of the company." [111] A retired shipmaster of the British India Steam Navigation Company confirmed that the "lascar [took] a greater interest in a ship than the British seaman."[112] Such statements were repeated time and again but clearly need to be taken with a pinch of salt. For the shipping industry, it was surely easier to occupy the moral high ground by conjuring up paternalistic bonds with the 'lascar' while deploring the depravity of British seafarers than by admitting that considerations of cost played a role in the increasing displacement of the latter by the former. And yet, other evidence, including the memoirs and reminiscences of seafarers, corroborate a certain stability of maritime village links in areas as far apart as interior Goa, coastal Gujarat, northern Punjab, and Sylhet in eastern Bengal, as well as the importance of family links for gaining access to the maritime labour market.[113]

There is also evidence that the age range of Indian trimmers and firemen was somewhat wider than that of their European colleagues and competitors, who were usually younger adults. Less than a third of all British seamen on foreign-going ships were older than 35 between 1891 and 1911, while up to half of the stokehold crew was below 30.[114] A study of a sample of crew lists even found that the average age of a British worker in the fireroom was just over thirty between 1850 and 1950.[115] Indian shipping law as well as ILO conventions deviated from European legislation, however, in that, well into the 1930s, it was permitted to employ Indian adolescents as trimmers and stokers. This was justified by British officials with the fantastical claim that "in a tropical climate a boy reaches maturity much earlier than in Europe."[116] Among Indian crews, the recruitment of trimm-

---

Problem" in Ravi Ahuja, ed., *Working Lives and Worker Militancy: The Politics of Labour Colonial India* (Delhi: Tulika, 2013).

110 Ahuja, "Networks of Subordination."

111 *MaC*, vol. II: Evidence: 582 on.

112 *MaC*, vol. II: Evidence: 781.

113 Ahuja, "Networks of Subordination"; Yousuf Choudhury, *The Roots and Tales of Bangladeshi Settlers* (Birmingham: Sylheti Social History Group, 1993), 42, 57–59.

114 Burton, "Counting Seafarers": 316.

115 Kennerley, "Stoking the Boilers": 202.

116 League of Nations, *International Labour Conference, 2ⁿᵈ Session, Genova 1920* (Geneva: International Labour Office, 1920), 146 (Captain Duncan Vines, delegate of the Government of India). See

ers in their late teens, at times even at the age of 10 or 12, appears to have been rather common.[117] "A young man who intends to qualify for employment in the engine-room," an official letter from Bengal stated in 1911, "usually commences his career as a coal trimmer at about 16 years of age; he seldom goes away in a vessel by himself, but is almost invariably accompanied by a relative holding some post in the engine-room."[118] At the same time, it was also known that middle-aged men continued to be recruited by *serangs* even when their physical strength was beginning to ebb: "[T]here have been instances of grandfather, father, and son in the same ship," reported the P&O Company's nautical inspector.[119] This permitted a skill transfer that could begin at an earlier age while preserving the experience of seasoned stokers in the workforce for a longer period to be utilised for purposes of supervision and on-the-job training. Those in their twenties and thirties could be relied upon for full performance, while Indian village boys were groomed for future service as they took care of auxiliary tasks. Management-by-'race' thus also provided means for the maintenance of uncertified skill: a certain stabilisation (or, in the nautical inspector's words, "institutionalisation") of the workforce, and the harnessing of inter-generational modes of supervision and skill transfer held substantial advantages for managing the zone of uncertainty in the stokehold.

This wider generational scope certainly contributed to the size of 'lascar' boiler-room crews, which exceeded that of European 'black gangs' often by 50 percent. This takes us back to the question as to why larger 'lascar' crews were increasingly being hired at the very time when freight rates were dropping and shipowners sought to reduce the wage bill. When official commissions interviewed British stokers, many respondents would opt for the language of white supremacism to deny 'coloured' labour market competitors any physical prowess or skill, any efficiency or courage.[120] Some, however, avoided racial stereotyping and hinted at uneven relations of power and issues of labour management. Thomas Alty, a fireman, stated for instance that British officers preferred "foreign" crew because "they seem to do

---

also OIOC, BoMP P/8587, A205–8, A393–95; OIOC, BoMP P/8838, A49–50 (February 1911): Despatch from Government of India to Secretary of State, 20 October 1910; OIOC, BoMP P/11535, A35–36 (January 27, 1926); Rajani Kanta Das, *History of Indian Labour Legislation* (Calcutta: University of Calcutta, 1941), 126–129; E.C. Tsandis, "International Maritime Labour Law. A Case Study of the ILO's Attempts to Develop Aspects Thereof," Ph.D. thesis, London School of Economics, 1992), 120–125.

117 See, for example, Minutes of the Evidence recorded by the Indian Mercantile Marine Committee, n.l., n.d.: 643.

118 OIOC, BoMP P/8587, A319–20 (July 1911): Letter from the Government of Bengal to the Government of India, Department Commerce & Industry, 29 March 1911.

119 *MaC*, vol. II: Evidence: 582 on.

120 See e.g.: *MMC*, vol. II: Evidence: 347 on.

as they like with them; they think we can speak our mind too freely." As for numerical proportions, he observed that work in the boiler room was "very trying, but there are a couple of them ['lascars'] to do the work of only one of our men, and that makes a lot of difference down in a stokehold."[121] Many spokesmen of the shipping industry, too, were comfortable with racist cliché and loudly repeated the presumably 'scientific' calculations of comparative racial efficiency to justify the unevenness of manning scales. Some, however, also claimed that the larger size of 'native' crews meant that ships "are better worked, kept in better order, and generally more efficient as mail and passenger ships than they would be with European crews."[122] More specifically, it was stated that steam pressure was maintained more evenly and that coal consumption reduced when employing 'native' firemen. The spokesman of the Liverpool Shipowners' Association contended, for instance, that

> the inferiority of the Lascar firemen in physique is an advantage, as he cannot put on a great deal of coal at a time, and he is, therefore, constantly stoking[,] putting on small quantities of coal, so that the steam pressure is evenly maintained. The European fireman, on the other hand, will put on a great deal, and have a rest, and the consequence is loss of pressure, and the result is that ships which employ Lascars are able to keep better time than ships employing European firemen.[123]

The Board of Trade's principal Marine Department official for London concurred that "since the introduction of Lascars I am told that the consumption of coal has decreased, and the speed of ships has increased."[124] If such claims were often couched in the jargon of racist stereotypes by referring to the 'lascars'' presumed "inferior physique" and lesser sensitivity to heat, the gist of the matter, in terms of actual labour management, was clearly that less restrictive manning scales enabled the stokehold crew to tend to the fires more efficiently, namely to feed them more frequently and regularly with smaller quantities of coal rather than tossing in heavy shovelfuls at longer intervals. More men made "a lot of difference down in a stokehold," too, regarding those unending and crucial ancillary tasks, which had to be seen to immediately and without letting off in the production of steam.

---

121 *MMC*, vol. II: Evidence: 333 on.
122 The quote is from the testimony of J. C. Almond, Nautical Inspector of the P&O Company to the Manning Committee in 1894: *MaC*, vol. II: Evidence: 582. See also *MaC*, vol. II: Evidence: 771; *MaC*, Volume I: Report: 20.
123 *MaC*, Volume I: Report: 531. The Superintendent of Liverpool's Mercantile Marine Office held the same view: *MaC*, Volume I: Report: 21.
124 *MaC*, Volume I: Report: 137.

Conclusion

P&O supremo Sir Thomas Sutherland may have presented, in 1901, endemic insubordination among British seafarers as well as the climatic conditions of the tropics as the main reasons for his preference for 'native' crews. Yet, deeper causes lurked behind. Asian stokehold crews could facilitate uninterrupted operation at sea because their size could be augmented to comprise an internal labour reserve without increasing labour costs. This internal labour reserve permitted a levelling out of the typical fluctuations of workload in the stokehold and the high incidence of sickness in this work environment. It also enabled a closer supervision of the labour process by employing an additional layer of intermediaries while preserving and transferring skill among a wider range of age groups. In sum, the existence of this internal labour reserve explains the repeated assertions of shipping spokesmen that liners could be kept in a better shape and that tight schedules were fulfilled more reliably with a 'lascar' crew.[125] Indian seafarers were quite aware of the practise. Amir Haider Khan, remembering his first attempt to gain seafaring employment with a 'lascar' crew in early 1915 observed, for instance, that in "those days in most of the big coal-burning ships were employed some extra men who were signed on as firemen or coal passers" but were in fact deployed to cleaning tasks in the "engine room or other auxiliary work" and also served as substitutes when regular stokers and trimmers were taken ill.[126] If extra men were recruited in Bombay and Calcutta while undermanning was the rule in British ports this may well explain why an overseer for the Liverpool shipping company Gillison & Chadwick claimed that one engineer had told him "he would sooner go for less wages if we would give him Lascars."[127] The racist stereotypes commonly used to vindicate the larger size of these crews were thus ideologically supercharged verbalisations of perfectly workable and cost-saving management practises.

If the internal labour reserve of 'lascar' crews facilitated the uninterrupted operation at full capacity of the steamer's power plant at sea, a combination of racialised maritime labour contracts and anti-Asian immigration restrictions served to keep the workforce available even in ports of call, push down the rate of attrition, and stabilise the workforce without raising costs of employment. If similar elements of contractual unfreedom remained justifiable, in the twentieth century,

---

125 *MaC*, vol. I: Report: 20; *MaC*, vol. II: Evidence: 582, 771, 775; *MMC*, vol. II: Evidence: 531, 543.
126 Khan, "I Break with the Old World": 156.
127 *MaC*, vol. II: Evidence: 692.

for 'white' wage workers only under crisis or war conditions,[128] management-by-'race' offered a route of circumvention available at all times: the structural tension between the compulsion to continuity in the labour intensive work processes of the steamship, on the one hand, and the disruptive potential of formally free wage labour, on the other, could be resolved, without raising labour costs, through the racialisation of maritime employment and labour management. The practical relevance of such calculations was rarely laid bare and remained enshrouded in the robe of racial taxonomy.

When oil increasingly came to replace coal as the preferred fuel of maritime transport after the First World War, the labour intensity of maritime propulsion was much reduced. Enormous boiler-room crews like that of the *Titanic*, where each of the three watches had comprised, in 1912, as many as 81 men,[129] became a less common sight in ports. The coal-fueled steamer's demise into technological obsolescence was, however, less rapid in the British merchant marine than among her United States and European competitors.[130] Britain's shipping industry faced greater obstacles in shifting from coal to oil, but also possessed superior, imperial means to compensate for the decreasing competitiveness of their fleet in terms of fuel efficiency.[131] If oil-fueled vessels appeared at a slower pace in the British merchant fleet, the proportion of 'native' seafarers employed in British ships increased sharply. Between 1914 and 1938, the overall annual employment in the British merchant marine declined from 295,652 to 192,375 (or by 35 percent), while the annual employment of 'lascars' remained constant at about fifty thousand (or rose from 17 to 26 percent).[132] The steady supply of cheap and disenfranchised steamship labour from India and other colonies provided the beleaguered British shipping industry, and particularly its liner segment, with a certain competitive edge in terms of labour costs. Management-by-'race' thus prolonged the super-exploitation of stigmatised 'black gangs' in the stokehold.

---

128 Alessandro Stanziani, *Sailors, Slaves, and Immigrants. Bondage in the Indian Ocean World, 1750–1914* (Basingstoke: Palgrave Macmillan, 2014), 125–133.
129 de Kerbrech, *Down amongst the Black Gang*, 67.
130 Max E. Fletcher, "From Coal to Oil in British Shipping," *Journal of Transport History* 3, 1 (1975): 7.
131 Stephanie Jones, *Trade and Shipping: Lord Inchcape, 1852–1932* (Manchester and New York: Manchester University Press, 1989), 121–126. See also Christopher J. Napier, "Allies or Subsidiaries? Inter-Company Relations in the P&O Group, 1914–39," *Business History* 39, 2 (1997): 69–93.
132 Ahuja, "Networks of Subordination": 11–12.

Jonathan Hyslop

10 Southern Africa, Maritime Labour, and Steamship Imperialism c. 1875 to 1948

The period between the 1870s and the end of the Second World War was the era in which steamships dominated the oceans. Although there was some overlap in the early part of that period with sailing vessels, and in the latter part with oil-burning ships, steam was the technology that defined the maritime world. It was also this period that saw southern Africa transformed from a marginal region in the world economy, only partially colonised by Europe, to a global centre of mining and agricultural production dominated by British imperial power, British capital, and a strong South African settler colonial state. The contemporaneity of these transformations was not coincidental. Steamships were the crucial link between southern Africa and the rest of the world, transporting settlers, imperial armies, colonial officials, consumer goods, and heavy machinery to the region on a huge scale, and taking abroad gold and other minerals, agricultural and animal products, and colonial troops. Although a number of European powers had steam fleets that played a role in southern Africa, it was British shipping that predominated, as it did – as the world's largest merchant marine by far – across the world. And although there were other colonial powers – Germany before 1914 in South West Africa, Portugal in Angola and Mozambique, and Belgium in Katanga – Britain was the hegemon in the region, militarily, politically, and economically. The maritime world, and especially its British component, is therefore crucial to an understanding of southern Africa at that time.

Steam was a technology that completely transformed the labour process at sea. It replaced the highly skilled mariners of sailing ships with a new kind of workforce. Whereas sailors would need several years on the rigging to become really proficient, steamship work could be picked up fairly quickly. The fragmentation of labour into different "departments" – engine room, deck, and catering – made for recruitment in an ethnically and racially segmented way, splitting the workforce politically. This also coincided with the arrival of modern trade unionism but meant that the new labour organisations tended to be fragmented along racial lines.

The southern African history of the sea raises some important and difficult questions for labour history, which relate to the central concerns of the re:work project. First, the issue of writing a global labour history. There were in fact relatively few South African seafarers, with most sailors of the time in the region's ports coming from elsewhere in the world. How are we to understand the labour

https://doi.org/10.1515/9783111086552-011

history of global merchant fleets, with their travelling and transnationally recruited workforces, in the context of how they impact on a specific geographical region? Classic labour histories tend to focus on a particular factory, town, region, or country, and often feature a limited constellation of union organisations or workers' parties. This may well focus on migrant or itinerant workers, but their mobility through space and the lack of attachment to a particular geographical space is hardly ever as radical as it is for seafarers. Multiple places of origin and an almost infinite range of cultural and political traditions and organisational affiliations come into play when we turn to the sea. There is a good case for regarding the maritime labour force of the steamship era as the first global working class – but it was certainly not a unified one.

Second, there is the issue of free and unfree labour. Although we now understand the remarkable persistence of unfree labour in the twentieth century, the forms and temporalities of this were radically different in the oceanic world compared with the seafarers' home countries. This issue requires a rather specific theorisation, but also one that has broader implications for understanding the racial cleavages within the global labour force. The steamship era witnessed a complex politics, in which maritime workers from the metropolitan countries often fought to preserve their superior political status, with the associated economic advantages, in relation to colonial subject workers. Yet, while workers from the colonised world laboured under especially egregious forms of unfreedom, the maritime workers from industrialised countries, which were supposedly evolving a standard employment relationship of social and economic citizenship, were still significantly less free than their onshore fellow-citizens. Sailors of all races in the British merchant marine were criminalised if they broke their labour contracts; they were also often in a situation of near or actual debt-servitude to captains and labour brokers, and experienced great difficulty in accessing the rights to which they were formally entitled. Class and racial politics interacted in unusual ways in a labour world characterised by unfree labour.[1]

Finally, our understanding of the life courses of workers comes up short against the extraordinary brutality of life on a steamship. The notion of a life course has been a very useful and productive tool for understanding labour and social history. But if we think about the notion of the life course as a transition from childhood to youth, maturity, and old age, then the lethal nature of steamship work does not fit; so many sailors' lives were interrupted by death or mutilation at an early age. Steamship work was significantly more dangerous than most forms

---

[1] Jonathan Hyslop, "British Steamship Workers c. 1875–1945: Precarious Before Precarity," *Labour History* 116 (2019): 5–28.

of factory work, and often more so even than mining or logging, which were usually considered particularly hazardous. Many workers did not live to see old age, and, as such, I have posited the term "catastrophic life course" to describe the almost unique relationship of the lives of seamen during this era to mortality. To discuss maritime labour is to discuss death on a mass scale.

A key point here is that globalisation during this era was not a smoothly unfolding economic process.[2] It was closely connected with the political and military power of Empire, and with the unequal relations between the different colonial powers. This shaped the workforce, in that workers from both Britain itself and from the British Empire played a disproportionately central role in shipping in the southern African region. But the structure of this workforce was also determined by class conflicts, nationalist insurgency, and racial/ethnic politics in both the metropole and the colonies.

Questions of mobility and spatiality must be at the centre of any understanding of a maritime workforce. The very specific political context of each port shaped how sailors were able to move. In some places they were relatively free to come and go; in others – and South African ports tended to be at this end of the spectrum – they were either heavily constrained by legal regulation or prevented from landing altogether. This had a dramatic effect on the available strategies for survival. Tighter immigration regulation made it much harder to take onshore employment, to settle in a new country, or even to change ships. By the same token, while their continuous movement made it notoriously difficult for seafarers to organise, it also meant that on the relatively rare occasions that mass industrial strike action did take place, the impact would be amplified to an extraordinary degree, with work stoppages encompassing multiple countries. In the context of the globally dominant British merchant fleet, this was a major threat for imperial economic cohesion, often setting off contradictory political responses from London, from the settler colonial governments, and from the semi-devolved administrations of the colonies.

A maritime perspective poses new and challenging questions for our understanding of the working classes in southern Africa. The last 50 years have seen the development of a rich literature on labour history in the region.[3] The strengths of this body of work lie particularly in its recovery of the sense of African working-

---

2 To some extent this is the underlying assumption behind the otherwise admirable work of Michael Miller, *Europe and the Maritime World: A Twentieth Century History* (Cambridge: Cambridge University Press, 2014).
3 A very useful overview is found in Bill Freund, "Labour Studies and Labour History in South Africa; Perspectives from the Apartheid Era and After," *International Review of Social History* 58, 3 (2013): 493–519.

class agency and in its sophisticated discussion of the relationships between capitalism and race. But this historiography has often also been limited by what Marcel van der Linden has termed "methodological nationalism." There has been a tendency for the different countries of the region to be seen as having their own self-contained labour histories, and, moreover, the discussion of those histories to be subordinated to the nationalist histories of anti-colonialism. For example, the history of South African labour could be reduced to one of the rise of apartheid and resistance to it, with labour merely a supporting actor in the nationalist struggle. Since the 1990s, there have been attempts to globalise South African histories, but there is a considerable distance to go in this regard. In order to get away from a national framing of labour histories, we need to look simultaneously "down" towards specific local histories, "up" toward links between cities, and "sideways" at the lateral connections between regions and empires. Incorporating an oceanic perspective is a useful way of doing so.[4]

Workforces were also shaped by the infrastructural imperatives and capitalist rivalries of steam ports. Harbours organised around coaling and rail transport required vast concentrations of resources, and this resulted, at the international level, in a clear move away from a large number of smaller sail-based ports to a few major steam ports. The construction initiatives and political struggles of particular groups of capitalists affected the outcome of these contestations. There were battles for markets between ports – notably, in the case of southern Africa, in the struggle between Cape Town, Durban, and Lourenço Marques (Maputo) for the position of dominant regional harbour. These ports also had very specific connections with other metropolitan and colonial harbours, which, in turn, affected the employment opportunities for particular workers. It is also important to note that such configurations were often a product of the initiatives of local groups of capitalists, rather than simply being emanations of the decisions of the moguls of the City of London and other metropolitan financial centres.

A striking feature of this era was the complexity of political relationships governing decision-making across the British Empire concerning the maritime industry. This was especially significant in relation to "lascars" – the very large group of Indian, Arab, and Horn of Africa workers on British ships. In general, the British merchant fleet was regulated by legislation passed by the Westminster parliament, as well as the Board of Trade in London. The board was subject to pressures from

---

4 This chapter does not deal with the question of dock labour. There has been some excellent work on this subject, notably, in recent years by Ralph Callebert, *On Durban's Docks: Zulu Workers, Rural Households, Global Labor* (Rochester, NY: Rochester University Press, 2017); and Peter Cole, *Dockworker Power: Race and Activism in Durban and San Francisco Bay Area* (Urbana, Chicago and Springfield: University of Illinois Press, 2018).

shipowners, but also increasingly by the trade unions as they gradually became more powerful. Lascars on British ships, however, could be affected by administrative decisions made by the government department in control of the Raj, the India Office. To make matters more complicated, the Viceroy's government in India was able to pass its own measures to regulate Indian maritime workers. This multiplicity often led to competing policy imperatives. While shipowners were keen to use Indian workers, who were seen as cheap and docile, British unions wanted to exclude them. As time went on, the government of India wanted to buy off nationalist agitation by improving the lascars' working conditions, but shipowners were not willing to foot the bill. The consequence was a Byzantine complexity as to which policies should be implemented, with shipping employers often able to achieve their goals within the space that this opened up.

There was also a complex relationship between the metropolitan and settler colonial governments. Despite the formal autonomy of the Cape and Natal colonies before 1910, and of the new South African state after that, the British government succeeded in insisting that its own draconian legislation regarding seafarers, which imposed criminal penalties for leaving a job, be imposed by magistrates in all British Empire ports. The sea marked the limits of Dominion self-government.

1870 to 1910: The Conquest Era

The 1870s marked a turning point in the history of the sea. Although experiments with steam technology dated back half a century, it was only at this time, with shipyards mastering the key technologies of the steamship, that steam began to prevail. Most important was the triple-expansion steam engine, which utilised three cylinders operating at different pressures for a far more efficient use of steam power than the previous single- or double-chamber models. Screw propellors replaced cumbersome and fragile paddle wheels, and metallurgical and structural advances in the building of metal hulls made ships more resilient. For the first time, steam came to predominate over sail on the world's oceans. The new technology of steam drastically disrupted the organisation of maritime work. Sailing ship labour was, in a sense, artisanal. It required several years to become effective at managing the rigging and to master the complex maintenance tasks. The sense of pride taken in the skill this produced, together with the cooperation among the crew needed for survival, made for a strong *esprit de corps.* It also, I would argue, tended to soften ethnic, racial, and religious cleavages among the mutually reliant crew members.[5] The era of steam, on the other hand, can be characterised as a time of mechanisation and industrialisation of the sea. Steam produced a three-way split in the labour force. The engine rooms required muscle. Coal was kept in bunkers, from where it was shovelled into barrows by trimmers, who then pushed these barrows, often at a very fast pace, toward the furnaces attended by firemen. The firemen then fed the coal into the furnaces with their shovels. They were responsible for maintaining the fires at the right level of intensity, raking them with a long bar, known as a slicer. This generated an enormous amount of ash, which was usually carried away in buckets. Every stage of this work was fraught with dangers. Although there were definite elements of skill involved, the primary requirement was physical strength, and the basics of the job could be learned quickly. Conditions below deck were hellish; workers were burned by flames and hot surfaces, crushed by sliding heaps of coal, mutilated in falls and explosions, and, in the long run, choked by respiratory diseases caused by the dust. The labour process was supervised by foremen and, above them, ship's engineers. This system of control often coincided with, and reinforced, important racial and ethnic social cleavages – white engineers oversaw colonial workers while, for example, Scottish Protestant engineers exercised a tense supervision over Irish Catholic firemen.[6]

Deck workers performed a wide range of functions, but much of their time was taken up with the repetitive and uninspiring work of scraping and painting the metal surfaces. Catering departments grew substantially, as the new technology permitted the construction of big liners. Cooks, waiters, cabin staff, and stewardesses performed work that had almost all the disadvantages of their shorebound counterparts, but with no home to retreat to. Cramped, ill-ventilated accommodation, poor food, and harassment from peers and officers were commonplace for all categories of worker, although inequalities were usually intensified along racial gradients. This compartmentalisation of labour also lent itself to a stronger ethnic and racial segmentation of the workforce. Recruitment to particular tasks was often carried out on a regional, racialised, or ethnicised basis, supported by ideologies concerning the suitability of particular peoples for particular work. For example, on lascar-crewed ships there was a stereotypical allocation of jobs in different parts of the vessel to different ethnic and regional groups. Goans were widely employed in the catering departments and East Bengalis and Punjabis in the stokehold, while a range of other ethnic groups were assigned to deck work

---

5 The African-American seaman James Williams, for example, gave a remarkably positive evaluation of his experiences of working on British sailing ships in the relevant period ; James Williams, *Blow the Man Down: A Yankee Seaman's Adventures Under Sail* (New York: E.P. Dutton, 1959).
6 Stephen Fox, *The Ocean Railway: Isambard Kingdom Brunel, Samuel Cunard and the Revolutionary World of the Great Atlantic Steamships* (London: Harper and Collins, 2003), 324.

– a structure that certainly helped to keep workers politically fragmented. Moreover, as the system of officer promotion by examination was elaborated, and merchant marine officers, especially on the liners, attained greater status, the gap between officers and crew widened.

There was a technical hierarchisation in the shipping labour force as well. Although seafarers were radically insecure, in that they were hired by the voyage, workers on regularly scheduled liner services were often able, somewhat informally, to secure steady employment. This enabled them to build relatively stable family lives in their home ports, with a cycle of voyages and leave. Workers on tramp steamers – the workhorses that took cargo around the world – had much more insecure lives. Ships would arrive in a port and arrangements for the next cargo would be made by telegraph. Voyages were thus lengthy and unpredictable. An even lower rank was occupied in the early part of the period by workers on the surviving sailing vessels, which continued until the 1920s to carry cargo where speed was not of the essence, such as bringing timber from the Pacific Coast of North America to southern Africa. American sailing ships had a particularly lurid reputation for brutality by their (often of Scandinavian-origin) officers.[7]

Until the 1870s, the colonial hold on southern Africa had been tenuous. British rule was secure only in the Cape Colony and the southern part of Natal. The Boer states of the southern African interior were weak, contemporary Namibia, Zambia, Zimbabwe, Malawi, and Katanga were not colonised at all, and Portuguese colonial power was feeble beyond the costal footholds. The last decades of the nineteenth century changed all this, with a "mineral revolution" supported by military power transforming the region. A major rise in world commerce with southern African ports took place, driven first by the diamond boom in the Cape and then by the gold rushes in the Transvaal, especially after the discovery of the great gold fields of the Witwatersrand/Johannesburg in 1886. The late 1870s and 1880s saw the conquest of Zululand, the Eastern Cape, and the Pedi Kingdom, and the 1890s, of the Rhodesias. In Angola and Mozambique, in the face of British and German colonial competition, the Portuguese finally crushed the African polities of the interior. The carving out of boundaries at the conference at Berlin from 1884 to 1885 included the allocation of South West Africa to Germany.

In the 1870s, the passenger shipping trade to the Cape was dominated by two companies, the Union Line and the Castle Line. Sir Donald Currie, the chairman of the Castle Line, set out to gain dominance in this field. He began by manoeuvring the Union Line to share the lucrative mail contract with the colony, and went on to

---

7 E. Kay Gibson, *Brutality on Trial: "Hellfire" Pedersen, "Fighting" Hansen and the Seaman's Act of 1915* (Gainesville: University of Florida Press, 2006).

establish a network of political patrons ranging from Gladstone to the Hohenzollerns, receive subsidies from the British government for building ships adaptable to wartime purposes, and act as a negotiator in important southern African political disputes. By 1900, he had unified the two companies into the Union Castle Line.[8] The merger took place at the height of the Boer War, when the British Empire was sustaining armies of several hundred thousand in southern Africa. Union Castle became the dominant shipping line on the United Kingdom's southern Africa route for the next three quarters of a century, and also took a large chunk of the region's trade under its wing. The key point here is that Union Castle's rise was not the outcome of simple economic competition, but of an eminently political process. British maritime economic power in the region was bound up with military and political interests. Union Castle's dominance was not the result of a simple globalising extension of the world market, but of its imbrication with British imperial power.

The shape of the Union Castle workforce was determined by key points of articulation with the ports of the Empire. Southampton was Union Castle's operational base. Developed as a specialist liner port, under the leadership of the Giles family in the mid-nineteenth century, the harbour's extensive facilities and fast rail links to London attracted a number of the world's key liner companies.[9] The large concentration of deck and engine room workers in Southampton and Portsmouth, as well as the ability to draw on the vast reserves of catering workers both there and in the London area, provided a solid foundation for a relatively stable workforce. Cape Town remained, throughout Union Castle's life, the major passenger port, with Durban taking a substantial share of its cargo.

Up until 1910, there was very little formal labour organisation in southern Africa's ports and on the shipping lines that served them. In the United Kingdom, seamen's unions had emerged in the 1890s under the leadership of Havelock Wilson's National Sailors' and Firemen's Union (NSFU). The union's impact was uneven, for seamen were a difficult group to organise. But it did scare employers. It also coincided with the increasing political leverage of the United Kingdom's working class. 1884 saw a broad extension of the franchise to "respectable" male workers; 1893, the formation of the Independent Labour Party of Keir Hardie; and 1906, a major electoral breakthrough in which a significant number of representatives of the Labour Representation Committee won seats at Westminster, forming the

---

8 Marischal Murray, *Union-Castle Chronicle 1853–1953* (London: Longman's, Green, 1953); Jonathan Hyslop, "Southampton to Durban on the Union Castle Line: An Imperial Shipping Company and the limits of globality c. 1900–1939," *Journal of Transport History* 38, 2 (2017): 171–195.
9 F.E. Wentworth-Shields, "The Port of Southampton," *The Scottish Geographical Magazine*, 42, 1 (1926): 1–11; Jean Cottier, "Le Port de Southampton," *Annales de Géographie* 45, 255 (1936): 240–256.

basis of the parliamentary Labour Party. Faced with a seafaring workforce that was becoming increasingly assertive and enjoying partial political citizenship, shipping employers looked for ways to contain them. For lines trading with the Indian Empire, a clear solution lay in a shift from British to lascar crews. Asian seamen, as rightless colonial subjects, could be hired at a fraction of the wages of British sailors, were subject to lower legal requirements in terms of onboard living conditions, and did not yet have labour unions.[10] Moreover, their hiring could be sub-contracted to Indian labour-brokers, or *Ghat Serangs*, who could police them and to whom workers were conventionally in debt bondage. Thus in the case of the Bullard King Company, which specialised in a direct run from Britain to Durban and in shipping indentured labour from India to Natal, crew lists show a clear shift in the last decades of the nineteenth century from British, Irish, and northern European crews to a pattern of British officers and Indian crews (including, at times, crews from many other nationalities as well).[11] A similar composition of Asian crews and British officers is observable in the ships of other lines that sailed the Indian Ocean route to southern Africa, such as the British India Steam Navigation Company and the Clan Line. Ideologically, there was a great deal of tension around this shift. It produced a backlash among white workers, who bought into the ideology of racial protection that gained traction in British maritime unionism. A propaganda war took place, in which captains and shipping companies stressed the sober and disciplined character of the lascars and presented British seamen as dissolute and unreliable.[12] At the same time, proponents of white labour, which included both trade unionists and some imperial ideologues, exalted the supposedly unique moral fibre of the British seaman.

Amid the relative absence of formal labour organisation, informal resistance to employers was frequent. Seafarers worked under conditions of great coercion but were able to resist on an individual or small-group basis through tactics of evasion and non-cooperation. Desertion played a crucial role. Moreover, whenever seamen were legally discharged, they would put the captain in the difficult position of having to round up the full crew. To take one example, on 8 January 1901, the Berlin-born captain Richard Kessler came to the Merchant Marine Office at Poplar, in the East End of London, to sign on a crew for a voyage on Bullard King's *SS Um-*

---

10 Gopalan Balachandaran, *Globalizing Labour? Indian Seafarers and World Shipping c.1870–1950* (Delhi and Oxford: Oxford University Press, 2012); Ravi Ahuja, "Mobility and Containment: The Voyages of South Asian Seamen, c.1900–1960," *International Review of Social History* 51, Supplement (2006): 111–141.

11 This can be seen in the crew lists for Natal Direct Line ships held in the Maritime History Archive, Memorial University of Newfoundland (hereafter MHA/MNU).

12 Captain W. H. Hood, *The Blight of Insubordination* (London: Spottiswoode, 1903).

bilo to Durban and India, and back to Durban.[13] The crew was unusually polyglot, perhaps because of the demand for labour generated by the Boer War. As originally intended, most of the able seamen and a couple of the firemen and trimmers recruited in London were let go at Calcutta. But Ali Hassan from Aden and Willa Swami from Madras received their discharge at Port Natal. Abdul Rahman from Calcutta and Mahomed Hassan deserted in Durban. Mauritian deckhand A.M. David deserted in the Cape Colony's East London. A Jamaican fireman, Stuart King, deserted in Colombo. Four Muslim stokers from Bombay were taken on at Port Elizabeth and discharged on the second visit to Durban. They appeared to have been in southern Africa for some time, and not to have been earning their living at sea immediately before signing on. Four firemen/trimmers from Singapore were taken on at Natal in May, of which one deserted in Colombo and the others took their discharges in Natal.[14]

Such informal resistance also involved clashes with the global authority of the British state. Under the legislation passed in 1894, seamen could be convicted and imprisoned for desertion, and this was enforced not only by magistrates in Britain but throughout the Empire. Seafarers were the only category of British workers for whom leaving their job was a criminal offence after 1875. In this respect, they were almost on the level of colonial subjects. In the British colonies of Natal and the Cape, settler colonial officials were strongly committed to racially exclusionary policies and sought with particular enthusiasm both to punish desertion and strongly limit the landing of Asian and African sailors as legal immigrants.[15] But they also tended to see white sailors as potentially poor whites, who would be socially disruptive and an economic burden. Thus, they made it very difficult for sailors to get ashore, and as a consequence the British ports of southern Africa tended to lack the sailortowns typical of harbour cities. In Durban, the chief immigration officer, Harry Smith, waged a particular campaign against the animal attendants on ships from Buenos Aires, Trieste, New Orleans, and other ports specialised in the export of livestock to southern Africa. He saw these workers as lumpen, ethnically or racially inferior, and difficult to move on because they did not have experience in normal maritime work.

---

13 MHA/MUN 98050 Umbilo Crew Agreements 1901.
14 MHA/MUN 98050 Agreement 1901.
15 Jonathan Hyslop, "Oceanic Mobility and Settler-Colonial Power: Policing the Global Maritime Labour Force in Durban Harbour c. 1890–1910," *Journal of Transport History* 36, 2 (2015): 248–267; Uma Dhupelia-Mesthrie, "Betwixt the Oceans: The Chief Immigration Officer of Cape Town, Clarence Wilfred Cousins (1905–1915)," *Journal of Southern African Studies* 42, 3 (2016): 463–481.

1910 to 1926: The Apogee of White Labour Militancy

Imperial connections tightened in the fifteen years after South African unification in 1910, and the dominance of Union Castle on the South African run intensified. Especially in the 1920s, a huge citrus fruit trade to the United Kingdom developed, carried by Union Castle ships to the extensive cold storage facilities of Southampton and then to the British rail networks. Union Castle during the 1920s also began successfully marketing southern Africa as a tourist destination for affluent British and European tourists, utilising an extensive regional network of luxury trains. Although German, Dutch, and American ships provided Union Castle with some competition, the company was able to use its dominant political position to impose agreements with the South African government to effectively constrain the share of the market accessible to these rivals.[16]

There were other global linkages as well. South Africa's long-running maritime connections with India survived the end of traffic in indentured labour at around the time of unification. A dense network of connections between the relatively prosperous, largely Gujarati Indian diasporic merchant community and the motherland, and the political interests of the semi-autonomous government of India, would ensure the continuation of a strong passenger and merchant service between South Africa and the Raj over the next decades. There was also a parallel connection between the small Portuguese colony of Goa in India and Lourenço Marques and Beira. Germany had gone to quite formidable lengths to become a maritime power in the region. Before 1914, the Woermann Line had built strong links along the western coast to German South West Africa and Cape Town to become a key player in retail trade, while on the east coast, the Deutsche Ost-Afrika Linie had created a highly reputed service through Lisbon and the Suez Canal to Lourenço Marques and Durban.[17] These companies even made an impressive attempt to regain a foothold after the loss of German African territories in 1919.

Between 1910 and 1926, white settler workers in southern Africa began to get a taste for political power. Although relatively few of them were seafarers, their racial politics created a more favourable dynamic for the European-based seamen's unions in the ports of the region, and an even more hostile one for the seamen who were colonial subjects. In South Africa, a significant British immigrant-led,

---

16 Geoff Berridge, *The Politics of the South African Run: European Shipping and Pretoria* (Oxford: Clarendon, 1987), 4–10.

17 Gert Uwe Detlefsen, *Die Deutschen Afrika-Linien* (Bad Segeberg: Verlag Gert Uwe Detlefsen, 2013).

but increasingly also Afrikaner, trade union movement fought the government in a series of apocalyptically violent strikes in 1913, 1914, and 1922. In Mozambiquan Lourenço Marques and (probably to a lesser extent) Angolan ports, Portuguese worker organisations influenced by syndicalist ideas flourished in the railway and harbour industries, and benefitted from the relatively liberal political regime at home, which had been inaugurated with the new republic in 1910.[18]

As we will see, these local developments would shape subsequent events in the maritime labour realm. But so did the political developments in the metropolitan centres and the contingencies of the First World War. Havelock Wilson's NSFU reached the apogee of its militancy in 1911, when it cooperated with transport workers in a number of northern European countries and on the United States East Coast to stage what was arguably the first transnational strike.[19] However, the NSFU went on to become increasingly dominated by Wilson's autocratic and irascible personality and was British-chauvinist and racist in its politics. A financial dispute led to a breakaway of NSFU members in Southampton and the Clydeside to form the British Seafarer's Union (BSU). The union did not expand far beyond these two centres, but it enjoyed exceptional leaders: Thomas Lewis in Southampton and Emmanuel Shinwell in Glasgow, who built strong organisational structures. The union, while not free of xenophobia, was much less driven by the issue of racial competition in the labour market and more internationalist than the NSFU.[20] Because Southampton was the home port for Union Castle (as for a number of other major liner companies), this had massive implications for southern Africa. The BSU energetically represented its members against Union Castle over issues of pay, conditions, and compensation. When war broke out in 1914, a large proportion of British ships were requisitioned for use as war transport, and Union Castle vessels began to be operated out of other ports, notably London.[21]

This could have been an opportunity for the company to break away from its reliance on the Southampton labour force. Lewis was, however, able to use his union's organisational strength to negotiate a contract with Union Castle for the company's ships to continue to be manned by Southampton and Portsmouth crews. This had long-term consequences, ensuring that Union Castle retained regionally

18 Jeanne Marie Penvenne, "Labor Struggles at the Port of Lourenço Marques, 1900–1933," *Review (Fernand Braudel Center)* 8, 2 (1984): 249–285.
19 Marcel van der Linden, "Transport Workers Strike, Worldwide", *St. James Encyclopedia of Labor History* (Detroit: St. James, 2003), 334–336.
20 Basil Mogridge, "Militancy and Inter-Union Rivalries in British Shipping, 1911–1929," *International Review of Social History* 6, 3 (1961): 375–412.
21 Edward Frederick Knight, *The Union-Castle and the War, 1914–1919* (London: Union-Castle Steamship Co., 1920).

based British crews, right up until the demise of its South Africa run in the 1970s. This workforce suffered devastating casualties in the wartime sinking of merchant ships but emerged initially strong from the ordeal. However, the British maritime union landscape became more complex in the aftermath of the war with the steep decline in global demand for shipping capacity.

In the supposedly Roaring Twenties, seafarers were actually struggling to find work, a situation that was obviously favourable for employers. Wilson used his now cosy relationships with employers to attack rival unions. The BSU defensively fused with a ship stewards' union to form the Amalgamated Marine Workers Union (AMWU). The rise of the militant Communist-led National Minority Movement (NMM), which had a seamen's wing, meant that there was a new level of militancy in the workforce, although Lewis and Shinwell were Labour Party-oriented. In 1925, Wilson's NSFU, under pressure from employers, accepted a pay cut. The AMWU, with support from the NMM, called an international strike.

Although it had limited effects in British ports, the strike had a massive impact on British ships abroad, especially in New Zealand, Australia, South Africa, and even Mozambique. The South African situation was particularly propitious, because in 1924, the white electorate had voted out the pro-Empire government of Jan Smuts and replaced it with a coalition of the Afrikaner Nationalists of the new prime minister, JBM Hertzog, and the largely British immigrant supported South African Labour Party (SALP), which took a strong white labour protectionist position. Hertzog was annoyed by the economic disruption caused by the strike, but he found himself under pressure to support it from both his SALP allies and some middle-class British loyalists who sympathised with the seamen. Although a large number of seafarers were interned in Cape Town, in Durban the strikers enjoyed a great deal of public support and local officials were reluctant to act against them. For about a month, normal trade was severely disrupted. Union Castle exacerbated the situation by threatening to recruit lascars in Bombay to replace the strikers, which inflamed the racial protectionist politics of the SALP, of settler colonial leaders in Natal, and of some British seamen. In the end, the strike crumbled.[22] In the wake of this defeat, legal manoeuvres by Wilson hobbled the AMWU, causing it to fall apart. The subsequent failure of the British General Strike of 1926 finally put an end to a decade and a half of exceptional British sailor militancy.

The involvement of southern Africa-based labour in sea-going work across the maritime industries remained relatively low, with few exceptions other than

---

22 Baruch Hirson and Lorraine Vivian, *The Seamen's Strike of 1925 in Britain, South Africa and Australasia* (London: Clio, 1992); Jonathan Hyslop, "A British Strike in an African Port: The Merchant Marine and Dominion Politics in Durban, 1925," *The Journal of Imperial and Commonwealth History* 43, 5 (2015): 882–902.

among the quite numerous coastal fishermen, especially amongst the Coloured communities in the Cape and the Indians in Natal. White South Africans seem to have been reluctant to work at sea, though there was a thin trickle as well as a government attempt to train merchant marine officers on the ship *General Botha*. During the First World War there seems to have been a brief surge in black South Africans going to sea to escape being forced into military service by local chiefs. A number of African workers, mainly recruited from the Eshowe region of Natal, were involved in a small whaling industry, operated out of Durban harbour by Norwegian entrepreneurs.[23] A few African labourers also worked on a service run by the South African railways which brought Jarrah wood from Australia for use as sleepers.

Were these African sailors cosmopolitan or anti-colonial insurgents, as some scholarship would suggest? It is a complex question. Given the lack of organisational structures, they were really more focused on strategies of evasion and trading, with a combination of parochial and open-minded attitudes. The fascinating autobiographical reminiscences of seaman George Magodini, a Qwabe from Mzimkhulu, who worked across the oceans in the early 1920s, suggests that African seamen do not fit easily into categories of resistance or co-option. Magodini had a lively curiosity about the places to which he travelled. He was intrigued both by traditional bead work and modern maritime technology. He appears to have accepted the paternalism of white officers at face value, but harboured extreme suspicions toward Somali, Adenese, and Chinese sailors.[24] Isolated in small clusters or as individuals, transnational southern African sailors tended to adopt picaresque survival strategies. The radicalism of seamen in southern African ports was more likely to come from visiting syndicalists or Garveyites. Created by the Jamaican activist, Marcus Mosiah Garvey, the Universal Negro Improvement Association became a mass black political movement in the United States in the immediate aftermath of the First World War. Its millenarian message of the return of the African diaspora to the mother continent in order to create an African political rebirth had immense appeal across the colonial world. The postwar period saw frequent reports of visiting West Indian and African-American Garveyite sailors speaking or

---

23 D.I. Børreson, "'Three Black Labourers Did the Job of Two Whites': African Labourers in Modern Norwegian Whaling", in *Navigating Colonial Orders*, edited by Kirsten Alsaker Kjerland and Bjørn Enge Bertelsen (New York and Oxford: Berghahn, 2015), 127–152.

24 James Stuart, "Testimony of George Magodini," James Stuart Archive, Killie Campbell Library, Durban; Jonathan Hyslop, "Zulu Seafarers in the Steamship Era: The World Voyage Narratives of Fulunge Mpofu and George Magodini, 1916–1924," in *Critical Perspectives on Colonialism: Writing the Empire from Below*, edited by Fiona Paisley and Kirsty Reid (London: Routledge, 2014), 123–140.

distributing propaganda in South African ports.[25] Garveyism influenced the Industrial and Commercial Workers Union, the first black working-class movement in the region, which spread across South Africa, Namibia, and the Rhodesias in the 1920s.

In the Portuguese colonies, the liberal republic of 1910 to 1926 enabled the development of a strong, syndicalist trade unionism among port and rail employees in Mozambiquan Lourenço Marques, and to a lesser extent in Angolan Lobito, which made considerable gains for skilled workers. This unionism was white dominated, but not exclusively white. By the end of this period, Durban had become the central port of the region linked to an interior rail network extending to Belgian Katanga. This network granted the white rail and mining workers a strategic position, which led to some considerable upsurges of white labour. But outside South Africa, this would be tamed by capital. With the coming of a Portuguese dictatorship in 1926, the labour movement of the Lusophone ports was crushed.

1926 to 1938: Stasis

The defeat of the British seamen's strike was a prelude to a more general weakening of the British labour movement, symbolised by the defeat of the General Strike in 1926. The coincidence of this event with the 1926 coup in Portugal, ushering in a near half-century of authoritarian rule and an intensification of repression in its Angola and Mozambique colonies, brought about a new conjuncture in the southern African maritime labour field.

The end of the First World War did see a shift in the global maritime industry from the construction of steamships to that of oil burners. These new ships had a completely different configuration of labour, with the firemen and trimmers in the stoke holds and bunkers replaced with a small group of engine room workers tending the oil-fired engines in a much cleaner environment. But Britain was slow to make this move, compared with the more enterprising Scandinavian shipping industries, and British construction of the new type of ships plunged downward in the Great Depression. The consequence was that, throughout the interwar period, it was the steamship, with its distinctive organisation of labour, that remained the basis of the British maritime industry. Although engine and hull-building technology was refined over time, the way work was carried out on steamships changed remarkably little over the lifetime of the technology. Changes in the experience of

---

25 Robert Trent Vinson, *"The Americans Are Coming": Dreams of African American Liberation in Segregationist South Africa* (Athens: Ohio University Press, 2012).

work were more related to organisational changes, such as adjustments to the watch (shift) system,[26] and very limited reforms in, for example, sleeping arrangements and food quality.

As Leon Fink has shown, the International Labour Organisation did, in the interwar years, start to make a real impact on state regulation of seamen's conditions of work at an international and nation state level.[27] In this sense, metropolitan seafarers' unions and their social democratic allies could be argued to have had an effect. Even in the colonial context, there was pressure on European states to ameliorate the position of colonial subject seamen in order to head off nationalist agitation. In the Indian case, a great deal of the literature has focused on the flagrantly racist 1925 Alien Seamen's Order, which tried to exclude seamen of colour from British ports. But in reality the implementation of the order was largely ineffective, and there were a number of initiatives from the British authorities in India during the 1930s that sought to close the differentials between lascar and British seamen in the interests of managing nationalist demands. On the other hand, the ILO was starting from a very low base in terms of the atrocious conditions of maritime work and implementing any reforms in the semi-autonomous social world of the ship was always going to be hard. On the more radical end of the political spectrum, the Comintern-led International of Seamen and Harbour Workers did have a small presence in South African ports, but its influence was more strongly felt among harbour workers than seamen. When the Comintern dispatched its emissary, Eugene Dennis, to the region, Dennis (a future head of the United States Communist Party) made extensive promises about organising maritime workers in South African ports, but ultimately failed to deliver on them.[28]

The coming of the Great Depression further tipped the scales against seamen's organising, as the collapse of world trade crushed the already limited demand for maritime labour. Union Castle nearly failed. Its chairman, Lord Kylsant, went to jail for fraud and the company was only saved because the City of London and the British government saw it as an essential strategic interest.[29] After the death of Wilson in 1929, the NSFU was reorganised from a personality-cult to something more like a conventional British trade union and renamed the National Union of Seamen

---

26 Ben Bright, *Shellback: Reminiscences of Ben Bright, Mariner.* Edited by Ewan MacColl and Peggy Seeger (Oxford: History Workshop, 1974), 21.
27 Leon Fink, *Sweatshops at Sea: Merchant Seamen in the World's First Globalized Industry* (Chapel Hill, NC: University of North Carolina Press, 2011).
28 Letter from E. Dennis to ECCI on 22 October 1932 in Apollon Davidson et. al., *South Africa and the Communist International: A Documentary History volume II* (London: Frank Cass, 2003), 38–39.
29 Edwin Green and Michael Moss, *A Business of National Importance: The Royal Mail Shipping Group, 1902–1937* (London: Methuen, 1982), 1–34.

(NUS). But unions had little leverage under the cost-cutting coalition government of Ramsay MacDonald and the subsequent Conservative administrations of Baldwin and Chamberlain. European dictatorial regimes also destroyed labour organisation and pushed workers into strategies of evasion. In Angola and Mozambique, the transmutation of the military government in Portugal into the quasi-fascist regime of the Estado Novo closed any space for worker organisation. Salazar's government established a labour regime of bogus, powerless trade unions (*sindicatos*). Effectively a police state, it shut down the possibility of real political expression by workers in the region until the collapse of the Lisbon regime in 1974.

With little possibility of formal organisation, and an extraordinarily harsh environment for employment, seamen in southern African ports were more likely to engage in informal strategies of resistance such as smuggling and petty trading, in collaboration with dock workers, than in political initiatives. Desertion did continue to be a strategy but was perhaps more difficult to achieve in southern Africa than elsewhere in the world, as both the South African and Portuguese authorities were vigilant against seamen's attempts to get ashore. An interesting paradox of the white states of southern Africa in the interwar years was their strongly exclusionary policies – not only concerning people of colour but also white immigrants, fearful of a deepening of the so-called poor white problem; indigent whites threatened to blur racial boundaries. However, some sailors did manage to reach the shore. An added incentive to do so was that, at least for white sailors, South Africa offered a more promising place to live than the dictatorial states of Europe from which many of them came. An underground German trade union bulletin mentioned Cape Town as one of the ports where "many German seafarers use the opportunity once and for all to shake off the blessings that National Socialism has brought to them."[30]

1938 to 1948: War and the End of Empire

The coming of the Second World War strengthened the position of British Empire maritime labour, both in general and in South African ports in particular. The British war effort was crucially reliant on shipping to keep the home island supplied with foodstuffs and military equipment. This meant that there was a politically driven move to maximise shipping capacity and to ensure an abundant supply

---

30 Zeitschriften der Internationalen Transportarbeiterföderation, Bibliothek der Friedrich Ebert Stiftung, *Die Schifffahrt*, 5–6, 1937, p. 6, https://library.fes.de/itf//schiffahrt-1937.htm downloaded 29 January 2023.

of maritime labour. Both lascar and white British seamen found that their labour-power was in demand and this strengthened their bargaining position. The British government was anxious to placate seamen's grievances in order to prevent disruption to maritime transport. The entry of the Labour Party into the wartime coalition government in the United Kingdom also meant that organised labour had a little more influence. South Africa was strategically essential to the British war machine between 1940 and 1943, when Italy's entry into the war virtually closed off the Mediterranean, forcing the British to use a round-the-Cape route to supply the armies in North Africa, the Far East, and India.[31] Despite the disruption of normal trade, the amount of shipping passing through Cape Town and Durban approximately doubled.

The rise of the nationalist movement in India in the interwar period had already led to an emergence by the late 1930s of substantial seamen's unions, notably the All-India Seamen's Union run by Aftab Ali from Calcutta, and the Bombay Seamen's Union, led by the Goan socialist O.C. Mendes. There had also been work organising Indian seamen in British ports by Surat Ali, a former sailor who had lived in London since 1919, and more recently by Tahsil Miya, a newly arrived seaman, both aligned with the British Communist Party. The India League of V. Krishna Menon, operating from London and ambiguously placed between Nehru's wing of the Indian Congress and the Communists, also played a role in supporting these organisers.[32]

The changing political situation produced a new assertiveness among Indian seamen, with Bombay Seamen's Union members participating in a fierce labour insurgency in their home port in 1938.[33] Almost immediately following the declaration of war by Britain in 1939, there was a worldwide wave of strikes by Indian seamen on British ships, beginning in South Africa. First to go on strike were the Muslim seamen from the Bullard King *SS Umvoti* in Durban.[34] They were followed by revolts in Cape Town on the Clan Line *SS Clan Alpine*, and later in the month on the same company's *SS Clan Buchanan*. The dispute spread quickly to British ports,

---

31 Archie Munro, *The Winston Specials: Troopships Via The Cape 1940–1945* (Liskeard: Maritime Books, 2006).
32 British Library, India Office Records (hereafter IOR) L/P and J /12/630/12 "V.K. Menon and the India League," 1939.
33 Dinkar Desai, *Maritime Labour in India* (Bombay: Servants of India Society, 1939); A. Colaco, *A History of the Seamen's Union, Bombay* (Bombay: Vaz, 1955). On Aftab Ali, see IOR L/P& J/12/630/153–4 "Copy of letter dated 17.4.44 sent by DIB," 1944.
34 Durban Municipal Archives, Magistrate's Court Record.

as well as to Australia and Burma.[35] Coming at the beginning of a war in which shipping would play an important part, this was a serious threat to British security. The London cabinet applied pressure on the shipping companies to settle the disputes, leading to significant concessions being made for the strikers. The British government was certainly anxious to avoid a repetition of this episode; the strike was followed by major reforms, in which the government forced employers effectively to double lascar wages and to improve conditions on lascar ships. The trade unionist and British Labour minister Ernest Bevin even discouraged the use of the by-now somewhat pejorative term "lascar." But Indian seafarers remained restive, and in 1942 there was a spectacular riot in Durban harbour by the lascar crew of *SS Jeypore*.[36]

The war situation led to a reassertion of British authority in South African shipping. A former director of the Glen Line, Charles Wurzburg, was installed by the British Ministry of War Transport (MWT) as a plenipotentiary authority over British ships in South African ports, with the acquiescence of the South African government. Reflecting the uneasy compromise between Conservatives and Labour in the British government, the MWT regime in South African harbours exercised its authority with a mixture of coercion and welfarism. NUS representatives were established in South Africa to work with the MWT, both bringing forward their members' grievances and helping to discipline them. Local committees of South African and British interested parties were established to help provide for the welfare and health needs of visiting sailors, victims of shipwreck or sinkings, and hospitalised mariners.[37] The churches and especially the Anglican Missions to Seamen played a great role in providing accommodation and recreation facilities.[38] This was accompanied by efforts on the part of the British government to project a vision of a postwar modern, cleaner, and safer Merchant Marine comprising oil-burner ships, in which technological change would bring an end to the grim labour of firemen and trimmers, with the new ships offering more spacious and hygienic accommodation and eating facilities for their crews. There was a very conscious – and, in the case of British crews, largely successful – attempt to manage their role in the war effort by incorporating them into the national consensus. After the invasion of the Soviet Union by Germany in 1941, Communist seamen also devoted

---

35 IOR LP& J /12/630/3 Inspector A.P. Newman, New India Dock to the Chief Police Officer, 30 October 1939.

36 http://www.historybuffs.co.za/mutiny-in-durban-harbourhttpwww-historybuffs-co-zawp-con tentuploads201207ss-jeypore1-300x119-jpg/, accessed 10 January 2023.

37 National Archives of South Africa, Pretoria (hereafter NASA) VWN 1037 SW 443/2, Minutes of Port of Durban Seamen's Welfare Committee.

38 Annual Reports of the Missions to Seamen, Mission to Seafarers Office, Durban.

their energy and resources to subordinating labour issues to the needs of the war effort. This had a considerable effect on British seamen, but probably less so among lascars, where the non-cooperation policies of the Indian National Congress were a more powerful influence.

The xenophobic and particularly anti-Indian South African immigration policies, which had previously impacted on lascar sailors, were strikingly relaxed for the duration of the war under pressure from the MWT. Large numbers of Indian seamen were allowed ashore for lengthy periods and accommodated in hostels or boarding houses. This development, however, created a powerful political dynamic in Durban. Many of the seamen were placed in commercial boarding houses run by Indian merchants. There was a great deal of corruption involved and investigations revealed appalling conditions in this sector. The scandal around this was grist to the mill of Natal's white anglophone anti-Indian politicians and may have been a factor in the imposition by the Smuts government of highly discriminatory measures to restrict Indian property ownership. This, in turn, engendered considerable radicalisation in the Indian community, with a generation of young Communists breaking the hold of the previously rather moderate community leadership around the country. This was crucial to the part that Indians were to play in the ANC-alliance in subsequent decades.[39]

Aftermath

The steam empire of the British merchant marine was torn apart by the war. A concatenation of major events completely changed the existing configuration of maritime labour in the years after the conflict. The pre-war steam merchant fleet had been decimated by wartime sinkings. As the ships went to the bottom, they were replaced by massive numbers of oil-burners, notably the Liberty Ships, constructed in American yards. The oil-burners eliminated the need for firemen and trimmers, making for much smaller crews, thus disrupting existing recruitment patterns. As part of the price for wartime Lend-Lease aid to Britain, the United States was given access to British Empire markets. American goods thus started to feature more prominently in the economies of the weakened Empire, increasing shipping connections across the South Atlantic to Africa.

Although the postwar Labour government did attempt to deliver on promises of better conditions for British mariners, they were operating in the context of the beginning of the fall of British maritime hegemony. The trend toward flags of con-

---

39 NASA VWN 1037 SW 443/2, Minutes of Port of Durban Seamen's Welfare Committee.

venience took off almost immediately after the war. Shipowners, confronted with increasing regulation of the shipping industry and its labour conditions in the advanced economies, sought to avoid the expensive changes to safety standards, accommodation, and pay levels this would entail. They instead began to register ships in countries such as Panama and Liberia, which placed almost no controls on how they operated. This development resulted in another major round of the elimination of British and European seamen, and their replacement with low-paid workers from the global periphery.

These changes interacted with the weakening of South Africa's long-running connections to Britain and India. With Indian independence in 1947, there was no longer a question of a distinct category of lascar labour within a British-owned merchant marine. New Delhi was at daggers drawn with the Smuts government over its treatment of Indians, and there would be no special maritime cooperation across the Indian Ocean. With the coming to power of a militant nationalist Afrikaner regime on a manifesto of apartheid in 1948, South Africa's ties to Britain, at least at a political level, began to weaken. South Africa pushed a not-particularly-successful attempt to develop an autonomous shipping line, *Safmarine*. Although Union Castle continued to ply the South African route – with English crews – until 1977, the advent of mass international air travel in the early 1960s rendered it a lost cause.

Conclusion

Although technological determinism is always a dangerous game, there is no doubt that the transition from sail to steam fundamentally transformed maritime labour. A different labour process laid the conditions for social and political changes in the workforce. The replacement of a relatively cohesive, highly skilled multi-national workforce with one that was fragmented by task and segmented and divided by race and ethnicity was dramatic. This new sea-going working class possessed strong elements of antagonism toward employers, but the difficulties of organising in an ultra-mobile world meant that resistance often appeared as evasion and illegal trade rather than head-on confrontation. The metropolitan workforce was in a more powerful political position than that of colonised workers, and yet they were also, to an important extent, less free than their fellow-workers at home. This racial disparity in power made for a racial and ethnic politicisation of trade unionism, which saw ordinary trade union conflicts become bound up with attempts by white workers to maintain a differential position in the employment hierarchy.

In southern Africa, this global labour world impacted in a complex way on the regional polity and economy. The steamship labour force was the crucial connection between the region and the world, and yet only a very minimal proportion of it actually came from there. Thus, the dynamics of the politics of home ports were crucial to those workers' struggles and protests. Yet, as the ships came into the ports, the sailors encountered a very specific local set of political dynamics. The racial exclusionism of South Africa heavily affected sailors of colour, and the authoritarianism and anti-unionism of both the South African and Portuguese states limited the scope of political activity for all sailors. But these local dynamics would play out in unforeseen ways. The existence of a strong white labour trade unionism in South Africa brought support to the 1925 British seamen's strike. The intra-imperial politics of World War Two led to the remarkable success of the 1939 Indian seamen's strike, which began in Durban, and to lascar seafarers gaining a foothold in Durban.

The racial politics of steam-era seafaring as it affected southern Africa in this period traced a complicated arc. With only a very small proportion of its own workforce employed at sea and a relatively tiny regional shipping fleet, the countries of the sub-continent were reliant on metropolitan, mainly British, shipping companies to connect them to the world. But the workers on these ships were racially fragmented. Some companies, like Union Castle, hired all-British or mostly-British crews. Initially the formula of a British-officered ship with colonial subject crews seemed enormously attractive to capitalists, who saw this as a safe and profitable alternative to increasingly less compliant British workers. But the project backfired as political conditions in the colonial world changed. By the end of the 1930s, Indian crews were becoming mobilised and organised in the context of the rise of Indian nationalism. In the end, there was no refuge for employers from the conflictual nature of steamship labour.

Daniel Tödt

11 Power after Work: The Un-free Time of Congolese Seafarers in the Belgian Empire (1910–1940)

Introduction

In 1923, the Congolese workers employed on the steamship *SS Anversville* received an unusual guest.[1] A suited white man with a moustache and goatee came below deck to investigate their workplace and sleeping quarters. The stokers and firemen told him all about the unequal pay conditions and the unpaid time on shore leave. The white man who took notes was Joseph Wauters, a renowned Belgian socialist and former minister for employment who had pushed through far-reaching social reforms for many Belgian workers. Yet, Wauters' concern was not to fight for better working conditions of Congolese seafarers. He simply did not want to wait until he arrived in Matadi to get on with his fieldwork on colonial labour. Later, his book *Le Congo au travail* would recount how impressed he was by the way the "natural-born traders" improved their salary by importing "buckets, knives, boxes, boots, hats, liquids, and above all [...] bikes."[2]

For Wauters, "Congolese labour" encompassed workers on the palm oil plantation in Leverville, the miners of Katanga, but also these seafarers in the ship's boiler room.[3] Indeed, the labour relations on the steamship could be understood

---

1 Earlier versions of this article were presented at conferences at the University of Gothenburg (organised by Christina Reimann and Martin Öhman), at the annual meeting of the African Studies Association in Germany (on a panel organised by Susann Baller), and at the final conference of the International Research Center "Work and Human Lifecycle in Global History" (re:work) at the Humboldt-Universität zu Berlin. I would like to thank the participants of these events, as well as the editors of this volume, for their advice and critical comments. I am also grateful for the kind support that I have received in my research from many colleagues and archivists.
2 Joseph Wauters, *Le Congo au travail* (Brussels: L'Églantine, 1924), 8–10. All translations in this essay from French and Dutch into English are my own.
3 For an overview on colonial labour in the Belgian Congo, see Julia Seibert, *In die globale Wirtschaft gezwungen. Arbeit und kolonialer Kapitalismus im Kongo (1885–1960)* (Frankfurt am Main: Campus, 2016). For mining, see Jean-Luc Vellut, "Les bassins miniers de l'ancien Congo belge: essai d'histoire économique et sociale (1900–1969)," *Les cahiers du CEDAF* 7 (1981): 1–70. For the Leverville plantation, see Benoît Henriet, *Colonial Impotence: Virtue and Violence in a Congolese Concession (1911–1940)* (Berlin: De Gruyter, 2021). For publications that touched upon Congolese seafarers, see Johan Lagae et al., "Koloniale Haven," in *Antwerpen Wereldhaven: over handel en scheepvaart,*

as an extension of the colonial working world. However, there are two major differences. First, these "sweatshops at sea"[4] were mobile workplaces with a travelling factory gate. Once the "floating factory"[5] had anchored, the clear demarcations and strict rules on board gave way to a social life that was much less easy to control. Port cities such as Antwerp, which would become hubs of world trade and imperial expansion,[6] brought together "workers, employers, and state officials with varieties of experiences and approaches to organizing work, space, and social relations."[7] Like other colonial seafarers, the Congolese crews were confronted with these sites of working struggles and enjoyed far greater – yet confined – spatial mobility than other workers on land.[8] Second, as global historians have recently foregrounded, instead of simply connecting two shores, the ship voyages created specific interactions with transformative potential.[9] By taking into account the spatiality of their floating workplace and the regular stays on shore, we will see that

---

edited by Els De Palmanaer et al. (Antwerp: Museum aan de Stroom, 2012), 101–125; Kivilu Sabakinu, "Histoire de la population et des conditions de vie à Matadi, 1890 à 1959, " Ph.D. thesis, Université Nationale du Zaire, 1981; Johan Lagae and Kivilu Sabakinu, "'Good Grief, is Antwerp City Centre Where the Jungle Begins Now?' Urban Traces and Congolese Memories of Exclusion in the Port Cities of Antwerp and Matadi (Congo), 1920–1960," Paper presented at the EAUH Conference, Rome, 29 August – 1 September 2018; Emile Lambert, *Le Marin Congolais* (Ecoles Sociales du Louvain, 1958); Laura Kottos, "L'anticolonialisme de gauche en Belgique durant l'entre-deux-guerres (1917–1939)," Master thesis, Université Libre Bruxelles, 2005; Frederik Larter, "Les marins congolais de la Compagnie maritime belge (1925–1960)," Master thesis, Universite Libre Bruxelles, 2007.

4 Leon Fink, *Sweatshops at Sea. Merchant Seamen in the World's First Globalized Industry, 1812 to the Present* (Chapel Hill: UNC Press, 2011).

5 Peter Linebaugh and Marcus Rediker, *The Many-Headed Hydra: Sailors, Slaves, Commoners, and the Hidden History of the Revolutionary Atlantic* (Boston: Beacon Press, 2013), 150.

6 For a critical discussion on the current historiography of port cities, see Lasse Heerten, "Mooring Mobilities, Fixing Flows. Port Cities and Globalization in the Age of Steam," *Journal of Historical Sociology* 34, 2 (2021): 350–374. On imperialism and port cities, see Lasse Heerten and Daniel Tödt, "Some Reflections on Imperial Port Cities in the Age of Steam," https://globalurbanhistory.com/2016/10/29/some-reflections-on-imperial-port-cities-in-the-age-of-steam/, accessed 14 March 2022.

7 Frederick Cooper, "Dockworkers and Labour History," in *Dock Workers. International Explorations in Comparative Labour History, 1790–1970*, edited by Sam Davies et al. (Burlington: Aldershot, 2000), 523–541.

8 For a focus on confined spaces of Indian seafarers, see Ravi Ahuja, "Capital at sea, Shaitan Below Decks? A Note on Global Narratives, Narrow Spaces, and the Limits of Experience," *History of the Present* 2, 1 (2012): 78–85; Gopalan Balachandran, "Indefinite Transits: Mobility and Confinement in the Age of Steam," *Journal of Global History* 11, 2 (2016): 187–208.

9 Martin Dusinberre and Roland Wenzlhuemer, "Editorial – Being in Transit: Ships and Global Incompatibilities," *Journal of Global History* 11, 2 (2016): 155–162.

the socialising effect of being Congolese workers on a Belgian steamship was able to make big waves.

Labour history from below deck mainly relies on a few written sources that were produced as a result of conflicts and tragedies.[10] While many travellers, or so-called explorers, and captains have documented their – often orientalist – impressions of their journey,[11] little is known about what actually went on below deck. By contrast, a vast quantity of ink was spilled by shipping companies and colonial officials documenting both their suspicions about the shore leave of colonial maritime workers and the companies' dependence upon colonial labour. Combining sea-based and land-based sources,[12] this essay sounds out the extent of possibilities and conditions for Congolese seafarers to determine their work and free time. Contrary to the intentions of the colonial authorities and management, who sought to control and stabilise the workforce by means of a complex and interlocked policy of segregation, the working and living conditions of Congolese seafarers entailed a close proximity that empowered them to stage a series of collective unrests in the interwar period. It will be argued that an explanation for their ability to protest against the strict regulation on shore can be found in the labour processes on board.

A brief introduction to the history of the imperial transport infrastructure of the Congo Free State and Belgian Congo is followed by a discussion on the place of Congolese workers within the complex and compartmentalised labour division on board. The racialised spaces of work on the ship that gave form to colonial power relations assured not only segregation from the white crew, but also regular interaction and a stable structure of cooperation among Congolese colleagues. The next section argues that the labour market and the recruitment patterns in Matadi aimed at stabilising the pool of Congolese seamen while also limiting their mobility. I will analyse how company managers and missionaries, colonial officials and captains, communists and anti-communists all tried to win over the Congolese in interwar Antwerp. The power that shipping companies and the state wielded over colonial labour after work arose out of a home built for seafarers, where the "frontier of control"[13] was constantly extended beyond the end of a hard-working day.

---

10 See Alston Kennerley, "Stoking the Boilers: Firemen and Trimmer in British Merchant Ships, 1850–1950," *International Journal of Maritime History* 20, 1 (2008): 219.

11 Michael Pesek, "Deutsche Passagiere auf der Dampferpassage in die Kolonie Deutsch-Ostafrika," *Werkstatt Geschichte* 53 (2009): 68–88.

12 For this approach, see Martin Dusinberre, "Writing the On-board: Meiji Japan in Transit and Transition," *Journal of Global History* 11, 2 (2016): 293.

13 Carter L. Goodrich, *The Frontier of Control. A Study in British Workshop Politics* (London: Harcourt, Brace and Howe, 1920).

By blurring the distinction between work and free time, the home echoed similar management policies in colonial Africa, where authorities and employers saw workers' leisure first and foremost as an "instrument of social control."[14] Yet, the "heteronomous management"[15] of a colonial workforce, whose unwanted presence in the metropole had to be temporally accepted in order to keep the Belgian imperial transport infrastructure as cheap as possible, turned into a struggle over the boundaries of labour and leisure, as well as over the shaky balance between public order and profits. It will be argued that the racialised management of Congolese seafarers gave birth not only to the twin approaches of segregation and stabilisation – but also to an unwanted child, solidarisation.

The Making of a Belgian Shipping Line to the Congo (1884–1910)

When Léopold II was granted ownership over the Congo Free State during the Berlin Conference 1884/1885, this vast territory was intended to be accessible for international and foreign investors and companies. Despite the proclamation of free trade, the king preferred merchants and capitalists from Belgium to open up and exploit the Congo. There was a scramble not only for the Congo itself, but also for physical access to its resources. Almost entirely land-locked, the Free State's only direct access to the sea consisted of a short strip along the Atlantic coast at the mouth of the Congo river. As the Congo proved difficult to navigate, the inland port of Matadi was conceived as a transloading point, for transferring shipments from sea vessels to rail. The railway line connecting the docks of Matadi with the later capital city of Léopoldville was built by a subsidiary company of the Compagnie du Congo pour le Commerce et l'Industrie (CCCI, later Banque d'Outremer), which was founded in 1886 by Albert Thys, a Belgian businessman and early supporter of the king's imperial ambitions. The CCCI was fuelled by mostly Belgian capital and sought to finance Belgian colonial expansion while reducing British economic influence in the Congo.[16]

---

14 Emmanuel Akyeampong and Charles Ambler, "Leisure in African History: An Introduction," *The International Journal of African Historical Studies* 35, 1 (2002): 9.

15 Marcel van der Linden, "Work Incentives and Forms of Supervision," in *Handbook Global History of Work*, edited by Karin Hofmeester and Marcel van der Linden (Berlin: De Gruyter Oldenbourg, 2018), 439–489.

16 Guy Vanthemsche, *La Belgique et le Congo* (Brussels: Éditions Complexe, 2007), 195; Jean-Luc Vellut, "Réseaux Transnationaux dans l'économie politique du Congo Léopoldien, c. 1885–1910," in *Af-*

Building up a Belgian-owned imperial shipping company to establish a regular maritime connection between Belgium and the Congo, however, proved more difficult.[17] In the first years, the Free State was serviced by the British and German lines that dominated world shipping. Still pursuing his dream of a shipping company under the Belgian flag, Léopold II applauded the creation of the Compagnie Belge Maritime du Congo (CBMC) and the Société Maritime du Congo (SMC) in 1895. Yet, these rival companies with a seat in Antwerp depended on foreign capital, foreign ships, and foreign labour forces. The CBMC was part of the Elder Dempster Group from Liverpool, whose owner, Alfred Lewis Jones, had befriended Léopold II and become a consul for the Free State in 1891. The SMC was a subsidiary of the Woermann line in Hamburg. These direct lines enjoyed a profitable quasi-monopoly on the shipping of goods, mail, and passengers between the Free State and Belgium. Until 1900, colonial trade boomed and Antwerp was the world's largest market for ivory and rubber.[18]

While colonial trade meant prosperity in Antwerp, it meant atrocities in the Free State. The first reports of abuses and deaths of African labourers concerned construction workers who had been forcefully recruited to build the railway line connecting Matadi and Léopoldville. Later, Edmond Morel, a British clerk from Elder Dempster employed on the docks of Antwerp, took it upon himself to investigate why steamships would arrive fully loaded with rubber and return to the Congo with firearms and chains. Together with another former Elder Dempster clerk employed in the Free state, Roger Casement, these two whistleblowers created the Congo Reform Association, which would go on to unveil the bloody rubber system. A highly mediatised international campaign resulted in the take-over of Léopold's private colony by Belgium in 1908.

The Belgian state inherited the shipping agreements between the CBMC and the Free State. Yet, after the death of Alfred Jones, the Elder Dempster group loosened its grip on the company. In 1910, Albert Thys successfully renegotiated to give the Banque d'Outremer a 60 percent share in CBMC holdings, allocating 20 percent

---

rican Networks, Exchange and Spatial Dynamics, edited by Laurence Marfaing and Brigitte Reinwald (Berlin: LIT, 2001), 134.

17 On imperialism and global shipping, see Frances Steel, "Shipping – Imperial," in *The Encyclopedia of Empire*, edited by John Mackenzie (New Jersey: Wiley, 2016), 1–12.

18 Greta Devos and Guy Elewaut, *CMB 100, a Century of Commitment to Shipping* (Tielt: Lanoo, 1995), 19–35; Zana Etambala, "Antwerp and the Colony, from 1885 until ca. 1920," in *De panoramische droom; Antwerpen en de wereldtentoonstellingen 1885/1894/1930*, edited by Jan-Lodewijk Grootaers and Mandy Nauwelaerts (Antwerp: "Antwerpen 1993," 1993), 185–192; Lagae et al., "Koloniale Haven"; Daniel Tödt, "Making Second Imperial Cities: Modern Ports, Colonial Connectivity and Maritime Globalization," *Moderne Stadtgeschichte*, 2 (2019): 115–139.

to the British and Germans respectively. From now on, the capital and managing directors of the CBMC would be intertwined with numerous Belgian companies operating in the Congo under the financial umbrella of the Banque d'Outremer. The imperial transport infrastructure became ever more Belgian: more ships were built there, coal came from the mines of Wallonia, and cargo from the Congo was handled by local agents in Antwerp. Furthermore, the Belgian state was granted a greater say in the imperial shipping company. Contracts with the colonial ministry gave maritime transport between the Congo and Belgium a quasi-monopoly. When in 1930 the company bought out its rival, Lloyd Royal Belge, the Compagnie Maritime Belge (CMB) became the biggest Belgian shipping line handling most Congo exports by calling at numerous ports along the shores of southern and eastern Africa, where the railway lines from the colony terminated. The CMB guaranteed both the state and colonial enterprises regular speedy connections and reduced freight rates at a time of economic crisis. In return, the company could count on state subsidies. Yet, the external influence of colonial politics and the dependency on Congo exports would shape the company's room for manoeuvre. [19]

Decisive in this regard is that the making of a Belgian shipping line was accompanied by a reconfiguration of the maritime workforce manning the steamships, and these two events occurred synchronically on a global and imperial scale.

Colonial Labour on Board: Segregating Belgian and Congolese crews

The gradual transition from sail to steam in the shipping industry entailed a transformation of the nature of on-board work.[20] The materiality of the steamship produced a multi-layered compartmentalisation of work and labour processes. While sailing vessels relied on cooperative work, steamships included many discrete tasks that were not specific to maritime labour. A passenger liner was a hotel and a restaurant relying on waiters, cleaners, and cooks. It was a factory where industrial labour was performed in the engine rooms. Thus, a steamship did not have a single, unified crew, but a number of different working crews.

When, around 1910, steam-driven shipping finally replaced the sail, not only was there a need for more coal to fulfil the speed and predictable schedules of

---

19 Devos and Elewaut, *CMB 100:* 78; Vanthemsche, *La Belgique et le Congo:* 236–237.
20 Jonathan Hyslop, "Steamship Empire: Asian, African, and British Sailors in the Merchant Marine c. 1880–1945," *Journal of Asian and African Studies* 44, 1 (2009): 49–76.

the passenger and cargo lines, but also for more low-skilled workers.[21] Since the late nineteenth century, the labour division was further accentuated by the "racializing of work and the racializing of skill" that embodied colonial power relations.[22] Maritime workers from Asia or Africa became more numerous on steamships as they were considered more suitable for the subaltern cabin, cleaning, or cooking duties, as well as for the low-skilled but dangerous jobs as trimmers and firemen. Until 1914, every fourth worker on a British-owned or flagged steamship came from colonial India. However, companies under the Belgian flag relied on low-skilled trimmers and firemen from Belgium and Ireland. Highly qualified positions such as the masters and engineers were still held by British, Scandinavian, and German staff.[23] The first Belgian captain took office not until in 1908.

Against this backdrop, the configuration of the CMB workforce in 1910 was unique. As national flagships, the state obliged the company to recruit Belgians for two-thirds of the total working crew and half of the officer positions. Belgian graduates from newly established maritime schools and experienced seafarers were favoured and took high ranking positions in the hierarchy on board. The lower positions were giving to another newly established workforce that was supposed to make up the remaining third of the crew: Congolese seafarers.[24] They were a replacement for the Kru from Sierra Leone, who had performed low-skilled jobs on the steamers of the Anvers-Matadi connections previously, and belonged to a group that had already manned British ships during the slave trade and after abolition.[25] Recruiting Irish and Belgians for the stokehole and serving tasks was out of question for the colonial ministry. The labour division and hierarchy in the maritime workforce clearly aimed to reproduce the social order of the Belgian Congo.

---

21 John Darwin, *Unlocking the World: Port Cities and Globalization in the Age of Steam, 1830–1930* (London: Allen Lane: 2020), 144–145.

22 Laura Tabili, "A Maritime Race: Masculinity and the Racial Division of Labor in British Merchant Ships, 1900–1939," in *Iron Men, Wooden Women: Gender and Seafaring in the Atlantic World, 1700–1920*, edited by Margaret S. Creighton and Lisa Norling (Baltimore: The Johns Hopkins University Press: 1996), 173.

23 Kristof Loockx, "Migration Trajectories of Seafarers During the Transition from Sail to Steam: Change and Continuity in Antwerp, 1850–1900," *The International Journal of Maritime History* 32, 3 (2020): 628–629.

24 Devos and Elewaut, *CMB 100:* 78; Vanthemsche, *La Belgique et le Congo:* 236–237.

25 Jeffrey Gunn, *Outsourcing African Labour in the Nineteenth Century. Kru Migratory Workers in Global Ports, Estates and Battlefields* (Berlin: De Gruyter, 2021); Diane Frost, *Work and Community among West African Migrant Workers since the Nineteenth Century* (Liverpool: Liverpool University Press, 1999).

Yet, at the very moment that the CMB working crews were about to be restructured, the global labour market for colonial seafarers came under fire. Seafarers' unions in Great Britain, in particular, were agitating against the wage dumping of mainly Indian "lascars."[26] In June 1911, the recently created Belgian seafarers' union – whose members had many British colleagues – stood in solidarity with the militant strikes of the National Amalgamated Sailors' and Firemen's Union at British ports. Echoing calls against colonial seafarers, which in Cardiff turned into open violence,[27] Belgian unionists pressed the CMB to privilege white crews instead of Congolese. The company argued that Africans were more "heat resistant" and "naturally" suitable for working along the Equator.[28] The Belgian shipping company quickly learned the language of racist justification for recruiting colonial workers that had been long practised by their British, German, and French counterparts. Most importantly, the Congolese were attractive because of their significantly lower wages. Compared with the unionised Belgian maritime workers, they were considered to be more "docile," obviously a euphemism for the structural "difference in access to political participation."[29]

How can we imagine the workforce on a Belgian vessel? For instance, a voyage of the passenger ship *SS Elisabethville* counted 216 workers in the late 1920s.[30] Among them were 111 Belgians (including the captain, officers, mechanics, and barkeepers) and another 14 white Europeans (eight Scandinavians, two Italians, and one Chilian, French, Greek, and English each). The remaining ninety-one crew members were Congolese. Divided across three departments, only nine of the colonial workers were employed as deckhands to maintain and clean the upper deck. A majority of 51 belonged to the machine department, mainly stokers and firemen in the coal bunkers and boiler rooms below deck. They worked under conditions resembling an "industrial hell."[31] They were joined by six greasers and a boy for their cabin. The remaining 31 workers constituted the cabin department, who serviced the passengers and cleaned their facilities, and the captain had one personal boy for his cabin and another worked in the kitchen. The Congolese all acted under

---

26 Ravi Ahuja, "Mobility and Containment: The Voyages of South Asian Seamen, c. 1900–1960," *International Review of Social History* 51, Supplement (2006): 111–141; Gopalan Balachandran, *Globalizing Labour? Indian Seafarers and World Shipping, c.1870–1945* (Oxford and New York: Oxford University Press, 2012).

27 Baruch Hirson and Lorraine Vivian, *Strike Across the Empire. The Seamen's Strike of 1925: in Britain, South Africa and Australasia* (London: Clio, 1992).

28 Lambert, *Marin Congolais*, 14.

29 Hyslop, "Steamship Empire": 59.

30 Shipping crew of *SS Elisabethville*, Voyage 42, 18 December 1929, State Archives in Antwerp-Beveren, R452, Fonds PK Antwerpen 2001 C, 333.

31 Hyslop, "Steamship Empire": 56.

the orders of Belgian superiors. They were additionally supervised by a Congolese foreman, the so-called capita, who also exerted some influence on recruitment. Yet, that the capita of a cargo vessel was fired when it came to light that he was squeezing money out of his crew[32] points to the fact that these foremen did not take as much advantage of their position as the *serang*, the foremen of the lascars on British steamships.[33] As we will see later, what was uniformly referred to as the "Congolese" crew consisted of men intentionally recruited from numerous linguistic and regional backgrounds. By systematically appointing the capita, based on many years of loyal service, from a group different to those he supervised, the CMB aimed to undermine the sense of solidarity and identity that should have been associated with the notion of "Congolese seamen."

Nevertheless, the racial segregation of the Congolese from the Belgian workers on board laid the groundwork for their identification with a common fate. Notwithstanding their employment in different departments and the mixed teams, the Congolese workers were literally in the same boat. With the exception of the capita, there was little in the way of professional hierarchies among them that would have institutionalised division on the job, and they shared the fate of subordinated rank. Trustful cooperation was essential for the life-threatening tasks in the machine rooms. Furthermore, racial segregation was built into the steamship, creating spatial proximity among the Congolese workers during the weeks-long journeys. Their space for recreation was far apart from the Europeans, it was less spacious and more poorly equipped, their cabins had minimal sleeping space, and the food was of lower quality. But unlike the separation of the white workers' sleeping facilities along the respective departments,[34] the Congolese crew shared a common space. Thus, the highly racialised "spatial configuration"[35] on board assured not only segregation from the white crew but also constant interaction and a stable structure of cooperation among Congolese colleagues.

In the following, we will see how not only the working life on board but also the recruitment, control, and stabilisation of Congolese seamen on shore constituted part of the shipping companies' and colonial officials' policy for segregating the colonial workforce. Yet, this segregation-oriented management created another

---

32 Letter from Captain of *SS Katanga* to Cruyen, 3 November 1929, KADOC, BE/942855/1262/7110/5.
33 Gopalan Balachandran, *Globalizing Labour?*, chapter two; Ravi Ahuja, "Die 'Lenksamkeit' des 'Lascars'. Regulierungsszenarien eines transterritorialen Arbeitsmarktes in der ersten Hälfte des 20. Jahrhunderts," *Geschichte und Gesellschaft* 31, 3 (2005): 338–340.
34 On the spatial separation of different working crews on steamships, see Kennerley, "Stoking the Boilers".
35 Dusinberre, "Writing the On-board": 293.

layer of spatial proximity, which further strengthened a structure of cooperation to – albeit unintentionally – serve as a breeding ground for self-organisation.

Narrowing Spaces: The Labour Pool in Matadi and Shore Leave in Antwerp

When, in 1910, the CMB agreed to recruit every third crew member in the Belgian Congo, a maritime labour market for seamen in Matadi quickly began to take shape that could be best characterised by amounting insularity. The first Congolese seamen were either recruited from Banana, a small town at the Congo estuary on the Atlantic coast where workers embarked to perform the tasks of cargo handling in Matadi,[36] or from further inland. In urgent need of an experienced workforce in the machine department, the CMB recruited men from the Upper Congo provinces who had served on smaller steamships navigating on the Congo river.[37] Matadi's population was roughly 5,000 in the mid-1910s and rose to more than 11,448 in 1938,[38] when a total of 542 Congolese workers were officially registered by the CMB. Their numbers had peaked in 1929, with around 900 regularly employed seamen and declined throughout the global depression to 300.[39] Official numbers from the mid-1930s show that 40 percent of the seafarers came from Matadi's surrounding areas, slowly approaching the numbers of those recruited further inland. The percentage of those from up the Congo river was much higher in the group of seafarers than among the total working population of Matadi[40] – which can be explained by the intentional mixing of crews on board.

Most of the seafarers ended up settling in Matadi with their families. The regularity of the timetable made the stays of seafarers – especially those on passenger ships – more predictable. Shore leave between journeys was at least 10 days. But it was also the stabilisation policy of the colonial state and the shipping company that socially anchored them in their home port. On shore leave in Matadi, the seafarers remained neighbours, dwelling in designated districts within the African part of

---

36 Wauters, *Le Congo au travail*, 52, 217; Lambert, *Marin Congolais,* 37.

37 Lambert, *Marin Congolais,* 14; William J. Samarin, *The Black Man's Burden. African Colonial Labour on the Congo and Ubangi Rivers 1880–1900* (London: Routledge, 1990); Sabakinu, "Histoire de la population": 253.

38 Sabakinu, "Histoire de la population": 96–97.

39 Statistics of 1937, Archives CMB, 27/III/100; Interview with Cruyen in *La Tribune Congolaise*, 15 July 1935, cited in Larter, "Les marins congolais": 37.

40 Sabakinu, "Histoire de la population": 219.

town.[41] Similarly to other colonies in Africa, in the 1920s former migrant workers employed in factories, mines, or fields of the Belgian Congo were encouraged by the companies to settle with their families. Especially in the industrialised mining regions of Katanga in southern Congo, camps run with the help of missions provided housing, education, leisure, and health in order to stabilise and control the social reproduction of the colonial workers. As Julia Seibert has shown for the mining compounds of Elisabethville, the spatial proximity in the living conditions coupled with stable crews on the job enabled workers to overcome their different origins and occasionally organise themselves for their causes.[42] The situation of the seafarers, who shared narrow social spaces both on board and on shore, was comparable.

Furthermore, the working conditions fostered an insularity of the maritime labour market. Their recruitment, conducted by a CMB-affiliated company, obliged the seafarers to enter into a tacit agreement for a roundtrip to Belgium that would always start and end in Matadi – pay-day was not until their arrival home.[43] In this respect, the limited mobility resembled the early lascar agreements of British shipping companies, which restricted the discharge of Indian seamen to the subcontinent although longer stays in Britain were not unusual.[44] The CMB favoured a stable and experienced crew for their vessels that would complement each other. Nevertheless, it enjoyed a strong bargaining position thanks to strong discretionary powers.[45] In the absence of a contract, the Congolese had to comply with the unwritten rule of regularly embarking on their usual vessel. Missing onward journeys, changing vessel, or repeatedly refusing to enrol came with the risk that they would not be hired anymore. Only those who accepted the lot of becoming "permanent casual workers" could hope for privileges such as being granted unpaid leave. Congolese workers themselves seemed to have been keen to avoid the types of conflicts that could easily have occurred. For being dismissed by the

---

41 On Matadi, see Johan Lagae, Kivilu Sabakinu, and Luc Beekmans, "'Pour Matadi la question [de la ségrégation] est encore plus grave qu'ailleurs.' The Making and Shaping of a Congolese Harbour City During the Interwar Years," unpublished paper, 2015.

42 Julia Seibert, "'Kazi' – Konzepte, Praktiken und Semantiken von Lohnarbeit im kolonialen Kongo," in *Semantiken von Arbeit: Diachrone und vergleichende Perspektiven*, edited by Jörn Leonhard and Willibald Steinmetz (Böhlau: Köln, 2016), 209–224.

43 "Loi portant réglementation du contrat d'engagement maritime, 5 June 1928," *Moniteur Belge* 98 (1928).

44 Balachandran, *Globalizing Labour?*, 28–29.

45 See "Letter Territorial Administrator in Matadi to Cruyen," 3 June 1931, KADOC, BE/942855/1262/ 7105.

ship's captain or minor infractions such as disobeying orders meant being added to the list of "undesirable seamen."[46]

Being formally free to quit after a round journey had little meaning in practise. Earning not even half the salary of Belgium seafarers for the same task still meant belonging to the better-off Congolese in Matadi. The low-skilled jobs performed on the steamship only qualified them for employment that would be paid much less in other parts of the Belgian Congo. Most importantly, the petty trade that the seafarers could conduct along their journeys promised additional income. It afforded them a privileged position in Matadi for trade in imported items that the workers – as we will see – were determined to defend.

Desertion in Belgium was not an exit-option either. After the First World War, only a few Congolese seamen jumped ship in Antwerp, although until 1922 they were not considered deserters because they were not employed under the labour regime of the Belgian merchant marine but only for a single voyage.[47] Dismissing migration from the Congo, the authorities pressured the CMB to regulate their labour regime to make recruitment for a round journey an obligation. In the face of the infraction of desertion, very few deserted. For instance, even between June 1930 and March 1935, when unemployment was high, no more than 44 took their chances.[48] Given the small number of Congolese in Belgium, they could not blend in and were repatriated in most cases. It might seem contradictory at first sight that the Belgian government in the early 1930s decided that any deserters who succeeded in remaining unnoticed in Belgium for more than three months should stay.[49] Yet, the biggest fear for the authorities was that these Congolese could have been meanwhile infiltrated with subversive ideas; sending them back to the Congo would jeopardise the colonial order.

Although maritime workforces in sailor towns throughout the imperial world were seen as subversive,[50] the unwanted but necessary stay of Congolese seamen in Antwerp created particularly severe anxieties for numerous Belgian actors. With

---

46 "List of undesirable seamen," 13 March 1935, Archives CMB, 27/III/99.

47 "Letter from Commissaire en Chef de Police Liège an Administrateur Directeur Général de la Sûreté Publique de Bruxelles," 1 February 1921, Archives générales du Royaume, Ministry of Justice, Police des étrangers, 774.

48 For statistics, see "list of undesirable seamen, 13 March 1935," Archives CMB, 27/III/99; CMB list of deserters November 1932, KADOC, BE/942855/1262/7105.

49 Correspondence between Colonial Ministry and Ministry of Justice, 1 September 1933, Archives générales du Royaume, Ministry of Justice, Police des étrangers: 774.

50 Harald Fischer-Tiné, "Flotsam and Jetsam of the Empire?: European Seamen and Spaces of Disease and Disorder in Mid-nineteenth Century Calcutta," in *The Limits of British Colonial Control in South Asia. Spaces of disorder in the Indian Ocean region*, edited by Ashwini Tambe and Harald Fischer-Tiné (New York: Routledge, 2009), 121–154.

the exception of some priests and servants, seafarers were the only Congolese to regularly set foot in Belgium.[51] Having the precarious privilege to commute between colony and metropole, they were considered prone to indoctrination with anticolonial or communist ideas. Therefore, the Belgian authorities did all they could to limit their radius of action. In Matadi, for instance, only impeccable candidates were granted a travel permit, a document colonial subjects in the Belgian Congo had to carry when leaving their home region. Local police in the interior considered seafarers who only wanted to visit their extended family as "undesirable transients" and prevented them from going ashore along the Congo river.[52]

Against this backdrop, the recruitment patterns and the stabilisation of the labour pool in Matadi became a means of reducing the mobility of Congolese seafarers within the colony and therefore lessening the danger of infiltration. Yet, the aim of maintaining a "cordon sanitaire"[53] to shield the Belgian colony from metropolitan or international influence was in conflict with the temporal presence of Congolese seafarers in Antwerp.[54]

Congolese Only: A Seafarers' Home in Antwerp and Communist Overtures

In the mid-1920s, the recently founded Belgian Communist Party started to target Congolese seamen as a potential vehicle for propagating their ideology in the colony.[55] Notwithstanding the fact that the Belgian Communist Party remained rather marginalised compared with communist parties in other parts of interwar Europe,

---

51 Even in the mid-1950s, no more than approximately 300 to 400 Congolese lived in Belgium. For an overview of the Congolese migration to Belgium, see Zana Etambala, *In het land van de Banoko: de geschiedenis van de Kongolese/Zaïrese aanwezigheid in België van 1885 tot heden* (Leuven: Hoger instituut, 1993); Anne Cornet, "Migrations subsahariennes en Belgique. Une approche historique et historiographique," in *Migrations subsahariennes et condition noire en Belgique*, edited by Jacinthe Mazzochetti (Paris: Harmattan, 2014), 39–64.
52 Nancy Rose Hunt, *A Nervous State: Violence, Remedies, and Reverie in Colonial Congo* (Durham, NC: Duke University Press, 2016), 109.
53 Jean-Luc Vellut, "Episodes anticommunistes dans l'ordre colonial belge (1924–1932)," in *La peur du rouge*, edited by Pascal Dewit and José Gotovitch (Brussels: Université de Bruxelles, 1996), 186.
54 On the "imperial immobility" that characterised Belgian colonial rule, see Matthew G. Stanard, "Belgium, the Congo, and Imperial Immobility: A Singular Empire and the Historiography of the Single Analytical Field," *French Colonial History* 15 (2014): 87–109.
55 Holger Weiss, *Framing a Radical African Atlantic. African American Agency, West African Intellectuals and the International Trade Union Committee of Negro Workers* (Leiden and Boston: Brill, 2014), 486–488.

it represented the only radical opposition to colonialism in Belgium. Their adherence to the anticolonial agenda that had been propagated by the Comintern fuelled the "red scare" that soon reigned over the country.[56]

When, in September 1925, *Le Drapeau Rouge*, under the editorship of party leader Joseph Jacquemotte, launched the Kimbanguist campaign, instrumentalising ongoing revolts in the western region of the Congo,[57] local authorities in Matadi found several copies of the newspaper in the hands of Congolese seafarers on the *SS Anversville*.[58] That, generally speaking, the large majority of those who would be dismissed as communists happened to be cabin boys[59] can be explained by the nature of their job: their direct and unobserved contact with passengers placed them within easy reach of the propagandists. In any case, this single incidence left newspapers in Léopoldville demanding "strict surveillance of the African seaman,"[60] while the conservative Catholic newspaper *La Metropole* in Antwerp began advertising the idea of a permanent seafarers' home for Congolese during their time in the metropole. The article featured Alphonse Cruyen, a Catholic missionary of the Scheut order who returned to Belgium in 1919 after over a decade in the colony.[61] On his daily visits to the CMB steamships, he offered religious services and an evening school for the mostly illiterate Congolese workers, paternalistically depicting himself as providing guidance for the "children" in need of "a comprehensible and firm surveillance on board."[62] In February 1927, *La Metropole* called once again for the creation of a seafarers' home – with greater success. The anti-communist newspaper put Cruyen's project on the front page, alongside coverage of the "congress against colonial oppression and imperialism" that was taking place in Brussels at the same time and constituted the inaugural meeting of the League against Imperialism (LAI).[63] The international congress was keenly followed by the Société d'Études Politiques, Economiques et Sociales

---

56 Ibid.; Benoit Verhaegen, "Communisme et anticommunisme au Congo (1920–1960)," *Brood en Rozen* 4 (1999): 113–127.

57 "Aide efficace aux prolétaires coloniaux," *Le Drapeau Rouge*, 5–6 July 1925: 1, cited in Kottos, "L'anticolonialisme de gauche en Belgique": 50.

58 See Sabakinu, "Histoire de la population": 499; Vellut, "Episodes anticommunistes dans l'ordre colonial belge": 185.

59 For the period 1930 to 1935, nine out of 12 who fired on grounds of "communist tendencies" were cabin boys. See "list of undesirable seamen, 13 March 1935," Archives CMB, 27/III/99.

60 A. Brenez, "Les communistes et les noirs. Une dangereuse campagne," *L'Avenir colonial Belge*, 2 July 1925: 1, cited in Kottos, "L'anticolonialisme de gauche en Belgique": 55.

61 Marcel Storme, "Cruyen," in *Biographie Belge d'Outre-Mer* VI, edited by Académie Royale des Sciences d'Outre-Mer (1968), 250.

62 "Les noirs à bord des malles congolaise," *La Métropole* (9 September 1925).

63 "A quand le Home pour gens de couleur?," *La Métropole* (11 February 1927).

(SEPES), a Belgian organisation that documented putative communist activities and gathered information for employer organisations and companies such as the CMB. Facing reports that their crews were being targeted by the Antwerp branch of the International Seamen's Club to be ambassadors for the communist and anticolonial struggle,[64] the CMB decided to support a safe house for Congolese seafarers. Alex Van Opstal, since 1923 director of CMB, assumed the presidency over the committee and from now on would collaborate closely with father Cruyen. While the CMB paid most of the costs, additional funds came from the city and province, the colonial ministry, and individual donors. One main supporter was Willy Friling from the Bunge enterprise, which made its fortune dominating the rubber trade with the Congo.[65] He had an economic interest in the safe passage of colonial commodities and raw material. Close cooperation of this sort between state authorities, enterprises, and missions was typical for Belgian management of the colonial workforce in the Congo – and it was now spilling over into the metropolitan waterfront.

Ndako Ya Bisu, Lingala for "our home," opened in May 1928. Located in a former hotel directly opposite the inner-city quays where the CMB steamships berthed, it consisted of a living room, a kitchen, and a café where the seafarers predominantly bought beer and cigarettes. It offered games and newspapers, a radio and a gramophone, as well as instruments from the Congo. Evening classes and catholic masses could be attended, and a variety of movies were screened. Forty seafarers, half of the regular Congolese crew, frequently visited the home in its first year.

Ndako Ya Bisu corresponded to the seafarers' homes that had been set up since the mid-nineteenth century in numerous ports around the world. Depicting the transient seafarers with their cash as vulnerable and easy victims for crimps and prostitutes, different actors such as missionaries, social reformers, and shipping companies ran boarding houses in the sailor towns. Especially in the ports where the national shipping lines regularly called, such homes were created to welcome specific nationals and foster the loyalty of the mobile seamen to both their nation and their wives.[66] Similarly to other seafarers' homes, Ndako Ya Bisu aimed to keep the Congolese seafarers away from the "urban-maritime cul-

---

64 Anne-Sophie Gijs, *Le pouvoir de l'absent: Les avatars de l'anticommunisme au Congo (1920– 1961)* (Brussels: Peter Lang, 2015), 61–71; Kottos, "L'anticolonialisme de gauche en Belgique"; Marc Swennen, "Les mouvements anticommunistes dans les années 1920," *Courrier hebdomadaire du CRISP* (2010) 14: 5–51.
65 Ndako Ya Bisu leaflet, 1 October 1928, KADOC, BE/942855/1262/7110/1.
66 Graeme J. Milne, *People, Place and Power on the Nineteenth-Century Waterfront: Sailortown* (Basingstoke: Palgrave, 2016); David Brandon Dennis, "Mariners Seduction on the Waterfront: German Merchant Sailors, Masculinity and the 'Brücke zu Heimat' in New York and Buenos Aires, 1884–1914," *German History* 29, 2 (2011): 175–201.

tures"[67] and to turn them into moral and god-fearing family fathers. It was built on moral and political panic: According to father Cruyen, who directed the home, shore leave was considered dangerous because of the "places of debauchery" and the "communism that wants to get a hold of these new souls that are easily fascinated when it comes to race equality and illusory material interests".[68] His mission also mirrored widespread racist fears about sexual relations of colonial seafarers with white women because virile masculinity and miscegenation was seen as a threat to the colonial order.[69] Ndako Ya Bisu is a striking example of how "imperial states produced racialized spaces"[70] in sailor towns. While the other crew members returned to their homes in other parts of Belgium, the Congolese were progressively contained in a "home" right next to their workplace, intentionally segregated from their colleagues and other houses that welcomed sailors from all around the world.

Fig. 1: The visit of Prince Leopold III of Belgium (second from right) to the Ndako ya Bisu in Antwerp. The first row includes Alphonse Cruyen (first from right), director of the seafarers' home. Unnamed Congolese workers are standing in the background. KADOC-KU Leuven. Archives of the Generalate of CICM. 7110. ©Gazet van Antwerpen, January 1934.

---

67 Brad Beaven et al., eds., *Port Towns and Urban Cultures. International Histories of the Waterfront, c.1700–2000* (London: Palgrave, 2016).
68 Cruyen, Note sur l'Oeuvre du Ndako Ya Bisu, 20 August 1930, KADOC, BE/942855/1262/7110/1.
69 On this subject, see Carina E. Ray, "The White Wife Problem: Sex, Race and the Contested Politics of Repatriation to Interwar British West Africa," in *Navigating African Maritime History*, edited by Carina E. and Jeremy Rich (Newfoundland: International Maritime Economic History Association, 2019), 163–188.
70 Milne, *People, Place and Power,* 234.

The welcoming culture of Ndako Ya Bisu towards the formally free seafarers was encroaching. From the outset, the home was a centrepiece for extending the limits of control over the colonial workers' free time. For the CMB, the mission, and the colonial ministry, Ndako Ya Bisu was a Belgian flagship that provided a stage for the good treatment of and good behaviour by Congolese workers, while keeping their segregation under surveillance even after work. For the seafarers, who would experience the home as a means of narrowing their space on shore leave, it quickly came to resemble a gunboat.

Home-made Resistance

After the inauguration of the seafarers' home, fears of communist infiltration kept knocking at its door. Internal documents of the Belgian Communist Youth leaked by the SEPES claimed to have established connections to Congolese seafarers in the International Seamen's Club.[71] It is hard to say what was fact or what was propaganda, as the Belgian Communist Party admitted difficulties in winning over Congolese seafarers.[72]

In any case, the communist activities laid bare a conflict of interests between the colonial ministry and the shipping company as to whether the employment of Congolese seafarers should be continued. For the state, the company's financial gains from recruiting Congolese came at the cost of potentially endangering the public order in the colony. The growing malaise to pay this prize made the minister ask for them to be successively replaced. The company fiercely opposed this, arguing that such a restructuring of the labour force would put them at a disadvantage to other shipping lines who were able to profit from cheap colonial workers. Van Opstal begged for more time, announcing "energetic measurements of surveillance."[73] Advised by Cruyen, he introduced new rules for shore leave, which the Congolese workers had to accept before recruitment, forcing them to return on board before midnight and to avoid certain bars and streets. Furthermore, they were obligated to carry an identity card to facilitate the sanctioning of rule breakers with disciplinary penalties.[74] But these means of control turned out to be coun-

---

71 SEPES newsletter, 15 May 1929; Kottos, "L'anticolonialisme de gauche en Belgique": 103.
72 Kottos, "L'anticolonialisme de gauche en Belgique": 119–120.
73 Letter from Van Opstal (CMB) to colonial minister, 1929, cited in Vellut, "Episodes anticommunistes dans l'ordre colonial belge": 186.
74 Notes by Cruyen, 24 August 1930, KADOC, BE/942855/1262/7110/1; letter from state prosecutor, 30 May 1930, State Archives in Antwerp-Beveren, R452, Fonds PK Antwerpen 2001 C, 333.

terproductive. Rather than preventing unrest, the regulation of free time triggered the first broad series of collective resistance and strikes.

It started with an anonymous handwritten letter that was sent to the shipping company in early November 1929. In the name of the "black staff," complaints were directed at father Cruyen, who, it alleged, would prevent them from visiting any other place but the home and enforced a curfew. They wanted to be "free again like before" and asked to have the missionary replaced by a Congolese.[75] Their threat to otherwise collectively quit their job indicated an awareness that the replacement of coordinated crews was not in the interests of a company whose fleet was at full capacity in the flourishing colonial economy. Only a few weeks later, a Congolese representative of the *SS Anversville* didn't shy away from sending a typed letter with nearly the same wording to the General Governor, the highest representative of the colonial state in the Congo. Subsequent investigations brought to light that capitas of different steamships had sent similar protest letters.[76] The colonial ministry defended Cruyen against these "accusations" and any capitas who acted as spokesmen for their crews instead of overseeing them were punished.[77] In the aftermath, 40 workers of the *SS Anversville* alone were fired, suggesting that the action was not a lone initiative of a handful of foremen.[78] Despite these sanctions, the shared interest among the Congolese seafarers in deciding over their free time in Antwerp led to an intensified mobilisation across working departments and the passenger liners.

In March 1930, recruitment started in Matadi for the *SS Léopoldville*, a brand-new vessel built in the Cockerill shipyard with a capacity of 355 passengers. It was the first journey under the shore leave regulations and the 102-man strong Congolese crew unanimously refused to accept the identity cards.[79] After some leaders were arrested, the workers apparently agreed to do their job on the round-journey but continued to oppose the documents.[80] On the way to the Congo, the ship's captain sent a cable to the colonial authorities about the "rebellious spirit" of the crew. That the situation did not escalate until the steamship berthed in Matadi is telling, for work stoppages at sea would be classed as mutiny. Once in the quay, the district

---

75 Letter to director of CMB, November 1929, KADOC, BE/942855/1262/7105.
76 Letter from CMB to Cruyen, 12 November 1929. KADOC, BE/942855/1262/7105.
77 Ministry of Colony to General Governor, January 1930, KADOC, BE/942855/1262/7105.
78 Minutes of Captain Biebuyck, April 1930, State Archives in Antwerp-Beveren, R452, Fonds PK Antwerpen 2001 C, 333.
79 Letter from state prosecutor, 30 May 1930, State Archives in Antwerp-Beveren, R452, Fonds PK Antwerpen 2001 C, 333.
80 Minutes of Captain Biebuyck, April 1930, State Archives in Antwerp-Beveren, R452, Fonds PK Antwerpen 2001 C, 333.

commissioner, joined by the captain, faced ongoing resistance when they tried to hand out the identity cards. Meanwhile on board, nine workers in the machine department collectively laid down their tools and left the vessel, unauthorised, in protest.[81] As the capita of the second engineer later reported, the Congolese stokers had worked at a sluggish pace during the shift, slowing down the vessel. One of the firemen was then slapped by the Belgian second engineer, whose job was to keep the appropriate pressure in the steam boiler. Together with another two cabin boys who had threatened their superior, the nine workers from the machine department were arrested.[82] In the quay, word spread that the suspended protestors of the *SS Anversville* were involved in collective resistance and that strikebreakers would face violence.[83] Immediately detained and waiting on the port's train platform for banishment, these 40 workers were brutally thrown to the ground by their own ship captain, a scene witnessed by the crew of the *SS Léopoldville.*

A few days later, the unruly Congolese workers were supposed to be recruited for the next voyage of the *SS Léopoldville,* showing the reliance of the CMB on coordinated crews and the belief that resistance had broken. Yet, when the Congolese workers collectively refused to enrol, they ended up in prison. That their incarceration was legal even though nothing formally obliged them to accept the job was due to the fact that the Congolese were managed on the basis of the *indigénat,* a legal system for colonial subjects allowing coercion and corporal punishment.[84] Colonial labour laws also legalised such disciplinary means guaranteeing strong discretionary powers over formally free workers.[85] Keen to avoid losing their job over the new shore leave regulations, the incarcerated crew finally agreed to carry identity cards and boarded the ship.

In total, 50 seaman from *SS Léopoldville* and *SS Anversville* were fired, and 34 were banished.[86] To teach the "blacks sailing on our ships" a "lesson," as the captain noted, the strike leaders – a chain around their neck – were embarked on a

---

81 For this section, see: police protocol, 17 April 1930, State Archives in Antwerp-Beveren, R452, Fonds PK Antwerpen 2001 C, 333.
82 Minutes of Captain Biebuyck, 16 April 1930, State Archives in Antwerp-Beveren, R452, Fonds PK Antwerpen 2001 C, 333..
83 Minutes of Captain Biebuyck, April 1930, State Archives in Antwerp-Beveren, R452, Fonds PK Antwerpen 2001 C, 333.
84 Loi portant réglementation du contrat d'engagement maritime, 5 June 1928, Moniteur Belge 98 (1928): 333–334.
85 Julia Seibert, *In die globale Wirtschaft gezwungen,* 103.
86 Sabakinu, "Histoire de la population": 495.

smaller boat for relegation to the eastern province of Kivu.[87] The rationale behind these harsh sanctions was that the local authorities were convinced that these Congolese "had been consulted by socialists or communists."[88] By seeing colonial workers fighting for better treatment and working conditions as nothing more than puppets of communism, the Belgian authorities delegitimised any resistance against the control measures.

Throughout the various sources, there is no indication that the strikes were incited by communist activists. Yet, the protest had offered the Belgian Communist Party an opportunity to mobilise.[89] While the SS *Léopoldville* was still on her way to Antwerp, *Le Drapeau Rouge* – which must have had informants among Belgium workers in Matadi[90] – was already reporting about the "savage imperialist repression" and the "brutality used against the strikers."[91] When the ship berthed in Antwerp, members of the party unrolled posters showing a policeman with the CMB sign on his uniform clubbing a naked black man with a baton. Later that day, some 20 members of the Congolese crew once again rebelled against the rules for shore leave. They returned to the ship after midnight, refused to show their identity cards, and made a mess of their cabins. Three of them were taken away by the port police to a cargo ship leaving the same night for Matadi.[92] Among the disobedient workers was the captain's cabin boy, showing how pressing the need was for the authorities to punish the renewed flare up of resistance.

Communist and anti-communist actors tended to interpret the strikes as evidence of ideological conversion. In the chamber of representatives, Jacquemotte even proclaimed a "resistance of the black population" against capitalism.[93] Yet, an investigation by the state attorney brought to light that the Congolese seafarers were protesting against the interference in their free time in Antwerp. They had turned their back on the Catholic home not to meet communists, but prostitutes.[94] More importantly, being under constant surveillance had prevented them from

---

87 Minutes of Captain Biebuyck, April 1930, Matadi, State Archives in Antwerp-Beveren, R452, Fonds PK Antwerpen 2001 C, 333.

88 Letter from district commissioner of Boma to provincial governor, Boma, 20 April 1930, cited in Sabakinu, "Histoire de la population": 498.

89 Police report to state prosecutor, 30 May 1930, State Archives in Antwerp-Beveren, R452, Fonds PK Antwerpen 2001 C, 333.

90 Kottos, "L'anticolonialisme de gauche en Belgique": 115.

91 *Le Drapeau Rouge*, 10 May 1930, cited in Larter, "Les marins congolais": 29.

92 Report of state prosecutor Henri Verhoven in Antwerp, 31 May 1930, State Archives in Antwerp-Beveren, R452, Fonds PK Antwerpen 2001 C, 333.

93 Minutes of Chamber of Representatives, 2 July 1930.

94 Police report to state prosecutor, 30 May 1930, State Archives in Antwerp-Beveren, R452, Fonds PK Antwerpen 2001 C, 333.

buying and importing goods for their petty trade in the colony. [95] This clandestine trade, once tolerated by the company, came under general suspicion and thorough scrutiny in the port of Antwerp. It was one of the main pillars of an onshore household, enabling women and children to sell prestigious goods on the market at a profit in order to keep the family afloat during the husband's regular absence.[96] Rather than communists-to-be, the Congolese protestors were capitalists-to be.

Understandably, the new shore-leave regulations crossed a line. While the fear of financial losses explains the timing of the first and most important collective strike in the history of Congolese seafarers, its location was also not accidental. The SS Léopoldville was the most popular passenger vessel and its journeys and arrivals in the docks of Antwerp's inner city attracted much attention; it set the public stage for the workers' demands. Compared with cargo ships carrying no more than two dozen colonial workers, this passenger vessel also regularly recruited 120 Congolese, and so constituted a critical mass for collective action.

Finally, it should be noted that the long-standing captain of the SS Léopoldville, who had been working on the Congo lines since 1912, highlighted in his report that "the black refused en bloc and without distinction of race."[97] He was astonished that the tried and tested strategy of recruiting heterogeneous working crews from different parts of the Congo in order to undermine solidarity had been proved wrong. Deprived of any formal way to protest and negotiate labour conflicts, the Congolese organised a collective strike that aimed at literally immobilising the steamship, reminiscent of the resistance practise of the "motley crew" sailors striking the sail. Yet, in the age of sail, the frequently successful mutinies were based on the unifying effects of "common cooperative work."[98] On the steamship, however, the compartmentalisation of labour processes, where "hierarchies of class intersected with hierarchies of race,"[99] reinforced racialised borders of solidarity. Tellingly, on the SS Léopoldville, it was the white crew members that temporally took over the subaltern tasks in the machine room necessary to get the "en-

---

95 *Le Drapeau Rouge*, 10 May 1930, cited in Larter, "Les marins congolais": 28.
96 For the challenges that women and children of Nigerian seafarers faced who were away for three to six months, see Lynn Schler, *Nation on Board. Becoming Nigerian at Sea* (Athens: Ohio University Press, 2016), 33–35.
97 Minutes of Captain Biebuyck, April 1930, Matadi, State Archives in Antwerp-Beveren, R452, Fonds PK Antwerpen 2001 C, 333.
98 Linebaugh and Rediker, *The Many-Headed Hydra*; Marcus Rediker; "Afterword: Reflections on the Motley Crew as Port City Proletariat," *International Review of Social History* 64, Special issue (2019): 255–261.
99 Schler, *Nation on Board*, 2.

gines of empire"[100] running, while the Congolese unanimously refused to work. The Congolese workers' ability to have collectively mobilised across the crews of different departments and even across different steamships was based on the "proximity in segregation" that preconditioned both their work on board and life on shore. Their forced stay in the seafarers' home and their fierce resistance against it only strengthened solidarity and created favourable conditions for self-organising.

Tightening the Grip and Tightening the Belt

The following year, the colonial ministry began to warn the CMB that the replacement of Congolese would be enforced for the sake of upholding public order in the colony.[101] When the general strike that broke out in summer 1932 in the coal mines of unemployment-struck Belgium, the Congolese seafarers felt encouraged to make demands for shorter shifts and more homogenous working crews.[102] However, these would ultimately go unfulfilled. When the global depression started to be felt in the shipping industry, the company managed to convince the ministry of ever-stronger reliance on cheap Congolese labour for their remaining vessels. Between 1932 and 1935, only 300 out of 900 registered workers were regularly employed in Matadi.[103]

Once again, the company opted to strengthen the surveillance of Congolese seamen by limiting their mobility and coercing them to accept the rules on shore leave. While immediately after the strikes some seafarers "systematically boycotted" the Ndako Ya Bisu,[104] attendance became mandatory in 1932. A card was introduced for Congolese workers, which had to be stamped on each stay. Although it is unclear how many workers were fired on these grounds, acceptance of the forced leisure programme increased. The company was able to impose the tightened controls. The insecurely employed seafarers who remained in Matadi throughout the economic crisis provided an ever-ready source of labour to replace any insubordinate workers. The seafarers themselves appear to have preferred to wait to until they were re-hired instead of taking less advantageous jobs in Mata-

---

100 Douglas R. Burgess Jr., *Engines of Empire. Steamships and the Victorian Imagination* (Stanford, CA: Stanford University Press, 2016).
101 Internal document Ministry of Colony, 6 October 1931, Archives Africaines, Bruxelles, AI/1396.
102 Territorial Administrator, "Note succincte et confidentielle sur le communisme à Matadi," 24 July 1933, KADOC, BE/942855/1262/7109.
103 Interview with Cruyen in La Tribune Congolaise, 15 July 1935, cited in Larter, "Les marins congolais": 37.
104 Cruyen, Note sur l'Oeuvre du Ndako Ya Bisu, 20 August 1930, KADOC, BE/942855/1262/7110/1.

di.[105] To reassure the colonial ministry, who feared that unemployment would pre-pare the ground for communist activities even though the local administration in Matadi reported no such incidences,[106] surveillance was extended.[107] A sister-house of Ndaku ya Bisu was created by Van Opstal and Cruyen in Matadi[108] and inaugurated in 1933. Financially supported by the CMB and other local transport companies belonging to the Banque d'Outremer, it was a means of gaining more control over the social lives of the crew.[109] The land on which the house was built was provided for free by the General Governor, who hoped to "have a serious control over the conduct and the tendencies of the black sailors."[110]

Knowing the economic constraints of the active seamen, the company appa-rently felt in a position to expand control over their shore leave in Antwerp, too. In 1935, any seamen who failed to supply evidence of their visit to the home and return on board before 11 o'clock would face a cut in wages corresponding to between a tenth or twentieth of their monthly wages. Should the offence be re-peated, they were suspended.[111] The way Congolese seafarers spent their free time began to determine the amount of remuneration.

These new regulations incited resistance that followed the protocol of the 1930 strikes on the passenger vessels. When, in June 1935, the SS *Thysville* landed in Ant-werp, the whole Congolese crew refused to go to Ndako ya Bisu. When they were forced to stay on board for seventeen days before returning to the Congo, Jacque-motte, who had already made public the strikes of the Congolese in 1930, asserted his right to visit the boat.[112] *Le Drapeau Rouge* reported that the "Prisoners on the Thysville" were "treated like slaves in Anvers." Some days later, the Congolese crew on another steamship, the SS *Anversville*, refused to visit Cruyen's home because

---

105 Sabakinu, "Histoire de la population": 487–497; Territorial Administrator, "Note succinte et con-fidentielle sur le communisme à Matadi," 24 July 1933, KADOC, BE/942855/1262/7109.

106 Territorial Administrator, "Note succinte et confidentielle sur le communisme à Matadi," 24 July 1933, KADOC, BE/942855/1262/7109.

107 Colonial minister to General Governor, 16 December 1932, Archives Africaines, Bruxelles, AI/1405, cited in: Larter, "Les marins congolais": 32.

108 Letter from CMB to Cruyen, 2 March 1931, KADOC, BE/942855/1262/7109.

109 Letter from Ndako Ya Bisu to colonial ministry, 29 September 1931, Archives Africaines, Brux-elles, AI/1396.

110 Telegram from Cruyen to CMB, 1 May 1931, Report on the visit of General Governor before the inauguration, Archives Africaines, Bruxelles, AI/1396.

111 "Le conflit sur le Thysville à Anvers", *Le Drapeau Rouge*, 27 July 1935, cited in Larter, "Les mar-ins congolais": 36.

112 Sabakinu, "Histoire de la population": 496.

he had been condemned in the communist journal as a "religious snitch".[113] The ship became their prison, too. Again, the company and the authorities reacted with the most severe sanctions. Some protestors were relegated within the colony; others were transferred to cargo vessels with no stopover in the Congo.[114] With Belgian steamships, the relegation practise was complemented by a mobile form of banishment.

The strike was less spectacular than in 1930. Yet, for the colonial ministry it confirmed their suspicions that Congolese seafarers would ally with the Belgian Communist Party and that all mechanisms to control their shore leave had failed. However, for a CMB that still depended on government loans to make up for the induced reduction of cargo transport fees, the low wages for Congolese workers were a necessary means of weathering the global economic crisis. Therefore, the colonial minister waited until 1937, a record year in cargo and passengers,[115] to ask the finally sound company to replace the Congolese crew.[116]

The constant conflict between capital and state as to whether profit on the basis of low wages outweighs the importance of public security would finally be resolved. That the shipping company asserted itself can be partly explained by its new head of management. Already in 1932, the deceased Van Opstal had been superseded as chairman of CMB by Félicien Cattier, a well-known and highly influential Belgian lawyer and financier. Cattier was director of the Banque d'Outremer, to which, besides the CMB, other colonial enterprises such as the mining company of Katanga belonged, and which filled not only the ship's hold but also the coffers of the colonial ministry. It was also due to his ability to play the two segregated racialised workforces off against each other. On a meeting at the colonial ministry, CMB representatives repeated well-worn arguments for colonial workers.[117] Defending the profitable racialisation of maritime labour tasks, the CMB provided detailed statistics demonstrating that an increase in white workers would nearly double the personnel costs and imply more cabin space, which would necessarily lead to increased transport fees. Tapping into the maritime labour pool of the Kru in western Africa, as had been done before 1911, was dismissed as a violation of

---

113 "Le conflit sur le Thysville à Anvers," *Le Drapeau Rouge*, 27 July 1935: 2, "Contre l'esclavage et le mouchardage religieux," *Le Drapeau Rouge*, 10 August 1935: 2, cited in Larter, "Les marins congolais": 36.

114 "Six nègres relégués," *Le Drapeau Rouge*, 9 November 1935, cited in Larter, "Les marins congolais": 37.

115 Devos and Elewaut, *CMB 100:* 112, 155.

116 Colonial minister to CMB, 9 January 1937 and 29 May 1937, Archives CMB, 27/III/100.

117 Meeting between CMB and colonial minister on indigenous seafarers, 5 June 1937, Archives CMB, 27/III/100.

the agreement with the colonial ministry to employ only Belgians and Congolese on their vessels. Turning on its head the argument that the employment of Congolese would threaten public order in the colony, the CMB underlined that white workers actually caused more trouble. Contrasting the long-standing idea of docile colonial seafarers and their structurally weak bargaining position with politically organised white workers, the company depicted Europeans as "much better agents for propaganda of subversive ideas than the indigenous". Referring to the Belgian general strike of 1936 that started in Antwerp and paralyzed the country, Cattier highlighted that it was only thanks to the Congolese seamen that the maritime connection between the colony and metropole had been maintained. Similar to what happened during the Congolese workers' strike in 1930 but with roles reversed, the company made use of the racial segregation of their maritime labour force to undermine collective claim-making and solidarity. While the white unionised working class with no interest in the fate of colonial workers achieved major concessions, the Congolese acted as strike breakers. After this meeting, the colonial ministry once and for all gave in to the company's line of argument, meaning that the recruitment of Congolese workers would continue until independence in 1960.

Conclusion

The life and work of Congolese seafarers on Belgian steamships reflects the room for manoeuvre of colonial labourers both at and after work. Similarly to Indian seafarers, the labour management of Congolese seafarers is a comparatively extreme example of "reducing the freedom of movement of a potentially highly mobile occupational group."[118] Furthermore, the Belgian maritime connections to the Congo reinforce arguments that "the movement of capital and labour in the shipping industry were, spatially and socially, tightly constrained."[119]

The control and stabilisation of this – quite literally – floating group was achieved through segregated social spaces spanning metropole and colony, docks and decks. The Congolese seafarers were recruited only by one Belgian company at a single port, the shipping routes were limited to always starting and ending in Matadi. These formally free labourers were encapsulated by bounded labour recruitment and forced to spend their un-free leisure time in a seafarers' home. Restrictive policies of immigration made jumping ship and entering the metropolitan

118 Ahuja, "Mobility and Containment": 119.
119 Jonathan Hyslop, "Southampton to Durban on the Union Castle Line: An Imperial Shipping Company and the limits of globality c. 1900–1939," *The Journal of Transport History* 38, 2 (2017): 4.

labour market almost impossible, while other employment in the colony remained unattractive. On both sides of the Belgian empire, the shore for Congolese was a narrow place.

The management of colonial workers on land interlocked with their management on board. The racial segregation on the steamship defined the ways in which maritime labour was organised, performed, negotiated, controlled, and coerced. Replicating the colonial order on board, the subordinated Congolese seamen were separated from the white crew members. During the long ship-journeys, transformative potential developed as the stable and inescapable collegiality on the job and in their cabins enabled constant interaction between workers who had been originally recruited from different regions of the Congo. Being part of the Congolese crew meant sharing the same subordinate position in the ship's hierarchy, the same weak bargaining position, the same exposure to coercion, the same reduced cabin space, and the same disconnection from national labour organisations and communist internationalism. The sense of community was, not least, strengthened by the onshore regulations that constituted another layer of the ambivalent labour management that aimed at control but allowed proximity in segregation.

Conceived as an extension of the more easily controlled free time aboard, Ndako Ya Bisu was the centrepiece of ever-increasing surveillance. While the steamships at times turned into "vessels of confinement,"[120] the shore leave of the Congolese crew could resemble the day leave of prisoners. While working time and free time are considered mutually constitutive and separated periods for labourers in industrial capitalism, the "erosion of the work-life distinction" was fundamental for the Congolese seafarers.[121] The blurred boundaries of leisure and labour made it therefore necessary to place the conditions and tipping points for their mobilisation both at sea and on land within a single analytic frame. The narrow shore and tight working spaces set the stage for collective strikes of formally free labour over their un-free time after work.

The two attempts to resist and formulate grievances across steamships in the 1930s demonstrated the ability of Congolese seamen for collective action. The punitive reaction of their employer and the state also demonstrated their strong discretionary powers over these formally free workers. The outcry in Belgium about working conditions and repression was limited to some members of the communist party, whose mission to close ranks with the Congolese compromised efforts

---

120 Balachandran, "Indefinite transits": 189.
121 Klaus Dörre, Nicole Mayer-Ahuja et al., eds., *Capitalism and Labor. Towards Critical Perspectives* (Frankfurt am Main: Campus, 2018), 22.

of self-organisation and claim-making. The colonial ministry and other state authorities constantly interpreted grievances as a sign of communist infiltration. The maritime bottleneck of the Belgian Congo along with the ports in Antwerp and Matadi enabled different regimes of mobility: While cargo and resources flowed, any process of mobilisation and politicisation was filtered out.

Nevertheless, the ongoing struggles of Congolese seafarers to escape surveillance and to enlarge their room for manoeuvre on shore showed their determination to defend their low scale yet profitable economic niches within the Belgian imperial transport network. These structurally discriminated colonial labourers were ironically empowered by a spatial proximity at work that was intended to prevent solidarity and mobilisation. The strikes in the 1930s can be seen as the collateral damage of the colonial state's and companies' labour management techniques based on racial segregation. That the seafarers' home in Antwerp would include a shop in the 1950s, where Congolese could buy their trading goods at advantageous prices, marked a late victory in their power struggle.[122]

---

122 Report on Goals and Activities of the Association des Marins Congolais, c. 1956, City Archive Antwerp, 1072#64.

Nicole Mayer-Ahuja

12 Power at Work: Approaching a Global Perspective

This volume focuses on control and resistance on the shopfloor and beyond. Under capitalist conditions, the relationship between capital and labour is always shaped by a structural imbalance of power. Although they depend on each other, their interests diverge: while companies are keen to get the most out of their investment in labour, it is crucial for workers to safeguard their labour power against over-exploitation. This is the only way of ensuring that their labour power can be sold and reproduced continuously, with regard to one's daily regeneration, to the up-keeping and development of labour power over the course of a lifetime, as well as to its intergenerational reproduction, implying, for instance, the raising of children. For this reason, labour relations are full of potential conflict: surrounding wages and contracts, as well as the organisation of the labour process, since the transformation of workers' labour capacity into actual labour on the shopfloor lies at the heart of capitalist production and service provision.

There is no labour process without organisation, coordination, and control. This introduces an element of coercion into (most) labour relations, and the capitalist enterprise in particular is no democratic sphere, as Elizabeth Anderson[1] points out. However, management control can take on fundamentally different shapes, as Marcel van der Linden argues in the introduction to this volume. It can be discretionary, or bound by formal and informal rules. It can be based mainly on coercion, or on workers' consent. It can imply a direct control of the labour process (whether through personal or technological forms of supervision), or involve "responsible autonomy" (to use Friedman's terms),[2] when the actual cooperation is left to the workers as long as they meet the targets and deadlines as defined by their superiors. The relative roles of autonomy and heteronomy are constantly being contested, with workers doing their best, in many different ways, to respond to management power, and to establish counter-power, using hidden or overt resistance. This may imply strikes, shirking, machine breaking, and other acts of violence, but also collective organisation, for instance in trade unions, and the struggle for collective standards. Such standards, whether in the form of

---

1 Elizabeth Anderson, *Private Government. How Employers Rule Our Lives and Why We Don't Talk About It* (Princeton: Princeton University Press, 2017).
2 Andy Friedman, "Responsible Autonomy Versus Direct Control Over the Labour Process," Capital and Class (1) Issue 1 (1977): 43–57.

https://doi.org/10.1515/9783111086552-013

state laws or collective agreements, reduce the competition between workers (which is unavoidable under capitalist conditions), thus countering management strategies of divide and rule (along the lines of ethnicity or gender, for instance). As a result, "there is a constantly shifting 'frontier of control,' that is an ongoing struggle for control in the workplace, with managers and supervisors trying time and again by direct and indirect means to increase their power over their subordinates, and the subordinates reacting and trying to maintain and increase their relative autonomy" (van der Linden, p. 3).[3]

In this volume, the complex influences upon power at work on the shopfloor and beyond are discussed in ten case studies, focusing on different world regions between the mid-nineteenth century and the present. In order to approach a global perspective on the shifting frontiers of control, some of the most important lines of argument are summarised and rearranged in the following paragraphs. This is also an attempt to continue the unconventional but thought-provoking search for unlikely connections, similarities, differences, and interrelations which has characterised the discussions that have taken place at re:work.

Rationalising the Labour Process: An Ubiquitous Managerial Approach

"Rationalisation" refers to management strategies aiming at an ever more efficient utilisation of labour power, including all mechanisms (whether organisational or technological) apt to secure a maximum "return on investment" in human labour. Since power at work is a highly contested terrain, it does not suffice to focus solely on management strategies of rationalising the labour process. Instead, we need to analyse the complex interplay between, on the one hand, these strategies and actual management practises and, on the other hand, the ways in which workers accept, openly counter, tacitly pervert, or evade these strategies.

Toby Boraman presents an especially striking example of how organisational and technological rationalisation contributed to a weakening of labour in the meat industry in New Zealand (p. 162). During the postwar period, the industry was shaped by its highly organised workforce. However, during the long 1980s, "an astonishing inversion in social relations occurred in the meat industry. Employers gained the upper hand by thoroughly restructuring the industry in order to render it more profitable. They closed most older abattoirs and as good as cut the workforce in half, while also constructing new, highly automated slaughterhouses, in

---

3 Unless indicated otherwise, page numbers refer to this volume.

which they re-asserted their 'right to manage' the work process." Workers' widespread resistance to this "destructuring," as restructuring was termed by some unionists, did not prove successful, and by 1990, markedly less strikes were occurring in the industry.

Such rationalising efforts were not restricted to developed capitalist countries, and they had early predecessors. Even on the tea plantations of Assam, Rana Behal argues, where the cultivation process was "almost entirely based on manual labour," "the cultivation and manufacturing methods were further refined and modified [...] to improve production and productivity" (p. 31). Technological and organisational rationalisation even seems to have gained particular impetus in countries where a socialist state supported the rationalising zeal of local management. As Sabine Rutar notes, with regard to the 3. Maj shipyard in Titoist Yugoslavia, the economic plan for 1966 to 1970 formulated very detailed goals, including specifications for the relative share of shipbuilding, constructing diesel engines, and equipment production and development. "Construction deadlines were to be shortened once more by about 30 percent. To achieve this target, parallel construction lines were introduced, the assembly flow re-arranged, and pre-assembly blocks were established." This implied a considerable extension of the shipyard's capacities, "making 3. Maj look more like a construction site than a facility for the construction of ships: Larger halls, new cranes, and new devices for drying and painting sheets were introduced, as were new machines for sheet-metal cutting and for the hydraulic bending of sheets, along with a fully automated panel line, stronger engines, reconstructed slipways, a floating production unit for the building of larger ships, and new buildings to house 3. Maj's administration" (p. 200).

Even agricultural work "under the collectives" in China during the 1950s, Jacob Eyferth emphasises in his contribution (p. 52), "came to resemble industrial work – not in terms of prestige and remuneration, which remained low, but in the fact that most such work was performed by teams of people working in close cooperation and under the supervision of collective leaders, that work rhythms were regulated by the clock, and that remuneration was closely tied to the intensity of labour effort" (p. 52). Moreover, "[o]perational sequences were increasingly standardised, and planners resorted to almost-Taylorist prescriptions on how workers should position their bodies, bend their backs, move their hands, and coordinate hands and eyes while at work" (p. 51). Despite this formal resemblance to Taylorist principles of organising factory work, however, the methods of control were strikingly different. "Coercion alone" was not feasible, according to Eyferth, since "[l]eaders were elected by team members, had no expectation beyond the village, and usually returned to the rank and file after a few years of service." Team members could be neither dismissed, nor promoted or demoted. Moreover, there were incentives linking "income to individual effort, but overall cash and grain incomes were capped and did not grow over time" (p. 61). Hence "ideological mobilisation" played a much more important role than in classical Taylorist approaches. After all, even if the Chinese state "pursued an almost-Taylorist standardisation of the labour process, [...] the ideal rural labourer, from the state's perspective, was not a mindless automaton but rather a proactive, self-improving agent, willing to learn from others and on the constant lookout for new challenges" (p. 60). This combination of Taylorist features and management's appeal to the subjectivity and creativity of working men and women might appear improbable at first glance. However, this has also shaped industrial production in capitalist countries, from the 1980s onward, when Toyotism advocated "continuous improvement," in an attempt to access workers' implicit knowledge of the production process. Taylorist features were only partially abandoned, despite a new emphasis on teamwork. The most advanced capitalist manufacturers of automobiles thus seem to have relied upon a similar combination of coercion and commitment as state planners in 1950s China.

Materiality of Production and the Contingencies of Organising the Labour Process

Organisational and technological rationalisation in any given context depends on the materiality of production, since the growing of cotton poses different challenges to the building of ships, or to the slaughtering of animals. In order to grasp the potentialities of rationalisation, to judge management measures adequately, and to be able to envisage alternatives, a careful analysis of the respective labour process is crucial. At the same time, objective material requirements can be translated into a wide range of different practises with regard to the organisation, coordination, and control of the labour process. Again, Eyferth provides an interesting observation, stating that "collective-era farming technologies," and especially the ways in which Chinese farmers pruned and shaped their cotton plants, were characterised by "their labour intensity, compared not only with earlier Chinese practise but also the rest of the world" (p. 68). After all, it was access to international cotton markets, which required "careful and timely picking" and a type of industrial processing, that resulted in a higher quality of clean cotton than the one that used to be produced for the subsistence of small farmers (p. 68). The practises of growing, harvesting, and processing cotton described by Eyferth thus had less to do with material requirements of the cotton plant itself than with the organisation of rural society in 1950s China. And this cannot be understood without reference to the economic, political, social, and cultural developments that shaped this very specific spatio-temporal constellation.

The argument that the labour process is shaped by the materiality of production, while the technological and organisational challenges associated with the introduction of modern machinery can translate into different management approaches to rationalisation, is reinforced in the contributions on maritime labour by Ravi Ahuja, Jonathan Hyslop, and Daniel Tödt. When sailing ships were replaced by steamships, Hyslop (p. 259) argues, "[a] different labour process laid the conditions for social and political changes in the workforce. The replacement of a relatively cohesive, highly skilled multi-national workforce with one that was fragmented by task and segmented and divided by race and ethnicity was dramatic." Ahuja (p. 220) confirms this observation, with an even stronger emphasis on changes in the labour process. The firemen or stokers who fed the new steam machines with coal experienced a marked deskilling compared with former sailors, since the ship owners defined their tasks ever more narrowly, centralised responsibility with the (chief) engineer, and exerted a (slightly) more efficient remote control over the "black gangs" that could not be supervised directly on their long-distance journeys. However, organisational rationalisation had its limits. First, it did not explicitly imply technological rationalisation, apart from the introduction of steam machines. The actual labour process of firemen remained unaltered over decades: the simple tools they used were not replaced with more refined and potentially labour-saving technology. The result was a "curious combination of cutting-edge technology with a cannibalistic overexploitation of labour power, almost entirely indifferent to the reproduction of the latter" (p. 217). Secondly, although stokehold labour was typically regarded as unskilled, it in fact required a wide range of skills and specific forms of cooperation, which had to be heeded in the process of rationalisation to safeguard the proper functioning of the steamship. Thirdly, the materiality of production limited the scope of managerial control, and an organisational "zone of uncertainty" persisted: "In front of the furnace, the widely varying combustion qualities of different types of coal, as well as the particularities and high susceptibility to failure of the machinery, were among the multiple variables requiring a deep experiential – even sensory – knowledge that defied verbalisation and was, therefore, not recognised as a formally teachable and certifiable 'skill'." Yet, it was "crucial to avoid pressure drops, wastage of fuel, damage to the boilers, and risks for the security of the ship: all of this required knowledge" (p. 219). Even engineers had to rely on the competencies of experienced firemen, despite all formal hierarchies. Hence the new technology of steam influenced the balance of power between workers and their superiors in contradictory ways. On the one hand, it became possible to promote a further segmentation of the workforce, both horizontally (through task division) and vertically (in new hierarchies), which was considered desirable in terms of efficiency. On the other hand, management fantasies of a clear division of labour along these new lines and of total control proved hard to implement – and again, it was the materiality of production (here: the crucial importance of implicit knowledge at the furnace) that created "objective" necessities that could not be ignored. This shifted the frontiers of control in favour of experienced firemen.

Moreover, Ahuja points out that the new steam technology could be used in different ways. Steamships used as tramps (i. e., as vessels for the relocation of staple goods, whose exact arrival time in ports was not of utmost importance) were typically manned with workers on short-term contracts. They often left the ship in a port along the route, since their unstable labour contracts and poor working conditions prevented the emergence of loyalty to a shipping company, to a captain, or to the crew on board a specific ship. On liners, by contrast, which carried post and passengers, it was crucial to keep to timetables; thus the workforce in the stoke room had to be stable and reliable. In order to achieve this aim, however, ship owners had two options. Some operated with the formal employment of (typically European) seamen, offering better wages, long-term contracts, etc., thus boosting a formalisation of employment. Others employed "lascars," mostly from India, and safeguarded stability in the stokehold by drawing upon colonial subjects, whose labour was much more strictly regulated (implying, for instance, that contracts were hard to terminate). It was thus not the steam technology as such that necessarily resulted in specific organisational features. Instead, we need to look at economic dynamics, at differences between economic sectors, at variations in organising the labour process according to different modes of operation (for example, tramps versus liners), and at political regulation supporting a particular utilisation of labour power (such as the colonial regulation of Indian labour).

How, then, does technological and organisational rationalisation contribute to shifts in the frontiers of control? Obviously, the sheer availability of a new technology does not necessarily have direct repercussions on the relations between capital and labour, given that it can be used in different ways and might not be implemented at all. Automatic stokers (a technical adaptation of the conveyor belt to the steamship), for instance, were never considered sufficiently reliable or to have a sufficiently cost-saving effect for wider distribution (Ahuja, p. 218). The level of automation that Boraman describes for New Zealand's abattoirs from the 1980s onward (p. 179) was never reached in Western Germany, where, even today, "the automated slaughterhouse remains a 'factory of the future.'"[4] Current debates about the effects of digitisation would benefit from the simple observation that technological innovation shapes the labour process intrinsically, but does not

---

4 Peter Birke, *Grenzen aus Glas. Arbeit, Rassismus und Kämpfe der Migration in Deutschland* (Wien: Mandelbaum, 2022), 203. My translation.

determine it. Organisation and control are not a natural consequence of technological innovation, but closely interrelated with management power and workers' counterpower.

Re-composing the Workforce: The Recruitment of Women

Apart from technological and organisational rationalisation, several contributions to this volume discuss management efforts to render labour more docile or more skilled, more flexible or more stable, through a systematic re-composition of the workforce, especially in terms of gender and ethnicity.

Increasing the employment of women, for instance, is among the most prominent strategies applied by companies to respond to labour shortages, with direct consequences for the labour process and for management control. In her contribution on factory work in Kemalist Turkey (p. 100), Görkem Akgöz argues that women were systematically recruited for industrial production during and after the Second World War, with active ideological support by the state. Under conditions in which "[e]conomic nationalism combined an intense dislike for foreign capital with protectionism, autarky, and industrialism" (Akgöz, p. 100), the recruitment of women was part of the state's effort to secure a stable and skilled industrial workforce, to raise productivity, and to "modernise" Turkish society. The specific ways in which a female labour force was constructed in the process had direct implications for the frontiers of control. According to Akgöz, "a specific female industrial labour control regime" was established, "combining a new set of external labour discourses with older forms of shopfloor labour control" (p. 101). The latter involved a traditional division of labour based on gendered stereotypes. It was advocated, for instance, by a German industrial expert in the 1930s: "Spinning is much easier than operating weaving looms, the expert wrote. In fact, it was so easy that virtually anybody could master it. [...] [S]ince the task required no intellect, women – or better still, girls – should be employed in the spinning shop." By contrast, weavers' skills were indispensable, according to this "expert", both for the quality of the cloth and overall productivity. "Unsurprisingly, therefore, weaving in Turkish textile factories was almost exclusively a job for men" (p. 123). This limited women to specific and predominantly low-skilled occupations like spinning, which had always been considered less demanding than weaving. "Because all of the managerial, and almost all of the supervisory, staff were male, the shopfloor environment of the 1930s and 1940s was highly gendered and male-controlled," Akgöz (p. 121) argues.

The employment of women increased the discretionary power of management in mainly two respects. First, many companies recruited young and unmarried women, who constitute an especially vulnerable part of the workforce. For Kemalist Turkey, Akgöz notes that in order to "break women's resistance to factory work," an especially "ambitious factory director devised the strategy of employing girls 'while they were too young to be spoilt by their mothers' and familiarise them with the mixed-gender world of the factory" (p. 108). When a new Labour Code was implemented in 1947, a parliamentary inspection report on sixty factories documented the "widespread employment of girls under twelve and the common practise of falsifying their age" (p. 114). Even if the employment relationships of (very) young women formally constitute free wage labour, they tend to enjoy less personal freedom than other workers, being subject as they are to parental authority. Hence even in the early twenty-first century, factories in China and India systematically recruit girls to join the workforce at their parents' command with the objective of earning some money for their dowry. In order to safeguard impeccable moral behaviour, parents agree to working arrangements that bind girls to an employer for a fixed period of time. Managerial control is thus extended far beyond the actual labour process. After work, these young women are confined to dormitories, rendering them available for the company 24/7. Under these conditions, it is difficult to build up resistance to management. This is noteworthy, given that working and living together has always been an important source of power for workers, for instance in Chinese state-owned factories, where workers enjoyed lifetime employment, as Li emphasises in her contribution to this volume. "There were so many people behind me," one worker told her. "Such mass solidarity within this generation of workers came both from their shared working and living experiences as well as the communal public spaces they occupied." Even at a public sector enterprise like Nanfang Steel, a younger generation of workers faced less favourable conditions as labour policies had changed profoundly. In Kemalist Turkey, as in present-day China and India, however, the barracking of young women results in almost total management control and confronts workers with a loss of voice as well as exit options.

Second, managers used the employment of mothers as a strategy to overcome labour shortages. As Akgöz states in her contribution, many women workers in Turkey during and after the Second World War had household and parental responsibilities, and accepted work in the factory only because they had no other options. This gave rise to the "question that preoccupied the minds of all the poor working mothers: Us, women workers, what should we do when our children are sick? If I work, my child will die. If I don't work, we will all starve to death" (p. 112). From a management perspective, it was certainly a welcome side effect that the recruitment of these women increased productivity levels. Albeit not limited to Kemalist Turkey, Akgöz notes that "female work intensification is associated with the utilisation of so-called feminine characteristics, and women's high productivity is cited as a natural product of their female qualities such as diligence and endurance for fast, monotonous work," with middle-class observers applauding "the patience and the endurance of the Turkish women worker" in the tobacco, cigarette box, and textile factories (p. 129). As a matter of fact, however, high labour intensity is generally observed in settings in which women with reproductive obligations work part-time, reaching levels of productivity that are difficult to maintain for a full working day. With regard to shifting frontiers of control, then, the employment of mothers has similarly problematic consequences for workers as the employment of young girls. In the Kemalist case, "[t]he combination of a state feminist discourse and work intensification under the authority of the foreman enabled employers to get high levels of productivity from their female workers with little resistance. Reinforcing each other, these two forces created a passive female labour force employed in jobs that required rapid performance of repetitive tasks" (p. 132). This meant that women had even fewer opportunities to "fraternise" (or better: sororise) than their male colleagues.

Relocating Production – Relocating Workers

A second strategy of re-composing the workforce, which has been applied by management in different times and places to combat labour shortages and to shift the frontiers of control in favour of the company, involves the relocation of labour. The contributions to this volume indicate that this strategy tends to produce ambivalent results.

In the 3. Maj shipyard in Yugoslavia studied by Rutar, for instance, management tried to fight "trends of labour fluctuation and massive emigration" (p. 202) during the 1960s by recruiting unskilled rural labour. Thus, a category of workers, who had been (mis)used by managers in order to lower wages and worsen working conditions ever since Frederick Engels described the fate of freshly migrated Irish workers in the industrial districts of England in the nineteenth century,[5] were offered especially advantageous conditions: Skilled workers continued to be hard to come by. The workforce at 3. Maj was predominantly unskilled, many of its workers recent migrants from the countryside. Ongoing efforts to transform them into fully qualified workers were never sufficient. The measures taken in

---

5 Frederick Engels, "The Condition of the Working Class in England," *Collected Works of Karl Marx and Frederick Engels: Volume 4* (New York: International Publishers, 1975), 295–596.

this regard included professional training, the bestowal of social benefits, as well as offerings related to cultural, sport, and other leisure activities: in sum, the ship-yard adopted a comprehensive approach to a lifestyle centred on the workplace. (p. 201)

Such incentives were especially crucial since the new migrants lacked the net-works that would otherwise stabilise social relations among long-term residents of working-class neighbourhoods. Even if they could (and would) be used as a basis for collective organisation, such networks were traditionally supported by many companies with the intention of tightening management control. After all, they helped to stabilise the new local workforce, which enabled the company to recruit suitable staff among the friends, neighbours, and children of employees as well as to reinforce formal control using informal disciplinary mechanisms, through peer pressure on the job or the soothing influence of fathers, grandfathers, and other relatives on the more hot-headed of the younger generation. Although, in the case of 3. Maj, workers were additionally offered various options to participate in the running of the company, efforts to "counter this churn" and to bind workers to the workplace "were only mildly successful. The expressed goal of self-manage-ment to strengthen the workforce's loyalty largely failed" (p. 203).

Recruiting migrants from the countryside, in this case, seems to have been a last resort for managers who did not have sufficient access to skilled urban labour – and this improved the negotiating position of unskilled rural workers. A striking-ly different constellation occurred in New Zealand's meat industry, when compa-nies relocated to the countryside in quest of a new, cheaper, and more docile work-force. In order to "maximise profitability and to minimise labour unrest," large plants in urban areas were closed, "while opening smaller yet more automated plants in rural areas situated on cheaper land. These rural meatworks were locat-ed closer to stock and in areas without strong union traditions (indeed, several were opened as anti-union plants)" (Boraman, p. 178). In the process of relocation, the companies cut their core workforces and recruited local agency workers, some on daily contracts. The relocation of these companies to the countryside constitut-ed a "spatial fix"[6] that weakened the power resources of workers decisively.

Immobilising Labour – Controlling Reproduction

Rana Behal and Christian Strümpell, in their contributions, both focus on manage-ment strategies involving a move to the Indian countryside (in one case, to the hills

---

6 David Harvey, "Globalization and the Spatial Fix," *Geographische Revue* 2 (2001): 23–30.

of Assam, in the other, to the jungle of Rourkela in Orissa/Odisha) without any intention of recruiting from the local workforce. Instead, workers were systematically "imported" to these places where the natural conditions (soil and climate in Assam, mineral resources in Rourkela) were suitable for the establishment of tea plantations and a steel plant respectively, but the local people were considered unsuitable for the tasks required. The implications for workers' capacity to negotiate the frontiers of control were, however, strikingly different.

Employment on the tea plantations of Assam, Behal (p. 28) argues, was directly shaped by the interventions of the colonial state. These could imply worker protection, for instance, when "[m]assive mortality during the transit and on arrival in the plantations in the early 1860s warranted state intervention in the form of labour legislation". More importantly, however, and with detrimental effects, planters were able to use a law of the British colonial state, namely the Workman's Breach of Contract Act XIII, to establish a system of indentured labour, from 1859 onward. "The main provision of the legislation lay in the power to arrest labourers bestowed upon the planters for breach of contract and desertion without a warrant within the limits of the district." Under these conditions, workers could not leave their job without facing a prison sentence. "Thus, despite formalising the minimum wage and labour contract, the law turned unfreedom into an integral part of the indenture system" (Behal, p. 29). The colonial state played an ambivalent role: "While it claimed to protect the interests of labour, in reality it legitimised the exercise of extra-legal authority by the planters" (p. 35). In this case, relocating the workforce was accompanied by a policy of binding workers locally: "After being mobilised in the recruitment process, the labour force was strictly immobilised within the plantation complex in Assam" (p. 49). Since leaving the job would be considered "desertion" and punished accordingly, the loss of an exit option evidently reduced workers' capacity to voice dissent as well. By way of curtailing workers' freedom of movement, the British colonial state ensured tea planters' access to labour power. This was further invigorated by the fact that "coolies" and their families worked and lived on the plantations in "coolie-lines" provided by the planters under the close supervision of managers and could hardly leave the premises. Company control over the reproduction of labour power in this case implied that the latter was severely obstructed, since workers had little opportunity for regeneration after a long working day, could hardly maintain and develop their physical strength and competencies over their life course, and could not raise their children in a healthy environment, let alone provide them with decent schooling. As we learn from Behal, the living conditions on the plantations caused illness, hunger, and desperation. Even after Independence (1947) and to the present day, this situation has not improved. Those who had lost their jobs on the plantations settled in nearby slums and returned to the fields as contract workers. Utterly inadequate support from the company for social reproduction gave way to no support at all. The power resources of the plantation workers that had been extremely restricted under colonial conditions through indenture were now curtailed even further in the process of informalisation.

When the Indian state decided to establish the enormous public sector steel plant in rural Orissa/Odisha in the 1950s, managers could no longer make use of the coercive power of colonial legislation. Instead, Strümpell argues, they "had to attract workers to their remote locations and turn them into a stable workforce" (p. 136). Given the crucial importance of steel as a key industry for economic development, the young independent state "was interested in co-opting workers, all the more so since a wave of strikes in the aftermath of World War Two had shown that labour was able to seriously flex its muscle. The fear of a radicalisation of industrial workers was widespread among politicians, bureaucrats, and capitalists." Under these conditions, the management of the Rourkela Steel Plant (RSP) took pains to create an attractive working and living environment. This included relatively high wages, lifetime employment, social security provisions, professional training, and clearly defined career paths (based on a system of guaranteed, time-bound promotions), in order to boost workers' commitment to the company. In the same vein, workers were offered company housing in a "spacious company township" (p. 157). Again, this was an attempt by managers to control the reproduction of labour power on a daily, life-long, and intergenerational basis after relocating the workforce. The results were strikingly different, however, compared with the Assam tea plantations. Whereas the settlement of workers in the plantation "coolie lines" had guaranteed managers almost absolute access to labour in Assam and obstructed reproduction, the eligibility for company housing at RSP provided the privileged core workforce of this public sector plant with the opportunity to reproduce their labour power on an ever-increasing level. RSP's company workers were "relatively well remunerated and securely employed" (p. 138) and did not have to stay in slums, like the many "precariously employed contract workers" who were hired in increasing numbers from the late 1960s onward. They could also afford to spend more time and money on their children's education than contract workers (p. 156). Even when the core workforce was cut drastically in the name of liberalisation from around 1980, "[m]ost of the RSP company workers, whether Odia or Adivasi, also seemed confident that if their children did well at school and college they would be sufficiently well equipped to compete successfully for the employment opportunities in the private sector that India's economic liberalisation was opening up elsewhere in the country. Consequently, they were more concerned about their children's education than about the lack of employment prospects in the public sector" (p. 157). Based on formal employment and company support for the reproduction of labour power (including company housing), then, Rourkela's younger generation of workers had acquired the exit options which their parents had lacked, and which contract workers continued to lack.

Li's account of the marked difference between the power resources of former workers at Nanfang Steel, a public sector factory in China, and its current workforce, under conditions of increasing market pressure and contract work, bears an obvious resemblance to the Rourkela constellation. The pensioners, who had moved to the region from the mid-1960s onward, found it much easier to stand up collectively and in big numbers, for instance, when the plant's management suggested pension cuts or an inadequate distribution of new company flats. "Most had come to Nanfang Steel during the earliest period of the Third Front construction and had spent their lives together in this factory community. Before retirement, they had worked together; after retirement, they shopped at the same markets, exercised in the same parks, and played cards or *Mahjong* in the same teahouses" (p. 82). Again, the fact that this company not only organised the production process, but also exerted a direct influence upon the reproduction of labour power (by providing company housing and the public spaces around it), seems to have strengthened the power resources of workers: "[W]hile these pensioners never formed any kind of organisation with an administrative or functional structure in the strict sense, they were nevertheless able to act in quite effective and prompt ways" (p. 82). Among the current generation of workers at Nanfang Steel, these "subcultures of resistance to outside claims" (p. 82) had virtually vanished. "[D]uring the 1980s, no collective protest ever took place among the younger workers who then made up the labour force, although different kinds of everyday resistance could be argued to have widely occurred." According to Li, "a paternalistic factory regime accompanied by improved living standards and an emerging flexible labour management system [...] were more effective as a carrot and stick for current workers rather than those who had already retired." (p. 84). Again, lifetime employment during the 1960s and 1970s (and, in the case of China, the lack of capitalist pressure on wage labour) seems to have shifted the frontiers of control in favour of former migrant workers, who were then able to plan ahead and advance their children's prospects without too much anxiety about the future. The backlash of liberalisation in India, and of China's integration into the capitalist world market, however, weakened their position and strengthened management's discretionary power.

For the rural population of 1960s China, the immobilisation of labour through a coupling of work and state support for social reproduction proved ambivalent in terms of power resources. As Eyferth (p. 73) argues, the introduction of a household registration system markedly reduced the chances for rural people to leave the countryside, or even their village. On the one hand, being part of an agricultural collective implied "secure tenure: short of sending them to a labour camp, a team could not get rid of unwanted members. On the other hand, it meant that villagers were deprived of the exit option – migration to the city or to some distant border region – that had traditionally allowed them to express their discontent" (p. 73). In present-day China, the fact that access to social security provisions is still tied to one's place of origin does not prevent young men and women from migrating to big cities in search for better-paying jobs. Still, this specific state policy of immobilising labour renders the position of rural migrant workers especially precarious, and also weakens their capacity to oppose employers.

Finally, ships constitute a workplace that is permanently in motion. This means that "[q]uestions of mobility and spatiality must be at the centre of any understanding of a maritime workforce," as Hyslop argues (p. 241). The very fact that seamen were not tied to any specific locality had turned sailors (among others) into an impersonation of the "many-headed hydra" that was the early labour movement.[7] Even after the advance of steamships, management, church, and the state all regarded seamen with deep mistrust, as Tödt has emphasised with regard to the Congolese seamen on Belgian ships who were commuting regularly between Matadi and Antwerp in the early twentieth century. "Having the precarious privilege to commute between colony and metropole, they were considered prone to indoctrination with anticolonial or communist ideas. Therefore, the Belgian authorities did all they could to limit their radius of action" (p. 273). The immobilisation of maritime labour on shore could take on different shapes, however, depending on the political context of a specific port. As Hyslop argues, seamen were "relatively free to come and go" in some places, whereas in others, "they were either heavily constrained by legal regulation or prevented from landing altogether. This had a dramatic effect on the available strategies for survival. Tighter immigration regulation made it much harder to take onshore employment, to settle in a new country, or even to change ships" (p. 241). Control over maritime labour was based not only on the labour contract or specific modalities of organising the labour process (as discussed above); it also implied a tight grip on the reproduction of labour power, even and especially when seamen spent time ashore. In this sense, the efforts of a Belgian pastor, Father Cruyen, to establish seafarers' homes for Congolese seamen in Antwerp, for instance, were not only an expression of Christian charity, but also an "instrument of social control" (Tödt, p. 264). What was initially intended as a means of controlling the seamen's daily regeneration also had repercussions for the lifetime reproduction of their labour power: Their contact with the local population was curtailed, thus preventing them

---

7 Peter Linebaugh and Marcus Rediker, *The Many-headed Hydra. Sailors, Slaves, Commoners, and the Hidden History of the Revolutionary Atlantic* (Boston: Beacon Press, 2000).

from establishing new networks and exploring alternative employment or business opportunities.

Just as spatial immobility could entail either an empowerment of workers (in the case of lifetime employment for public sector enterprises in India or China) or their oppression due to a loss of exit options (on the tea plantations of colonial Assam and the cotton fields of Maoist China), the seamen's spatial mobility also had differing results. Especially under colonial conditions, the British and Belgian states made sure that these workers, who occupied a strategic position for their respective Empire's economy, did not shift the frontiers of control in their favour, and they did this by subjecting seamen to especially rigid labour laws. At the same time, these workers were able to exert much more effective pressure on shipping companies and the state than was available to more place-bound labour. "[O]n the relatively rare occasions that mass industrial strike action did take place, the impact would be amplified to an extraordinary degree, with work stoppages encompassing multiple countries," Hyslop (p. 241) notes. "In the context of the globally dominant British merchant fleet, this was a major threat for imperial economic cohesion" (p. 241). However, management strategies of recomposing the workforce along the lines of ethnicity weakened the power resources of (not only) maritime labour considerably.

Dividing the Workforce Along Lines of Ethnicity

Capitalist production is based on inequality and competition. Companies, but also working men and women, are constantly positioned in opposition to each other in an everlasting quest for better conditions, and sometimes for survival. For this reason, the working class has never been homogeneous, and it is notoriously hard (though of course not impossible) for workers to act collectively and to practise solidarity against all odds, as the history of the labour movement shows. Shifting the frontiers of control, then, entails management efforts to make use of lines of segmentation between workers that exist beyond the corporate sphere, and to accentuate them even further in order to divide the workforce and to impede collective organisation – and it also entails workers' struggles to counter such strategies, by standing united. The recruitment of women, for instance, has long been a particularly efficient way of deepening divisions among workers and undermining solidarity. Trade unions have the option to respond to this either with chauvinist resistance to these female "cheap competitors" or with emancipatory approaches that bring together men and women workers on the basis of experiences shared across the working class. Much the same is true for ethnicity. As the contributions to this volume show, however, segmentation along the lines of regional origin, language, religion, or caste, in different places and at different times, mainly hampered the workers' fight for their common interests.

The combined relocation of production and workers to remote regions, for instance, implied the active constitution of ethnic minorities. On Assam's tea plantations, the fact that the newly recruited plantation workers came from far-away regions made it much easier to cut them off from neighbourly exchanges with the local population. "The key emphasis throughout was on controlling labour mobility, preventing desertion, and curbing workers' contact with the world outside the plantations. Both strategies aimed at preventing the formation of labour organisations" (Behal, p. 37): "One of the major consequences of the fact that plantation workers have been forced into an immobilised residential existence for a very long time is their isolation from wider Assamese society outside the plantations" (ibid.). This isolation persists to the present day, even though the families of many plantation workers have lived in Assam for generations and settled nearby after their contracts expired. "While the forced enclave existence left the tea plantation labouring communities socially and politically isolated, this was further exacerbated by the general attitude of indifference on the part of the Assamese intelligentsia and political leadership, both during and after colonial rule" (ibid.). The fact that "these communities continue to be treated as outsiders in the Assamese public narrative" (ibid.) weakened the power resources of plantation workers decisively, given the lack of exit options and of alternative employment in the local economy. Ethnic segmentation thus implied a massive shift of the frontiers of control in favour of management.

At the Rourkela Steel Plant (RSP), the recruitment of non-locals had a contrary effect. Here, the new arrivals (mostly from Punjab and Bengal) enjoyed a privileged position with access to the most attractive, skilled, stable, and well-paid jobs, including those of supervisors. Since these new migrants constituted roughly two-thirds of the workforce in the first decade of the company's existence, it was local workers who were turned into an ethnic minority on the shopfloor (Strümpell, p. 142). The fact that the local population felt discriminated against in the process of staffing the new and prestigious public sector plant fuelled Odia nationalism, which spread from local elites to local workers at RSP, and formed the ideological basis for the establishment of a new union. Its Odia nationalism "also attracted many workers identifying as Odia because it offered space to manoeuvre, first into RSP employment and, once in place, in conflicts between management and labour as well as among workers" (p. 148). Political segregation and chauvinism outside the plant (as part of state politics of production, in Michael Burawoy's terms) and the organisational structures, hierarchies, and divisions of labour within it (which constituted the basis for specific politics in production) thus reinforced each other. Ethnic differences were utilised and further strengthened by management to tighten its control over the workforce, as well as to impede solidarity between different groups of workers. Even though new migrants and local workers cooperated closely in the labour process, the fact that they were treated as unequal, that access to tasks and hierarchical positions was based on their ethnic origin, made it much easier to keep the workforce divided.

In many ways, such management strategies reflected older, often colonial, practises of dividing and ruling. They implied a systematic segmentation of the workforce, by assigning certain tasks to specific ethnic groups. As Strümpell (p. 140) points out, "[c]lerks were largely Malayalam, from the southern Indian state of Kerala, skilled operators were Punjabi, Bengali, or Bihari, while the semi- and unskilled workers under their supervision had an Odia and Adivasi background" (ibid.). As a result of such management policies at RSP, "caste and ethnic difference was exacerbated, especially among the first generation of workers" (ibid.). Local Adivasis, who occupied the lowest strata of Odia society, were also appointed to the most unattractive jobs on offer: "In Rourkela, the same stereotypes saw RSP personnel managers assign Adivasis to RSP's iron and steel zone or to its 'hot shops', the coke ovens, blast furnaces, and the steel melting shop where fumes, dust, and heat made working conditions extremely hazardous." This specific position in the company's division of labour was typically explained by "RSP executives, workers, and unionists [...] with reference to the low levels of schooling and technical training among Adivasis". However, "even the few who were better qualified ended up toiling in the hot shops" (ibid.). At the same time, most RSP company workers recruited in the 1950s and 1960s occupied more prestigious positions, despite a very similar lack of schooling, literacy, and professional training. "Adivasis, then, were not exceptional in their lack of formal education and technical skills. What set them apart was their lack of connection to those with discretionary powers, be it RSP executives or state representatives" (ibid.). The position of Adivasis was further weakened by racist stereotypes: "Upper-caste interlocutors usually assumed Adivasi to be uneducated and wild (*jungli*), and to drink excessively and eat all kinds of impure meats" (ibid.). Such "tribal characteristics" were typically cited to explain "what made Adivasis ideal manual labourers." This stereotypical representation "closely resembles colonial perceptions of the alleged distinctiveness of Adivasis, 'aboriginals,' or 'tribals,' which made them the perfect 'coolie nation' to withstand the harsh working conditions in the Assam tea plantations. In Rourkela, the same stereotypes saw RSP personnel managers assign Adivasis to RSP's iron and steel zone or to its hot shops" (p. 148).

It is on nineteenth-century steamships, however, that "management by 'race'" (as a historical predecessor of such management practises) can be studied in a nutshell. Ahuja argues (p. 212) that the transition from sailing ships to steamers had entailed a much more rigid division of labour and the establishment of steeper hierarchies. "This intentional, owner-managed division of the workforce along lines of status and skill was not necessarily marked out racially." But when "Indian 'lascars' as well as African, Yemeni, and Chinese ship workers were recruited in large numbers to toil as trimmers and stokers in coal bunkers and boiler rooms" from the 1850s onward, the "language of racial difference" gained importance, as "shipping lords discovered management-by-'race' as an ideologically irrational but perfectly profitable option" (p. 212). After the labour process had become increasingly segmented, tasks were thus ascribed to workers from different ethnic backgrounds based on racist stereotypes "concerning the suitability of particular peoples for particular work," as Hyslop notes (p. 244). "Goans were widely employed in the catering departments and East Bengalis and Punjabis in the stokehold, while a range of other ethnic groups were assigned to deck work – a structure that certainly helped to keep workers politically fragmented."

For Belgian vessels, Tödt emphasises "the tried and tested strategy of recruiting heterogeneous working crews from different parts of the Congo in order to undermine solidarity" (p. 281). He also highlights one instance of unity among different groups of Congolese seamen. When distress mounted, due to an ever more consistent encroachment of the representatives of state, capital, and church on the seamen's leisure time, "the black refused en bloc and without distinction of race" to carry identity cards, as a Belgian captain noted. "Deprived of any formal means to protest and negotiate labour conflicts," Tödt remarks, "the Congolese organised a collective strike that aimed at literally immobilising the steamship, reminiscent of the resistance practise of the 'motley crew' sailors striking the sail." However, the "compartmentalisation of labour processes" that had accompanied the transition from sailing ships to steamships "reinforced racialised borders of solidarity. Tellingly, on the SS *Léopoldville*, it was the white crew members that temporally took over the subaltern tasks in the machine room necessary to get the 'engines of empire' running, while the Congolese unanimously refused to work" (pp. 205–282).

This systematic division of maritime workforces along ethnic lines, according to Ahuja, resulted in an enormous wage difference between British and "lascar" seamen. In the late nineteenth and up until the late twentieth century, "[t]he pay of an Indian seafarer was believed to range between a quarter and a third of that of a British seaman" (p. 227). The low wages paid to "lascars" also allowed for human resource strategies of "overmanning", with implications for the organisation of shift systems and working times. Whereas British seamen could insist on two four-hour shifts, the "'khalasi watch' system, by contrast, explicitly required 'lascars' to be available whenever needed", which seems to have implied "three four-hour watches" in many cases. "As in more openly 'unfree' labour relations, working time was not separated from off-time by legal regulation, while customs as well as the conditions for terminating a labour contract were racially defined" (p. 231).

In the case of maritime labour, not only was a segmentation of the workforce originating in social structures of inequality outside the company, and especially in ethnic differences, utilised and reinforced by a management that wished to save on labour costs, raise the efficiency of the labour process in the stokeholds, and impede solidarity among different groups of workers; this segmentation was also systematically intensified by the state.

Shifting the Frontiers between Free and Unfree Labour

According to Karl Marx, workers under capitalism need to be personally free in order to be entitled to sell their own labour power. At the same time, they are free from the means of production. And it is this negative freedom, in the first place, that results in the structural imbalance of power between capital and labour, since the lack of other means of subsistence introduces a strong element of coercion into capitalist labour relations. Even if some global labour historians advocate moving beyond Marx's definition,[8] it is widely agreed that 'formally' free wage labour can imply a strikingly different scope of 'actual' freedom.

First of all, for many formally free wage labourers, especially from the colonies, the long shadows of slavery served as a powerful disciplinary device. When the strike, mentioned above, carried out by Congolese seafarers on Belgian ships was defeated in 1929, "the strike leaders – a chain around their neck – were embarked on a smaller boat for relegation to the eastern province of Kivu" (Tödt, pp. 279–280). Obviously, this was supposed to remind these workers that their freedom was in fact at stake and depended on good behaviour.

In Behal's contribution on indentured labour in Assam, he discusses a specific variety of forced labour based on a contract under which workers were required to relinquish their status as formally free wage labourers for a fixed period of time. This bears some resemblance to the seafarers in the British and Belgian Empires, where, even if they had not signed an indenture contract, their freedom would also be suspended for the duration of a voyage, especially if they came from the colonies. As Ahuja argues, "the labour relations of 'lascars' and other 'native seamen' differed substantially from those of 'European' seamen not only in re-

---

8 Marcel van der Linden, *Workers of the World. Essays Toward a Global Labor History* (Leiden: Brill, 2008), 15–37.

gard to wages and other forms of compensation but, even more importantly, in respect of their level of personal subordination." There was "a separate category of work contract for 'native seamen' that was referred to as 'lascar (or, Asiatic) articles of agreement'", which severely restricted their right to terminate their contract (p. 230). In the same way as for indentured workers on Assam tea plantations, who could be arrested by planters "for breach of contract and desertion without a warrant within the limits of the district" (Behal, p. 28), seamen were also legally bound to their places of work, thus curtailing their right both to quit their job and to leave the ship. State intervention was crucial for this means of disciplining labour, since the indenture system had been established through legislation (see above), whereas the restrictions on the freedom of colonial seamen were based on a combination of labour contracts and immigration rules. As Ahuja argues, the fact that "Indian seafarers could be denied shore leave in port while being prevented, by immigration laws, from disembarking in several important shipping destinations" implied that they could be "compelled to work continuously even in port, while desertion rates were pushed down", and both supported "the uninterrupted and punctual performance of liner operations" (p. 231). In the Belgian Empire, Tödt argues, the "forced leisure" (p. 282) of Congolese seafarers, who were increasingly compelled to spend their free time in seafarers' homes, to carry identity cards, and to report daily to the colonial authorities in case of unemployment, limited their opportunities to organise collectively or to find alternative sources of subsistence, thus weakening their power resources considerably.

A similarly ambiguous status between unfree and free labour can be attributed to the peasantry in Maoist China, as Eyferth points out, and again, the state played a crucial role. In contrast to independent farmers, Chinese peasants "worked in collective agriculture, growing crops and raising animals under the supervision of collective leaders to specifications handed down by the State Planning Committee and the Ministry of Agriculture" (p. 51). Even though they were not employed as wage labourers and did not contribute to capitalist profit-making, their working situation resembled formally free wage labour in some respects, given their "experience of working under supervision, following impersonal routines, and earning a fixed wage per task or per labour day" (p. 52). At the same time, however, "Chinese rural workers were unfree in the specific sense that they were tied to a community and a place, and thus also to a workplace that they could not leave." According to Eyferth, it was not so much the "discretionary power of team leaders" that "drove people to work", but hunger. "Members of rural collectives were thus free not to work in the same way as the early factory proletariat, namely in the sense that they were free to choose between work and starvation" (p. 74). Moreover, they had little chance to leave their agricultural collectives: "The household registration system, formalised in 1960, made it all but impossible for rural people to leave their place of birth (or place of marriage, in the case of women who married into another village)" (p. 73). Hence Chinese agricultural workers also lacked the freedom to terminate their contract and leave their job, which discerns formally free wage labour from other, more unfree, forms of employment. To the extent that the actual freedom of wage labour could be compromised, suspended, or called into question altogether by management, the frontiers of control shifted toward the company.

Formalising "Free Wage Labour"

In the abattoirs of New Zealand (Boraman), on the 3. Maj shipyard in Titoist Yugoslavia (Rutar), in the Chinese state-owned Nanfang Steel company (Li), in Kemalist textile factories (Akgöz), and in the Indian Rourkela Steel Plant (Strümpell), the status of workers came very close to the ideal type of formally free wage labour. Yet, it took on markedly different shapes depending on the complex interrelations between the politics in production – on the shopfloor – and state politics of production.

Especially (but not only) under conditions of colonial capitalism, political regulation had directly influenced the power relations between capital and labour – in favour of the former. After the Second World War, however, the situation appears to have changed in different parts of the world, as several contributions to this volume indicate. What Rutar (p. 191) describes as "'[t]he peak phase of organized capitalism' from 1945 to 1975, characterised by 'the expansion of the welfare state and labour legislation, the cooperation of organized interests and the state, economic politics with increasingly Keynesian approaches, as well as a solid share of sectors put under state control and state-led master plans,'" had profound implications for the relationship between capital, labour, and the state. This can be studied across the globe, with more similarities than differences to be found in countries of the Global East and West, North and South.[9] In Titoist Yugoslavia, for instance, "[t]hese features made this [peak phase of organised capitalism] an 'economically mixed order,'" as Rutar argues (p. 192). The state was supposed to "wither away," handing over its power to self-managed work collectives, where "self-management mechanisms [...] would ultimately regulate the forces of the market successfully" (p. 209). Within companies, "all major decisions concerning shopfloor organisation, such as income distribution and capital investments, had

---

9 Jan Breman, Kevan Harris, Ching Kwan Lee, and Marcel van der Linden, *The Social Question in the Twenty-First Century. A Global View* (Oakland: University of California Press, 2019).

to be ratified by the entire work collective. [...] The Law on Associated Labour was, ultimately, to replace the constitution, and the self-managed bodies were to assume responsibility for all tasks previously performed by the state" (p. 210). But even in Yugoslavia, the state did not withdraw to the extent originally envisaged. In capitalist countries, instead, the state assumed an ever more active role after the Second World War, and its interventions often tended to strengthen the position of labour. Workers' legal rights were extended through state legislation and collective agreements, thus increasing their room for manoeuvre vis-à-vis employers. Systems of social security provision were established and expanded, protecting workers against the risks inherent in wage labour (such as illness, unemployment, or poverty in old age). Together with the strengthening of public infrastructure and public services, Castel argues, this entitled workers to a collective "social property," thus reducing (though never abolishing) their dependence on continuously selling their labour power.[10] Moreover, the state increasingly functioned as employer in many countries, as discussed in this volume for India (RSP), China (Nanfang Steel), and Yugoslavia (3. Maj). Public sector enterprises pioneered stable fulltime employment with comprehensive social security coverage and labour laws, with workers represented by particularly strong works councils and trade unions. This formalisation of wage labour, which culminated in specific forms of "standard employment," not only in the Global North but also in the Global South,[11] reduced "employers' discretionary power, both on the shopfloor and beyond" (van der Linden, p. 4), in public as well as in private enterprises.

The RSP public sector enterprise in India is a particularly good example of this tendency, and also of its limitations. Ever since the company was established in the 1950s, according to Strümpell (p. 135), it belonged to those public sector companies "supposed to set the standards for the relation between (state) capital and labour in India." What had been achieved by Tata workers in the first half of the twentieth century with regard to "security of employment, maximum working hours, minimum wages, paid holidays, pensions, and the right to union representation" set the stage for the three post-Independence public sector steel plants, supposed "to act as model employers, providing the same standards as Tata from the outset." Under conditions of recently acquired Indian Independence, even the recruitment of different ethnic groups from all over India was explicitly supposed to serve the purpose of nation building in the 1950s. The founders of RSP expected that "[b]y

---

10 Robert Castel, *Les Métamorphoses de la Question Social. Une Chronique du Salariat* (Paris: Fayard, 1995).
11 Nicole Mayer-Ahuja, "Die Globalität unsicherer Arbeit als konzeptionelle Provokation: Zum Zusammenhang zwischen Informalität im Globalen Süden und Prekarität im Globalen Norden," *Geschichte und Gesellschaft. Zeitschrift für Historische Sozialwissenschaft* 43, 2 (2017): 264–296.

working together in a modern steel factory, as well as living together in the modern townships that were built on the green field sites alongside the plants, and all under the guidance of a benevolent state employer, public sector steel workers and their families would inevitably transcend their 'primordial' identities of ethnicity, religion, and caste" (p. 136). Just like the establishment of formalised employment, this kind of recruitment could have paved the way for a reduction in difference and competition on the shopfloor. Instead, both management and the Indian state, on a national and regional level, chose to pursue strategies that would keep the workforce divided, even during the prosperous decades following the Second World War, through a (horizontal and vertical) division of labour along the lines of ethnicity, language, and caste. "The fear of a radicalisation of industrial workers was widespread among politicians, bureaucrats, and capitalists. To avert working-class unity, they also encouraged the affiliation of trade unions to different, rival parties" (p. 136).

While, then, managerial divide and rule strategies did not disappear during the 1950s and 1960s, they were now being confronted with conflicting goals of nation building and class compromise after the distortions of the Second World War (in the capitalist centres) or Independence (in the former colonies), as well as in the context of the Cold War. Under these conditions, new standards for the regulation of wage labour were established, both with regard to the employment relationship (which became more stable and plannable for workers) and to the utilisation of labour power on the shopfloor (concerning working time, for instance), which were (in principle) applicable to all workers without distinction. In reality, they did not eradicate difference and competition between men and women, or between locals and migrants, altogether, but they did have a mitigating effect to some extent. Even if "standard employment relationships," for instance, were established predominantly among the male workforces in the big industries, and especially in public sector enterprises, the sheer existence of universal standards strengthened the position even of traditionally discriminated parts of the working population. When women were actively recruited for industrial employment in Kemalist Turkey, for instance, "industrial policymakers and middle-class intellectuals underlined two points: Turkish women 'could' work at factories ('the right to work') and Turkish women 'should' work at factories ('the duty to work')" (Akgöz, p. 107). Despite being subject to various kinds of gender stereotyping, remunerated with lower wages, and stuck in less demanding and rewarding jobs, an increasing number of Turkish women were now able to earn their own wages and acquire some economic independence. In many countries (like Germany, for instance),[12] women (including wives and mothers) increasingly took up wage labour after the Second World War, developed professional identities, and started to organise collectively in pursuit of better working and living conditions. Still, they never fully bridged the gap to male-dominated "standard employment". However, if compared with earlier forms of economic activity accessible to women (like doing outwork from home, which was the background of many of the Turkish women workers who entered Kemalist textile factories), they moved much closer to contemporary standards of socially protected wage labour. Being formally employed with a work contract, labour rights, social security provisions, and the chance to cooperate with colleagues on the shopfloor represented a decisive step toward the "standard employment" that was in the process of being established in many countries at the time.

All in all, the role of the state changed profoundly after the Second World War. Instead of contributing to a further segmentation of the workforce, as in earlier periods, state policies of formalisation were now expected to reduce difference between workers, at least in theory and to some extent. Under conditions of a booming economy, a lack of skilled (and sometimes even unskilled) labour, and (in the case of former colonies) with the need for import substitution, the frontiers of control could thus be shifted in favour of workers. This even strengthened the position of migrants and women at the lower end of social hierarchies, within the confines of the company and beyond. The formalisation of employment made standing up to management easier: Workers had more jobs to choose between, and if their formal rights were violated, they could either opt for an exit and change jobs or reassert their entitlement, whether in court, through collective action, or a combination of the two.

Turning the Tide: Weakening Workers' Power Through Informalisation

From the 1970s and 1980s onward, after three decades of more or less continuous growth, the world economy cooled down. Many jobs were lost and competition among workers for adequate working and living conditions mounted. In many countries, both in the Global North and South, state policies, again, underwent a fundamental change. In order to create employment, the new economic paradigm of neoliberalism or neoconservatism assumed that capital had to be freed from

---

12 Nicole Mayer-Ahuja: *Wieder dienen lernen? Vom westdeutschen „Normalarbeitsverhältnis" zu prekärer Beschäftigung seit 1973* (Berlin: Edition Sigma, 2003).

legal restrictions, including labour regulation. Thus many states around the world created new opportunities for work contracts that were less stable than "standard employment relationships" (such as contract work, or agency work), and labour courts tended to interpret workers' rights much more restrictively than before – if labour conflicts were even brought before the court at all. Moreover, governments cut down on social security provisions and public services, and privatised public sector enterprises. Stable full-time employment with social security coverage, labour rights, and subsistence wages lost importance under conditions that were now shaped by state policies of informalisation. As the contributions to this volume indicate, managers across the world utilised the opportunities provided by market-friendly governments to increase their discretionary power, whether in capitalist countries (New Zealand), socialist countries (China), or non-aligned countries (India).

In New Zealand's meat industry, for instance, where "[a]ssembly-line workers were frequently at the forefront of the major wave of workplace conflict that occurred in high-income countries during the long 1970s" (Boraman, p. 161), "[t]hey subsequently bore much of the burden of de-industrialisation, automation, neo-liberal de-regulation, and globalisation in the long 1980s. Meat processing workers suffered from such a fate, as a wave of plant closures rippled around the world from Argentina to Australia, the United States, Aotearoa/New Zealand, and beyond." This resulted, Boraman states, in "startling reversals in power relations in that industry during the 1970s and 1980s" (ibid.).

A strikingly similar scenario is described by Li (p. 78) for the public sector steel plant in China she has analysed, even if the most important changes only occurred after the mid-1990s. "During its heyday of the late 1980s and early 1990s," Nanfang Steel employed around thirty thousand workers. "Between the mid-1990s and the early 2000s," however, "a variety of radical market-oriented means – mergers, partial privatisation, downsizing, burden alleviation, large-scale lay-offs, and so on – [...] brought tremendous destruction and chaos to the factory." Nanfang Steel was not closed, "largely for the sake of social stability," but entered "a painful process of slow death, with a streamlined despotic factory regime on the shopfloor, a pauperised working class, and a disintegrated factory community." According to Li, this marked "the epitome of the eventually victorious establishment of capitalist labour relations in the workplace, evolving from its more cautious and hesitant early stages to the more determined later years."

At the Rourkela Steel Plant in India, managers were equally eager to explore the new opportunities provided by the Indian government in the context of liberalisation. The segmentation of the workforce in terms of employment status had already gained momentum during the late 1960s, when the RSP management had begun to increasingly hire contract workers and "greatly succeeded in dividing labour along the lines of formal and informal employment" (Strümpell, pp. 136–137). Whereas many public sector enterprises had "relied on supplementary informal labour in the 1970s and 1980s," during the "liberalisation of the Indian economy – slowly and by stealth since the early 1970s, and officially and faster since the 1990s," they "increasingly employed informal labour to replace the formal workforce" (ibid.). When RSP tried to make substantial job cuts around 1990, "[t]he security of employment enjoyed by regular workers prevented management from achieving such a large-scale reduction of the workforce by retrenchment." Hence the company offered voluntary retirement schemes to "the first generation of RSP workers [who] reached the age of superannuation at fifty-eight" (ibid.). The "smaller number of workers" who were hired to replace them were no longer employed directly by RSP, "but through chains of privately operating labour contractors and subcontractors" (ibid.). These contract workers "did not enjoy legally sanctioned employment security, union representation, and standards of working conditions." This rendered them "cheaper and politically weaker": "In contrast to RSP company workers, contract workers could be hired and fired at will, and, depending on their skill and gender, they would earn effectively between one-third and one-fifth of the amount earned by a regular worker" (p. 152). And still, workers at the Rourkela Steel Plant found ways of countering management strategies of dividing and ruling the workforce by informalising employment. When RSP decided to cut down on staff, this posed a serious threat to contract workers, who would then have fewer opportunities to join the regular workforce, but also to company workers. After all, the "curtailment of vacancies" at RSP "also curtailed the chances of their grown-up children being able to follow in their footsteps," which raised "concerns about the reproduction of class positions" (pp. 155). Under these conditions, "across all ethnic-cum-caste divides RSP workers quickly started rallying behind a new union" that had just been formed by an RSP clerk "who had gained local fame for a case he had filed for the regularisation of RSP contract workers" (ibid.). This initiative proved successful: "In 1994, the Indian supreme court indeed obliged RSP to employ as regular company workers 4,500 of its contract labour force." A success that Strümpell attributes to "the overwhelming combined support [...] from RSP's contract workers and company workers" (p. 155).

During the following decades, even at RSP "[t]he gulf between contract and company workers remained wide." By 2008, contract workers still earned roughly one-fifth of the wages paid to company workers. Moreover, although workforce cuts implied stricter management controls even for company workers, they "rarely faced dismissal." Under these conditions, competition between workers increased, and former experiences of solidarity could not be repeated. Many contract workers "complained that 'our sweat never dries but they [the company workers] sit around eating air' (idling around)." In fact, employment status proved an ever more significant dividing line, superseding even ethnic difference, as Adivasi company workers enjoyed a relatively secure position, whereas it was "largely Adivasi contract workers who actually did most of the real hard work. This shows that it is nowadays not so much caste that determines one's power on the RSP shopfloor, but employment status" (Strümpell, p. 156). In the long run, then, RSP's recruitment strategies created a new dividing line between contract workers and company workers, whose short-term solidarity was eradicated over the years. As economic pressure and competition for jobs increased, company workers no longer tried to confront management. Instead, they took to defending their privileges against contract workers, villainising them in order to justify their lack of support for these colleagues: "Regardless of caste background, RSP company workers unanimously considered these contract workers unfit for and undeserving of regular employment. That is a far cry from the late 1980s and early 1990s, when we saw RSP company workers supporting the struggle of contract workers for regularisation" (p. 117).

As workforces became increasingly fragmented, and employment informalised, the discretionary power of management reached its peak. Under these conditions, solidarity and collective action were hard to achieve, as Li reports with regard to Nanfang Steel in China, which also underwent severe restructuring in a quest to increase competitiveness in an increasingly global market. The older generation of workers, who were now retired, "still harboured vivid memories of the more militant working-class traditions that emerged during the Cultural Revolution" and "had launched quite a few successful contentious collective actions during the 1980s." The current workforce, who were "more directly influenced by carrot and stick policies, were largely compliant and even cooperative" (p. 24). In the absence of proper unions, Li argues, present-day workers at Nanfang Steel could still use "weapons of the weak," such as "ostensible conformity, backstage rumours and curses, and shopfloor non-confrontational resistance" (p. 90). After management had introduced financial sanctions for "absenteeism, tardiness, and resistance to discipline," many workers employed "foot-dragging and indifference" as "the most prevalent forms of daily resistance." According to Li, workers took revenge on their supervisors by "remaining aloof, watching the machine break down again and again, and revelling in their managers' inability to do anything." Withholding labour and skill "endowed the workers with a secret power to counterbalance, even if only to a small degree, the arbitrary and dominant power of management" (p. 93). At the same time, however, this kind of "everyday resistance, expressed as it is in passive and negative ways, actually went against the moralities generally held by most Nanfang Steel workers." Assuming a distanced attitude toward their work, these workers were left with "feelings of inadequacy and powerlessness" (p. 94). "In other words, these strategies of resistance could be argued to

have deprived workers of the pride and even legitimacy that could have been derived from clearly claiming their rights and proudly confronting management" (p.
95). Even these public sector Chinese workers were now painfully aware that they
might easily face the "fate of joining the millions upon millions of dislocated labourers in the export-oriented globalised sweatshops in the south, or simply becoming unemployed." This "created a permanent possible threat, constantly reminding the workers of the fragility of their jobs and how easily and sometimes
arbitrarily these could be taken away" (p. 91). State policies of informalising labour
have thus weakened the position of workers all over the globe, in public as well as
private enterprises, and in formal as well as informal jobs. Under these conditions,
keeping up workers' counterpower and defending decent working and living conditions has become an ever bigger challenge.

Conclusion

The contributions to this volume are based on detailed case studies spanning three
centuries and different parts of the world. Still, they speak to each other in many
ways, highlighting the fact that power at work, whether on the shopfloor or beyond, results from a wide range of complex interrelations. Between technological
innovations and the ways in which they are actually implemented. Between the
division of labour at the site of production or service provision and changing
standards of social segmentation beyond the premises of the company, which
can be reinforced – or weakened – by management strategies of utilising labour
power as well as workers' reaction to these strategies. Finally, between politics
in production, which shape the relations between capital and labour on the shopfloor, and state politics of production, which cannot be understood without reference to broader developments in economy and society.

In order to approach a global perspective on shifting frontiers of control, then,
a threefold process of analysis is required. First of all, it is important to realise that
these interrelations shape the power resources of capital and labour in very different spatio-temporal constellations. Second, the specificities of these constellations
need to be scrutinised. As argued above, the actual potential of rationalisation, for
instance, depends upon the materiality of production, but also on the power resources of workers in a specific economic sector and with regard to a particular
working task. They can take varying shapes, in response to labour market dynamics, to changing standards of segmentation between groups of working people, or
to state policies of labour regulation, which may differ from country to country and
over time. Third, it is necessary to move beyond the logics of detailed case studies.
In order to proceed to a more global perspective, overarching dynamics and inter-

relations between developments in different nation states need to be identified – such as the worldwide shift from policies of formalisation to policies of informalisation around 1980.

This approach to changes in the world of work is not only productive in analytical terms, as this volume hopefully illustrates. It is also essential, in political terms, for emphasising that power at work is no quasi-natural outcome of technological, economic, or political dynamics that evolve spontaneously and cannot be shaped, or stopped, by workers, whether individually or collectively. Instead, the frontiers of control are contested, and it is crucial to identify the factors that influence the power resources available to management and workers respectively.

During the last decades, the worldwide trend toward an informalisation of labour, as well as the concomitant dismantling of standards with regard to job stability, social and legal protection, and collective interest representation, has severely weakened workers' power, both in the Global North and South. Contrary to the claims of politicians and managers, however, there are alternatives. If there is any lesson to be learned from global labour history, it is the possibility (and necessity) of adapting technological and organisational change to the needs and interests of working men and women, in order to establish and maintain solidarity, despite state policies of segmentation and managerial divide and rule strategies, and to reduce the differences and the competition among workers through collective organisation and state policies that expand labour's space of manoeuvre. It is possible, as Marx stated in his *Contribution to the Critique of Hegel's Philosophy of Right*, "to overthrow all relations in which man is a debased, enslaved, abandoned, despicable essence."

Notes on Contributors

Ravi Ahuja is Professor of Modern Indian History at the Centre for Modern Indian Studies of Georg-August-University Göttingen. His publications include *Die Erzeugung kolonialer Staatlichkeit und das Problem der Arbeit. Eine Studie zur Sozialgeschichte der Stadt Madras und ihres Hinterlandes zwischen 1750 und 1800* (Stuttgart: Franz-Steiner-Verlag, 1999) and *Pathways of Empire. Circulation, 'Public Works' and Social Space in Colonial Orissa (c. 1780–1914)* (Hyderabad: Orient Blackswan, 2009). He was a research fellow at re:work in Berlin in 2010 to 2011.

Görkem Akgöz is a postdoctoral student at Humboldt University in Berlin, and co-founder of the Workplaces: Pasts and Presents Group of the European Labour History Network. Her articles have appeared in *International Review of Social History, Labor History*, and *Toplumsal Tarih*. Her book *Between Nation and Class: Industrialisation, Nation-Building and Working-Class Politics in Turkey* is forthcoming (Leiden: Brill). She was a research fellow at re:work in Berlin in 2017 to 2018.

Rana Partap Behal taught history at Deshbandhu College, University of Delhi and at Cornell University, Syracuse University and Oberlin College. He is the author of articles published in *International Review of Social History, Journal of Peasant Studies* and *Modern Asian Studies*, of *One Hundred Years of Servitude: Political Economy of Tea Plantations in Colonial Assam* (New Delhi: Tulika, 2014), and, with Marcel van der Linden, edited *India's Labouring Poor. Historical Studies, 1600–2000* (New Delhi: Foundation Books, 2007). In Berlin he was research fellow at re:work in 2009 to 2010 and the Centre for Development Studies, and in Erfurt at the Max-Weber-Kolleg, 2018 to 2019.

Toby Boraman is Lecturer in Politics at the School of People, Environment and Planning, Massey University/Te Kunenga ki Pūrehuroa, New Zealand. He is the author of *Rabble Rousers and Merry Pranksters. A History of Anarchism in Aotearoa/New Zealand from the Mid-1950s to the Early 1980s* (Christchurch, NZ: Katipo Books, 2007), and of articles in *Counterfutures, International Review of Social History, Journal of Labor and Society*, and *Labour History*. He was a research fellow at re:work in Berlin in 2013 to 2014.

Jacob Eyferth is Associate Professor of Modern Chinese History in the department of East Asian Languages and Civilizations of the University of Chicago. He is the author of *Eating Rice from Bamboo Roots: The Social History of a Community of Handicraft Papermakers in Rural Sichuan, 1920–2000* (Cambridge, MA: Harvard University Press, 2009), and editor of *How China Works: Perspectives on the Twentieth-Century Industrial Workplace* (London: Routledge 2006). He was a research fellow at re:work in Berlin in 2009 to 2010.

Jonathan Hyslop is Professor of Sociology and Anthropology and African & Latin American Studies at Colgate University, Hamilton, NY, and Extraordinary Professor at the University of Pretoria. His articles have been published in edited volumes and in a variety of journals, including *International Labor and Working Class History, International Review of Social History, Journal of Global History, Journal of Imperial and Commonwealth History, Journal of Southern African Studies, Journal of Transport History, Scientia Militaria: South African Journal of Military Studies, South African Historical Journal*. He was a research fellow at re:work in Berlin in 2015 to 2016.

https://doi.org/10.1515/9783111086552-014

Ju Li is an Associated Researcher at the Frontlines of Value Programme, Department of Social Anthropology, University of Bergen, and taught at the Central European University in Budapest. She is the author of *Enduring Change: The Labor and Social History of One Third-Front Industrial Complex in China from the 1960s to the Present* (Berlin: Walter de Gruyter, 2019). Her articles have been published in *Eszmélet*, *Global Labour Journal*, *International Labor and Working Class History*, *International Review of Social History*, *Review of Radical Political Economics*, and *Journal of Historical Sociology*. She was a research fellow at re:work in Berlin in 2013 to 2014.

Marcel van der Linden is Senior Research Fellow at the International Institute of Social History in Amsterdam, where he served for 14 years as Research Director. He is the author, editor or co-editor of some 50 books, including *Workers of the World. Essays toward a Global Labor History* (Leiden: Brill, 2008; French, German, Portuguese, Spanish and Turkish translations), and the two-volume *The Cambridge History of Socialism* (Cambridge: Cambridge University Press, 2023 [2023]). In 2010 he joined the re:work advisory board.

Nicole Mayer-Ahuja is Professor of Sociology at Georg-August-University in Göttingen. Her publications include *Wieder dienen lernen? Vom westdeutschen "Normalarbeitsverhältnis" zu prekärer Beschäftigung seit 1973* (Berlin: Edition Sigma, 2003); *Everywhere is becoming the same? Regulating IT-work between India and Germany* (New Delhi: Social Science Press, 2014); *Verkannte Leistungsträger:innen. Berichte aus der Klassengesellschaft* (Berlin: Edition Suhrkamp, 2021; edited with Oliver Nachtwey). She was a Research Fellow at re:work in Berlin in 2010 to 2011 and 2020 to 2021. In 2015 she joined the re:work advisory board.

Sabine Rutar is a Senior Research Associate at the Leibniz Institute for East and Southeast European Studies, Regensburg, and the Editor-in-Chief of *Comparative Southeast European Studies* (De Gruyter). She is the author of *Kultur – Nation – Milieu. Sozialdemokratie in Triest vor dem Ersten Weltkrieg* (Essen: Klartext, 2004), and recently (co-)edited *No Neighbors' Lands. Vanishing Others in Postwar Europe* (London: Palgrave, 2022); *Beyond the Balkans. Towards an Inclusive History of Southeastern Europe* (Vienna, Zürich, Berlin: Lit, 2014); and *Violence in Late Socialist Public Spheres* (*European History Quarterly*, 45, 2 [2015]). She was a research fellow at re:work in Berlin in 2014 to 2015.

Christian Strümpell is Research Associate at the Institute of Social and Cultural Anthropology, Universität Hamburg. He is the author of *'Wir arbeiten zusammen, wir essen zusammen' : Konvivium und soziale Peripherie in einer indischen Werkssiedlung* (Berlin: Lit, 2006), and has published articles in *Contributions to Indian Sociology*, *Citizenship Studies* and *Modern Asian Studies* as well as blogs and an online exhibit in *TRAFO – Blog for Transregional Research* and in *Workplaces: Pasts and Presents*. He was a research fellow at re:work in Berlin in 2015 to 2016.

Daniel Tödt is Assistant Professor of African History at the Humboldt University in Berlin. His books include *The Lumumba Generation. African Bourgeoisie and Colonial Distinction in the Belgian Congo* (Berlin: De Gruyter, 2021), and *Vom Planeten Mars. Rap in Marseille und das Imaginäre der Stadt* (Münster: LIT, 2011). He was a research fellow at re:work in Berlin in 2017–19.

Index

abattoirs *see* slaughterhouses
Abin (steel worker)   92–93, 94–95
absenteeism, at Tōmoana slaughterhouse   169
abuses, of African workers   265
accidents, in New Zealand slaughterhouses
  178
Adivasi
  education of children   157, 300–301
  exploitation of   149
  inequalities at RSP   144–145
  labour resistance   149
  Odia, opinion on   156
  position at RSP   150, 305
  in RSP township   157
  in slums   151
  stereotypes   305–306
  upper-caste view of   148
  working conditions in RSP   148–149
Africa *see* Belgian Congo; southern Africa; Sudan
African workers
  abuses of   265
  see also Congolese sailors
age
  of engine-room crews   233–234
  of Turkish girls as factory workers   114, 119
agricultural products
  purchase and marketing in PRC   54–55
  quotas in PRC   72–73
  targets in Chinese collective farms   59
  see also cotton; tea
agricultural work
  characteristics   51
  as factory work   52, 74–75, 291
  Plantation Labour Act (India)   44
  as vehicle to socialism   52
agricultural workers *see* Assam tea plantation
  workers; Chinese agricultural workers
agriculture
  development in PRC   55–56
  transformation of landscape for   56–57
  see also farms; plantations
Allied Corporation, work at   21

anger
  of Nanfang Steel workers   87, 92
  of Turkish factory worker on woman co-work-
    er's skills   125
antagonism, towards own work   94
Antić, Zdenko   206
Antwerp
  Ndako Ya Bisu   275–277, 276 fig.
  shore leave of Congolese sailors   283
Anversville (steamship)   261, 278, 279, 283–284
Aotearoa *see* New Zealand
apartments, disputed distribution of at Nanfang
  Steel factory   82–83
arrest, of retired Nanfang Steel worker   81–82
ash removal, from engine rooms   215–216
Asia *see* China; India
Assam tea plantation workers
  character   40–41
  exclusion   48
  health issues   45
  living conditions   45, 50, 299–300
  malnutrition   45
  mortality   39
  recruitment   27, 28, 29, 299
  residential compulsion   30, 299
  resistance   41–43, 47–49, 50
  Scheduled Tribe status denied   48
  standard of living   38–40
  wages   38–39, 48–49
  women   38, 39, 45–46
Assam tea plantations
  contribution overview   23
  expansion   27–28, 39
  indenture labour regime   35–40, 49–50, 299
  isolation   46, 47, 304
  labour legislation   28–29
  opening up   27
  power of employers   28–29, 30
  production process   30–35
  violence   42
  working conditions   44–45, 46–47, 48–49
assembly-line workers *see* New Zealand meatworkers

https://doi.org/10.1515/9783111086552-015